SWITZERLAND

T0293512

DOING BUSINESS, INVESTING
IN SWITZERLAND GUIDE
VOLUME 1
STRATEGIC AND PRACTICAL INFORMATION

International Business Publications, USA
Washington DC, USA - Switzerland

SWITZERLAND
DOING BUSINESS, INVESTING IN SWITZERLAND GUIDE
VOLUME 1 STRATEGIC AND PRACTICAL INFORMATION

UPDATED ANNUALLY

We express our sincere appreciation to all government agencies and international organizations which provided information and other materials for this guide

Cover Design: International Business Publications, USA

International Business Publications, USA. *has used its best efforts in collecting, analyzing and preparing data, information and materials for this unique guide. Due to the dynamic nature and fast development of the economy and business environment, we cannot warrant that all information herein is complete and accurate. IBP does not assume and hereby disclaim any liability to any person for any loss or damage caused by possible errors or omissions in the guide.*
This guide is for individual use only. Use this guide for any other purpose, included but not limited to reproducing and storing in a retrieval system by any means, electronic, photocopying or using the addresses or other information contained in this guide for any commercial purposes requires a special written permission from the publisher.

2017 Updated Reprint International Business Publications, USA
ISBN 1-5145-2792-8

For additional analytical, business and investment opportunities information,
please contact Global Investment & Business Center, USA
at (703) 370-8082. Fax: (703) 370-8083. E-mail: ibpusa3@gmail.com
Global Business and Investment Info Databank - www.ibpus.com

Printed in the USA

For additional analytical, business and investment opportunities information,
please contact Global Investment & Business Center, USA
at (703) 370-8082. Fax: (703) 370-8083. E-mail: ibpusa3@gmail.com
Global Business and Investment Info Databank - www.ibpus.com

SWITZERLAND

DOING BUSINESS, INVESTING IN SWITZERLAND GUIDE

VOLUME 1
STRATEGIC AND PRACTICAL INFORMATION

TABLE OF CONTENTS

For additional analytical, business and investment opportunities information,
please contact Global Investment & Business Center, USA
at (703) 370-8082. Fax: (703) 370-8083. E-mail: ibpusa3@gmail.com
Global Business and Investment Info Databank - www.ibpus.com

For additional analytical, business and investment opportunities information,
please contact Global Investment & Business Center, USA
at (703) 370-8082. Fax: (703) 370-8083. E-mail: ibpusa3@gmail.com
Global Business and Investment Info Databank - www.ibpus.com

For additional analytical, business and investment opportunities information,
please contact Global Investment & Business Center, USA
at (703) 370-8082. Fax: (703) 370-8083. E-mail: ibpusa3@gmail.com
Global Business and Investment Info Databank - www.ibpus.com

For additional analytical, business and investment opportunities information,
please contact Global Investment & Business Center, USA
at (703) 370-8082. Fax: (703) 370-8083. E-mail: ibpusa3@gmail.com
Global Business and Investment Info Databank - www.ibpus.com

For additional analytical, business and investment opportunities information,
please contact Global Investment & Business Center, USA
at (703) 370-8082. Fax: (703) 370-8083. E-mail: ibpusa3@gmail.com
Global Business and Investment Info Databank - www.ibpus.com

STRATEGIC AND DEVELOPMENT PROFILES

Capital		None (de jure)
		Bern (de facto)
		46°57′N 7°27′E46.950°N 7.450°E
	Largest city	Zürich
	Official languages	German; French; Italian; Romansh
	Demonym	English: Swiss,
		German: Schweizer(in),
		French: Suisse(sse),
		Italian: svizzero/svizzera, or elvetico/elvetica,
		Romansh: Svizzer/Svizra
	Government	Federal multi-party directorial republic with thorough elements of direct democracy
•	Federal Council	Doris Leuthard (Vice President)
		Ueli Maurer
		Didier Burkhalter
		Simonetta Sommaruga
		Johann Schneider-Ammann (President)
		Alain Berset
		Guy Parmelin
•	Federal Chancellor	Walter Thurnherr
	Legislature	Federal Assembly
•	Upper house	Council of States
•	Lower house	National Council
	History	
•	Foundation date	c. 1300 celebrated on 1 August 1291
•	Treaty of Basel (1499)	22 September 1499
•	Peace of Westphalia	24 October 1648
•	Restoration	7 August 1815
•	Federal state	12 September 1848[2]
	Area	
•	Total	41,285 km² (135th)
		15,940 sq mi
•	Water (%)	4.2
	Population	
•	September 2014 estimate	8,211,700[3] (96th)
•	2013 census	8,139,600[4]
•	Density	198/km² (65th)
		477.4/sq mi
GDP (PPP)		2016 estimate
•	Total	$493.126 billion (39th)
•	Per capita	$59,150 (9th)
GDP (nominal)		2016 estimate
•	Total	$651.770 billion (19th)
•	Per capita	$78,179 (2nd)
Gini (2014)		28.5
		low · 18th
HDI (2014)		0.930
		very high · 3rd

For additional analytical, business and investment opportunities information, please contact Global Investment & Business Center, USA at (703) 370-8082. Fax: (703) 370-8083. E-mail: ibpusa3@gmail.com Global Business and Investment Info Databank - www.ibpus.com

Currency	Swiss franc (CHF)
Time zone	CET (UTC+1)
• Summer (DST)	CEST (UTC+2)
Date format	dd.mm.yyyy (AD)
Drives on the	right
Calling code	+41
Patron saint	St Nicholas of Flüe
ISO 3166 code	CH
Internet TLD	.ch
Website	https://www.admin.ch

Switzerland officially the **Swiss Confederation** (Latin: *Confoederatio Helvetica*, hence its abbreviation CH), is a federal parliamentary republic consisting of 26 cantons, with Bern as the seat of the federal authorities, the so-called *Bundesstadt* ("federal city").The country is situated in Western and Central Europe, where it is bordered by Italy to the south, France to the west, Germany to the north, and Austria and Liechtenstein to the east. Switzerland is a landlocked country geographically divided between the Alps, the Swiss Plateau and the Jura, spanning an area of 41,285 km^2 (15,940 sq mi). While the Alps occupy the greater part of the territory, the Swiss population of approximately 8 million people is concentrated mostly on the Plateau, where the largest cities are to be found. Among them are the two global cities and economic centres of Zürich and Geneva.

The establishment of the Swiss Confederation is traditionally dated to 1 August 1291, which is celebrated annually as Swiss National Day. It has a long history of armed neutrality—it has not been in a state of war internationally since 1815—and did not join the United Nations until 2002. It pursues, however, an active foreign policy and is frequently involved in peace-building processes around the world. Switzerland is also the birthplace of the Red Cross and home to numerous international organizations, including the second largest UN office. On the European level, it is a founding member of the European Free Trade Association and is part of the Schengen Area – although it is notably not a member of the European Union, nor the European Economic Area. Switzerland comprises four main linguistic and cultural regions: German, French, Italian and the Romansh-speaking valleys. Therefore, the Swiss, although predominantly German-speaking, do not form a nation in the sense of a common ethnic or linguistic identity; rather, the strong sense of identity and community is founded on a common historical background, shared values such as federalism and direct democracy, and Alpine symbolism.

Switzerland has the highest nominal wealth per adult (financial and non-financial assets) in the world according to Credit Suisse and eighth-highest per capita gross domestic product on the IMF list. However, Switzerland is also the most expensive country in the world to live in, as measured by the price level index.

Swiss citizens have the second-highest life expectancy in the world on the UN DESA list. Switzerland is tied with the Netherlands for the top rank on the Bribe Payers Index indicating very low levels of business corruption. Moreover, for the last five years the country has been ranked first in economic and tourist competitiveness according to the Global Competitiveness Report and the Travel and Tourism Competitiveness Report respectively, both developed by the World Economic Forum. Zürich and Geneva have each been ranked among the top cities with the highest quality of life in the world, with the former coming second globally according to Mercer. However, Mercer also rates those two cities as the fifth- and sixth- most expensive cities in the world to live in

For additional analytical, business and investment opportunities information, please contact Global Investment & Business Center, USA at (703) 370-8082. Fax: (703) 370-8083. E-mail: ibpusa3@gmail.com Global Business and Investment Info Databank - www.ibpus.com

SWITZERLAND: STRATEGIC PROFILE

Background: Switzerland's independence and neutrality have long been honored by the major European powers and Switzerland did not participate in either World War I or II. The political and economic integration of Europe since World War II may be rendering obsolete Switzerland's concern for neutrality.

GEOGRAPHY

Location: Central Europe, east of France, north of Italy
Geographic coordinates: 47 00 N, 8 00 E
Map references: Europe

Area:
total: 41,290 sq km *land:* 39,770 sq km *water:* 1,520 sq km

Area—comparative: slightly less than twice the size of New Jersey
Land boundaries:
total: 1,852 km
border countries: Austria 164 km, France 573 km, Italy 740 km, Liechtenstein 41 km, Germany 334 km

Coastline: 0 km (landlocked)
Maritime claims: none (landlocked)

Climate: temperate, but varies with altitude; cold, cloudy, rainy/snowy winters; cool to warm, cloudy, humid summers with occasional showers

Terrain: mostly mountains (Alps in south, Jura in northwest) with a central plateau of rolling hills, plains, and large lakes
Elevation extremes:
lowest point: Lake Maggiore 195 m
highest point: Dufourspitze 4,634 m
Natural resources: hydropower potential, timber, salt

Land use:
arable land: 10% *permanent crops:* 2% *permanent pastures:* 28%
forests and woodland: 32% *other:* 28%

Irrigated land: 250 sq km
Natural hazards: avalanches, landslides, flash floods
Environment—current issues: air pollution from vehicle emissions and open-air burning; acid rain; water pollution from increased use of agricultural fertilizers; loss of biodiversity

Environment—international agreements:
party to: Air Pollution, Air Pollution-Nitrogen Oxides, Air Pollution-Sulphur 85, Air Pollution-Sulphur 94, Air Pollution-Volatile Organic Compounds, Antarctic Treaty, Biodiversity, Climate Change, Desertification, Endangered Species, Environmental Modification, Hazardous Wastes, Marine Dumping, Marine Life Conservation, Nuclear Test Ban, Ozone Layer Protection, Ship Pollution, Tropical Timber 83, Tropical Timber 94, Wetlands, Whaling
signed, but not ratified: Air Pollution-Persistent Organic Pollutants, Antarctic-Environmental Protocol, Climate Change-Kyoto Protocol, Law of the Sea

Geography—note: landlocked; crossroads of northern and southern Europe; along with southeastern France and northern Italy, contains the highest elevations in Europe

PEOPLE

Population: 7,275,467
Age structure:
0-14 years: 17% (male 639,970; female 611,876)
15-64 years: 68% (male 2,509,988; female 2,417,580)
65 years and over: 15% (male 444,482; female 651,571)

Population growth rate: 0.2%

Birth rate: 10.53 births/1,000 population
Death rate: 9.06 deaths/1,000 population
Net migration rate: 0.49 migrant(s)/1,000 population

Sex ratio:
at birth: 1.05 male(s)/female
under 15 years: 1.05 male(s)/female
15-64 years: 1.04 male(s)/female
65 years and over: 0.68 male(s)/female
total population: 0.98 male(s)/female

Infant mortality rate: 4.87 deaths/1,000 live births

Life expectancy at birth:
total population: 78.99 years
male: 75.83 years
female: 82.32 years

Total fertility rate: 1.46 children born/woman

Nationality:
noun: Swiss (singular and plural)
adjective: Swiss
Ethnic groups: German 65%, French 18%, Italian 10%, Romansch 1%, other 6%
Religions: Roman Catholic 46.1%, Protestant 40%, other 5%, no religion 8.9% (1990)
Languages: German 63.7%, French 19.2%, Italian 7.6%, Romansch 0.6%, other 8.9%

Literacy:
definition: age 15 and over can read and write
total population: 99% (1980 est.)
male: NA%
female: NA%

GOVERNMENT

Country name:

conventional long form: Swiss Confederation
conventional short form: Switzerland

local long form: Schweizerische Eidgenossenschaft (German); Confederation Suisse (French); Confederazione Svizzera (Italian); Confederaziun Svizra (Romansh)

local short form: Schweiz (German); Suisse (French); Svizzera (Italian); Svizra (Romansh)

Government type:

formally a confederation but similar in structure to a federal republic

Capital:

name: Bern

geographic coordinates: 46 55 N, 7 28 E
time difference: UTC+1 (6 hours ahead of Washington, DC, during Standard Time)
daylight saving time: +1hr, begins last Sunday in March; ends last Sunday in October

Administrative divisions:

26 cantons (cantons, singular - canton in French; cantoni, singular - cantone in Italian; Kantone, singular - Kanton in German); Aargau, Appenzell Ausserrhoden, Appenzell Innerrhoden, Basel-Landschaft, Basel-Stadt, Bern/Berne, Fribourg/Freiburg, Geneve, Glarus, Graubuenden/Grischun/Grigioni, Jura, Luzern, Neuchatel, Nidwalden, Obwalden, Sankt Gallen, Schaffhausen, Schwyz, Solothurn, Thurgau, Ticino, Uri, Valais/Wallis, Vaud, Zug, Zuerich

note: 6 of the cantons - Appenzell Ausserrhoden, Appenzell Innerrhoden, Basel-Landschaft, Basel-Stadt, Nidwalden, Obwalden - are referred to as half cantons because they elect only one member to the Council of States and, in popular referendums where a majority of popular votes and a majority of cantonal votes are required, these six cantons only have a half vote

Independence:

1 August 1291 (founding of the Swiss Confederation)

National holiday:

Founding of the Swiss Confederation in 1291; note - since 1 August 1891 celebrated as Swiss National Day

Constitution:

previous 1848, 1874 (extensive revision of 1848 version); latest adopted by referendum 18 April 1999, effective 1 January 2000; amended several times, last in 2014 (2012)

Legal system:

civil law system; judicial review of legislative acts, except for federal decrees of a general obligatory character

International law organization participation:

accepts compulsory ICJ jurisdiction with reservations; accepts ICCt jurisdiction

Suffrage:

18 years of age; universal

Executive branch:

chief of state: President of the Swiss Confederation Johann N. SCHNEIDER-AMMANN (since 1 January 2016); Vice President Doris LEUTARD (since 1 January 2016; note - the Federal Council, which is comprised of 7 federal councillors, constitutes the federal government of Switzerland; council members rotate in a 1-year term as federal president (chief of state and head of government)

head of government: President of the Swiss Confederation Johann N. SCHNEIDER-AMMANN (since 1 January 2016); Vice President Doris LEUTARD (since 1 January 2016)

cabinet: Federal Council or Bundesrat (in German), Conseil Federal (in French), Consiglio Federale (in Italian) indirectly elected usually from among its members by the Federal Assembly for a 4-year term

elections/appointments: president and vice president indirectly elected by the Federal Assembly from among members of the Federal Council for a 1-year, non-consecutive term; election last held on 9 December 2015 (next to be held in early December 2016)

election results: Johann N. SCHNEIDER-AMMANN elected president; Federal Assembly vote - 196 of 208; Doris LEUTHARD elected vice president

Legislative branch:

description: bicameral Federal Assembly or Bundesversammlung - in German, Assemblee Federale - in French, Assemblea Federale - in Italian consists of the Council of States or Staenderat - in German, Conseil des Etats - in French, Consiglio degli Stati - in Italian (46 seats; members in multi-seat constituencies representing cantons and single-seat constituencies representing half cantons directly elected by simple majority vote; members serve 4-year terms) and the National Council or Nationalrat - in German, Conseil National - in French, Consiglio Nazionale - in Italian (200 seats; 195 members in cantons directly elected by proportional representation vote and 5 in half cantons directly elected by simple majority vote; members serve 4-year terms)

elections: Council of States - last held in most cantons on 18 October 2015 (each canton determines when the next election will be held); National Council - last held on 18 October 2015 (next to be held in October 2019)

election results: Council of States - percent of vote by party - NA; seats by party (as of 18 October 2015) - Christian Democratic People's Party 13, FDP.The Liberals 13, SDP 12, Swiss People's Party 6, other 2; National Council - percent of vote by party - SVP 29.4%, SPS 18.8%, FDP 16.4%, CVP 11.6%, Green Party 7.1%, GLP 4.6%, BDP 4.1%, other 8.0%; seats by party - SVP 65, SPS 43, FDP 33, CVP 27, Green Party 11, GLP 7, BDP 7, other 7

Judicial branch:

highest court(s): Federal Supreme Court (consists of 38 judges and 31 substitutes and organized into 5 sections)

judge selection and term of office: judges elected by the Federal Assembly for 6-year terms; note - judges are affiliated with political parties and are elected according to linguistic and regional criteria in approximate proportion to the level of party representation in the Federal Assembly

subordinate courts: Federal Criminal Court (began in 2004); Federal Administrative Court (began in 2007); note - each of Switzerland's 26 cantons has its own courts

Political parties and leaders:

Christian Democratic People's Party (Christlichdemokratische Volkspartei der Schweiz or CVP, Parti Democrate-Chretien Suisse or PDC, Partito Popolare Democratico Svizzero or PPD, Partida Cristiandemocratica dalla Svizra or PCD) [Christophe DARBELLAY]

Conservative Democratic Party (Buergerlich-Demokratische Partei Schweiz or BDP, Parti Bourgeois Democratique Suisse or PBD, Partito Borghese Democratico Svizzero or PBD, Partido burgais democratica Svizera or PBD) [Martin LANDOLT]

Free Democratic Party or FDP.The Liberals (FDP.Die Liberalen, PLR.Les Liberaux-Radicaux, PLR.I Liberali, Ils Liberals) [Philipp MUELLER]

Green Liberal Party (Grunliberale or GLP, Parti vert liberale or PVL, Partito Verde-Liberale or PVL, Partida Verde Liberale or PVL) [Martin BAEUMLE]

Green Party (Gruene Partei der Schweiz or Gruene, Parti Ecologiste Suisse or Les Verts, Partito Ecologista Svizzero or I Verdi, Partida Ecologica Svizra or La Verda) [Adele THORENS GOUMAZ and Regula RYTZ]

Social Democratic Party (Sozialdemokratische Partei der Schweiz or SPS, Parti Socialiste Suisse or PSS, Partito Socialista Svizzero or PSS, Partida Socialdemocratica de la Svizra or PSS) [Christian LEVRAT]

Swiss People's Party (Schweizerische Volkspartei or SVP, Union Democratique du Centre or UDC, Unione Democratica di Centro or UDC, Uniun Democratica dal Center or UDC) [Toni BRUNNER] other minor parties

International organization participation:

ADB (nonregional member), AfDB (nonregional member), Australia Group, BIS, CD, CE, CERN, EAPC, EBRD, EFTA, EITI (implementing country), ESA, FAO, FATF, G-10, IADB, IAEA, IBRD, ICAO, ICC (national committees), ICCt, ICRM, IDA, IEA, IFAD, IFC, IFRCS, IGAD (partners), ILO, IMF, IMO, IMSO, Interpol, IOC, IOM, IPU, ISO, ITSO, ITU, ITUC (NGOs), LAIA (observer), MIGA, MINUSMA, MONUSCO, NEA, NSG, OAS (observer), OECD, OIF, OPCW, OSCE, Pacific Alliance (observer), Paris Club, PCA, PFP, Schengen Convention, UN, UNCTAD, UNESCO, UNHCR, UNIDO, UNITAR, UNMISS, UNMOGIP, UNRWA, UNTSO, UNWTO, UPU, WCO, WHO, WIPO, WMO, WTO, ZC

Diplomatic representation in the US:
chief of mission: Ambassador Martin DAHINDEN (since 18 November 2014)
chancery: 2900 Cathedral Avenue NW, Washington, DC 20008
telephone: (202) 745-7900
FAX: (202) 387-2564
consulate(s) general: Atlanta, Chicago, Los Angeles, New York, San Francisco
consulate(s): Boston
Diplomatic representation from the US:
chief of mission: Ambassador Suzan G. LEVINE (since 2 June 2014); note - also accredited to Liechtenstein

embassy: Sulgeneckstrasse 19, CH-3007 Bern
mailing address: use Embassy street address
telephone: [41] (031) 357-70-11
FAX: [41] (031) 357-73-44
Flag description:
red square with a bold, equilateral white cross in the center that does not extend to the edges of the flag; various medieval legends purport to describe the origin of the flag; a white cross used as identification for troops of the Swiss Confederation is first attested at the Battle of Laupen (1339)
National symbol(s):
Swiss cross (white cross on red field, arms equal length); national colors: red, white
National anthem:
"Schweizerpsalm" [German] "Cantique Suisse" [French] "Salmo svizzero," [Italian] "Psalm svizzer" [Romansch] (Swiss Psalm)
lyrics/music: Leonhard WIDMER [German], Charles CHATELANAT [French], Camillo VALSANGIACOMO [Italian], and Flurin CAMATHIAS [Romansch]/Alberik ZWYSSIG
note: unofficially adopted 1961, officially 1981; the anthem has been popular in a number of Swiss cantons since its composition (in German) in 1841; translated into the other three official languages of the country (French, Italian, and Romansch), it is official in each of those languages

ECONOMY

Switzerland is a peaceful, prosperous, and modern market economy with low unemployment, a highly skilled labor force, and a per capita GDP among the highest in the world. Switzerland's economy benefits from a highly developed service sector, led by financial services, and a manufacturing industry that specializes in high-technology, knowledge-based production. Its economic and political stability, transparent legal system, exceptional infrastructure, efficient capital markets, and low corporate tax rates also make Switzerland one of the world's most competitive economies.

The Swiss have brought their economic practices largely into conformity with the EU's to enhance their international competitiveness, but some trade protectionism remains, particularly for its small agricultural sector. The fate of the Swiss economy is tightly linked to that of its neighbors in the euro zone, which purchases half of all Swiss exports. The global financial crisis of 2008 and resulting economic downturn in 2009 stalled export demand and put Switzerland in a recession. The Swiss National Bank (SNB) during this period effectively implemented a zero-interest rate policy to boost the economy as well as prevent appreciation of the franc, and Switzerland's economy began to recover in 2010. The sovereign debt crises currently unfolding in neighboring euro-zone countries pose a significant risk to Switzerland's financial stability and are driving up demand for the Swiss franc by investors seeking a safe-haven currency.

The independent SNB has upheld its zero-interest rate policy and conducted major market interventions to prevent further appreciation of the Swiss franc, but parliamentarians have urged it to do more to weaken the currency. The franc's strength has made Swiss exports less competitive and weakened the country's growth outlook; GDP growth fell below 2% per year during 2011-13. Switzerland has also come under increasing pressure from individual neighboring countries, the EU, the US, and international institutions to reform its banking secrecy laws.

Consequently, the government agreed to conform to OECD regulations on administrative assistance in tax matters, including tax evasion. The government has renegotiated its double taxation agreements with numerous countries, including the US, to incorporate the

OECD standard, and is considering the possibility of imposing taxes on bank deposits held by foreigners. These steps will have a lasting impact on Switzerland's long history of bank secrecy.

GDP (purchasing power parity):
$371.2 billion (est.)
country comparison to the world: 37
$363.9 billion
$360.1 billion (2011 est.)
note:data are in 2013 US dollars

GDP (official exchange rate):
$646.2 billion (est.)

GDP - real growth rate:
2% (est.)
country comparison to the world: 146
1%
1.8% (2011 est.)

GDP - per capita (PPP):
$54,800 (est.)
country comparison to the world: 11
$53,300
$50,900 (2011 est.)
note:data are in 2013 US dollars

Gross national saving:
31.5% of GDP (est.)
country comparison to the world: 23
31.5% of GDP
27.3% of GDP (2011 est.)

GDP - composition, by end use:
household consumption:
57.4%
government consumption:
11.5%
investment in fixed capital:
20.3%
investment in inventories:
0.7%
exports of goods and services:
50.4%
imports of goods and services:
-40.2%
(2013 est.)

GDP - composition, by sector of origin:
agriculture:
0.7%

industry:
26.8%
services:
72.5% (est.)

Agriculture - products:
grains, fruits, vegetables; meat, eggs

Industries:
machinery, chemicals, watches, textiles, precision instruments, tourism, banking, insurance

Industrial production growth rate:
2.2% (est.)
country comparison to the world: 121

Labor force:
4.976 million (est.)
country comparison to the world: 77

Labor force - by occupation:
agriculture:
3.4%
industry:
23.4%
services:
73.2% (2010)

Unemployment rate:
3.2% (est.)
country comparison to the world: 25
2.9%

Population below poverty line:
7.6% (2011)

Household income or consumption by percentage share:
lowest 10%:
7.5%
highest 10%:
19% (2007)

Distribution of family income - Gini index:
28.7
country comparison to the world: 123
33.1 (1992)

Budget:
revenues:
$217.8 billion

For additional analytical, business and investment opportunities information,
please contact Global Investment & Business Center, USA
at (703) 370-8082. Fax: (703) 370-8083. E-mail: ibpusa3@gmail.com
Global Business and Investment Info Databank - www.ibpus.com

expenditures:
$208.5 billion
note:includes federal, cantonal, and municipal budgets (est.)

Taxes and other revenues:
33.7% of GDP (est.)
country comparison to the world: 71

Budget surplus (+) or deficit (-):
1.4% of GDP (est.)
country comparison to the world: 23

Public debt:
33.8% of GDP (est.)
country comparison to the world: 110
34.9% of GDP
note:general government gross debt; gross debt consists of all liabilities that require payment or payments of interest and/or principal by the debtor to the creditor at a date or dates in the future; includes debt liabilities in the form of SDRs, currency and deposits, debt securities, loans, insurance, pensions and standardized guarantee schemes, and other accounts payable; all liabilities in the GFSM 2001 system are debt, except for equity and investment fund shares and financial derivatives and employee stock options

Fiscal year:
calendar year

Inflation rate (consumer prices):
-0.4% (est.)
country comparison to the world: 6
-0.7%

Central bank discount rate:
0.5% (31 December 2010 est.)
country comparison to the world: 132
0.75% (31 December 2009 est.)

Commercial bank prime lending rate:
2.7% (31 December 2013 est.)
country comparison to the world: 171
2.69% (31 December 2012 est.)

Stock of narrow money:
$525.9 billion (31 December 2013 est.)
country comparison to the world: 11
$534.4 billion (31 December 2012 est.)

Stock of broad money:
$1.36 trillion (31 December 2013 est.)
country comparison to the world: 14
$1.215 trillion (31 December 2012 est.)

Stock of domestic credit:
$1.395 trillion (31 December 2013 est.)
country comparison to the world: 14
$1.247 trillion (31 December 2012 est.)

Market value of publicly traded shares:
$1.079 trillion (31 December 2012 est.)
country comparison to the world: 14
$932.2 billion (31 December 2011)
$1.229 trillion (31 December 2010 est.)

Current account balance:
$65.6 billion (est.)
country comparison to the world: 8
$63.82 billion

Exports:
$229.2 billion (est.)
country comparison to the world: 25
$226 billion
note:trade data exclude trade with Switzerland

Exports - commodities:
machinery, chemicals, metals, watches, agricultural products

Exports - partners:
Germany 18.5%, United States 11.61%, Italy 7.61%, France 6.96%, United Kingdom 5.67% (est.)

Imports:
$200.5 billion (est.)
country comparison to the world: 26
$197.9 billion

Imports - commodities:
machinery, chemicals, vehicles, metals; agricultural products, textiles

Imports - partners:
Germany 28.19%, Italy 10.46%, France 8.49%, United States 6.08%, China 5.75%, Austria 4.4% (est.)

Reserves of foreign exchange and gold:
$536.3 billion (31 December 2013 est.)
country comparison to the world: 5
$536.4 billion (31 December 2012 est.)

Debt - external:
$1.544 trillion (31 December 2012 est.)
country comparison to the world: 12

For additional analytical, business and investment opportunities information,
please contact Global Investment & Business Center, USA
at (703) 370-8082. Fax: (703) 370-8083. E-mail: ibpusa3@gmail.com
Global Business and Investment Info Databank - www.ibpus.com

$1.424 trillion (31 December 2011)

Stock of direct foreign investment - at home:
$968.9 billion (31 December 2013 est.)
country comparison to the world: 9
$955.1 billion (31 December 2012 est.)

Stock of direct foreign investment - abroad:
$1.432 trillion (31 December 2013 est.)
country comparison to the world: 5
$1.381 trillion (31 December 2012 est.)

Exchange rates:
Swiss francs (CHF) per US dollar -
0.9542 (est.)
0.9374
1.0429 (2010 est.)
1.0881 (2009)
1.0774 (2008)

ENERGY

Electricity - production:
68.02 billion kWh
country comparison to the world: 41

Electricity - consumption:
58.97 billion kWh
country comparison to the world: 41

Electricity - exports:
34.57 billion kWh
country comparison to the world: 5

Electricity - imports:
32.25 billion kWh
country comparison to the world: 6

Electricity - installed generating capacity:
18.07 million kW
country comparison to the world: 42

Electricity - from fossil fuels:
3.1% of total installed capacity
country comparison to the world: 200

Electricity - from nuclear fuels:
24.3% of total installed capacity
country comparison to the world: 5

For additional analytical, business and investment opportunities information,
please contact Global Investment & Business Center, USA
at (703) 370-8082. Fax: (703) 370-8083. E-mail: ibpusa3@gmail.com
Global Business and Investment Info Databank - www.ibpus.com

Electricity - from hydroelectric plants:
68% of total installed capacity
country comparison to the world: 24

Electricity - from other renewable sources:
5.5% of total installed capacity
country comparison to the world: 43

Crude oil - production:
3,613 bbl/day
country comparison to the world: 100

Crude oil - exports:
0 bbl/day (2011 est.)
country comparison to the world: 187

Crude oil - imports:
258,200 bbl/day
country comparison to the world: 28

Crude oil - proved reserves:
0 bbl (1 January 2013 est.)
country comparison to the world: 192

Refined petroleum products - production:
96,710 bbl/day
country comparison to the world: 74

Refined petroleum products - consumption:
258,200 bbl/day
country comparison to the world: 50

Refined petroleum products - exports:
7,585 bbl/day
country comparison to the world: 87

Refined petroleum products - imports:
157,600 bbl/day
country comparison to the world: 36

Natural gas - production:
0 cu m
country comparison to the world: 195

For additional analytical, business and investment opportunities information,
please contact Global Investment & Business Center, USA
at (703) 370-8082. Fax: (703) 370-8083. E-mail: ibpusa3@gmail.com
Global Business and Investment Info Databank - www.ibpus.com

Natural gas - consumption:
3.2 billion cu m
country comparison to the world: 71

Natural gas - exports:
8.494 billion cu m
country comparison to the world: 31

Natural gas - imports:
11.77 billion cu m
country comparison to the world: 26

Natural gas - proved reserves:
0 cu m (1 January 2011 est.)
country comparison to the world: 196

Carbon dioxide emissions from consumption of energy:
41.84 million Mt

COMMUNICATIONS

Telephones - main lines in use:
4.382 million
country comparison to the world: 38

Telephones - mobile cellular:
10.46 million
country comparison to the world: 77

Telephone system:
general assessment: highly developed telecommunications infrastructure with excellent domestic and international services
domestic: ranked among leading countries for fixed-line teledensity and infrastructure; mobile-cellular subscribership roughly 125 per 100 persons; extensive cable and microwave radio relay networks
international: country code - 41; satellite earth stations - 2 Intelsat (Atlantic Ocean and Indian Ocean)

Broadcast media:
the publicly owned radio and TV broadcaster, Swiss Broadcasting Corporation (SRG/SSR), operates 7 national TV networks, 3 broadcasting in German, 2 in Italian, and 2 in French; private commercial TV stations broadcast regionally and locally; TV broadcasts from stations in Germany, Italy, and France are widely available via multi-channel cable and satellite TV services; SRG/SSR operates 18 radio stations that, along with private broadcasters, provide national to local coverage (2009)

Internet country code:
.ch

Internet hosts:
5.301 million
country comparison to the world: 20

Internet users:
6.152 million
country comparison to the world: 42

TRANSPORTATION

Airports:
63
country comparison to the world: 78
Airports - with paved runways:
total: 40
over 3,047 m: 3
2,438 to 3,047 m: 2
1,524 to 2,437 m: 12
914 to 1,523 m: 6
under 914 m: 17 (2013)
Airports - with unpaved runways:
total: 23
under 914 m:
23 (2013)
Heliports:
2 (2013)
Pipelines:
gas 1,800 km; oil 94 km; refined products 7 km (2013)
Railways:
total: 4,876 km
standard gauge: 3,846 km 1.435-m gauge (3,591 km electrified)
narrow gauge: 1,020 km 1.000-m gauge (1,013 km electrified); 10 km 0.800-m gauge (10 km electrified) (2008)
country comparison to the world: 37
Roadways:
total: 71,464 km
paved: 71,464 km (includes 1,415 of expressways) (2011)
country comparison to the world: 65
Waterways:
1,292 km (there are 1,227 km of waterways on lakes and rivers for public transport and another 65 km on the Rhine River between Basel-Rheinfelden and Schaffhausen-Bodensee used for the transport of commercial goods) (2010)
country comparison to the world: 57
Merchant marine:
total: 38
by type: bulk carrier 19, cargo 9, chemical tanker 5, container 4, petroleum tanker 1
registered in other countries: 127 (Antigua and Barbuda 7, Bahamas 1, Belize 1, Cayman Islands 1, France 5, Germany 2, Hong Kong 5, Italy 13, Liberia 25, Luxembourg 1, Malta 20, Marshall Islands 12, NZ 2, Panama 15, Portugal 3, Russia 3, Saint Vincent and the Grenadines 7, Singapore 3, Spain 1) (2010)
country comparison to the world: 76
Ports and terminals:

For additional analytical, business and investment opportunities information,
please contact Global Investment & Business Center, USA
at (703) 370-8082. Fax: (703) 370-8083. E-mail: ibpusa3@gmail.com
Global Business and Investment Info Databank - www.ibpus.com

river port(s): Basel (Rhine)

MILITARY

Military branches:
Swiss Armed Forces: Land Forces, Swiss Air Force (Schweizer Luftwaffe) (2013)
Military service age and obligation:
19-26 years of age for male compulsory military service; 18 years of age for voluntary male and female military service; every Swiss male has to serve at least 260 days in the armed forces; conscripts receive 18 weeks of mandatory training, followed by seven 3-week intermittent recalls for training during the next 10 years (2012)

Manpower available for military service:
males age 16-49: 1,828,043
females age 16-49: 1,786,552

Manpower fit for military service:
males age 16-49: 1,493,509
females age 16-49: 1,459,450
Manpower reaching militarily significant age annually:
male: 46,562
female: 42,585

Military expenditures:
0.64% of GDP (2014)
0.69% of GDP (2013)
0.76% of GDP (2012)
0.75% of GDP (2011)
0.76% of GDP (2010)
country comparison to the world: 117

TRANSNATIONAL ISSUES

Disputes - international:

none
Refugees and internally displaced persons:
refugees (country of origin): 15,065 (Eritrea) (2014)
stateless persons: 79

Illicit drugs:
a major international financial center vulnerable to the layering and integration stages of money laundering; despite significant legislation and reporting requirements, secrecy rules persist and nonresidents are permitted to conduct business through offshore entities and various intermediaries; transit country for and consumer of South American cocaine, Southwest Asian heroin, and Western European synthetics; domestic cannabis cultivation and limited ecstasy production

IMPORTANT INFORMATION FOR UNDERSTANDING SWITZERLAND

PROFILE

OFFICIAL NAME: Swiss Confederation

Geography
Area: 41,285 sq. km. (15,941 sq. mi.); about the size of Vermont and New Hampshire combined.
Cities: *Capital*--Bern (population about 123,000). *Other cities*--Zurich (341,000), Geneva (176,000), Basel (165,000), Lausanne (116,000).
Terrain: 60% mountains, the remainder hills and plateau. Switzerland straddles the central ranges of the Alps.
Climate: Temperate, varying with altitude and season.

People
Nationality: *Noun and adjective*--Swiss (singular and plural).
Population: 7,523,934.
Annual growth rate: 0.43%.
Ethnic groups: Mixed European.
Religions: Roman Catholic 42%, Protestant 33%, Muslim 4.3%, others 5.4%, no religion 11%.
Languages: German 63.7%, French 20.4%, Italian 6.5%, Romansch 0.5%, other 9.4%.
Education: *Years compulsory*--9. *Attendance*--100%. *Literacy*--100%.
Health: *Infant mortality rate*--4.3/1,000. *Life expectancy*--men 77.7 yrs., women 83.5 yrs.
Work force (3.81 million): *Agriculture and forestry*--4.2%. *Industry and business*--25.6%. *Services and government*--70.2%.

Government
Type: Federal state.
Independence: The first Swiss Confederation was founded in August 1291 as a defensive alliance among three cantons. The Swiss Confederation established independence from the Holy Roman Empire in 1499.
Constitution: 1848; extensively amended in 1874; fully revised in 2000
Branches: *Executive*--Federal Council, a collegium of seven members, headed by a rotating one-year presidency. *Legislative*--Federal Assembly (bicameral: Council of States, 46 members; National Council, 200 members). *Judicial*--Federal Tribunal.
Administrative subdivisions: 26 cantons (states) with considerable autonomy.
Political parties: Swiss People's Party (SVP), Social Democratic Party (SP), Free Democratic Party (FDP), Christian Democratic Party (CVP), and several smaller parties representing localities or views from extreme left to extreme right.
Suffrage: In federal matters, universal over 18.

PEOPLE

Switzerland sits at the crossroads of several major European cultures, which have heavily influenced the country's languages and cultural practices. Switzerland has four official languages--German, French, Italian, and Romansch (based on Latin and spoken by a small minority in the Canton Graubunden). The German spoken is predominantly a Swiss dialect, but newspapers and some broadcasts use High German. Many Swiss speak more than one language. English is widely known, especially among professionals.

For additional analytical, business and investment opportunities information, please contact Global Investment & Business Center, USA at (703) 370-8082. Fax: (703) 370-8083. E-mail: ibpusa3@gmail.com Global Business and Investment Info Databank - www.ibpus.com

More than 75% of the population lives in the central plain, which stretches between the Alps and the Jura Mountains and from Geneva in the southwest to the Rhine River and Lake Constance in the northeast. Resident foreigners and temporary foreign workers make up about 20% of the population.

According to the Swiss Federal Office of Statistics, the population in Switzerland increased to 7,523,934 (July estimate) in 2006. Three-quarters of this growth was attributed to migration. Switzerland naturalized 22% more people in 2006 compared to 2005, totaling 46,700 persons. By the end of 2006, there were 850,000 foreigners working legally in Switzerland. The rise of German immigrants, as confirmed in earlier reports, increased by 10.6% (+10,000). Portuguese workers also increased by 7.4% (+7000). On the other hand, the number of the Italians continued to drop by –3.2% (-5000).

Almost all Swiss are literate. Switzerland's 13 university institutes enrolled 111,100 students in the academic year of 2004-05. About 25% of the adult population holds a diploma of higher learning.

The Constitution guarantees freedom of worship, and the different religious communities co-exist peacefully.

Switzerland consistently ranks high on quality of life indices, including highest per capita income, one of the highest concentrations of computer and Internet usage per capita, highest insurance coverage per individual, and high health care rates. For these and many other reasons, it serves as an excellent test market for businesses hoping to introduce new products into Europe.

HISTORY

Originally inhabited by the Helvetians, or Helvetic Celts, the territory comprising modern Switzerland came under Roman rule during the Gallic wars in the 1st century BC and remained a Roman province until the 4th century AD. Under Roman influence, the population reached a high level of civilization and enjoyed a flourishing commerce. Important cities, such as Geneva, Basel, and Zurich, were linked by military roads that also served as trade arteries between Rome and the northern tribes.

After the decline of the Roman Empire, Switzerland was invaded by Germanic tribes from the north and west. Some tribes, such as the Alemanni in central and northeastern Switzerland, and the Burgundians, who ruled western Switzerland, settled there. In 800, the country became part of Charlemagne's empire. It later passed under the dominion of the Holy Roman emperors in the form of small ecclesiastic and temporal holdings subject to imperial sovereignty.

With the opening of a new important north-south trade route across the Alps in the early 13th century, the Empire's rulers began to attach more importance to the remote Swiss mountain valleys, which were granted some degree of autonomy under direct imperial rule. Fearful of the popular disturbances flaring up following the death of the Holy Roman Emperor in 1291, the ruling families from Uri, Schwyz, and Unterwalden signed a charter to keep public peace and pledging mutual support in upholding autonomous administrative and judicial rule. The anniversary of the charter's signature (August 1, 1291) today is celebrated as Switzerland's National Day.

Between 1315 and 1388 the Swiss Confederates inflicted three crushing defeats on the Habsburgs, whose aspiration to regional dominion clashed with Swiss self-determination. During that period, five other localities (cantons in modern-day parlance) joined the original three in the Swiss Confederation. Buoyed by their feats, the Swiss Confederates continuously expanded their

For additional analytical, business and investment opportunities information,
please contact Global Investment & Business Center, USA
at (703) 370-8082. Fax: (703) 370-8083. E-mail: ibpusa3@gmail.com
Global Business and Investment Info Databank - www.ibpus.com

borders by military means and gained formal independence from the Holy Roman Empire in 1499. Routed by the French and Venetians near Milan in 1515, they renounced expansionist policies. By then the Swiss Confederation had become a union of 13 localities with a regularly convening diet administering the subject territories. Swiss mercenaries continued for centuries to serve in other armies; the Swiss Guard of the Pope is a vestige of this tradition.

The Reformation led to a division between the Protestant followers of Zwingli and Calvin in the German and French parts of the country respectively, and the Catholics. Despite two centuries of civil strife, the common interest in the joint subject territories kept the Swiss Confederation from falling apart. The traffic in mercenaries as well as the alienation between the predominantly Protestant Swiss and their Catholic neighbors kept the Swiss Confederation out of the wars of the European powers, which formally recognized Swiss neutrality in the Treaty of Westphalia in 1648. The Swiss remained neutral during the War of the First Coalition against revolutionary France, but Napoleon, nonetheless, invaded and annexed much of the country in 1797-98, replacing the loose confederation with a centrally governed unitary state.

The Congress of Vienna in 1815 re-established the old confederation of sovereign states and enshrined Switzerland's status of permanent armed neutrality in international law. In 1848, after a brief civil war between Protestant liberals seeking a centralized national state and Catholic conservatives clinging on to the old order, the majority of Swiss Cantons opted for a Federal State, modeled in part on the U.S. Constitution. The Swiss Constitution established a range of civic liberties and made far-reaching provisions to maintain cantonal autonomy to placate the vanquished Catholic minority. The Swiss amended their Constitution extensively in 1874, establishing federal responsibility for defense, trade, and legal matters, as well as introducing direct democracy by popular referendum. To this day, cantonal autonomy and referendum democracy remain trademarks of the Swiss polity.

Switzerland industrialized rapidly during the 19th century and by 1850 had become the second most industrialized country in Europe after Great Britain. During World War I serious tension developed between the German, French, and Italian-speaking parts of the country, and Switzerland came close to violating its neutrality but managed to stay out of hostilities. Labor unrest culminating in a general strike in 1918 marked the interwar period, but in 1937 employers and the largest trade union concluded a formal agreement to settle disputes peacefully, which governs workplace relations to the present day. During World War II, Switzerland came under heavy pressure from the fascist powers, which after the fall of France in 1940 completely surrounded the country. Some political and economic leaders displayed a mood of appeasement, but a combination of tactical accommodation and demonstrative readiness to defend the country helped Switzerland survive unscathed.

The Cold War enhanced the role of neutral Switzerland and offered the country a way out of its diplomatic isolation after World War II. Economically, Switzerland integrated itself into the American-led Western postwar order, but it remained reluctant to enter supranational bodies. Switzerland did not join the United Nations, even though Geneva became host to the UN's European headquarters, and the country played an active role in many of the UN's specialized agencies. Switzerland also remained aloof in the face of European integration efforts, waiting until 1963 to join the Council of Europe. It still remains outside the European Union. Instead, Switzerland in 1960 helped form the European Free Trade Area, which did not strive for political union. Following the Cold War, Switzerland joined the Bretton Woods institutions in 1992 and finally became a member of the United Nations in 2002.

GOVERNMENT

For additional analytical, business and investment opportunities information, please contact Global Investment & Business Center, USA at (703) 370-8082. Fax: (703) 370-8083. E-mail: ibpusa3@gmail.com
Global Business and Investment Info Databank - www.ibpus.com

Switzerland is a federal state composed of 26 cantons (20 are "full" cantons and six "half" cantons for purposes of representation in the federal legislature) that retain attributes of sovereignty, such as fiscal autonomy and the right to manage internal cantonal affairs. Under the 2000 Constitution, cantons hold all powers not specifically delegated to the federation. Switzerland's federal institutions are:

A bicameral legislature--the Federal Assembly;

A collegial executive of seven members--the Federal Council; and

A judiciary consisting of a regular court in Lausanne--the Federal Tribunal--and special military and administrative courts. The Federal Insurance Tribunal is an independent division of the Federal Tribunal that handles social security questions; its seat is in Lucerne. The Federal Criminal Court, located in Bellinzona, is the court of first instance for all criminal cases under federal jurisdiction.

The Constitution provides for separation of the three branches of government.
The Federal Assembly is the primary seat of power, although in practice the executive branch has been increasing its power at the expense of the legislative branch. The Federal Assembly has two houses--the Council of States and the National Council. These two houses have equal powers in all respects, including the right to introduce legislation. Legislation cannot be vetoed by the executive nor reviewed for constitutionality by the judiciary, but all laws (except the budget) can be reviewed by popular referendum before taking effect. The 46 members of the Council of States (two from each canton and one from each half canton) are directly elected in each canton by majority voting. The 200 members of the National Council are directly elected in each canton under a system of proportional representation. Members of both houses serve for 4 years.
The Federal Assembly meets quarterly for 3-week plenary sessions. The parliamentary committees of the two houses, which are often key in shaping legislation, meet behind closed doors, but both majority and minority positions are presented during the plenary sessions. The Federal Assembly is a militia parliament, and members commonly retain their traditional professions. Individual members of parliament have no personal staff.

The Assembly can be legally dissolved only after the adoption of a popular initiative calling for a complete revision of the Constitution. All citizens 18 or older have the right to vote and run for office in national, cantonal, and communal elections unless individually disqualified by the relevant legislature.

A strong emphasis on ballot votes arises out of the traditional Swiss belief that the will of the people is the final national authority. Every constitutional amendment adopted by parliament is automatically brought to the ballot and has to carry a double majority of votes and states in order to become effective. The voters themselves may actively seek changes to the Constitution by means of the popular initiative: 100,000 voters may with their signatures request a national vote on a proposed constitutional amendment. New federal legislation also is subject to popular review, under the so-called referendum: 50,000 signatures suffice to call a ballot vote on any federal law adopted by parliament. The Assembly can declare an act to be too urgent to allow time for popular consideration, but this is rare. At any rate, an act passed urgently must have a time limit and is later subject to the same constitutional provisions on popular review as other legislation.

The top executive body is the seven-member cabinet called the Federal Council. The Federal Assembly individually elects the seven Federal Councilors in a joint session of both houses at the opening of a new legislature. Federal Councilors are elected for 4-year terms; there are no term limits and no provision to recall the cabinet or individual members during the legislature. Each

For additional analytical, business and investment opportunities information,
please contact Global Investment & Business Center, USA
at (703) 370-8082. Fax: (703) 370-8083. E-mail: ibpusa3@gmail.com
Global Business and Investment Info Databank - www.ibpus.com

year, the Federal Assembly elects from among the seven Federal Councilors a president and vice president, following the principle of seniority. The member who is vice president one year traditionally is elected president the next. Although the Constitution provides that the Federal Assembly chooses and supervises the cabinet, the latter has gradually assumed a preeminent role in directing the legislative process as well as executing federal laws.

Under an arrangement between the four major parties called the "magic formula" which was introduced in 1959 but ended in December 2003, two Federal Councilors (ministers) were elected each from the Christian Democrats, the Social Democrats, and the Free Democrats and one from the Swiss People's Party. Under the new magic formula starting January 1, 2004, the new party composition of the cabinet changed to the following composition: 1 Christian Democrat, 2 Social Democrats, 2 Free Democrats, and 2 representatives of the Swiss People's Party.

The Constitution requires that Federal Councilors act collectively in all matters, not as individual ministers or as representatives of their parties. Each Councilor heads one of seven federal departments and is responsible for preparing legislation pertaining to matters under its jurisdiction. The president, who remains responsible for the department he heads, has limited prerogatives and is first among equals (there is no formal prime minister).

The administration of justice is primarily a cantonal function. The Federal Tribunal is limited in its jurisdiction. Its principal function is to hear appeals of civil and criminal cases. It also hears complaints of violations of the constitutional rights of citizens and has authority to review cantonal court decisions involving federal law as well as certain administrative rulings of federal departments. However, it has no power to review federal legislation for constitutionality. The Tribunal's 30 full-time and 30 part-time judges are elected by the Federal Assembly for 6-year terms. The Federal Criminal Court is the court of first instance for criminal cases involving organized and white-collar crime, money laundering, and corruption, which are under federal jurisdiction. The Court's 11 judges are elected by the Federal Assembly for 6-year terms. The cantons regulate local government. The basic unit of local government, which administers a village, town, or city, is the commune or municipality. Citizenship is derived from membership in a commune and can be conferred on non-Swiss by a commune. Cantons are subordinate to federal authority but keep autonomy in implementing federal law.

Principal Government Officials - Federal Council Members

Member of Council	Joined Council	Party	Canton	Function
Doris Leuthard	Aargau	Christian Democrats	Aargau	Head of the Federal Department of Environment, Transport, Energy and Communications
Eveline Widmer-Schlumpf	Graubünden	Conservative Democrats	Graubünden	Head of the Federal Department of Finance
Ueli Maurer	Zurich	Swiss People's Party	Zurich	Head of the Federal Department of Defence, Civil Protection and Sports
Didier Burkhalter	Neuchâtel	FDP.The Liberals	Neuchâtel	Head of the Federal Department of Foreign Affairs
Simonetta Sommaruga	Bern	Social Democrats	Bern	President for 2015; Head of the Federal Department of Justice and Police
Johann Schneider-Ammann	Bern	FDP.The Liberals	Bern	Vice President for 2015; Head of the Federal Department of Economic Affairs, Education and Research

For additional analytical, business and investment opportunities information, please contact Global Investment & Business Center, USA at (703) 370-8082. Fax: (703) 370-8083. E-mail: ibpusa3@gmail.com
Global Business and Investment Info Databank - www.ibpus.com

Alain Berset	Fribourg	Social Democrats	Fribourg	Head of the Federal Department of Home Affairs

Switzerland maintains an embassy in the United States at 2900 Cathedral Avenue NW, Washington, DC 20008. Consulates General are in Atlanta, Chicago, Houston, Los Angeles, New York, and San Francisco. Swiss national tourist offices are in Chicago, New York, and San Francisco.

POLITICAL CONDITIONS

Although it has a diverse society, Switzerland has a stable government. Most voters support the government in the armed neutrality underlying its foreign and defense policies. Domestic policy poses no major problems, but the changing international environment has generated a significant reexamination of Swiss policy in key areas such as defense, neutrality, and immigration. Quadrennial national elections typically produce only marginal changes in party representation.

In recent years, Switzerland has seen a gradual shift in the party landscape. The rightist Swiss People's Party (SVP), traditionally the junior partner in the four-party coalition government, more than doubled its voting share from 11% in 1987 to 22.5% in 1999, and finally to 26.6% in 2003, thus overtaking its three coalition partners. This shift in voting shares ended the 44-year old "magic formula," the power-broking agreement of the four coalition parties, and gave a second seat in the 7-person Swiss cabinet to the Swiss People's Party at the expense of the Christian Democrats, now the weakest party with 14.4% of the votes. For the first time in Swiss history, the SVP has two seats in the government, reflecting its new status as Switzerland's most popular party.

On December 10, 2003, Christoph Blocher--a self-made industrialist and main figure of the right-populist Swiss People's Party known for his strong opinions on asylum and migration and law and order issues--was elected to the cabinet by parliament, replacing the incumbent Christian Democrat Justice and Police Minister Ruth Metzler. The parliament also elected the Free Democrat Hans-Rudolf Merz to replace retiring Finance Minister Kaspar Villiger. Both Blocher and Merz are strong advocates of drastic public spending cuts in order to reduce the country's mounting $102 billion francs state deficit and are staunch opponents to Switzerland's entering the European Union. On June 14, 2006, the Federal Council elected Doris Leuthard of the Christian Democratic Party. Leuthard replaced the retiring Joseph Deiss and has assumed the Economics and Trade portfolio that Deiss managed. Leuthard's election and Deiss' resignation do not change the dynamics of the Federal Council. The current makeup of the government remains fiscally conservative and against further integration with the European Union.

The Constitution limits federal influence in the formulation of domestic policy and emphasizes the roles of private enterprise and cantonal government. However, the Confederation has been compelled to enlarge its policymaking powers in recent years to cope with national problems such as education, agriculture, energy, environment, organized crime, and narcotics.

ECONOMY

Currency	1 Swiss franc (CHF 1)
Fiscal year	Calendar year
Trade organisations	EFTA, WTO and OECD
	Statistics
GDP	$362.4 billion (PPP, 2012 est.)
GDP rank	20th (nominal) / 35th (PPP)
GDP growth	1.7% (2014 est.)
GDP per capita	$54,600 (PPP, 2012 est)

GDP by sector	agriculture (1.3%) industry (27.7%) services (71.0%) (2012 est.)
Inflation (CPI)	-0.7% (CPI, 2012 est.)
Population below poverty line	7.9% (2010)
Gini coefficient	29.6 (2010)
Labour force	4.91 million (2012 est.)
Labour force by occupation	agriculture (3.4%) Industry (23.4%) services (73.2%) (2010)
Unemployment	2.9% (2012 est.)
Main industries	machinery, chemicals, watches, textiles, precision instruments, tourism, banking, insurance
Ease-of-doing-business rank	28th

External

Exports	$308.4 billion (2012 est.) Note: trade data exclude trade with Switzerland
Export goods	machinery, chemicals, metals, watches, agricultural products
Main export partners	Germany 19.8% United States 11.1% Italy 7.2% France 7.1% United Kingdom 5.4% (2012 est.)
Imports	$287.7 billion (2012 est.)
Import goods	machinery, chemicals, vehicles, metals; agricultural products, textiles
Main import partners	Germany 29.7% Italy 10.2% France 8.4% United States 5.6% China 5.6% Austria 4.2% (2012 est.)
FDI stock	$634.3 billion (31 December 2012 est.)
Gross external debt	$1.346 trillion (30 June 2011)

Public finances

Public debt	46.7% of GDP (2012 est.)
Revenues	$212.7 billion (2012 est.)
Expenses	$211.1 billion (2012 est.)Note: includes federal, cantonal and municipal accounts
Economic aid	donor: ODA CHF2.31 billion (0.47% of GDP)
Credit rating	Standard & Poor's: AAA (Domestic) AAA (Foreign) AAA (T&C Assessment) Outlook: Stable Moody's: Aaa Outlook: Stable Fitch: AAA Outlook: Stable

For additional analytical, business and investment opportunities information, please contact Global Investment & Business Center, USA at (703) 370-8082. Fax: (703) 370-8083. E-mail: ibpusa3@gmail.com Global Business and Investment Info Databank - www.ibpus.com

Foreign reserves	US$331.9 billion (31 December 2011)

The **economy of Switzerland** is one of the world's most stable economies. Its policy of long-term monetary security and political stability has made Switzerland a safe haven for investors, creating an economy that is increasingly dependent on a steady tide of foreign investment.

Because of the country's small size and high labor specialization, industry and trade are the keys to Switzerland's economic livelihood. Switzerland has achieved one of the highest per capita incomes in the world with low unemployment rates and a balanced budget. The service sector has also come to play a significant economic role.

Despite a dearth of natural resources, the Swiss economy is among the world's most advanced and prosperous. Per capita income is virtually the highest in the world, as are wages. Trade has been the key to prosperity in Switzerland. The country is dependent upon export markets to generate income while dependent upon imports for raw materials and to expand the range of goods and services available in the country. Switzerland has liberal investment and trade policies, notwithstanding agriculture, and a conservative fiscal policy. The Swiss legal system is highly developed, commercial law is well defined, and solid laws and policies protect investments. The Swiss franc is one of the world's soundest currencies, and the country is known for its high standard of banking and financial services. Switzerland is a member of a number of international economic organizations, including the World Trade Organization (WTO), the International Monetary Fund, the World Bank, and the Organization for Economic Cooperation and Development (OECD).

The Swiss economy expanded by 2.7% in 2006, the fastest rate in six years, thus confirming sustained growth over the last four years. GDP growth was primarily due to the positive evolution of private consumption and expansion of investment in fixed assets and software. For once, all export industries benefited from increased demand from foreign markets. With a surplus of $9.6 billion (SF 11.7 billion), the Swiss trade balance reached unprecedented levels. On the inflation side, import prices increased more rapidly than exports.

Switzerland was ranked as the most competitive economy in the World Economic Forum's 2006 Global Competitiveness Report for the first time, reflecting the country's sound institutional environment, excellent infrastructure, efficient markets, competent macroeconomic management, world-class educational attainment, and high levels of technological innovation, which boost Switzerland's competitiveness in the global economy. The country has a well-developed infrastructure for scientific research, companies spend generously on research and development, and intellectual property protection is strong. Business activity benefits from a well-developed institutional framework, characterized by the rule of law, an efficient judicial system, and high levels of transparency and accountability within public institutions. Higher education and training are rapidly growing in importance as engines of productivity growth.

Being a nation that depends upon exports for economic growth, and due to the fact that it is so closely linked to the economies of Western Europe and the United States, Switzerland was not able to escape recent slowdowns experienced in these countries. During most of the 1990s, the Swiss economy was Western Europe's weakest, with annual GDP growth averaging 0% between 1991 and 1997. Beginning in late 1997, the economy steadily gained momentum until peaking in 2000 with 3% growth in real terms. The economy returned to lackluster growth during 2001-2003, but has been growing at or above potential since 2004--2.5% per annum. The Swiss Economic Ministry reports that strong global demand, particularly in the U.S. and Asia, and better Euro zone growth has helped Switzerland's economic recovery. Long-run economic growth, however, is predicated on structural reforms. In order to maximize its economic potential, Switzerland will need to push through difficult agrarian and competition policy reforms. These are essential if the government is to reduce its budget deficits and meet its 3% growth target.

In 2005, the dollar/Swiss franc exchange rate continued to be shaped by geopolitical tensions. The dollar depreciated further against the Swiss franc from SF 1.49 in October 2002 to SF 1.31 in 2003, to 1.28 in 2005 to 1.23 in July 2006, and 1.22 in January 2007. The strengthening of the Euro, however, helped Switzerland to minimize the pressure from a weakening dollar. The Swiss National Bank raised interest rates on June 15, 2006 to 1.5%, the third increase since January 2006. The Swiss National Bank also said it expected economic growth to be a robust 2.5% in 2006 and 2007.

While the number of bankruptcies in Switzerland had been on the rise for four years, reaching alarming levels in 2005 (10,800), the rate dropped by 4.7% in 2006. Compared to other European countries, Switzerland's bankruptcy rates ranks fourth (1.35%) among the hardest hit countries, after Luxemburg (2.39%), Austria (1.9%) and France (1.49%).

The recent economic upswing had some positive impact on the labor market. Unemployment decreased from 4.1% in December 2003 to 3.1% in March 2007. Swiss in the 15-25 age bracket continue to fight unemployment numbers with a rate of 5.4%, and hotel and restaurant industry workers with 10.4%. One-fourth of the country's full-time workers are unionized. In general, labor/management relations are good, mostly characterized by a willingness on both sides to settle disputes by negotiations rather than by labor action. About 600 collective bargaining agreements exist today in Switzerland and are regularly renewed without major problems. However, the mood is changing. The massive layoffs that resulted from both the global economic slowdown and major management scandals have strained the traditional Swiss "labor peace." Swiss trade unions encouraged strikes against several companies, including the national airline SWISS, Coca-Cola, and Orange (the French telecom operator), but total days lost to strikes remain among the lowest in the OECD. Uncertainties concerning the proper management of pension funds, and the prospect of a potential hike in the retirement age from 65 to 67 have stirred heated political debate.

Switzerland's machinery, metals, electronics, and chemicals sectors are world-renowned for precision and quality. Together they account for well over half of Swiss export revenues. In agriculture, Switzerland is about 60% self-sufficient. Only 7.5% of the remaining imports originated from the U.S. Swiss farmers are one of the most highly protected and subsidized producer group in the world.

OECD estimates show that Switzerland is subsidizing more than 70% of its agriculture, compared to 35% in the EU. According to the newly adopted "2008-2011 Agricultural Program", Switzerland intends to reduce its subsidies from SF 14.1 billion (U.S. $11.6 billion) to SF 13.6 billion (U.S. $10.5 billion) over the next four years. In March 2007, the parliament increased the initial government bill by SF 150 million (U.S. $123 million) on the grounds that Swiss farm reforms were going too fast. The parliament also accepted international parallel imports for fertilizers and tractors. Swiss farmers will be allowed to import tractors produced in China or India and sold in the EU, and save up to $41 million (SF 50 million) annual in expenses. German fertilizer could save another $20 million (SF 25 million). A more general bill on parallel imports will be presented by the Justice Ministry to parliament by the end of 2007.

Tourism, banking, engineering, and insurance are significant sectors of the economy and heavily influence the country's economic policies. Swiss trading companies have unique marketing expertise in many parts of the world, including Eastern Europe, the Far East, Africa, and the Middle East. Not only does Switzerland have a highly developed tourism infrastructure (making it a good market for tourism-related equipment and services), the Swiss also are intrepid travelers. Per capita, more Swiss visit the United States every year than from any other country. Tourism is the most important U.S. export to Switzerland (earning almost $1.5 billion). In 2004, more than 285,000 Swiss came to the United States as tourists.

The Swiss economy earns roughly half of its corporate earnings from the export industry, and 62% of Swiss exports are destined for the EU market. The EU is Switzerland's largest trading partner, and economic and trade barriers between them are minimal. In the wake of the Swiss voters' rejection of the European Economic Area Agreement in 1992, the Swiss Government set its sights on negotiating bilateral sectoral agreements with the EU. After more than 4 years of negotiations, an agreement covering seven sectors (research, public procurement, technical barriers to trade, agriculture, civil aviation, land transport, and the free movement of persons) was achieved at the end of 1998. Parliament officially endorsed the so-called "Bilaterals I" in 1999, and the Swiss people approved them in a referendum in May 2000. The agreements, which had to be ratified by the European Parliament as well as legislatures in all 15 EU member states, entered into force on June 1, 2002. Switzerland has so far attempted to mitigate possible adverse effects of non-membership by conforming many of its regulations, standards, and practices to EU directives and norms. Full access to the Swiss market for the original 15 EU member states entered into force in June 2004, ending as a result the "national preference". The Swiss agreed to extend these preferences to the 10 new EU members on September 25, 2005.

The Swiss Government embarked in July 2001 on a second round of bilateral negotiations with the EU known as "Bilaterals II". Talks focused on customs fraud, environment, statistics, trade in processed agricultural goods, media, the taxation of savings, and police/judicial cooperation (dubbed the Schengen-Dublin accords). Amid a fierce political debate over the essence of Swiss-EU relations and populist warnings against EU workers and criminals entering Switzerland, the Schengen-Dublin package was approved on June 5, 2005 by a referendum of 54.6%. Fears of cheap labor coming from new EU member states have prompted the government to provide for tripartite surveillance committees to ensure that decent wages are enforced. The EU has still to ratify the extension of Schengen to Switzerland, and implement the bilateral agreements on research and development and media cooperation.

As part of the bilateral agreement on the taxation of savings signed in June 2003, Swiss banks will levy a withholding tax on EU citizens' savings income. The tax, which started on July 1, 2005, will increase gradually to 35% by 2011, with 75% of the funds being transferred to the EU. On November 26, 2006, the Swiss electorate approved a government bill to contribute 1 billion Swiss francs (about $800 million) to the 10 new EU member states. In a nation-wide referendum, 53.4% of voters accepted the "Eastern Europe Cooperation Act," which entitles the government to spend 1 billion Swiss francs on projects in primarily Central European states over the next 10 years. Switzerland had pledged this contribution to share the burden of the EU's eastern expansion in order to facilitate the conclusion of the second set of bilateral negotiations with the EU. The right-populist Swiss People's Party (SVP), which prompted the referendum, was disappointed, but pleased that it mobilized a 47% opposition.

The Eastern Europe Cooperation Act gives a new legal basis for Swiss aid to countries in Eastern Europe. The act has a 10-year term and replaces the former federal Law on Aid to Eastern Europe, which came into force in 1995. Since the fall of the Berlin Wall, Switzerland has spent SF 3.5 billion on about 1,000 aid projects in Central and Eastern Europe to help countries in the region transform into market economies. Sixty percent of the SF 1 billion is to come from the budget of the departments of foreign and economic affairs, mainly from cuts in aid programs to other parts of the world. The remaining 40% will be taken from the regular budget of the federal administration. The funds are to be used on projects chosen by Switzerland and focused on education, trade promotion, environment, and internal security. The money is paid directly to the projects and does not go the EU cohesion fund in Brussels. Switzerland has no formal agreement with the European Union concerning these contributions. Instead, there is a Memorandum of Understanding (MOU) that sets out the general conditions of the Swiss commitment to the ten new EU member states. Under the MOU, almost half of the funding will go to Poland. Hungary's benefit will be SF 131 million, while the Czech Republic will receive SF 110 million.

The Swiss federal government remains deeply divided over EU membership as its long-term goal, and in a March 2001 referendum more than 70% of Swiss voters rejected rapid steps toward EU membership. The issue of EU membership is likely to be shelved for several years, if not a decade. In May 2005, the government said it could sign a framework agreement with the European Union, as an alternative to joining the organization, to encourage dialogue and create a platform for closer cooperation.

Switzerland nevertheless expressed interest in reaching a third layer of bilateral agreements that would involve energy, the Galileo satellite navigation system, health, and agriculture. But recent harsh criticism by the European Commission against preferential cantonal tax treatment for foreign holdings cooled the political climate surrounding the EU. Unilateral trade retaliation--as threatened by the EU if the Swiss cantons do not change their cantonal tax regimes--has not occurred, but the political damage is done, including greater anti-EU feelings among the population. The pressure to negotiate with the EU could turn sour as the EU has already asked Switzerland to pay another SF 300-350 million ($240-280 million, on top of the SF 1 billion cohesion fund) to provide further financial aid to Romania and Bulgaria, which joined the EU on January 1, 2007. Unlike the November 2006 referendum, the newly enacted Eastern Europe Cooperation Act does not provide for an automatic referendum on further payments. The parliament will decide on the additional aid request.

The government also decided in November 2006 to once more consider adoption of the EU "Cassis-de-Dijon" principle for trade after a first setback in 2004. If adopted, EU products could be imported in Switzerland without having to go through the burdensome Swiss certification and Swiss language requirement process. Currently, Swiss retail prices are on average 20-40% higher than in the EU. If parallel imports are allowed under adoption of the Cassis-de-Dijion principle, prices could drop by 10%. Possible exceptions have been reduced from 129 products to 40, but hurdles remain on the labeling of alcohol contained in Alcopops, the Swiss ban of phosphates in washing machine powders, the real origin of "EU meat", and on the stringent Swiss generic food production requirements. The "Cassis de Dijon principle" will not apply to the many farming and industrial products already covered by mutual recognition agreements (MRAs) under the EU-Swiss Bilaterals I and II; nor will it apply to other products such as pesticides, motor engines, and weapons that require an authorization. The impact, as a result, may not be as large as expected. Another issue is that Swiss and EU MRAs concluded with third countries may also benefit from adoption of the Cassis-de-Dijon principle (these goods would also have to receive WTO most favored nation status).

The government has reaffirmed its wish to strengthen ties with other non-EU trading partners in Asia and America. Exploratory talks on a Free Trade Agreement between the U.S. and Switzerland failed to result in negotiations, due to Swiss problems with free trade in agriculture, but the two sides did agree to a new framework for economic, trade, and investment discussions. This new agreement is the Swiss-U.S. Trade and Investment Cooperation Forum (the "Forum") and is currently assessing areas where the two governments could facilitate greater trade and investment flows.

Switzerland ranks 17th among the main trading partners of the U.S. worldwide. The United States is the second-largest importer (11.5%) of Swiss goods after Germany (20%). The U.S. exports more to Switzerland each year than to all the countries of the former Soviet Union and Eastern Europe combined, and Switzerland imports more U.S. products and services than does Spain. In addition, the United States is the largest foreign investor in Switzerland, and conversely, the primary destination of Swiss foreign investment. It is estimated that 200,000 American jobs

For additional analytical, business and investment opportunities information, please contact Global Investment & Business Center, USA at (703) 370-8082. Fax: (703) 370-8083. E-mail: ibpusa3@gmail.com Global Business and Investment Info Databank - www.ibpus.com

depend on Swiss foreign investments. Total U.S.-Swiss bilateral trade increased from $15.33 billion during 2003 to $16 billion in 2004.

DEFENSE

On May 18, 2003, Swiss voters approved the military reform project "Army XXI" that will drastically reduce the size of the Swiss Army. In January 2004, the 524,000-strong militia started paring down to 220,000 conscripts, including 80,000 reservists. The defense budget of currently SF 4.3 billion ($3.1 billion) will be trimmed by SF 300 million, and some 2,000 jobs are expected to be shed between 2004 and 2011. The mandatory time of service will be curtailed from 300 to 260 days. All able-bodied Swiss males aged 20 to 30 must serve. Thereafter, most personnel are assigned to civil protection duties until the age of 37.

A new category of soldiers called "single-term conscripts" will discharge the total time of service of about 300 days of active duty in one go. Recruiting is on a voluntary basis and should not exceed 20% of a year's draft. The armed forces have a small nucleus of about 3,600 professional staff, half of whom are either instructors or staff officers, with the remainder mostly being fortification guards. The army has virtually no full-time active combat units but is capable of full mobilization within 72 hours. Women may volunteer to serve in the armed forces and may now join all units, including combat troops. About 2,000 women already serve in the army but, so far, have not been allowed to use weapons for purposes other than self-defense.
The armed forces are organized in four army corps and an air force and are equipped with modern, sophisticated, and well-maintained gear. In 1993, the Swiss Government procured 34 FA-18s from the United States.

FOREIGN RELATIONS

On September 10, 2002, Switzerland became a full member of the United Nations. Switzerland had previously been involved as party to the Statute of the International Court of Justice and member of most UN specialized agencies, as well as the International Atomic Energy Agency. Switzerland has long participated in many UN activities, including the Economic Commission for Europe, UN Environment Program, the UN High Commissioner for Refugees, UN Educational, Scientific and Cultural Organization, UN Conference for Trade and Development, UN Industrial Development Organization, and the Universal Postal Union (UPU). Prior to its formal accession, Switzerland had maintained a permanent observer mission at UN Headquarters since 1948.

Switzerland also is a member of the following international organizations: World Trade Organization, Organization for Economic Cooperation and Development, European Free Trade Association, Bank for International Settlements, Council of Europe, and Organization for Security and Cooperation in Europe (OSCE). In 1992, Swiss voters approved membership in the Bretton Woods organizations but later that year rejected the European Economic Area agreement, which the government viewed as a first step toward EU membership.

The Swiss Constitution declares the preservation of Switzerland's independence and welfare as the supreme objective of Swiss foreign policy. Below this overarching goal, the Constitution sets five specific foreign policy objectives: further the peaceful coexistence of nations; promote respect for human rights, democracy, and the rule of the law; promote Swiss economic interests abroad; alleviate need and poverty in the world; and the preservation of natural resources.

Traditionally, Switzerland has avoided alliances that might entail military, political, or direct economic action, but in recent years the Swiss have broadened the scope of activities in which they feel able to participate without compromising their neutrality. Swiss voters first rejected UN membership by a 3-to-1 margin in 1986 but in March 2002 adopted it, albeit in a very close election, making Switzerland the first country to join the UN based on a popular referendum decision. In similar fashion, the electorate rejected a government proposition to deploy Swiss

For additional analytical, business and investment opportunities information, please contact Global Investment & Business Center, USA at (703) 370-8082. Fax: (703) 370-8083. E-mail: ibpusa3@gmail.com Global Business and Investment Info Databank - www.ibpus.com

troops as UN peacekeepers (Blue Helmets) in 1994, but Switzerland joined NATO's Partnership for Peace and the Euro-Atlantic Partnership Council in 1996 and 1997, respectively, and deployed Yellow Berets to support the OSCE in Bosnia. In June 2001, Swiss voters approved new legislation providing for the deployment of armed Swiss troops for international peacekeeping missions under UN or OSCE auspices as well as closer international cooperation in military training.

Switzerland maintains diplomatic relations with almost all countries and historically has served as a neutral intermediary and host to major international treaty conferences. The country has no major dispute in its bilateral relations. Since 1980, Switzerland has represented U.S. interests in Iran. Switzerland played a key role in brokering a truce agreement between the Sudanese Government and Sudan's Peoples Liberation Army (SPLA) for the Nuba Mountain region, signed after a week's negotiations taking place near Lucerne in January 2002.

The Swiss feel a moral obligation to undertake social, economic, and humanitarian activities that contribute to world peace and prosperity. This is manifested by Swiss bilateral and multilateral diplomatic activity, assistance to developing countries, and support for the extension of international law, particularly humanitarian law. Switzerland (mainly Geneva) is home to many international governmental and nongovernmental organizations, including the International Committee of the Red Cross (whose flag is essentially the Swiss flag with colors reversed--the Red Cross historically being a Swiss organization). One of the first international organizations, the Universal Postal Union, is located in Bern.

The Swiss Government on June 25, 2003, eased most of the sanctions against the Republic of Iraq in accord with UN Security Council Resolution (UNSCR) 1483. The government lifted the trade embargo, flight restrictions, and financial sanctions in place since August 1990. The weapons embargo and the asset freeze, the scope of which was extended, remain in force, and restrictions on the trade in Iraqi cultural goods were newly imposed. Though not a member at the time, Switzerland had joined UN sanctions against Iraq after the invasion of Kuwait. Switzerland in recent years joined UN and EU economic sanctions imposed on Sierra Leone, UNITA (Angola), Liberia, Serbia and Montenegro, Burma, Zimbabwe, Sudan, Democratic Republic of the Congo, and Cote d'Ivoire. On October 15, 2003, the Federal Council ended the import restrictions on raw diamonds from Sierra Leone and lifted sanctions against Libya.

Switzerland in October 2000 implemented an ordinance to enforce UN sanctions against the Taliban (UNSCR 1267), which it subsequently amended in April 2001 in accord with tighter UN regulations (UNSCR 1333). On May 2, 2002, the Swiss Government eased the sanctions regime in accord with UNSCR 1388 and 1390, lifting the ban on the sale of acetic acid (used in drug production), Afghani Airlines, and Afghani diplomatic representations. The weapons embargo, travel restrictions, and financial sanctions remain in force. The Swiss Government in November 2001 issued an ordinance declaring illegal the terrorist organization al Qaeda as well as possible successor or supporting organizations. More than 200 individuals or companies linked to international terrorism have been blacklisted to have their assets frozen. Thus far, Swiss authorities have blocked about 72 accounts totaling 34 million francs.

Switzerland has furnished military observers and medical teams to several UN operations. Switzerland is an active participant in the OSCE, its foreign minister serving as Chairman-in-Office for 1996. Switzerland also is an active participant in the major nonproliferation and export control regimes.

Under a series of treaties concluded after World War I, Switzerland assumed responsibility for the diplomatic and consular representation of Liechtenstein, the protection of its borders, and the regulation of its customs.

For additional analytical, business and investment opportunities information, please contact Global Investment & Business Center, USA at (703) 370-8082. Fax: (703) 370-8083. E-mail: ibpusa3@gmail.com Global Business and Investment Info Databank - www.ibpus.com

U.S.-SWISS RELATIONS

Switzerland is a democratic country subscribing to most of the ideals with which the United States is identified. The country is politically stable with a fundamentally strong economy. It occupies an important strategic position within Europe and possesses a strong military capability. It has played an increasingly important role in supporting the spread of democratic institutions and values worldwide, as well as providing humanitarian relief and economic development assistance. U.S. policy toward Switzerland takes these factors into account and endeavors to cooperate with Switzerland to the extent consistent with Swiss neutrality.

The first 4 years of cooperation under the U.S.-Swiss Joint Economic Commission (JEC) invigorated bilateral ties by recording achievements in a number of areas, including consultations on anti-money laundering efforts, counter-terrorism, and pharmaceutical regulatory cooperation; an e-government conference; and the re-establishment of the Fulbright student/cultural exchange program.

The United States and Switzerland signed three new agreements in 2006 that will complement the JEC and will deepen our cooperation and improve our relationship. The first of the new agreements is the Enhanced Political Framework and was signed by Under Secretary of State for Political Affairs Nicholas Burns and Swiss State Secretary Michael Ambühl. The second agreement is the Trade and Investment Cooperation Forum and was signed by then-U.S. Trade Representative Robert Portman and then-Economics and Trade Minister Joseph Deiss. The last agreement is the revised Operative Working Arrangement on Law Enforcement Cooperation on Counterterrorism and was signed by U.S. Attorney General Alberto Gonzalez and Swiss Justice Minister Christoph Blocher.

The first official U.S.-Swiss consular relations were established in the late 1820s. Diplomatic relations were established in 1853. The U.S. ambassador to Switzerland also is accredited to the Principality of Liechtenstein.

Principal U.S. Officials
Anbassador - Suzan "Suzi" LeVine

Suzan "Suzi" LeVine took up her position as the United States Ambassador to Switzerland and Liechtenstein on June 2, 2014.

Charge d'Affaires--Jeffrey R. Cellars
Political/Economic Section--Richard Rorvig
Commercial Officer--Donald Businger
Consul General--Edward Birsner
Management Officer--Jonathan Schools
Regional Security Officer--Brian Murphy
Public Affairs Officer--Lisbeth Keefe
Defense Attache--Dorothea Cypher-Erickson
Legal Attache--Dan Boyd
Drug Enforcement Administration--Joe Kipp
Department of Homeland Security Attache--Joe Catanzarite

The U.S. Embassy in Switzerland is at Jubilaeumsstrasse 93, 3005 Bern, tel: (41) (31) 357-7011. The U.S. Mission to the European Office of the United Nations and other International Organizations is in Geneva at Route de Pregny 11, 1292 Chambesy, tel: (41) (22) 749-4111. The U.S. Mission to the WTO is in Geneva at Avenue de la Paix 1-3, 1202 Geneva, tel: (41) (22) 749-4111. The U.S. Delegation to the Conference on Disarmament (CD) is in Geneva at Route de

For additional analytical, business and investment opportunities information,
please contact Global Investment & Business Center, USA
at (703) 370-8082. Fax: (703) 370-8083. E-mail: ibpusa3@gmail.com
Global Business and Investment Info Databank - www.ibpus.com

Pregny 11, 1292 Chambesy, tel: (41) (22) 749-4407. America Centers and Consular Agencies are also maintained in Zurich and Geneva.

TRAVEL AND BUSINESS INFORMATION

The U.S. Department of State's Consular Information Program advises Americans traveling and residing abroad through Consular Information Sheets, Public Announcements, and Travel Warnings. **Consular Information Sheets** exist for all countries and include information on entry and exit requirements, currency regulations, health conditions, safety and security, crime, political disturbances, and the addresses of the U.S. embassies and consulates abroad. **Public Announcements** are issued to disseminate information quickly about terrorist threats and other relatively short-term conditions overseas that pose significant risks to the security of American travelers. **Travel Warnings** are issued when the State Department recommends that Americans avoid travel to a certain country because the situation is dangerous or unstable.

For the latest security information, Americans living and traveling abroad should regularly monitor the Department's Bureau of Consular Affairs Internet web site at http://www.travel.state.gov, where the current Worldwide Caution, Public Announcements, and Travel Warnings can be found. Consular Affairs Publications, which contain information on obtaining passports and planning a safe trip abroad, are also available at http://www.travel.state.gov. For additional information on international travel, see http://www.usa.gov/Citizen/Topics/Travel/International.shtml.

The Department of State encourages all U.S citizens traveling or residing abroad to register via the State Department's travel registration website or at the nearest U.S. embassy or consulate abroad. Registration will make your presence and whereabouts known in case it is necessary to contact you in an emergency and will enable you to receive up-to-date information on security conditions.

Emergency information concerning Americans traveling abroad may be obtained by calling 1-888-407-4747 toll free in the U.S. and Canada or the regular toll line 1-202-501-4444 for callers outside the U.S. and Canada.

The National Passport Information Center (NPIC) is the U.S. Department of State's single, centralized public contact center for U.S. passport information. Telephone: 1-877-4USA-PPT (1-877-487-2778). Customer service representatives and operators for TDD/TTY are available Monday-Friday, 7:00 a.m. to 12:00 midnight, Eastern Time, excluding federal holidays.

Travelers can check the latest health information with the U.S. Centers for Disease Control and Prevention in Atlanta, Georgia. A hotline at 877-FYI-TRIP (877-394-8747) and a web site at http://www.cdc.gov/travel/index.htm give the most recent health advisories, immunization recommendations or requirements, and advice on food and drinking water safety for regions and countries. A booklet entitled "Health Information for International Travel" (HHS publication number CDC-95-8280) is available from the U.S. Government Printing Office, Washington, DC 20402, tel. (202) 512-1800.

For additional analytical, business and investment opportunities information, please contact Global Investment & Business Center, USA at (703) 370-8082. Fax: (703) 370-8083. E-mail: ibpusa3@gmail.com Global Business and Investment Info Databank - www.ibpus.com

PRACTICAL INFORMATION FOR STARTING BUSINESS[1]

DOING BUSINESS IN SWITZERLAND BASICS

MARKET OVERVIEW

* Switzerland's population of 8 million is affluent and cosmopolitan
* GDP of about USD 631 billion; growth forecast of 2.2% for 2014
* In 2013 total exports from the U.S. to Switzerland amounted to USD 27 billion.
* U.S.-Swiss trade generally stable despite financial and economic crisis;
* World-class infrastructure, business-friendly legal and regulatory environment
* Highly educated, reliable, and flexible work force
* Consumer and producer of high-quality, value-added industrial/consumer goods
* Manufacturing sector is highly automated and efficient
* Strong market demand for U.S. components and production systems
* Strong demand for high quality products with competitive prices
* Highest per capita IT spending in the world
* Multilingual/multicultural European test market and business environment
* Many U.S. firms with European and regional headquarters in Switzerland

MARKET CHALLENGES

* Market is sophisticated, quality-conscious, high-tech and competitive
* An epicenter of European and global competition
* While EU-type regulations and standards exist in general, there are significant exceptions
* Unique Swiss requirements for pharmaceuticals, cosmetics, detergents, and chemicals

MARKET OPPORTUNITIES

* Products with relatively advanced technologies are best prospects
* Switzerland is strategically placed as a gateway to EU markets
* Ideal test market for introduction of new high tech and consumer products
* Excellent platform for marketing into Europe, Middle East and Africa
* High concentration of computer/Internet usage per capita
* Sophisticated market for U.S. devices
* Switzerland is becoming a European center for commercial aviation business
* Fast growing demand for highly sophisticated security equipment/systems
* One of the world's top countries for R&D
* Excellent opportunities for partnerships in biotech, nanotech, and renewable energies, especially solar
* Significant assets pooled from around the world under Swiss management, creating excellent opportunities for U.S. financial services providers

MARKET ENTRY STRATEGY

* Express commitment to the market and establish long term relationships
* Work directly with Swiss importers/distributors for maximum market penetration
* Be prepared to meet customer's needs and willing to sell in small volumes
* Offer high quality and environmentally friendly products
* Enter the market early to gain and maintain competitive edge

---

[1] US and Swiss Governmets materials

For additional analytical, business and investment opportunities information,
please contact Global Investment & Business Center, USA
at (703) 370-8082. Fax: (703) 370-8083. E-mail: ibpusa3@gmail.com
Global Business and Investment Info Databank - www.ibpus.com

* Evaluate carefully prospective partner's technical qualifications and ability to cover the German, French and Italian regions

SWITZERLAND INVESTMENT AND BUSINESS CLIMATE - STRATEGIC INFORMATION AND CONTACS FOR STARTING BUSINESS IN SWITZERLAND

Contact Point
Scott Woodard, Economic/Commercial Officer
Raphael Vogel, Economic Specialist
U.S. Embassy in Bern, Sulgeneckstrasse 17, 3003 Bern
+41 31 357 7319
Business-bern@state.gov

Switzerland welcomes foreign investment and accords it national treatment. Foreign investment is not hampered by significant barriers. The Swiss Federal Government adopts a relaxed attitude of benevolent noninterference towards foreign investment, allowing the 26 cantons to set major policy, and confining itself to creating and maintaining general conditions favorable to both Swiss and foreign investors. Such factors include economic and political stability, a transparent legal system, reliable and extensive infrastructure, efficient capital markets and excellent quality of life in general. Many US firms base their European or regional headquarters in Switzerland, drawn to the country's low corporate tax rates, exceptional infrastructure, and productive and multilingual work force.

Switzerland was ranked as the world's most competitive economy according to the World Economic Forum's Global Competitiveness Report in 2013. The high ranking reflects the country's sound institutional environment, excellent infrastructure, efficient markets and high levels of technological innovation. Switzerland has a developed infrastructure for scientific research; companies spend generously on R&D; intellectual property protection is generally strong; and the country's public institutions are transparent and stable.

Many of Switzerland's cantons make significant use of fiscal incentives to attract investment to their jurisdictions. Some of the more aggressive cantons have occasionally waived taxes for new firms for up to ten years but this practice has been criticized by the European Union, which has requested the abolition of these practices. Individual income tax rates vary widely across the 26 cantons. Corporate taxes vary depending upon the many different tax incentives. Zurich, which is sometimes used as a reference point for corporate location tax calculations, has a rate of around 25%, which includes municipal, cantonal, and federal tax. The **World Bank** , in its "Doing Business" survey ranks Switzerland as the 29th most attractive destination for doing business in the world and 2nd on the **IMD World Competitiveness Scoreboard**. However, the approval on February 9, 2014 of an initiative to restrict the principle of free movement of citizens from the European Union may strain relations with the EU going forward. This could have negative economic consequences for Switzerland; the Swiss government is currently in discussions with the EU on this matter.

Some former public monopolies retain their historical market dominance despite partial or full privatization. Foreign investors can find it difficult to enter these markets due to high entry costs and the relatively small size of the Swiss market.

OPENNESS TO, AND RESTRICTIONS UPON, FOREIGN INVESTMENT *ATTITUDE TOWARD FDI*

For additional analytical, business and investment opportunities information, please contact Global Investment & Business Center, USA
at (703) 370-8082. Fax: (703) 370-8083. E-mail: ibpusa3@gmail.com
Global Business and Investment Info Databank - www.ibpus.com

Switzerland welcomes foreign investment and accords it national treatment. Foreign investment is not hampered by significant barriers. No discriminatory effects on foreign investors or foreign-owned investments have been reported.

Other Investment Policy Reviews

The report states that "the Swiss Constitution allows national and foreigners to operate business in Switzerland, to form a company or to hold an interest in one. [...] Most economic sectors are open to investment by Swiss nationals and foreigners. However, investment restrictions continue to apply to areas under state monopolies, including certain rail transport services, some postal services, and certain insurance services and commercial activities (e.g. trade in salt). Restrictions (in the form of domicile requirements) are also applied in air and maritime transport, hydroelectric and nuclear power, operation of oil and gas pipelines, and transportation of explosive materials."

The same report states that "Liechtenstein has a stable and predictable investment regime. Most sectors are open to national and foreign investment, except for residency requirements; restrictions on the purchase of real estate; restrictions in production, trade, and transport of electricity, gas, and water (subject to state monopoly); and restrictions applied to a number of financial services (asset management, investment consulting, and assuming trusteeships) when these are provided on a professional basis by trustees or trust companies".

Laws/Regulations of FDI

The major laws governing foreign investment in Switzerland are the Swiss Code of Obligations, the Lex Friedrich/Koller, the Securities Law, and the Cartel Law. There is no screening of foreign investment. There are few sectoral or geographic preferences or restrictions. Several exceptions are described below in the section on performance requirements and incentives.

Some former public monopolies retain their historical market dominance despite partial or full privatization. Foreign investors can find it difficult to enter these markets due to high entry costs and the relatively small size of the Swiss market.

Industrial Strategy

The **WTO report** concluded that "the high living standards, highly skilled labour force, flexible labour laws, reliable infrastructure, as well as relatively low levels of taxation, are considered to make Switzerland one of the most attractive locations for foreign direct investment (FDI) in the world."

Switzerland Global Enterprise is the Swiss government's federal-level agency promoting investments into Switzerland (**http://www.s-ge.com**). The 26 cantons independently promote investments into their territories and have individual strategies to attract investments. Some cities and regions also have their own economic development organizations.

Limits on Foreign Control

Foreign and domestic enterprises may engage in various forms of remunerative activities and may freely establish, acquire and dispose of interests in business enterprises. However, the following legal restrictions apply:

For additional analytical, business and investment opportunities information,
please contact Global Investment & Business Center, USA
at (703) 370-8082. Fax: (703) 370-8083. E-mail: ibpusa3@gmail.com
Global Business and Investment Info Databank - www.ibpus.com

Corporate boards - - There are no laws authorizing private firms to limit or prohibit foreign investment or participation. The board of directors of a company registered in Switzerland must consist of a majority of Swiss citizens residing in Switzerland. At least one member of the board of directors authorized to represent the company (i.e., to sign legal documents) must be domiciled in Switzerland. If the board of directors consists of a single person, this person must have Swiss citizenship and be domiciled in Switzerland. Foreign controlled companies usually meet these requirements by nominating Swiss directors who hold shares and perform functions on a fiduciary basis. Mitigating these requirements is the fact that the manager of a company need not be a Swiss citizen and company shares can be controlled by foreigners (except for banks). The establishment of commercial presence by persons or enterprises without legal personality under Swiss law requires an establishment authorization according to cantonal law. The aforementioned requirements do not generally pose a major hardship or impediment for US investors.

Hostile takeovers - - Swiss corporate shares can be issued both as registered shares (in the name of the holder) or bearer shares. Provided the shares are not quoted on the stock exchange, Swiss companies may in their articles of incorporation impose certain restrictions on the transfer of registered shares to prevent unfriendly takeovers by domestic or foreign companies (article 685a of the Code of Obligations). Unwelcome takeovers can also be warded off by public companies, but legislation introduced in 1992 has made this practice more difficult. Public companies must now cite in their statutes significant reasons, relevant for the survival, conduct and purpose of their business, to prevent or hinder a takeover by an outsider. As a further measure, public corporations may limit the number of registered shares that can be held by any one shareholder to a certain percentage of the issued registered stock. In practice, many corporations limit the number of shares to 2-5% of the relevant stock. Under the public takeover provisions of the Stock Exchange and Securities Law (for which the implementing decree entered into effect in 1997), a formal notification is required when an investor purchases more than 3% of a Swiss company's shares. An "opt-out" clause is available for firms which do not want to be taken over by a hostile bidder, but such opt-outs must be approved by a super-majority of shareholders and well in advance of any takeover attempt (i.e., not to thwart an attempt already launched).

A reform of the corporation tax – implemented in early 2009 – reduces levies on dividends to investors with a stake of at least 10%. They are no longer taxed in full, but only at the rate of 50% for commercial investments and 60% for the private sector.

Banking - - The Swiss Federal Banking Commission (EBK), the Federal Office of Private Insurance and the Anti-Money Laundering Control Authority were merged in January 2009 to form the Swiss Financial Market Supervisory Authority (FINMA). This body aims to instill confidence in the financial markets and protect customers, creditors and investors.

Those wishing to establish banking operations in Switzerland must obtain prior approval from FINMA. This is generally granted if the following conditions are met: reciprocity on the part of the foreign state; the foreign bank's name must not give the impression that the bank is Swiss; the bank must adhere to Swiss monetary and credit policy; and a majority of the bank's management must have their permanent residence in Switzerland. Otherwise, foreign banks are subject to the same regulatory requirements as domestic banks. Banks organized under Swiss law have to inform FINMA before they open up a branch, subsidiary or representation abroad. Foreign or domestic investors have to inform FINMA before acquiring or disposing of a qualified majority of shares of a bank organized under Swiss law. In case of exceptional temporary capital outflows threatening Swiss monetary policy, banks can be obliged to seek approval from the Swiss national bank to issue foreign bonds or other financial instruments that would cause capital outflow. On December 20, 2008 government protection of current accounts held in Swiss banks was raised from CHF 30,000 to CHF 100,000.

For additional analytical, business and investment opportunities information,
please contact Global Investment & Business Center, USA
at (703) 370-8082. Fax: (703) 370-8083. E-mail: ibpusa3@gmail.com
Global Business and Investment Info Databank - www.ibpus.com

Insurance - - A federal ordinance requires the placement of all risks physically situated in Switzerland with companies located in the country. Therefore, it is necessary for foreign insurers wishing to provide liability coverage in Switzerland to establish a subsidiary or branch there.

With the exception of those few sectors in which Swiss-owned enterprises have been granted a legally established monopoly (i.e., railways, fire insurance, and certain utilities), non-discriminatory competition between foreign and domestic commercial entities prevails.

Cartels and Monopolies - - Foreign investments are subject to review by the Federal Competition Commission if the value of the investing firm's sales reaches a certain worldwide or Swiss-market threshold. An investment or joint venture by a foreign firm can be disapproved on the grounds of competition policy, although there is no evidence that regulators have applied these rules in a discriminatory manner.

Competition Law

The Federal **Competition Commission** may initiate investigations against entities suspected of hampering competition and issues a decision in light of an analysis of the prevailing conditions of competition in the sector. Secondly, the so-called **Price Controller**, like the Competition Commission is formally part of the Ministry of Economy, Education and Research, can suggest or insist on price modifications in the area of radio and television, the federal railway system, postal services, water, waste removal, and the medical sector.

The WTO **Trade Policy Review** concluded that "legislation on competition has not changed substantially since 2004. Four main laws continue to regulate competition: the Federal Law on cartels and other impediments to competition of October 6, 1995 (Cartels Law, LCart, RS 251), amended in 2004; the Federal Law against unfair competition of October 22, 1992 (LCD, LR 24), amended in 2002; the Federal Law on the internal market of October 6, 1995 (LMI, RS 943.02), amended in 2006; and the Law on price surveillance of December 20, 1985 (LSPr), which allows price investigations by the Price Controller when competition is deemed to be lacking."

Investment Trends

TABLE 1: The following chart summarizes several well-regarded indices and rankings.

Measure	Year	Rank or value	Website Address
TI Corruption Perceptions index	2013	7 of 177	http://cpi.transparency.org/cpi2013/results/
Heritage Foundation's Economic Freedom index	2013	4 of 177	http://www.heritage.org/index/ranking
World Bank's Doing Business Report "Ease of Doing Business"	2013	29 of 189	http//doingbusiness.org/rankings
Global Innovation Index	2013	1 of 142	http://www.globalinnovationindex.org/content.aspx?page=gii-full-report-2013#pdfopener
World Bank GNI per capita	2012	USD 80,970	http://data.worldbank.org/indicator/NY.GNP.PCAP.CD

For additional analytical, business and investment opportunities information,
please contact Global Investment & Business Center, USA
at (703) 370-8082. Fax: (703) 370-8083. E-mail: ibpusa3@gmail.com
Global Business and Investment Info Databank - www.ibpus.com

CONVERSION AND TRANSFER POLICIES

Remittance Policies

There are no restrictions on, or difficulties in, converting, repatriating or transferring funds associated with an investment (including remittances of capital, earnings, loan repayments, lease payments, royalties) into a freely usable currency and at the a legal market clearing rate.

Currency Manipulation

The U.S. Department of Treasury concluded in its semi-annual **report** to Congress on International Economic and Exchange Rate Policies on April 15, 2014 that "the Swiss authorities faced a constrained policy environment as external forces pushed the economy into deflation in the summer 2011. In September 2011, after a number of alternate policy measures failed to achieve the Swiss National Bank's (SNB) monetary policy objectives, it established a minimum exchange rate ("floor") of 1.20 Swiss francs per euro, temporarily changing the exchange rate regime from a floating to a managed rate. Through 2012 the SNB intervened repeatedly to prevent the franc form appreciating. [...] The SNB continues to reaffirm its commitment to a managed rate, noting that it is prepared to buy foreign currency in unlimited quantities to enforce the 1.20 exchange rate.

Since establishing the exchange rate floor, the SNB's foreign reserve assets have increased by $172 billion on a headline basis, and now total $492 billion as of February 2014. [...]

The exchange rate floor has contributed to the reduction of deflation and overall economic stability. Once economic conditions normalize, a return to a freely floating currency would be desirable."

DISPUTE SETTLEMENT

Legal System, Specialized Courts, Judicial Independence, Judgments of Foreign Courts

The organization of the judiciary differs from canton to canton. The larger the canton the more courts of first instance one finds. In smaller cantons, there is usually one. All the cantons have established a high court, but only four cantons (Zurich, Bern, St. Gallen and Aargau) have a specialized commercial court that is part of the high court. There are no specialized courts on matters related solely to intellectual property rights. The verdicts of the cantonal high courts can be appealed at the level of the Swiss Supreme Court. The court system is independent, competent and substantively fair.

Switzerland is party to a number of bilateral and multilateral treaties governing the recognition and enforcement of foreign judgments. Due to its close ties with the European Union, a multilateral treaty, the Convention on jurisdiction and the recognition and enforcement of judgments in civil and commercial matters (also called the **Lugano Convention**) entered into force on January 1, 201,1 replacing an older legal framework with the same name. A set of bilateral treaties is also in place dealing with judgments of foreign courts. There is no such agreement in place addressing the enforcement of judgments of foreign courts between the U.S. and Switzerland.

Bankruptcy

The World Bank's "Doing Business" survey ranks Switzerland as 47th out of 189 countries when it comes to resolving insolvency. The average time to close a business in Switzerland amounts to three years (as opposed to 1.7 years in the OECD) and 47.6 cents on the dollar are recovered by the claimants from the insolvent firm (as opposed to 70.6 cents in the OECD).

The **Swiss Federal Statute on Private International Law** (PILS, articles 166-175, in force since January 1, 1989) governs the recognition in Switzerland of foreign insolvency proceedings, including bankruptcies, foreign compositions and arrangements. Swiss law requires reciprocity on matters of the recognition of foreign insolvency orders and foreign administrators in Switzerland.

Investment Disputes

No investment disputes have been recorded involving U.S. or foreign entities in Switzerland in the past 10 years.

ICSID Convention and New York Convention

Switzerland is a member of the ICSID Convention since June 14, 1968 (entry into force of the convention) and member of the New York Convention since June 1, 1965 (ratification).

Duration of Dispute Resolution

The duration of dispute resolution depends on the parties. If a party appeals the decision of a first instance court and the (cantonal) high court up to the Supreme Court, a verdict may take one to two years.

PERFORMANCE REQUIREMENTS AND INVESTMENT INCENTIVES

WTO/TRIMS

The U.S. and Switzerland have only been on opposite sides of a WTO dispute once, when Switzerland (with other complainants) complained about the U.S. on matters related to Definite Safeguard Measures on Imports of Certain**Steel Products**. In December 2003, these safeguards were abolished by the U.S. The U.S. has never acted as a complainant against Switzerland in the framework of WTO.

Investment Incentives

The WTO Trade Policy Review notes "[b]oth Switzerland and Liechtenstein have a strong, export-oriented industrial base. Switzerland has a policy to support research and improve framework conditions for all economic sectors but it does not adhere to a policy of national champions. There are no cash subsidies in place to specific manufacturing industries other than measures open to all companies." Investment incentives are in the competence of the cantons and apply for domestic as well as foreign investors. Various tax privileges exist at the cantonal level for holding companies and mixed companies (for instance in rural areas). These companies remain, however, subject to ordinary taxation at the federal level.

Research and Development

Scholars and artists from the U.S. can apply to the State Secretariat for Education and Research for **Swiss Government Excellence Scholarships**. The Swiss National Fund's **strategy** states "universities, governments and research funding bodies negotiate and implement co-operation agreements with the aim of supporting the international component of research and creating an institutional framework to promote co-operation." Switzerland has various instruments in place to promote research and innovation such as the **national institutions for research and innovation promotion**, the **National Centres of Competences in Research (NCCR)**, the **National Research Programmes (NRP)** or the**Research in Swiss Government Departments**.

Data Storage

There is no "forced localization" laws designed to force foreign investors to use domestic content in goods or technology (i.e. storage of data within Switzerland). Businesses need to be aware that Switzerland follows strict privacy laws and certain data may not be legally collected in Switzerland as they are deemed personal and particularly "worthy of protection." The collection of certain data may need to be registered at the office of the **Federal Data Protection and Information Commissioner (FDPIC)**.

RIGHT TO PRIVATE OWNERSHIP AND ESTABLISHMENT

There is a right for foreign and domestic private entities to establish and own business enterprises and engage in all forms of remunerative activity

PROTECTION OF PROPERTY RIGHTS

Real Property

Interests in property is recognized and enforced.

Intellectual Property Rights

Switzerland effectively enforces intellectual property rights linked to patents and trademarks. However, since 2010 Swiss authorities have not vigorously enforced copyright on the internet, due to an interpretation of a court verdict in September 2010 (the so-called *Logistep* case). The Swiss High Court ultimately ruled in this case that internet protocol addresses were particularly worthy of protection and may not be used generally to identify violators of copyright on the internet. Although uploading of copyright-protected material remains *de jure* illegal, it has become *de facto* legal as prosecutors have generally refused to engage into any legal proceedings against alleged violators during the past three years. The relevant government authorities, including the **Institute of Intellectual Property** and the Federal Council may address this issue in the first half of 2014.

Contact at U.S. Embassy Bern:

Scott Woodard, Economic/Commercial Officer
Raphael Vogel, Economic Specialist
U.S. Embassy in Bern, Sulgeneckstrasse 17, 3003 Bern, Switzerland
+41 31 357 7319
Business-bern@state.gov

Country / Economy resources
Swiss American Chamber of Commerce
Talacker 41

8001 Zurich
+41 43 443 72 00
info@amcham.ch

WIPO Country Profile: ***http://www.wipo.int/members/en/details.jsp?country_id=33***

TRANSPARENCY OF THE REGULATORY SYSTEM

The Swiss government uses transparent policies and effective laws to foster competition. Proposed laws and regulations are open for public comment (including interested parties, interest groups, cantons and cities) then discussed within the bicameral parliamentary system and may be subject to facultative or automatic referenda that allow the Swiss voters to reject or accept the proposals.

EFFICIENT CAPITAL MARKETS AND PORTFOLIO INVESTMENT

Money and Banking System, Hostile Takeovers

Switzerland has a highly developed and sound banking system that provides credit to market terms. There is an effective regulatory system established to encourage and facilitate portfolio investment. Domestic and foreign bidders are treated equally when it comes to hostile takeovers.

COMPETITION FROM STATE-OWNED ENTERPRISES

OECD Guidelines on Corporate Governance of SOEs

The five Swiss State-Owned Enterprises (SOEs) in federal ownership are active in the areas of ground transportation (travel), information and communication, defense and aerospace (services) and are typically undertaking "public function mandates," but may also cover some hybrid activities (i.e. Swisscom in the area of telecommunications). The five companies, in which the Swiss Confederation is either the largest shareholder or the sole shareholder, are **CFF**,**Swisscom**, **Skyguide**, **Swiss Post** and **Ruag**. Other SOEs controlled by the cantons are active in the areas of energy and water supply and a number of subsectors. SOEs may benefit from exclusive rights and privileges (some of them are listed in the WTO **Trade Policy Review** in Table A3.1). The SOEs typically closely interact with private industry and are also active in foreign markets (i.e. Swisscom and Ruag). Generally, private sector competitors can compete with SOEs under the same terms and conditions with respect to access to markets, credit, and other business operations.

The **OECD** stressed in 2011 that Switzerland had adhered to the OECD Guidelines on Corporate Governance for SOEs. In its 2013 report the **OECD** concluded in another report that "in Switzerland the board [of SOEs] has the legal role of proposing the final candidate(s) to the AGM [Annual General Meeting] for appointment. For fully-owned SOEs, the Federal Council (executive authority), as the sole shareholder, decides on the nominees. Nevertheless, the board has a strong role in identifying potential nominees. When vacancies arise the Chair and/or board committee develop a requirement profile for board members and specifically define the board's needs in new appointments."

Swiss SOEs publish annual reports and report every year to the Federal Council on the achievement of their strategic goals. While consulting with the competent ministries the Federal Council approves the reports from the SOEs and their annual budget. The Swiss parliament then considers whether the Federal Council has supervised the SOEs appropriately.

For additional analytical, business and investment opportunities information, please contact Global Investment & Business Center, USA at (703) 370-8082. Fax: (703) 370-8083. E-mail: ibpusa3@gmail.com Global Business and Investment Info Databank - www.ibpus.com

Sovereign Wealth Funds

Switzerland does not have a Sovereign Wealth Fund (SWF) or an asset management bureau (AMB).

CORPORATE SOCIAL RESPONSIBILITY

OECD Guidelines for Multinational Enterprises

The Swiss government actively promotes the OECD Guidelines for Multinational Enterprise or the United Nations Guiding Principles on Business and Human Rights.

In 2014 Switzerland was ranked 1st out 100 countries evaluated in the **Environment Performance Index (EPI)**, and labor laws are respected.

In 2014, according to the World Bank Doing Business report, Switzerland only ranked 170th out of 189 rankings in the field of investor protection. This surprisingly low score has not damaged Switzerland's reputation as a major business hub and as one of the strongest economies in Europe. This is likely because of the particular methodology applied by the World Bank, and can be explained by the lack of disclosure obligations in Switzerland in general (i.e. transactions performed by the company, conflict of interests) and the lack of ease for shareholders to file suits.

POLITICAL VIOLENCE

Political violence is very rare in Switzerland.

The most prominent act in the recent years happened on April 1, 2011 when a letter bomb exploded and targeted employees of a lobbying organization promoting nuclear power. The militant attack is assumed to have been orchestrated by elements of an international anarchist network having also targeted Swiss embassies in the past. Nuclear power has contributed to the radicalization of certain small groups within Switzerland advocating for the immediate closure of the country's nuclear plants.

CORRUPTION

UN Anticorruption Convention, OECD Convention on Combating Bribery

Switzerland ratified the UN Anticorruption Convention on September 24, 2009 and signed the OECD Anti-Bribery Convention in 1997. It entered into force on May 1, 2000.

Switzerland has an effective legal and policy framework to combat domestic corruption. Laws are enforced effectively. US firms investing in Switzerland have not complained of corruption to the Embassy in recent years. Corruption is reportedly not pervasive in any area or sector of the Swiss economy. Switzerland maintains effective investigative and enforcement procedures to combat domestic corruption. The giving or accepting of bribes in Switzerland is subject to criminal and civil penalties, including imprisonment up to five years.

In February 2001, Switzerland signed the Council of Europe's Criminal Law Convention on Corruption and in December 2003 it signed the UN Convention against Corruption. In order to implement the Convention, the Parliament amended the Penal Code to make bribery of foreign public officials an offense (Title Nineteen "Bribery", Articles). These amendments entered into force on May 1, 2000. In accordance with the revised 1997 OECD Anti-Bribery Convention, Parliament amended the legislation on direct taxes of the Confederation, cantons and townships so as to prohibit the tax deductibility of bribes. These amendments became effective on January 1, 2001.

Under Swiss law, officials are urged not to accept anything that would "challenge their independence and capacity to act." According to the law, the range of permissible receipt of "individual advantages" is a sliding scale, depending on the role of the official. Some officials may receive no advantages at all (e.g., those working for financial regulators) to several hundred Swiss Francs. The upper-limit value of presents such as bottles of champagne and watches is a grey area that varies according to department and canton. Transparency International believes a maximum sum valid at the federal level should be fixed. Some multinationals have assisted with the fight against corruption by setting up internal hotlines to enable staff to report problems anonymously.

The law provides criminal penalties for official corruption, and the government generally implements these laws effectively. Investigating and prosecuting government corruption is a federal responsibility. A majority of cantons also require members of cantonal parliaments to disclose their interests. A joint working group comprising representatives of various federal government agencies works under the leadership of the Federal Department of Foreign Affairs to combat corruption.

Switzerland ratified the Council of Europe's Criminal Law Convention on Corruption on July 1, 2006. Switzerland's penal code was amended so that foreign diplomatic staff and members of international organizations can be brought to court if they accept bribes.

On September 24, 2009, Switzerland ratified the United Nations Convention against Corruption. Government experts believe this ratification will not result in significant changes since passive and active corruption of public servants is already considered a crime under the Swiss Criminal Code (Art. 322).

In October 2013, the Group of States against Corruption (GRECO, Council of Europe) welcomed Switzerland's efforts in its **Third Evaluation Round - Compliancy Report**. However, GRECO concluded "that the current low level of compliance with the recommendations is 'globally unsatisfactory' with the meaning of Rule 31, paragraph 8.3 of the Rules of Procedure." Areas which needed particular attention were transparency of party funding, criminalization of trading in influence, and the dual criminality requirement, for which Switzerland wishes to maintain its reservations and declarations on the relevant articles in the Criminal Law Convention on Corruption.

A number of federal administrative authorities are involved in combating bribery. The State Secretariat for Economic Affairs deals with issues relating to the OECD Convention, the Federal Office of Justice with those relating to the Council of Europe Convention, and the Department of Foreign Affairs with the UN Convention. The power to prosecute and judge corruption offenses is shared between the cantons and the Confederation. For the Confederation, the competent authorities are the Office of the Attorney General, the Federal Criminal Court and the Federal Police ("Fedpol"). In the cantons, the relevant actors are the cantonal judicial authorities and the cantonal police forces.

Resources to report corruption:

Contact at government agencies:

For additional analytical, business and investment opportunities information,
please contact Global Investment & Business Center, USA
at (703) 370-8082. Fax: (703) 370-8083. E-mail: ibpusa3@gmail.com
Global Business and Investment Info Databank - www.ibpus.com

Michel Huissoud
Director
Swiss Federal Audit Office
Monbijoustrasse 45
3003 Bern / Switzerland
Ph. +41 31 323 10 35
E-mail: **verdacht@efk.admin.ch**

Contact at "watchdog" organizations:
Delphine Centlivres
Executive Director
Transparency International Switzerland
Schanzeneckstrasse 25
P.O. Box 8509
3001 Bern / Switzerland
Ph. +41 31 382 3550
E-Mail: **info@transparency.ch**

BILATERAL INVESTMENT AGREEMENTS

Bilateral Taxation Treaties

To date, Switzerland has concluded numerous investment protection treaties with developing and emerging market economies. Around 115 remain in force.

Switzerland concluded an **Income Tax Treaty** with the U.S. in 1996. A 2009 Protocol to this Treaty has been ratified by Switzerland, but not yet by the U.S. Senate.

OPIC AND OTHER INVESTMENT INSURANCE PROGRAMS

Switzerland has not signed an investment protection agreement with any Western European country or the United States.

OPIC is not active in Switzerland. However, Switzerland is a member of the **Multilateral Investment Guarantee Agency** .

LABOR

The Swiss labor force is highly educated and skilled. Foreigners not only fill low-skilled, low-wage jobs, but also highly technical positions in the manufacturing and service industries. Roughly 29% of the estimated labor force of approximately 4.9 million people is foreign. Many foreign nationals are long-time Swiss residents who have not applied for or been granted Swiss citizenship. Only 3.3% of the workforce is employed in agriculture, where foreign "seasonal workers" take many low-wage jobs.

The Swiss economy is capital intensive and geared toward high value-added products and services. Wages in Switzerland are among the highest in the world.

The prohibition on strikes by federal public servants was repealed in 2000. The Federal Council may only restrict or prohibit the right to strike where it affects the security of the state, external relations, or the supply of vital goods to the country. Civil servants in a few cantons and municipalities are still denied the right to strike.

For additional analytical, business and investment opportunities information,
please contact Global Investment & Business Center, USA
at (703) 370-8082. Fax: (703) 370-8083. E-mail: ibpusa3@gmail.com
Global Business and Investment Info Databank - www.ibpus.com

Switzerland is in compliance with ILO conventions. Government regulations cover maximum work hours, minimum length of holidays, sick leave and compulsory military service, contract termination, and other requirements. However, there is no minimum wage law. Employees in the retail sector and in restaurants, bars, and the like, in cooperation with other interests, have been successful in slowing reform of the restrictive federal and cantonal laws governing opening hours. Shop-hour restrictions are nevertheless loosening gradually in centers such as Zurich, Geneva, and Bern.

Swiss voters narrowly accepted in 2005 the revision of the Swiss Federal labor law in order to provide for flexible working hours, such as Sunday openings in major railway stations and airports. The new regulation entered into force on April 1, 2006. Shopping hours outside of airports and railway stations remain regulated by cantonal laws. In a national initiative, Swiss voters on February 9, 2014 decided to abolish the principle of free movement for citizens of the European Union and to return to a quota regime to be able to limit immigration. In summer 2014, the Swiss Federal Council will publish proposals on how to implement this initiative that could potentially impact the Swiss labor market as it could become harder for companies within Switzerland to recruit labor from the EU market.

Approximately one-fourth of the country's full-time workers are unionized. In general, labor/management relations are good, with a willingness on both sides to settle disputes by negotiations rather than by labor action. Some 606 collective agreements exist today in Switzerland (of which approximately 1% concern the agriculture sector, 39% the secondary sector and 60% the third sector) and are usually renewed without major problems. Since 2002, trade unions have complained that too little of the Swiss labor force is covered by collective agreements. Although days lost to strikes in Switzerland are among the lowest in the OECD, Swiss trade unions have encouraged workers to go on strike on several occasions in recent years.

At the macro level, salaries increased by 1.5% in 2012.

The average unemployment rate amounted to 4.5% in 2013 (according to the ILO method of calculation). The average unemployment rate was 9.4% for foreigners and 3.1% for Swiss citizens. All cantons bordering EU countries suffer higher unemployment rates than the rest of Switzerland. Other cantons enjoy a better situation. Young workers aged 15-24 and persons aged between 25 and 39 were faced unemployment rates of 8.5% and 4.9%, respectively, in 2013.

FOREIGN TRADE ZONES/FREE PORTS

Swiss international airports have stores offering duty free shopping. Private companies can utilize duty-free warehouses to import goods tax and duty free into Switzerland as long as the goods are subsequently re-exported to third countries. In each of these examples, foreign-owned companies receive the same treatment as domestic firms. These warehouses have undergone significant expansions in recent years and may become the target for foreign tax authorities concerned with their role in abetting tax evasion and money laundering.

18. Foreign Direct Investment and Foreign Portfolio Investment Statistics

TABLE 2: Key Macroeconomic data, U.S. FDI in host country/economy

	Host Country Statistical source:	USG or international statistical source	USG or international Source of data (Source of Data: BEA; IMF; Eurostat;

For additional analytical, business and investment opportunities information,
please contact Global Investment & Business Center, USA
at (703) 370-8082. Fax: (703) 370-8083. E-mail: ibpusa3@gmail.com
Global Business and Investment Info Databank - www.ibpus.com

	State Secretariat for Economic Affairs				UNCTAD, Other)
Economic Data	Year	Amount	Year	Amount	
Host Country Gross Domestic Product (GDP) (Millions U.S. Dollars)	2012	584,007	2012	631,200	http://www.worldbank.org/en/country
Foreign Direct Investment	Host Country Statistical sources* Swiss National Bank State Secretariat for Economic Affairs		USG or international statistical source		USG or international Source of data: BEA; IMF; Eurostat; UNCTAD, Other
U.S. FDI in partner country (Millions U.S. Dollars, stock positions)	2012	92,571	2012	130,315	(BEA) click selections to reach. Bureau of Economic Analysis Balance of Payments and Direct Investment Position Data U.S. Direct Investment Position Abroad on a Historical-Cost Basis By Country only (all countries) (Millions of Dollars)
Host country's FDI in the United States (Millions U.S. Dollars, stock positions)	2012	214,723	2012	203,954	OECD Stat Extracts FDI positions by partner country (reporting country U.S.)
Total inbound stock of FDI as % host GDP (calculate)	2012	123	2011	89	OECD iLibrary Outward and inward FDI stocks World Bank Data 2011

Statistical discrepancies

The significant statistical discrepancies are due to different methodologies when measuring foreign direct investment.

As the **OECD Benchmark Definition of Foreign Investment** concludes there "are two possible approaches to identify the home country (of the direct investor) for inward FDI and the host country (of the direct investment enterprise) for outward FDI:

by immediate host country/investing country (IHC/IIC)

by ultimate host country/ultimate investing country (UHC/UIC)"

Switzerland uses the immediate investing country approach (IIC) and the U.S. uses the more complex ultimate investing country approach (UIC). The **OECD** report explains in great detail how the two different approaches generate different figures.

TABLE 3: Sources and Destination of FDI

TABLE 4: Sources of Portfolio Investment

Portfolio Investments Assets *Switzerland, June 2013* **Source: IMF**

Top Five Partners (Millions, US Dollars)								
Total			Equity Securities			Total Debt Securities		
World	1,152,606	100%	World	498,286	100%	World	654,320	100%
United States	181,081	16%	Luxembourg	138,813	28%	United States	89,528	14%
Luxembourg	160,772	14%	United States	91,553	18%	France	66,651	10%
France	89,308	8%	Ireland	32,328	6%	Netherlands	66,648	10%
Germany	83,206	7%	Germany	32,072	6%	Germany	51,134	8%
Netherlands	74,109	6%	Cayman Islands	30,721	6%	United Kingdom	38,486	6%

Liechtenstein

Liechtenstein's investment conditions are virtually identical in most key aspects to those in Switzerland, due to its intimate links with the Swiss economy. The two countries have a customs union, for example, and Swiss authorities are responsible for implementing import and export regulations. Liechtenstein has a stable and open economy that has created almost 38,000 jobs exceeding the country's domestic population of 37,000 – requiring a substantial number of foreigners (mainly Swiss and Austrians) to fill many of these jobs. It is also a very wealthy country – when adjusted for purchasing power parity, its per capita gross domestic product (GDP) is the highest in the world. According to the **Liechtenstein Statistical Yearbook** , the tertiary sector creates 56% of Liechtenstein's jobs, particularly in the finance sector, followed by the secondary sector (especially manufacturing tools, precision instruments, and dental products), which employs 43% of the work force. Agriculture accounts for less than 1% of the country's jobs.

The country reformed its tax system in 2011. The corporate tax rate, at 12.5%, is one of the lowest in Europe. Capital gains, inheritance, and gift taxes have been abolished. The Embassy has no recorded complaints from US businesses stemming from market restrictions in Liechtenstein.

IMPORTANT BUSINESS AND LEGAL CONTACTS

ENGLISH SPEAKING LAWYERS IN SWITZERLAND:

CANTON OF BASEL STADT

ALDER, Dr. Claudius Ph.; 21 St. Alban-Vorstadt, telephone 061-272-4511, fax 061-272-4535. Member of the law firm Hermann, Gelzer, Alder, Baumgartner. Born: Basel, BS, Switzerland, March 28, 1938. University of Basel; doctor of laws, 1961. Handles collection, estate and criminal cases, and trade disputes. Languages: English, German, French, Italian.

GELZER, Dr. Bernhard; 21 St. Alban-Vorstadt, telephone 061-272-4511, fax 061-272-4535. Member of the law firm Hermann, Gelzer, Alder, Baumgartner. Born: Basel, BS, Switzerland, July 13, 1928. University of Basel, doctor of laws, 1954. Handles collection, estate and criminal cases, and trade disputes. Notary public. Languages: English, German, French.

JENNY, Dr. David, LL.M.; Aeschenvorstadt 4, 4010 Basel; telephone: +41 61 279 33 49; fax: +41 61 279 33 10; e-mail: djenny@vischer.com; member of the law firm VISCHER AG; internet: www.vischer.com; born: Basel, June 3, 1960. University of Basel, Dr. of Laws, 1988; University of Michigan Law School, LL.M., 1989. Specialized in mergers & acquisitions, insolvency law and resolution of commercial disputes. Notary public attached to law firm. Languages: English, German, French.

LENZ, Dr. Peter; 15 Elisabethenstrasse, telephone 061-272-1330, fax 061-272-1595. Member of the law firm Lenz Caemmerer. Internet: www.lclaw.ch Born: Basel, BS, Switzerland, January 10, 1937. University of Basel; doctor of laws, 1964. Specialized in inheritance and company law. Handles collection and estate cases, and trade disputes. Notary public. Languages: English, German, French, Italian.

LIATOWITSCH, Dr. Felix H.; 28 Elisabethenstrasse, telephone 061-272-1455, fax 061-272-3807. Member of the law firm Liatowitsch, Bernstein & Günzburger. Born: Basel, BS, Switzerland, October 1, 1941. University of Basel; licentiate jur., 1965. Specialized in corporation law. Handles collection, estate and criminal cases, and trade disputes. Attended course of comparative law of New York University during academic year 1968/69. Languages: English, German, French, Italian.

THOMANN, Dr. Felix H.; Lerchenstrasse 42, 4059 Basel, telephone 061-283-9235, fax 061-283-9234; E-mail fhthomann@datacomm.ch. Counsel to the law firm of ThomannFischer. Born: Basel, BS, Switzerland, August 10, 1936. University of Basel; doctor of laws, 1960. Specialized in intellectual property, competition and information technology law. Languages: English, German,

Canton of Bern: Bern; Bienne/Biel; Burgdorf; Interlaken; Meiringen;Munsingen

FISCHER, Daniel David; 18 Schwarztorstrasse, 3007 Bern, telephone 031/382 08 08, telefax 382 26 30. Born: Bern, BE, Switzerland, 1953. University of Bern; licentiate jur., attorney 1980. 1/2 year practice in New York. Handles commercial and civil cases. Languages: English, German, French.

FRIEDLI, Georg; 5 Bahnhofplatz, telephone 031-326-5000, fax 031-326-5010, e-mail g.friedli@fslaw.ch. Member of law firm Friedli & Schnidrig. Born: Solothurn, SO. Switzerland, January 1, 1952. University of Bern; Bar Exam in 1977. Also studied at George Washington University; Master of Comparative Law 1981. Specialized in corporate investments, securities laws. Handles collection cases, estate cases, trade disputes. Languages: English, French, German.

GROSS, André; 7 Christoffelgasse, telephone 031-312-2112, fax 021-311-1281. Member of law firm Jaccard & Gross. Born: Aarau, AG, Switzerland, July 19, 1951. University of Bern; licentiate jur., 1976. One year experience with law firm in Santa Barbara, California. Specialized in International law, corporation law, tax law, entertainment law, labor law. Handles collection and estate cases, -trade disputes, criminal cases. Languages: English, French, German, Italian.

BERGER, Dr. Bernhard; 14 Kapellenstrasse, telephone 031-390-2525, fax 031-390-2526. Member of law firm Kellerhals Attorneys at Law (Berne/Basle/Zurich). Born: Langnau, BE, Switzerland, June 15, 1970. University of Bern, doctor juris 2000. Handles estate, criminal, collection cases, commercial and trade disputes. Studied law at Harvard Law School for 1 year (LL.M. '01). Languages: English, German, French.

ZUBLER, Bertrand H.; 29 Zeughausgasse, telephone 031-310-4646, fax 031-310-4642. Born: Bern, BE, Switzerland, June 19, 1953. University of Bern; licentiate jur. 1981. Specialized in civil, criminal and commercial law. Handles collection and estate cases, trade disputes, criminal cases. Notary public. Languages: English, French, German, Italian.

City of Bienne/Biel

UHLMANN, Max; 54 Bahnhofstrasse, telephone 032-328-1150, fax 032-328-1159. Member of law firm Uhlmann, Hoffet, Schürmann. Born: Wynigen, BE, Switzerland, January 31, 1949. Attorney at law November 21, 1975. Handles trade disputes and criminal cases. Languages: English, German and French.

WENDLING, Urs; 2 Bahnhofstrasse, telephone 032-323-1111, fax 032-323-1114. Member of law firm Wendling & Howald. Born: Biel, BE, Switzerland, October 31, 1950. University of Bern, graduated December 4, 1980. Handles collection, estate and criminal cases, and trade disputes. Languages: English, German, French and limited Italian.

CITY OF MEIRINGEN

SARTORIUS, Marcus A.; Rudenz 12, telephone 033 971 36 36, fax 033 971 61 17. From Basel. Born: May 16, 1953. Universities of Zurich and Bern; attorney at law May 27, 1980. Handles collection, estate and criminal cases, and trade disputes. Languages: English, German, French, Italian.

CITY OF MÜNSINGEN

DIENER-ALHO, Riitta; 5 Dorfplatz, telephone 031-721-5051, fax 031-721-7080. From: Bubikon, ZH, Switzerland. Born: May 8, 1948. University of Zurich; licenciate jur., 1975; University of Bern; attorney, 1986. Handles civil and criminal cases. Languages: English, German, Swedish, Finnish.

CANTON OF GENEVA: GENEVA

GRAZ, Jean Pierre; 11 bis, rue Rodolphe-Toepffer, telephone 00.41.22.346.52.60, telex 422 328, telefax 00.41.22.346.59.39. Henry, Graz, Vesley & Sekkiou. Born: Geneva, GE, Switzerland, July 27, 1942. University of Geneva; licentiate jur. Specialized in international business matters. Does not handle collection cases. Estate and criminal cases and trade disputes are accepted. Languages: English, French, German, Italian, Spanish.

JACQUEMOUD, Jean-Pierre; 2 rue Bellot, telephone 022/346 15 15, telex 28 800, telefax 022/346 89 64. Member of law firm Jacquemoud & Stanislas. Born: Switzerland, December 25, 1948. University of Geneva; licentiate jur., 1971. University of Texas; Master of Comparative Jurisprudence, 1977. New York Bar Exam 1979. One year in law firm Pillsbury, Madison & Sutro, San Francisco, CA, and one year with Sullivan & Cromwell, New York, NY. Specialized in comparative and business laws, licensing and distributorship agreement, and banking laws. Handles collection and estate cases, and trade disputes. Languages: English, French, German.

TURRETTINI, Dr. Maurice; 8-10, rue de Hesse, 1204 Geneva, telephone +41 22 319 11 11, fax +41 22 312 14 31, e-mail: maurice.turrettini@ptan.ch Partner of Poncet Turrettini Amaudrruz Neyroud & Partners since 1990, Born: Geneva, Switzerland. Law Degree, University of Geneva, 1984; LLM in International Banking Laws, Boston Unirversity, 1986; Geneva Bar Exams 1988. Controller of the Self-Regulatory Authority of the Swiss Lawyers Association since 2004. Member of various Board of Directors of Banks, Swiss and foreign companies in the financial industry. Specialized in commercial, corporate, estate and litigation laws. Languages: French, English and German

WILSON, David Wallace; 15bis Rue des Alpes, 1201 Geneva, telephone 022/707 80 00 , telefax 022 /707 80 01, e-mail: david.wilson@swlegal.ch Member of law firm Schellenberg Wittmer, Born: 1975. University of Geneva. licenciate jur., 1998; New York University , Master of Comparative Jurisprudence, 2002; Society of Trust and Estate Parctitioner, 2004. Admission to

New York Bar, 2002; Admission to Geneva Bar, 2003. Specialized in wills, succession and estate matter as well as trust law. Languages: English, French, German.

CANTON OF GRAUBÜNDEN: DAVOS

MATTLI, GEORG S.: Promenade 60, 7270 Davos-Platz. Tel. 081 413 10 43. Fax 081 413 13 70: Member of law firm of MATTLI & HEW. Swiss citizen. Born 1952 in Switzerland. University of Zurich. Doctor of Law, 1980. General practice; estate cases; trade disputes and collection cases. Does not handle criminal cases. Acts as a notary public. Languages: English German, French.

CANTON OF LUZERN: LUZERN

BREM, MARIUS, Certified Specialist SBA Inheritance Law, Luzernerstrasse 51a, 6010 Kriens, Tel: 041-318-4060; Fax 041-311-1832; email: brem@anwaelte-kriens.ch; member of law firm Kanzlei Luzernerstrasse Kriens, internet: http://www.anwaelte-kriens.ch, http://www.fachanwalt-erbrecht.ch. Born in 1966; dual national American/Swiss; University of Zurich 1995. Specialized in inheritance and business law. Handles collection cases on a time-spent basis; trade disputes. Notary Public. Languages: English, French, German.

HITZ, MARTIN F.: Schweizerhofquai 2, Postfach, 6004 Luzern. Tel. 041-417-4001. Telefax 041-417-4017. email: hitz@trollerlaw.ch Swiss citizen. Born 1937 in Switzerland. Member of law firm of TROLLER HITZ TROLLER & PARTNER. University of Bern. Doctor of Law 1962, University of Chicago M.C.L. 1963. Intellectual property law, corporate law, commercial law, arbitration, private international law, trade disputes. Does not handle criminal cases, acts as a notary public. Languages: English, French, German.

MOERI, PETER: Hertensteinstrasse 12, 6004 Luzern. Tel. 041-410-3130. Telefax 041-410-9616. Swiss citizen. Born 1957 in Switzerland. Licentiate of law, University of Bern. 4 Years of practice. Administration and civil law, collection and estate cases, trade disputes. Handles criminal cases. Acts as notary public. Languages: German, English, French.

TSCHUEMPERLIN, THOMAS: Zinggentorstrasse 4, 6006 Luzern. Tel. 041-419-3030. Telefax 041-410-4535. Member of law firm of FELLMANN, TSCHUEMPERLIN & LOETSCHER Swiss citizen. Born 1956 in Switzerland. University of Fribourg. Licentiate of Law 1982. Advisory and legal proceedings. Specialized in commercial, inheritance law; collection and estate cases; trade disputes. Acts as notary public. Languages: German, English, French.

CANTON OF NEUCHATEL: NEUCHATEL; LA CHAUX-DE-FONDS

KNOEPFLER, Dr. François; 4 rue de la Serre, telephone 032 729 02 10, fax 032 729 02 20. Member of law firm KGG et Associés. Born: Neuchâtel, NE, Switzerland, March 22, 1940. University of Neuchâtel; doctor of laws, 1963. Professor at University of Neuchâtel. Specialized in international private law, international commercial arbitration. Handles collection and estate cases, and trade disputes. Languages: English, French, German, Italian.

CITY OF LA-CHAUX-DE-FONDS

FAVRE, Maurice; 66 avenue Léopold-Robert, telephone 032-913-7324, fax 032-913-9396. Born: La Chaux-de-Fonds, NE, Switzerland, May 22, 1922. University of Neuchâtel; licentiate jur., 1943. Handles collection, estate and criminal cases, and trade disputes. Languages: English, French, German, Italian.

CANTON OF SOLOTHURN: OLTEN

GLAETTLI, Stephan; 9 Martin Disteli-Strasse, telephone 062-287-9060, fax 062-287-9066. Member of law firm Glaettli & Staeuble. Born: Switzerland, July 9, 1977. University of St. Gallen, lic. iur., 2003; Attorney-at-Law of the Canton St. Gallen, 2005; LL.M. University of Edinburgh 2006. Handles construction, environmental and planning law; social security law; criminal law; commercial and trade law. Languages: English, German.

Canton of St. Gallen: St. Gallen
BEELER, DANIEL: Untere Bahnhofstrasse 2, Postfach 1733, 8640 Rapperswil, and Haupstrasse 30, 9400 Rorschach. Tel: 055/ 214 40 50, Telefax: 055/ 214 40 51. Web: www.beelerlegal.ch. Member of law firm BEELER LEGAL. Swiss citizen. Born 1962 in Switzerland. University of Fribourg, Licentiates 1987. University of St Galen, M.B.L. 1997. General practice; estate cases; trade disputes; collection and criminal cases. Acts as notary public. International Bar Association. Languages: English, French, German, Italian.

SCHNEIDER, PHILIP: Poststrasse 23, 9001 St. Gallen. Tel: 071-228-2930. Telefax: 071-228-2940. Member of law firm SCHWAGER MAETZLER SCHNEIDER. Swiss citizen. Born 1961 in Switzerland. University of Zurich, Licentiates 1986. University of San Diego, California, M.C.L. 1990 Specialized in Business law & Civil law. Handles cases in estate law, corporate and commercial law, intellectual property law. Languages: English, French, German.

Canton of Ticino: Lugano; Locarno
MARIOTTA, ALFREDO: Via Cattedrale 4, 6900 Lugano.Tel: 091-922-9978. Telefax 091-923-1292. Swiss citizen. Born 1939 in Switzerland. University of Geneva. Licentiate of Law, 1963. 2 years practice at District and High Court. 1 year bank practice at local bank and at National Grundley's Bank, London. Specialized in international private law; taxation of individuals; succession law; divorces. Also handles estate and criminal cases; trade disputes. Acts as Notary public. Languages: English, German, French, Italian.

PIOTRKOWSKI, MARCO: Via Carducci 1, 6900 Lugano.Tel: 091-922-7452. Telefax: 091-923-8463. Swiss citizen. Born in 1951 in Switzerland. University of Zurich. Licentiate of law 1979. Commercial & corporate law; collection, estate, family and criminal cases; trade disputes. Specialized in civil law. Acts as a notary public. Languages: Italian, French, German, English and Spanish.

CITY OF LOCARNO

SALVIONI, SERGIO: Via della Gallinazza 6, 6600 Locarno. Tel: 091-751-1238. Telefax: 091-751-9484. email: info@salvionilaw.ch Member of law firm of SALVIONI & SALVIONI, internet: http://www.salvionilaw.ch Swiss citizen. Born 1927 in Switzerland. University of Bern. Doctor of Law, 1951. Specialized in fiscal law and trade disputes. Also handles estate and criminal cases. Acts as a notary public. Languages: English, German, French, Italian.

CANTON OF VALAIS: SION

DETIENNE, Bernard; 1 rue des Vergers, telephone 027-327-3040, fax 027-327-3041. Born: Riddes, VS, Switzerland, March 22, 1953. University of Geneva; licentiate jur., 1977. Handles collection, estate and criminal cases and trade disputes. Notary public. Languages: English, French

CANTON OF VAUD: LAUSANNE; MONTREUX

BOURGEOIS, Olivier; 2 avenue de Montbenon, Lausanne, telephone 021-321-4545, telex 455 148, fax 021-321-4546. Member of law firm Bourgeois & Cherpillod. Born: St-Loup, VD, Switzerland, October 5, 1938. University of Lausanne; doctor of laws, 1964. Specialized in tax law. Handles estate and criminal cases, and trade disputes. Languages: English, French, German.

DE PREUX Pascal; Rue du Lion d'Or 2, CP 5956, 1002 Lausanne. 021-343 2040, fax 021 312 2011. E-mail - pdepreux@lion-d-or.ch . Member of *LOROCH, ELKAIM & PARTNERS*. Attended University of Lausanne, 2002; LL.M. Boston University, May 2003. Specialized in mutual judicial assitance in criminal and civil matters, corporate law, commercial law, banking law. Handles commercial and criminal cases and international arbitration disputes. Languages: English, French, German and Italian.

CITY OF MONTREUX

HEIDER, Marcel; 8 avenue Nestlé, telephone 021-963-3038, fax 021-963-5485. Born: Lausanne, VD, Switzerland, February 22, 1931. University of Lausanne; doctor of laws, 1958. Specialized in common and commercial law. Handles estate cases, and trade disputes. Languages: English, French, German.

CANTON OF ZÜRICH: ZÜRICH

AFP Advokatur Fischer & Partner; FISCHER, Daniel David; Freigutstrasse 7, 8002 Zurich, telephone: 044/ 482 70 20 Fax: 044/ 286 20 49, email: info@swiss-advocate.com. Born: Bern, BE, Switzerland, 1953. University of Bern; licentiate jur., attorney 1980. 1/2 year practice in New York. Handles commercial and civil cases. Languages: English, German, French.

For additional analytical, business and investment opportunities information,
please contact Global Investment & Business Center, USA
at (703) 370-8082. Fax: (703) 370-8083. E-mail: ibpusa3@gmail.com
Global Business and Investment Info Databank - www.ibpus.com

ARPAGAUS, RETO: Bahnhofstrasse 106, P.O. Box 1130, 8021 Zurich; Tel: +41 58 258 11 00; Fax: +41 58 258 11 99. e-mail: reto.arpagaus@bratschi-law.ch internet: www.bratschi-law.ch Member of law firm of Bratschi Wiederkehr & Buob. Swiss citizen. Born in Zurich, Switzerland. Georgetown University Law Center, L.L.M., 1997, with distinction. University of Zurich, Doctorate, 1995. University of Zurich, Bachelors, 1989. Offers legal counsel and representation of corporations before state courts and arbitration tribunals. Specializes in contracts and corporate law; Intellectual Property law (trademark and competition law, distributorship and licensing); estate matters. Office in Bern acts as a notary public. Languages: English, German, French.

ERNI, LORENZ: Ankerstrasse 61, Postfach, 8026 Zurich; Tel: 044 296 88 99; Fax: 044 296 88 90. Member of law firm ESCHMANN & ERNI. Born 1950 in Switzerland. University of Zurich, University of Hamburg; Doctor of Law 1974. Specialized in criminal law. Does not act as a notary public. Languages: German, English French, Italian, Dutch.

FREY, MARKUS A.: Bahnhofstrasse 13, 8001 Zurich; Tel: +41 58 800 8000 . Fax: +41 58 800 8080 . email: markus.a.frey@nkf.ch. Member of law firm of NIEDERER, KRAFT & FREY. Swiss citizen. Born 1956 in Switzerland. University of Geneva, 1978, University of Zurich, Doctor of Law, 1986. University of Miami, School of law, LL.M 1988. Fiscal, corporate, financial, banking and commercial law; business and trade disputes; real estate ventures. Specialized in international tax and estate planning. Does not handle collection cases. Does not act as a notary public. Languages: English, German, French.

GUERRA, PATRICIA: Forchstrasse 452, P.O. Box 1432, 8032 Zurich; Tel: +41 44 396 91 91; Fax: +41 44 396 91 92. E-mail: patricia.guerra@mll-legal.com. Partner with Meyerlustenberger Lachenal. Swiss citizen. Born 1959 in Ecuador. Specialized in general corporate and contract law, international private law, matrimonial property law and inheritance law, wealth transfer, estate planning and charitable organizations. Languages: English, German, French, Spanish.

JÖRG, FLORIAN S.: Bahnhofstrasse 46, P.O. Box 1130, 8021 Zurich; Tel: +41 58 258 10 00; Fax: +41 58 258 10 99. e-mail: florian.joerg@bratschi-law.ch, internet: www.bratschi-law.ch, partner of the law firm of Bratschi Wiederkehr & Buob. Swiss citizen, born 1966. Admitted to the New York Bar (not practising), lecturer for private law at the University of St. Gallen. Member of the Swiss Bar Association, the American Bar Association and the New York State Bar Association. New York University (NYU) School of Law, MCJ, 1997. University of St. Gallen, Doctorate, 1997. Admitted to the Swiss Bars 1994. University of St. Gallen, Bachelors (lic.iur.), 1992. Offers legal counsel and representation before state courts and arbitration tribunals. Specializes in contracts and corporate law; mergers & acquisitions, banking law, international private law. Other offices of the firm offer notarial services. Languages: English, German, French.

RUTSCHI, FEDERICO M. : Tödistrasse 18, 8027 Zürich; Tel: 043 222 41 41; Fax: 043 222 41 49. E-mail: federico.rutschi@rutschilaw.ch URL: www.rutschilaw.ch. Attorney-at-Law, LL.M., NY Bar. The law office of Dr. F. M. Rutschi mainly concentrates on contract law, commercial and corporate law, debt collection and bankruptcy law, liability law, labor law, inheritance law, law of property, real estate law, tenancy law, administrative law and international law.

SOMARY, TOBIAS: Dreikönigstrasse 7, 8022 Zurich; Tel. 044 285 11 11; Fax: 044 285 11 22; tobias.somary@cms-veh.com; Partner of law firm CMS VON ERLACH HENRICI AG. Swiss-Irish double citizen. Born 1971 in Switzerland. University of Zurich 1998. Swiss Bar 2000, with distinction. Certified specialist SBA inheritance law. Stanford University, Law School, LL.M. 2004. Foreign associate with FENWICK & WEST LLP. Practice areas: commercial law, general corporate and contract law, private clients (inheritance law, matrimonial property law, estate planning), private international law (conflict of laws), life sciences, intellectual property law, as well as dispute resolution in the aforementioned areas. Languages: English, German, French.

STURGEON, JOHN C.: Wiesenstrasse 10, 8032 Zürich. Telephone: 044 387 1930 Fax: 044 387 4523 Email: jcsturgeon@gmx.net. Born 1950. Member Maryland/US Bar. Admitted as Foreign Legal Advisor in Germany. U.S. Military Academy, BS; University of Baltimore, MS; University of Akron, Juris Doctor. International private practice, company and commercial law, contracts and cross-border transactions, finance and investment, trusts and estates, tax, shipping law, intellectual property law. Offices also in Germany, Austria, United Kingdom. Languages: English, German.

WILDHABER, Christoph: Stockerstrasse 38, 8002 Zürich, Phone 044 208 25 25; Fax 044 205 25 26. Partner with Streichenberg Rechtsanwälte. Swiss citizen. Born 1964. University of St. Gall (Dr. iur. HSG 1991). Commercial and Corporate Law, National and International Distribution Law, especially Franchising, Licensing and Tax Law. Legal advice to national and international franchisors, particularly on legal organization, planning and negotiation of franchise and related agreements. Languages: German English, French.

CAGIANUT, Thierry: Zeltweg 44, 8032 Zurich, Phone 044 250 25 25, Fax 044 250 25 00. Email - tcagianut@bclaw.ch. Founded in 1977. This firm provides advice on Swiss law, with emphasis on international content, commercial and corporate law, banking law, taxation, fraud, employment laws and estate planning. Languages: German, English, French and Italian.

URBACH Simon, TRACHSLER Attorneys at law, Seefeldstrasse 283, 8034 Zürich, Phone 044 250 42 00, Fax 044 250 42 19, e-mail surbach@trachsler.ch . Advises Swiss and international clients in all aspects of corporate law, commercial law and general contract law. Particular focus on all legal matters related to employment law, tenancy law and real estate law including real estate transactions as well as white-collar crime.

SELLING U.S. PRODUCTS AND SERVICES

USING AN AGENT OR DISTRIBUTOR

Under Swiss law, agents are independent. They can work for several firms and are compensated by commission. A 1949 federal law on agency contracts governs their activities. Swiss law does not permit a principal to inspect the books of his/her Swiss agent. The law defines traveling salespeople (Handelsreisende) as employees of the company they represent. Under a 1941 federal law, they are entitled to a fixed salary, with or without commission, and reimbursement of travel and entertainment expenses.

For U.S. exporters interested in entering the Swiss market, finding and selecting the right person or firm for representation is important and sometimes difficult. Offering favorable terms may be required to obtain good representation for a new product or an unknown firm.

Viable Swiss firms are listed in the official trade registry. Once a potential partner has been identified, it is advisable to request a financial profile of the company. This can be obtained at a relatively low cost from Dun & Bradstreet in the United States.

ESTABLISHING AN OFFICE

The actual mechanics of forming and registering an office in Switzerland can be accomplished in two to four weeks, but the planning process can be more time-consuming and involves many factors. Probably the most important factor to consider for establishing an office in Switzerland is location. Tax laws, availability of work permits, availability of labor force, and availability and cost of business facilities vary widely among cantons. Some cantons may offer special incentives for foreign investors.

As a rule, any trading, manufacturing or other form of commercial enterprise is required to be registered in the commercial register. It is only after registration in the commercial register that legal entities receive their own legal personality and status. The firm or business name under which a commercial enterprise is operated can be freely chosen, as long as it companies with legal regulations. Registration documents contain the company name, amount of share capital, business purpose, names of directors and managers, and names of those who have signatory powers. Documents must be notarized and legalized by an "apostil" (legalization of the notary's signature) and, if required by the particular canton, translated by a recognized translator into German, French or Italian (the official languages of Switzerland).

The company's board of directors must consist of a majority of Swiss citizens, residing in Switzerland. However, with the exception of ownership interests in banks and real estate firms, foreigners may hold majority shares. Foreign-controlled companies usually meet this requirement by nominating Swiss directors who hold shares and perform functions on a fiduciary basis. The manager need not be a Swiss citizen, but at least one person authorized to sign with a sole signature or two persons authorized to sign by joint signature must be Swiss residents.

Registration also includes special wording that the company, if a branch of a foreign corporation, is relatively independent, economically and otherwise, from the corporation's head office. This basically enables the branch to exist as if it were a separate legal entity in Switzerland. The branch must have its own books of account, although such books may be kept by the company headquarters or by a third party. A branch does not enjoy limited liability. For that reason, American companies should normally set up a subsidiary.

For additional analytical, business and investment opportunities information, please contact Global Investment & Business Center, USA at (703) 370-8082. Fax: (703) 370-8083. E-mail: ibpusa3@gmail.com Global Business and Investment Info Databank - www.ibpus.com

Employment regulations and restrictions are often a concern to businesses once they have registered. Foreign employees must have work permits that are granted at the cantonal level (quotas apply) and approved at the federal level. Hiring Swiss residents is more straightforward. There is no minimum wage, but the company is liable for a host of benefits and compensations, ranging from pension plan contributions to health and accident insurance.

Compared to other countries, the legal regime governing the employment relationship in Switzerland is generally more liberal and favorable towards the employer than in many other countries. This is partly because labor unions are somehow less influential in Switzerland compared to, for example, labor unions in EU countries, but also because the unemployment rate traditionally has been and still is relatively low in Switzerland.

A final factor that needs to be taken into consideration when setting up a business is tax liability. As a rule, foreign companies have a tax liability on income attributable to a Swiss permanent establishment or income from immovable property located in Switzerland, including gains on the sale of such property. Withholding tax is levied on dividends and certain kinds of interest.

Under the U.S.-Switzerland treaty on double taxation, income from industrial and commercial activities is not taxed in either country unless derived from a permanent establishment in the taxing country. Switzerland taxes only those industrial and commercial profits of a U.S. permanent establishment in Switzerland attributable to in-country activities. The same deductions are allowed in determining taxable income as for

a Swiss corporation. Detailed information on investment in Switzerland is included in the Investment Climate Statement, Chapter 6.

Detailed information regarding setting up and staffing a business enterprise in Switzerland is available from the Swiss-American Chamber of Commerce and from the Handbook for Investors, Business Location in Switzerland (www.invest-in-switzerland.com) published by Osec, Business Network Switzerland.

LocationSwitzerland http://www.locationswitzerland.com/internet/osec/en/home/invest/us.html
Swiss-American Chamber of Commerce www.amcham.ch

FRANCHISING

Switzerland's small geographic size and population of 8 million makes it a challenging market for franchising. Although some well-known franchise names like Starbucks, Burger King and McDonald's are established, Switzerland's limited market size, high salaries and high cost of services are all factors that make it difficult for a Swiss master franchisee to be profitable. Since the margins in many sectors are shrinking, it is increasingly difficult to generate a substantial return from a franchise operation. Another factor that makes franchising challenging is the Swiss consumer preference for high quality, authentic products and innovative ideas. Also limiting the interest in franchising may be the lack of the availability of financing for the Swiss to operate their own distribution, retail chains or stores in Switzerland.

The key to establishing a franchise concept in the Swiss market is the master franchisee or a language area franchisee. Switzerland is a small and multilingual country. Therefore, franchises should be tested in different cultural and linguistic environments: French in Geneva and Lausanne; German in Zurich, Basel and Bern; and Italian in Lugano.

It is advisable to undertake a feasibility study coupled with a sound business plan prior to signing new franchisees. To achieve maximum market penetration, U.S. franchisers should therefore adapt to the norms, standards and high end user expectations. Only rarely can a franchise concept be implemented directly from the United States. Thus, a U.S. franchiser should show flexibility when entering the Swiss market. Since Switzerland is a high-priced country, potential franchisees may find it advantageous to centralize the purchase of supplies in order to offer attractive prices to the consumer.

The legal framework for franchising is the Swiss Code of Obligations, which covers legal situations in agency/licensing agreements, contracting, order placing, business formation and incorporation, as well as brand, trade name and commercial or intellectual property protection.

DIRECT MARKETING

Home shopping is popular in Switzerland. This method of direct marketing has grown enormously in the past few years. The Swiss home shopping boom has reached a record high, and products range from Tupperware and Mary Kay Cosmetics, to lingerie to new recipes and cleansing agents. More and more people are going online to fill their shopping basket with groceries, bringing success to outfits offering online grocery shopping. This market segment still accounts for less than one percent of Swiss retail sales, but is slated to grow substantially in the years to come. There are more than 5,700 members of the Swiss Association of Direct Marketing Companies (Schweizer Verband der Direktverkaufsfirmen VDF), excluding mail order companies.

Most of the products sold at so-called home shopping parties are top quality and innovative and cannot be found at retail stores. Within the VDF association only the British company Body Shop offers the identical cosmetic and personal hygiene products that can be found in company shops and for the same price. Most Swiss consider the advantages of home shopping to be the following: competent advice offered by the sales person; the relaxed and friendly atmosphere of the private location; the combined experience of shopping and meeting with friends; and the possibility of testing the products on the spot. The following paragraphs describe some of the most popular types of products sold through the direct marketing system in Switzerland.

Books and music: The Bertelsmann-Verlag (Random House) is an example of a large multimedia firm that sells books, CDs, DVDs, videos and a range of products and services.

Personal Hygiene: Beauty products are sold via personal demonstrations at private locations. Personal hygiene products ranging from soap to night creams are ideal for direct sale as home shoppers can try out the various products and profit from the personalized consultation. Amway is one of the strongest representatives in this sector, offering cosmetics and a whole variety of personal hygiene products. Other companies established in the Swiss market include Mary Kay Cosmetics, Deesse, Just, Jafra, Blidor AG and the Body Shop.

Jewelry and Apparel: Companies like Jenny Lane, Pierre Lang and Swiss Feeling AG successfully sell costume jewelry. The direct sale of clothing items has by and large failed due to the modest margins and the huge variety of products. However, direct sales of lingerie for women are gaining in popularity.

Cleansing Agents: "Just" brand products have been sold through home shopping for generations. Other companies that sell top quality, ecologically friendly cleansing products include Blidor, L. Zollinger AG, and Amway.

Household Articles: Items range from Tupperware (almost every Swiss household has at least one of their famous items) to special cooking pots and pans. A huge variety of electrical appliances and various cleaning devices can also be found in this sector. New-to-market products are especially popular with home shoppers. Borna, Bandar Genossenschaft and Lux are all active in this market segment.

Food/Nutrition: Direct sales are growing for food items like fat-free bouillon, sauces and salt-free spice mixes; multivitamin products and food supplements and power-drinks that

cover a whole day's requirement for vitamins, proteins and minerals. Nahrin AG, Edifors and NBC Nutrition & Bodycare Concept AG are the major competitors in the nutrition sector.

The members of the Swiss Association of Direct Marketing Companies (VDF) are obliged to comply with a code of honor, and by Swiss law, sales contracts may be rescinded within seven days. Many of the VDF members are willing to accept returns even after this time period has elapsed. The association offers assistance should consumers experience problems or misunderstandings that cannot be solved directly with the sales person or manufacturer. New companies that apply for VDF membership must undergo an extensive examination, conducted by the association.

Swiss Association of Direct Marketing Companies www.svdf.ch

JOINT VENTURES/LICENSING

Swiss government agencies use competitive bids for procurement. As a signatory to the WTO GPA, Switzerland complies with general international rules on procurement by government entities. Switzerland's federal government and cantonal governments are covered http://www.wto.org/english/tratop_e/gproc_e/appendices_e.htm#appendixI . Procurement at the federal level is generally limited to projects in sectors in which it has primary responsibility -- utilities, transportation, communications, defense and construction.

The Swiss Federal Government has put a priority on funding for research and education. U.S. manufacturers of scientific and laboratory instruments stand a realistic chance to supply a significant portion of the resulting procurement. Total federal government procurement averages over USD 6 Billion annually. The Defense Ministry has some restrictions on foreign purchases. The cantonal and communal governments implement public projects amounting to procurements of about USD 15 billion annually.

The federal government exercises a great deal of discretion in inviting bids, and selective, discretionary tenders are more common than are public tenders. Contrary to cantonal and communal practice, federal authorities are not required to inform an unsuccessful bidder of the tender award or reasons for the choice. In general, quality and technical criteria are more important than price in bid decisions. Cantons and communes usually prefer local suppliers. Foreign firms may be required to provide a Swiss bank guarantee if they have no local office or representation.

Notices of Swiss government tenders are published in the official trade journal *Handelsamtsblatt*. Tender documents can be obtained free from the Swiss government agency (www.simap.ch). While there is no requirement to have a local agent to bid, it is advantageous when equipment needs training, service or parts.

Swiss Official Gazette of Commerce www.shab.ch

SELLING TO THE GOVERNMENT

Procurement by armasuisse, part of the Federal Department of Defense, Civil Protection and Sports better known by its acronym DDPS, may involve offsets. With regard to national security and armament policy, offset or compensation transactions in cases of procurements abroad have proven successful. As in the past, offset transactions are expected to open up access to foreign markets for Swiss industry or to strengthen its position in these markets. In particular, offset transactions may lead to the acquisition of additional know-how and consequently to additional export value, if the Swiss industry can offer its services at competitive conditions. The Swiss defense department is heavily reliant upon cooperation and expertise from foreign companies due to limited capability in Switzerland.

Additional information may be obtained from armasuisse by visiting:
http://www.ar.admin.ch/internet/armasuisse/en/home.html

DISTRIBUTION AND SALES CHANNELS

The most effective method of importing into and distributing within Switzerland depends on the type of product and the location of manufacturing or distribution sites. Capital goods manufacturers may find direct exporting most desirable when contracts with a limited number of customers represent an appreciable share of the market. However, most new-to-market exporters and exporters with products that require training for use and after-sales service should engage the services of a technically qualified Swiss agent with good market knowledge. As a rule, Swiss buyers of raw materials use specialized importers. Large orders, however, may also be placed directly with foreign producers.

Some of the largest international trading and transit companies are based in Switzerland. They operate a network of bonded warehouses and other relevant facilities offering any kind of services needed in international trade.

Suppliers of consumer goods may deal with an importer/wholesaler, engage the services of a representative, or sell directly to buying offices of large retail chains, especially if dealing with mass-produced goods. Often a representative or agent, who usually specializes in one or more product groups, is responsible for distribution in the whole country.

Import and Wholesale Trade: Many Swiss wholesalers are also importers who generally expect exclusive regional or national rights for the imported product. Wholesalers maintain stocks of a range of products and provide quality control, transport, warehousing, and financing. Associations of wholesalers in various sectors protect their common interests and facilitate more effective competition with other forms of distribution. Most wholesalers and importers also belong, either through sector associations or individually, to the Federation of Swiss Importers and Wholesale Traders (Vereinigung des Schweizerischen Import- und Grosshandels http://www.vsig.ch/).

Retail Trade: Vertically integrated retailers dominate the Swiss market. Department stores, chain stores, consumer cooperatives, discount stores and supermarkets comprise the majority of such retailers that deal in a wide range of products and

services. Their vertical structure and centralized buying give them a competitive advantage over independent retailers. The structure of retail trade in Switzerland is changing fast. The number of independent retailers is decreasing, giving way to a growing number of discount stores and supermarkets. Retailers with competitive prices such as IKEA and Media Markt are gaining market share. Individual retailers have set up organizations to provide wholesale purchasing,

For additional analytical, business and investment opportunities information,
please contact Global Investment & Business Center, USA
at (703) 370-8082. Fax: (703) 370-8083. E-mail: ibpusa3@gmail.com
Global Business and Investment Info Databank - www.ibpus.com

importing, and other services to compete with the large, vertically integrated retail establishments. Most of the leading retailers are legally structured as cooperatives. In addition to the common department store product lines, they also carry textiles, leather goods, sports articles, pharmaceuticals, toys, and hardware.

Swiss retailers continue to streamline their operations in response to domestic and international competition. Scanner cash registers for bar-coded articles are now standard, and state- of-the-art systems for automated payments without cashiers are in the testing phase. The use of credit cards for payment is now acceptable in most shops.

SELLING FACTORS/TECHNIQUES

New-to-market U.S. exporters gain considerable market exposure through trade shows in Switzerland. Moreover, participation in trade shows demonstrates a commitment to the market. Swiss buyers, agents and distributors, to a greater extent than their U.S. counterparts, visit trade shows to find new products.

An exporter's offer must be accurate and comprehensive if it is to be taken seriously by the Swiss. The Swiss receive offers from all over the world, and they are unlikely to devote time to requesting additional details if not already included in marketing information. Relevant information must be provided at the outset with objective and detailed information, including the following: exact product description with technical specifications; price details (CIF or FOB) in U.S. dollars or Swiss francs; method of payment; quantities available; packaging; and transport and delivery terms. An offer should also include information on the exporting firm; production equipment available and quality control factors; and financial references. If minimum quantities for accepting orders are part of contract negotiations, the exporter should adapt to the Swiss importer's needs, taking into account the relatively small size of the Swiss market.

Commitments should be scrupulously observed or the likelihood of success in the market may be seriously compromised. In the relatively small Swiss market, maintaining a company's good reputation is critical. Prospective Swiss business partners place high value on a long-term business relationship and commitment to the market.

Payment terms are usually stipulated in the sales contract, can be negotiated, and depend upon the amounts involved. Most common terms are the following: payment 30-60 days net (from the date of the invoice); payment within 10-15 days with 2-3% discount; and payment after 30-60 days with an interest charge. Good customers may expect credit of up to three months. Except for single, one-time transactions, or first-time transactions where there is doubt about the recipient's credit-worthiness, the costly letter of credit (LC) procedure should be avoided. An LC is perceived as depriving the recipient of the means to make deductions for faulty products or shipping problems.

ELECTRONIC COMMERCE

With approximately 75 percent of the Swiss population regularly using the Internet, Switzerland is among the leading countries in the world in broadband Internet usage. Expenditures in telecommunication technologies per capita in Switzerland are among the highest in the world. Private Internet use is the second highest in Europe, and Switzerland ranks third in terms of E-commerce. Many Swiss use the Internet to buy travel services, to do grocery shopping, to order consumer electronics, computers and, increasingly, household and fashion items. Online sales of Switzerland's two largest retail supermarket chains, Coop and LeShop.ch, which is a subsidiary of retail giant Migros, are on the rise. The market was worth USD175 million in Switzerland in

2012 and is estimated that demand for online grocery shopping will increase to USD315 to USD420 million over the next five years. Online sales of drugs and pharmaceuticals are also growing, as is the popularity of mail-order shopping companies. Switzerland's manufacturers' representatives and dealers are increasingly using e-commerce for B2C sales.

Swiss companies use online procurement to accelerate and streamline B2B business processes and to optimize their supply chain and internal processes. On the whole, Swiss companies are currently investing in security, intranets, services (such as web-enabled process optimization), storage, mobile internet, integration of conventional IT and the internet, content management, CRM, ERP, networking, and web publishing. Initially the domain of large corporations, e-commerce is being embraced by more and more of Switzerland's 300,000 small and medium-sized enterprises.

TRADE PROMOTION AND ADVERTISING

Print Media: With much linguistic and cultural diversity, Switzerland has one of the highest per capita densities of newspapers in the world. As a result, many papers are geared to particular regions or localities. The number of dailies has changed only slightly in the past 50 years, but circulation figures have more than doubled. There are over 100 daily or weekly local papers distributed for free and supported by advertising. The Swiss also publish an extensive range of periodicals, trade, and special interest magazines, including those concentrating on travel, gastronomy, medicine, environment, and hobbies.

Given the diversity of publications and the intrinsic characteristics of Switzerland, it is advisable to work through a professional advertising firm, such as Publicitas, when planning an advertising campaign.

Publicitas Swiss Press
Holbeinstrasse 30
8022 Zurich
Tel. +41 44 250 37 00, Fax. +41 44 250 37 37
E-Mail: swisspress@publicitas.ch

MAJOR SWISS NEWSPAPERS AND PERIODICALS

Daily Newspapers (German):
Neue Zürcher Zeitung
Tages-Anzeiger
Der Bund
Daily Newspapers (French):
24 heures
Tribune de Genève
Le Matin
Le Temps
Daily Newspapers (Italian):
Corriere del Ticino
Giornale del Popolo
Weekly Newspapers (German):
Handelszeitung
Sonntagszeitung
Die Weltwoche
Business Magazines:
FACTS

Cash
Bilanz
Bilan
L'Hebdo

PRICING

In determining the selling price of a product, particularly for consumer goods, an exporter must take into account the difference between the price an importer is prepared to pay and the prevailing retail selling price. The costs of distribution combined with retail margins may increase the selling price substantially. Markups in Switzerland generally range from 20 to 100 percent and can be even higher.

Price controls, part of Swiss competition law since 1986, are primarily aimed at reducing abusive prices for goods and services resulting from a lack of competition and apply only to members of a cartel or similar organizations subject to this law. Parliament has established an office to look into prices that appear to be too high. Although this office maintains considerable informal clout, it cannot institute legal action. The prices of some products are directly influenced by government measures; these products are primarily agricultural goods and pharmaceuticals.

SALES SERVICE/CUSTOMER SUPPORT

Finding a reliable means of providing rapid and efficient quality service and after-sales customer support is absolutely essential in Switzerland. Concluding a sales contract is usually dependent upon the ability to provide this follow-up service which may involve one or more of the following measures: opening an office in Switzerland; finding a competent agent/distributor to provide after-sales service; and/or keeping replacement stock in a Swiss or European warehouse.

PROTECTING YOUR INTELLECTUAL PROPERTY

With the exception of Switzerland's deeply inadequate internet piracy laws (outlined in the United States Trade Representative's annual " Special 301 Report "), the Swiss legal framework ensures appropriate protection of intellectual property and its enforcement. This topic is discussed more thoroughly under Investment Climate section on "Protection of Property Rights" Patent applications, trademark or design registrations can be submitted t the Swiss Federal Institute of Intellectual Property (Eidgenössisches Institut für Geistiges Eigentum) (http://www.ige.ch/defaulte.htm). In almost all cases, foreign and domestic rights holders are afforded equal protection.

Several general principles are important for effective management of intellectual property rights in Switzerland. First, it is important to have an overall strategy to protect IPR. Second, IPR is protected differently in Switzerland than in the U.S. Third, rights must be registered and enforced in Switzerland, under local laws. Companies may wish to seek advice from local attorneys or IP consultants. The U.S. Embassy's Political/Economic Section can provide a list of local lawyers upon request.

It is vital that companies understand that intellectual property is primarily a private right and that the U.S. Government generally cannot enforce rights for private individuals in Switzerland. It is the responsibility of the rights holders to register, protect, and enforce their rights where relevant, retaining their own counsel and advisors. While the U.S. Government is willing to assist, there is little it can do if the rights holders have not taken these fundamental steps necessary to securing and enforcing their IPR in a timely fashion. Moreover, in many countries, rights holders who delay

For additional analytical, business and investment opportunities information,
please contact Global Investment & Business Center, USA
at (703) 370-8082. Fax: (703) 370-8083. E-mail: ibpusa3@gmail.com
Global Business and Investment Info Databank - www.ibpus.com

enforcing their rights on a mistaken belief that the USG can provide a political resolution to a legal problem may find that their rights have been eroded or abrogated due to doctrines such as statutes of limitations, laches, estoppel, or unreasonable delay in prosecuting a law suit. In no instance should USG advice be seen as a substitute for the obligation of a rights holder to promptly pursue its case.

It is always advisable to conduct due diligence on partners. Negotiate from the position of your partner and give your partner clear incentives to honor the contract. A good partner is an important ally in protecting IP rights. Keep an eye on your cost structure and reduce the margins (and the incentive) of would-be bad actors. Projects and sales in Switzerland require constant attention. Work with legal counsel familiar with Switzerland laws to create a solid contract that includes non-compete clauses, and confidentiality/non-disclosure provisions.

It is also recommended that small and medium-size companies understand the importance of working together with trade associations and organizations to support efforts to protect IPR and stop counterfeiting. There are a number of these organizations, both Switzerland or U.S.-based. These include:

- The U.S. Chamber and local American Chambers of Commerce
- National Association of Manufacturers (NAM)
- International Intellectual Property Alliance (IIPA)
- International Trademark Association (INTA)
- The Coalition Against Counterfeiting and Piracy
- International Anti-Counterfeiting Coalition (IACC)
- Pharmaceutical Research and Manufacturers of America (PhRMA)
- Biotechnology Industry Organization (BIO)

IPR Resources

A wealth of information on protecting IPR is freely available to U.S. rights holders. Some excellent resources for companies regarding intellectual property include the following:

- For information about patent, trademark, or copyright issues -- including enforcement issues in the U.S. and other countries -- call the STOP! Hotline: **1-866-999-HALT** or register at www.StopFakes.gov .

- For more information about registering trademarks and patents (both in the U.S. as well as in foreign countries), contact the US Patent and Trademark Office (USPTO) at: **1-800-786-9199**.

- For more information about registering for copyright protection in the U.S., contact the US Copyright Office at: **1-202-707-5959**.

- For U.S. small and medium-size companies, the Department of Commerce offers a "SME IPR Advisory Program" available through the American Bar Association that provides one hour of free IPR legal advice for companies with concerns in Brazil, China, Egypt, India, Russia, and Thailand. For details and to register, visit: http://www.abanet.org/intlaw/intlproj/iprprogram_consultation.html

- For information on obtaining and enforcing intellectual property rights and market-specific IP Toolkits visit: www.StopFakes.gov This site is linked to the USPTO website for registering trademarks and patents (both in the U.S. as well as in foreign countries), the

U.S. Customs & Border Protection website to record registered trademarks and copyrighted works (to assist customs in blocking imports of IPR-infringing products) and allows you to register for Webinars on protecting IPR.

DUE DILIGENCE

Although the vast majority of Swiss importers are financially reliable business partners for U.S. exporters, there are, nonetheless, occasional bankruptcies. Therefore, U.S. exporters should use normal precautions and analyze relevant company financial background information before establishing a business relationship.

The Swiss Trade Register is a key source for checking the background of Swiss companies. Swiss companies with annual sales of SFr. 100,000/ $ 110,000 or more must be listed in the Swiss Trade Register with the following information:

- name of firm
- legal form
- head office (legal domicile)
- list of branch offices, purpose
- owners, partners, managing directors
- persons having power of attorney
- number of shareholders
- year of establishment
- share capital
- registration number

Any firm listed in the Swiss Trade Register is considered a legitimate company and is required to keep accounts and to maintain a balance sheet. However, the register does not reveal information about a company's financial status and business practices.

Debt enforcement agencies provide information on whether or not any debt collections were made by Swiss companies. Debt enforcement agencies require a letter of interest in order to provide this type of information.

The Swiss Commercial Register is based on Federal Law, the Code of Obligations, and is implemented within the individual cantons. The Federal Office of Justice maintains Zefix (Central Business Names Index on the Internet), a listing of the cantonal registers of companies. Entries and changes in the commercial register are published in the Swiss Commercial Gazette (SHAB) . Each canton also maintains information on whether or not a registered company has defaulted on payments. That information can be obtained directly from the relevant cantonal debt enforcement office.

The Kompass Register, a listing of most Swiss companies, is roughly equivalent to the American Thomas Register. Provided by the listed companies, the information includes complete contact address, bank reference, name of president, members of the Board and managing director, a short description of company's activity, trademarks, share capital, number of employees, and year of establishment. The Kompass CD is available from:

Kompass Schweiz Verlag AG
Hagenholzstrasse 81
CH-8050 Zurich, Switzerland
Tel: +41 44 305 12 80, Fax: +41 44 305 12 14

E-Mail: info@kompassonline.ch

It should be noted that extensive information on Swiss companies can be obtained from the Federal Commercial Register (www.zefix.ch).

LOCAL PROFESSIONAL SERVICES

When American citizens are involved in disputes with either private individuals or business enterprises and the controversy cannot be settled amicably, the normal recourse is to seek remedy provided by the law of the appropriate cantonal jurisdiction. American diplomatic or consular officers may not act as attorney, agent, or representative in a fiduciary capacity in such matters. If legal action is to be undertaken in Switzerland, a local lawyer should be engaged either directly or via an American attorney. Since there are differences in the legal systems in Switzerland and the U.S., ignorance of those differences could jeopardize a case almost before it begins. The Swiss lawyer must file a complaint with the court, and the court then decides whether to serve or not. The Martindale-Hubbell Law Directory contains an extensive list of lawyers licensed to practice in Switzerland. The Embassy's Consular Section also maintains a list of lawyers by canton on its website below.

The only methods for a non-Swiss court or lawyer to obtain testimony or to serve process in civil matters in Switzerland are through the Hague Convention on taking of Evidence Abroad in Civil or Commercial Matters, the Hague Convention on the Service

Abroad of Judicial and Extra-judicial Documents in Civil and Commercial Matter and through a letter interrogatory. For information on this rather cumbersome legal process, contact either the Embassy Bern Consular Section bernacs@state.gov or the Office of Citizens Consular Services in the Department of State (202) 647-5226.

U.S. Embassy Bern Consular Section http://bern.usembassy.gov/judicial_asst.html

WEB RESOURCES

Swiss Official Gazette of Commerce , www.shab.ch
Swiss Franchise Association , www.franchiseverband.ch
Swiss Association of Direct Marketing Companies , www.svdf.ch
Swiss Federal Institute of Intellectual Property , www.ige.ch
Federal Commercial Register (Central Business Names Index), www.zefix.ch
Kompass Schweiz , www.kompass.ch
Swiss Bar Association , www.swisslawyers.ch

LEADING SECTORS FOR U.S. EXPORT AND INVESTMENT

AIRCRAFT AND PARTS

The total Swiss market demand for civilian aircraft and parts, including components and avionics, was valued at USD 1.490 billion and is expected to grow by 2-4%. U.S. suppliers garnered a market share of almost 30% of the overall import market. The market share gain can best be attributed to a larger export output of aircraft in 2012. Switzerland has a relatively large number of operators of aircraft given the small size of the country, including the national flagship carrier SWISS (part of the Lufthansa Group), operators of regional and business jets, air taxi services as well as a substantial number of privately held aircraft.

Switzerland's sole aircraft maker, Pilatus Aircraft Ltd., develops and produces high-performance single-engine turboprops: PC-12 business- and utility Aircraft, PC-21, PC-7MkII and PC-9 Turbo military trainer aircraft. The plane maker is particularly world renowned for its development of single-engine turboprop aircraft, the PC-12 civilian aircraft. The Swiss plane maker marked the delivery of the 1,200th PC-12 in 2013. This milestone is underscored by the high performance of the aircraft, rugged durability, versatile, and excellent operating economics. Pilatus launched the PC-24 Twin-Jet at the annual European Business Aviation Conference and Exhibition (EBACE) in Geneva in May 2013. The content of U.S.-sourced technology is substantial. The PC-24 will be powered by two Williams FJ44-4A turbines. Avionics will be provided by Honeywell. Pilatus expects FAA and EASA certification 2017.

The company reported solid results in 2012 in a very difficult market environment with an annual output of 86 aircraft deliveries, thereby ensuring demand for avionics, engines, parts and components from U.S. suppliers. U.S. content of the PC-12, Pilatus' flagship aircraft, is significant – this illustrates how intertwined the U.S. aviation industry is with the Swiss plane maker. Pilatus also produces the military trainer aircraft, the PC-21, newly developed for modern air forces around the world. The plane maker secured 79 orders for the sale of 25 PC-21 turboprop aircraft from Saudi Arabia and Qatar. Winning

the contract with the UAE constitutes an excellent boon for U.S., given the high U.S. content of the PC-21, thereby accelerating growth in the Swiss defense aviation industry. In addition to Pilatus, a string of Swiss aerospace companies source parts, components and avionics from U.S. suppliers.

Switzerland has over 30 manufacturers involved in the development, production and assembly of structural components, systems integration and services for aircraft, helicopter and systems that stem from defense and civilian aeronautics and space technology. These companies are receptive to the idea of broadening their U.S. supplier list and interested in new product offerings. One of the key players is Ruag Aviation, an international Technology Group, active in two segments: Aerospace & Technology and Defense & Security.

Although private jet aviation as a business productivity tool is already well accepted in the United States, Switzerland has been slower to embrace this concept. However, Swiss executives and politicians are increasingly taking advantage of business jets for flexibility and to avoid congested airports and flight delays, and demand is steadily increasing in the business/regional market segment. Corporate jets available in the market encompass a wide spectrum, ranging from twin-engine turboprops to reconfigured jetliners, although the number of propulsion airplanes dwarfs the number of twin-engine turboprops.

Federal Office for Civil Aviation (FOCA): http://www.aviation.admin.ch/

Swiss Aeronautical Industries Group (SAIG): http://www.swissmem.ch/

Annual European Business Aviation Convention & Exhibition (EBACE 2014) to be held in Geneva on May 20-22, 2014, URL: http://www.ebace.aero/

AUTOMOTIVE

The total Swiss market demand for automobiles, busses, automotive parts, equipment and accessories was assessed at USD 20.2 billion in 2012. With Switzerland coming out of an economic downturn, the GDP is forecast to grow is assessed at 1.3% in 2013. Industry sources are optimistic, predicting higher growth for automobiles, auto parts, accessories and aftermarket products in 2013. Consumers are continuing to exercise prudence when it comes to procuring new automobile purchases and accessories in order to weather the economic woes that might lie ahead. Imports from Germany have traditionally had a solid market share, capturing nearly 50% of the market, followed by France with 12% and Japan with 11%. In 2012, U.S. suppliers exported goods of nearly USD 1 billion, accounting for an approximately 7% market share. Demand for U.S. imports is expected to remain steady in 2013 as Swiss importers and distributors are capitalizing on the relative strength of the franc against the dollar, making U.S.-sourced automobiles, parts and components lucrative. The weak dollar against a strong Swiss franc makes U.S. products competitive and affordable for Swiss consumers. U.S. suppliers should carefully evaluate their pricing and sales terms to remain competitive.

Overall, Swiss automotive market demand, including sales of new and used automobiles and trucks, gasoline stations, repair and service facilities and providers of related services amounted to USD 105 billion in 2012. The overall automobile industry has established self as one of the mainstays of the Swiss economy. The overall car fleet in Switzerland is assessed at 3.85 million automobiles and is expected to grow marginally over the next two years as a result of higher retention rates of automobiles and the forecast for slow economic growth in 2012.

Although Switzerland does not manufacture automobiles, it has more than 300 enterprises involved in the production parts, components and systems for carmakers around the world, employing more than 34,000 people. Nearly 20% of the overall output is supplied to OEMs around the world. These companies yield a combined turnover of USD 15,5 billion per annum. Swiss manufacturers are heavily depended upon the German car industry; 75 of the companies are selling structures, parts and components to German OEMs.

The Swiss automotive market was liberalized on January 1, 2005, giving consumers greater choice in buying new automobiles. Many Swiss car dealers and repair facilities note that liberalization is bringing more competition into the market and is beginning to put downward pressure on prices. U.S. automobiles garnered 5% market share in 2010.

Effective January 2011, Swiss authorities no longer accept a Carfax report for used automobiles sourced from U.S. suppliers, which has had an adverse impact of the U.S. export volume of used automobiles to Switzerland. Negotiations are afoot with the appropriate Swiss authorities to find a solution to the need for appropriate documentation of the "first registration" of a U.S. car.

For additional analytical, business and investment opportunities information,
please contact Global Investment & Business Center, USA
at (703) 370-8082. Fax: (703) 370-8083. E-mail: ibpusa3@gmail.com
Global Business and Investment Info Databank - www.ibpus.com

RESOURCES / OPPORTUNITIES

Swiss Federal Roads Authority: http://www.astra.admin.ch/

Swiss Motor Trade and Repair Association (AGVS): http://www.agvs.ch/

84th International Motor Show in Geneva at Palexpo (fairgrounds) http://www.salon-auto.ch/en/
March 6-16, 2014

EDUCATIONAL EQUIPMENT AND SUPPLIES

The Swiss market for educational equipment and supplies was valued at an estimated USD 2,2 billion in 2012, and imports from the U.S. amounted to an estimated USD 235 million. Switzerland spends annually the equivalent of 5.8% of its GDP on education and related activities. Public funding amounted to an overall USD 26 billion for education – the cantons (states) spent USD 20 billion and the federal government USD 6 billion in 2010 (more current data is not available). Switzerland spends about USD 13,000 annually per student, USD 3,000 more per student than the average of the 29 OECD countries. The federal government focuses on tertiary education, which includes R&D. In addition, it finances the federal universities and research institutes ETH (Zurich), EPFL (Lausanne), PSI (Zurich), and EMPA (St.Gallen, Thun, Zurich) and contributes to the cantonal universities.

The Swiss education system is quite complex. On average, the Swiss attend school until the age of 17, which is one of the highest school-leaving ages in the world.

The education system is decentralized with the cantons and municipalities taking the majority of the responsibility. Compulsory schooling starts at six years old and is free of charge, followed by Lower Secondary level (12-16 years old); Upper Secondary level which is split into general and vocational education and Tertiary level: vocational and higher university degrees; higher technical schools, universities and teacher training.

There are 12 traditional universities, eight universities of applied science, 15 universities of teacher education and further university level institutions supported by the Confederation. These higher education institutions are based in the main cities throughout French, German and Italian speaking Switzerland. The Universities are adjusting to the Bologna declaration and changing their timetables for the Bachelors degree to three years and the Masters to 1.5 years.

In the fall 2006, the Swiss Federal Council decided to spend more on research and education, with an annual budget increase of 6% between 2008 and 2011. Most federal funding goes towards the universities with about USD 852 million spent annually on research and development. About USD 540 million of this amount is earmarked for combined educational and scientific programs that are managed by the Swiss National Science Foundation (SNF), an agency of the Swiss Federal Department of Science and Education and equivalent to the National Science Foundation (NSF). The public funds are matched about equally by the private sector. As a result of strong competition among Swiss universities, private sector funding is constantly increasing and plays an important and popular role. R&D will remain a top priority in Switzerland with strong support from both the private and public sector. U.S. manufacturers of scientific and laboratory instruments for universities have excellent opportunities in the Swiss market.

In addition to opportunities on the tertiary level, two significant factors and changes in the primary and secondary Swiss curricula will boost opportunities for U.S. firms in the near future: (1) the teaching of two foreign languages, including English, is mandatory at primary and secondary schools in the vast majority of cantons, and (2) the cantonal educational book publishers supplying public schools are expected to be privatized soon. This early English instruction is expected to boost market demand for English-language educational materials.

RESOURCES / OPPORTUNITIES

Rector's Conference of the Swiss Universities http://www.crus.ch/homenavigation/home.html?L=2
State Secretariat for Education and Research http://www.wbf.admin.ch/?lang=en

ELECTRIC POWER GENERATING AND DISTRIBUTION EQUIPMENT

In spite of the global downturn, demand for electric power generating equipment is forecast to grow approximately 3-5% in 2013. Switzerland's power companies are continually seeking equipment to streamline and upgrade operations, and demand will continue to grow for power management systems (IT), switching and distribution equipment. Of the power produced in Switzerland, 40% is generated from five nuclear power plants, and the other 60% is mostly generated from hydropower, which is distributed to surrounding countries, especially Northern Italy, in order to stabilize the European grid during periods of peak demand. Hydroelectric facilities still have a limited potential for expansion but will fall short of growing demand. Other sources of renewable energy in Switzerland are in their infancy with some efforts to promote solar, geothermal and wind energy.

To prevent a predicted energy shortfall by 2020 and avoid expensive power imports, Switzerland will require an estimated USD 20-30 billion of investment in new generating facilities over the next 15-20 years.

After a year that saw Switzerland officially renounce nuclear energy, the country now has to find alternatives. Politicians are calling for action. The questions raised after the May 2011 decision of the Swiss government to abandon nuclear energy have yet to be answered. While the disaster at Fukushima focused people's minds on the risks of atomic energy, there remains great uncertainty about the future of energy supply in this country.

By 2034, when the last nuclear power plant is due to close, the Swiss government will have to find other ways to make up the electricity now supplied by its five nuclear plants. This will be a considerable challenge, given that about 40 per cent of the electricity produced in Switzerland is nuclear-generated, equivalent to 25 terawatt hours (TWh) a year.

Consuming less, improving energy efficiency, and harnessing power renewable sources such as sun and wind are all officially encouraged. Alternatives to nuclear energy are not lacking in a country that ranks as one of the most innovative in the world, and which has made water the main domestic source of electricity.

The new Federal Law on Energy Supply entered into force on January 1, 2008. The law will allow the Electricity Commission to cap energy prices and business consumers of at least 100,000 Kwh to purchase their electricity freely, therefore bypassing the expensive cantonal monopolies. The major private sector utility companies are Romande Energie, FMB, Axpo, Atel and BKW. The Swiss national grid operator "Swissgrid" is the national transmission system operator and has full responsibility for operating the 6,700 kilometers of the Swiss high-voltage grid.

LABORATORY AND SCIENTIFIC INSTRUMENTS & EQUIPMENT

For additional analytical, business and investment opportunities information,
please contact Global Investment & Business Center, USA
at (703) 370-8082. Fax: (703) 370-8083. E-mail: ibpusa3@gmail.com
Global Business and Investment Info Databank - www.ibpus.com

The total Swiss market demand for laboratory equipment and scientific instruments amounted to an estimated USD 1,25 billion in 2012. Total imports in 2012, are estimated at USD 834 million and account for about 74% of the total market demand. The Swiss market is an attractive market for U.S. suppliers of analytical and process control

equipment and instruments, which enjoy an excellent reputation and are much in demand.

Switzerland's R&D activity, in relation to the size of the country, is rather impressive at an estimated USD 37 billion from 2007 through 2011. In addition to the wide range of research activities undertaken by Swiss universities and institutes, there is an enormous amount of research activity in the private sector, especially in the chemical, pharmaceutical, biotech, food, machinery and micro technology industries. The Swiss manufacturing industry is heavily export-oriented and depends upon the latest technology in order to retain its competitiveness on the world market. Therefore, state-of-the-art R&D remains a top priority in Switzerland.

There are a number of important new Swiss projects for research and development. Novartis Pharmaceutical is in the process of expanding its Basel global headquarters to encompass additional numerous research, production and administrative buildings in its Campus of Knowledge and Innovation. The first stages of this initiative have already been realized, and the whole project is to be completed by the year 2030. Hoffmann La Roche, the Swiss biotech company, intends to consolidate the 1,700 plus off-site workplaces in Basel at its headquarters there. In February 2011 Roche received the approval to build its 175 m high office building, which is planned for completion by the end of 2015. Since 2003, the Federal Institute of Zurich (ETH), one of Europe's premier universities, has been continually developing its location in Hoenggerberg as a model for universities in the 21st century. The ETH campus not only strengthens the knowledge base in Zurich, but also enhances Switzerland's reputation as a location for research and education.

The main end-users of laboratory equipment and scientific instruments are Swiss manufacturers, including about 180 chemical companies, 150 pharmaceutical producers, 200 biotech companies and 165 food manufacturers. Research institutes and universities, mostly federally funded, account for about 35% of the market demand and 20% of the end-user market are cantonal (state) and communal (city) laboratories.

OPPORTUNITIES / RESOURCES

LABOTEC Suisse, Basel, Switzerland, May 14 &15, 2014, New specialist annual trade show for laboratory equipment and scientific instruments, which had its debut in 2011 with 100 exhibitors.

ILMAC Basel, Switzerland, September 24-27, 2013, industrial exhibition and conference for research and development, environmental and process technology in pharmaceuticals, chemicals and biotechnology, 500 exhibitors, 17,000 trade visitors.

LABOTEC Suisse trade show for laboratory equipment and scientific instruments http://www .easyfairs.com/en/events_216/labotec-suisse2012
SWISS MEDLAB laboratory medicine congress and exhibition: http://www.swissmedlab.ch
ILMAC main Swiss scientific and lab equipment trade show: http://www.ilmac.ch
Swiss National Research Program: http://www.snf.ch
Federal Institutes of Technology in Zurich and Lausanne: http://www.ethz.ch , http://www.epfl.ch
Paul Scherrer Institute: http://www.psi.ch
Swiss Federal Department of Science & Education: http://www.bbt.admin.ch

For additional analytical, business and investment opportunities information,
please contact Global Investment & Business Center, USA
at (703) 370-8082. Fax: (703) 370-8083. E-mail: ibpusa3@gmail.com
Global Business and Investment Info Databank - www.ibpus.com

MEDICAL EQUIPMENT

With Europe's highest per capita income, Switzerland is an attractive, demanding market with one of the best national health care systems in the world. The country's liberal trade and investment policies favor access for a host of products and technologies. The dispersed nature of its health care system, which follows the pattern of its federal structure with 26 autonomous districts (cantons), contributes to the diversity of the market.

The combination of an aging population, rising living standards and new treatment methods is causing demand to grow at an above-average pace. Accordingly, as incomes rise, so do people's willingness to spend more on health services. Leading Europe on healthcare spending, Switzerland spends about 11.4% of its GDP on its national healthcare system, following the U.S., Netherlands, France and Germany. However, as in other national healthcare systems, cost-containment is a growing concern, and there is a clear trend to reduce hospital beds and to close down some hospitals.

U.S. equipment and supplies enjoy a good reputation in Switzerland. Many Swiss doctors and professors of medicine have been trained or have practiced in the United States, and there is considerable interchange in procedures and techniques. These factors create a strong demand for U.S. equipment and supplies.

Although Switzerland's market is relatively small, it is a highly sophisticated market with a strong demand for advanced technologies. It also offers the additional benefit of being a test market that is strategically placed in the heart of Europe. The country's 300 hospitals are mostly administrated by the 26 cantons or by local municipalities. In addition, a host of private clinics and medical homes (167) cater to the needs of a demanding local and international clientele and serve as professional training grounds for physicians. Specialized services, such as transplant capacities, are mainly offered at university clinics. In addition to laboratories in doctors' private offices, hospital, clinical and independent laboratories share the Swiss market.

OPPORTUNITIES / RESOURCES

Dental 2012, Bern, Switzerland, June 22-24, 2014, biannual dental congress and trade fair. http://www.dentalbern.ch/index.php?new_lang=en
IFAS, Zurich, Switzerland, October 2-5, 2014, biannual trade fair for medical and hospital equipment, 400 exhibitors, 16.500 trade visitors. www.ifas-messe.ch
FASMED (Swiss Association of the Medical and Hospital Trade): http://www.fasmed.ch
Swissmedic (Swiss Agency for therapeutic products): http://www.swissmedic.ch

SAFETY AND SECURITY EQUIPMENT

Switzerland (pop. 8 million) sits squarely in the heart of Western Europe. Although known as a very safe country, Switzerland is becoming significantly more security conscious. A key factor influencing this notion is the increase in immigration (both legal and illegal) has been connected in the public consciousness with a perceived increase in the number of assaults, threats, fraud and drug smuggling activities. Switzerland's demographic profile has changed within the last decade. Accompanying societal changes is a growing security consciousness among the Swiss at all levels of government and in the business community with measures being taken to protect data, access control, peripheral security, transportation and other critical infrastructure. There is growing demand for equipment used in access control, contraband detection, surveillance and law enforcement. Furthermore, there are ample opportunities for sales of security products in the fields of aviation, supply chain, and retail.

The Swiss safety and security market has grown steadily at the pace of 4-6% over the last decade. The overall market was valued at a USD 685 million in 2012, with total imports valued at USD 312 million. U.S. imports accounts for approximately 50% of the overall import market. U.S. suppliers enjoy excellent acceptance in the Swiss safety and security market.

Largely predicated on sales of CCTV, biometric applications and proximity systems, large and small-sized enterprises have begun to retrofit and incorporate new systems and technologies into existing security systems. The growing Swiss presence of regional and global headquarters of U.S. and other multinational corporations represents a significant end-user market segment. Airports represent another major purchaser category based on ongoing security enhancements to meet international agreements and bilateral agreements with the EU.

The most promising growth prospects are those in newer market segments, including airport passenger and baggage screening equipment, CCTV systems, perimeter protection systems, access control systems (including biometric identification systems), law enforcement equipment, explosives and metal detectors, forensic equipment, residential alarms and other advanced electronic systems. U.S. suppliers are especially competitive in access control equipment, biometrics applications, law enforcement supplies and equipment, forensics equipment, and surveillance equipment, including

CCTV systems, and residential alarms. Major prospective buyers include public/private sector agencies, the Federal Government and local state authorities, supply chains and retailers, and airport operators.

The federal system of Switzerland and the division into three levels, i.e. municipal, cantonal and federal level, is reflected in the structure of the country's law enforcement agencies. Basically, the 26 Swiss cantons (state) have jurisdiction over their own police matters. They are responsible for recruiting, training, equipment, armament and uniforms of the cantonal police force. Decentralization of the law enforcement agencies in Switzerland constitutes market opportunities for U.S. suppliers, as each police corps is responsible for its own procurement activities.

Notwithstanding its size, Switzerland is an attractive market for law enforcement equipment, accessories, hunting and sports arms, protective gear, crime scene investigation and forensic evidence collection supplies. U.S. suppliers garnered a significant market share in 2012 in this market segment. Demand for law enforcement equipment and accessories has grown over the past few years in order to combat rising crime in Switzerland. U.S. suppliers in all areas of law enforcement have traditionally enjoyed a high degree of receptivity among the different government authorities, guns smiths and end-users.

INFORMATION AND COMMUNICATION TECHNOLOGIES

Switzerland is one of the world's leading countries for Information and Communication Technologies (ICT). At both the individual and corporate level Switzerland is very receptive to ICT innovations. Altogether the ICT sector generates about USD 27.8 billion, accounting for approximately 8% of the gross domestic product (GDP). Switzerland is among the top ten countries worldwide in terms of the quality and depth of ICT infrastructure, as measured by the penetration of traditional fixed lines, broadband access lines, mobile phones, PCs Internet users and Internet servers. With 8% of Switzerland's GDP generated by the ICT sector, the country ranks third worldwide in this measure, behind only the U.S. (9%) and Sweden (8+%).

Telecommunications services and equipment account for almost half of the total value of the ICT market in Switzerland (43%). Software and IT equipment have about the same market share (15% and 18%), with the remaining 24% belonging to IT services (consulting and support).

Switzerland has an advanced telecom market, with one of the highest Internet and broadband penetration rates in Europe. Mobile services, including mobile Internet and broadband Internet access continue to drive the market. DSL networks have overtaken cable as the principal technology for broadband access. ADSL is available for more than 98% of telephone connections and is offered by 30 different suppliers.

The Swiss telecom market is divided primarily into the business fields of network-based communications, mobile communications, IP-based voice and data communications, and value-added services. One relatively recent branch of business is digital television, which is being marketed along with Internet access and telephony as a triple play offering via the Internet/cable network.

Swisscom is no longer the sole provider of telecommunication services. Orange and Sunrise, amongst others, operate their own networks for mobile communications and, to some extent, for fixed-line services. In February 2006, Sunrise signed a national roaming agreement with Swedish operator Tele2, which subsequently began operating as a mobile virtual network operator (MVNO). However, after being awarded its own GSM license, Tele2 launched its own mobile network and became a fully fledged network operator. In September 2008, Tele2 was acquired by Sunrise, reducing the number of mobile operators in Switzerland to just three.

In 2009 both Orange and Sunrise publicly announced their intention to merge their operations. The Competition Commission (Weko), however, blocked this deal in 2010, putting an end to any attempt to merge. On February 17, 2012, Weko agreed to allow the British firm Apax buy Orange from France Telecom. Weko announced that this sale would continue the competitive dynamics in the Swiss mobile phone market.

U.S. investments in the Swiss telecommunications market include Southern Bell Corporation's 9.5% stake in Sunrise's parent company (France Telecom), UPC Cablecom (100% owned by Liberty Global), a competitor offering VOIP and TV on demand services. Cablecom and other cable network providers deliver their communications services over the existing cable TV network. With over two million cable TV connections in Swiss households Cablecom controls the second largest network and is currently the only other company besides Swisscom that offers true triple play service (data, voice and television/radio) to its customers in Switzerland. Swisscom started its IPTV network in late 2006.

The Swiss parliament's decision in 2006 to open the "last mile" was a key event in the evolution of the Swiss telecoms market. It granted Swisscom's competitors full unbundled access to the copper-wire subscriber connection, cabling for leased lines, and high-speed bit-stream Internet access (within 4 years). Unbundling the last mile is an important step towards the full liberalization of the Swiss telecoms market and is expected to intensify competition among providers. As a result, the sector will continue to see declining prices.

Telecommunications in Switzerland are regulated by two bodies: the Federal Office of Communications (also known as OFCOM or BAKOM from its German name) and ComCom. OFCOM licenses all providers of fixed network services (without a tender procedure) and is responsible for the day-to-day management of the telecom sector.

For additional analytical, business and investment opportunities information,
please contact Global Investment & Business Center, USA
at (703) 370-8082. Fax: (703) 370-8083. E-mail: ibpusa3@gmail.com
Global Business and Investment Info Databank - www.ibpus.com

ComCom is responsible for awarding basic provision licenses, as well as licenses for the provision of mobile telephone and other radio services (through a tender procedure).

Forecasts include continued growth of information technology spending in Switzerland, a further decrease in mobile communication costs, and expanded services for third-generation mobile devices, such as IPTV. Continued strong growth is expected for VOIP solutions.

OPPORTUNITIES / RESOURCES

Infosocietydays 2014, Bern, Switzerland, March 4-7, 2014
Congress and exhibition for ICT usages http://www.infosocietydays.ch
Annual trade show for business software http://www.topsoft.ch OFCOM (Federal Office of Communications): http://www.bakom.admin.ch FOITT (Federal Office of Information Technology): http://www.bit.admin.ch ComCom (Federal Communications Commission) http://www.comcom.admin.ch
SWICO (Swiss Providers Association for ICT) http://www.swico.ch
Swiss Association of Telecommunications Users http://www.asut.ch

TRAVEL AND TOURISM

In 2012, a total of over 500,000 Swiss travelers visited the U.S., a 20% increase from the previous year. In spite of the many economic challenges, particularly in Europe, the Swiss travel trade expects another good USA year in 2012. The strong Swiss franc keeps providing travelers with attractive purchasing power.

The share of Swiss outbound travel sales made via the Internet is steadily growing. Internet sales were primarily for flights, individual hotels, and car rental reservations. About 90% of the growth in Internet sales is from travel within Europe, and Swiss travelers widely use the Internet as a source of information in planning a vacation.

Most Swiss still turn to travel agencies for purchases of packages above USD 1,000 per person as well as long haul travel. Switzerland's leading tour operators are noticing a growing trend towards more expensive trips and luxury hotels, and air travel in business class, as opposed to economy class.

The main factor supporting Swiss travel to the United States is the weak dollar, which lost value versus the Swiss franc. Other factors include the Swiss preference for safe destinations, and a relatively low language barrier. A strong additional incentive is easy accessibility with six airlines offering 17 daily direct flights to ten U.S. gateway cities on the East and West Coasts. The U.S. is becoming an alternative to typical beach vacation destinations on the Mediterranean coast, many of which are politically unstable or witnessing high crime rates. Some Swiss travel agencies that had reduced or even totally dropped their U.S. products in recent years are now back on the market and expanding their offers. Swiss media are covering U.S. cities, states and regions on a regular basis and introducing them as attractive travel destinations to their readers.

RESOURCES / OPPORTUNITIES

Swiss Travel Agency Association http://www.srv.ch
Swiss Travel Association of Retailers (STAR) http://www.star.ch
The Visit USA Committee http://www.vusa.ch
Schweizer Touristik (Trade magazine for the Swiss travel and tourism industry)_
http://www.schweizertouristik.ch

For additional analytical, business and investment opportunities information,
please contact Global Investment & Business Center, USA
at (703) 370-8082. Fax: (703) 370-8083. E-mail: ibpusa3@gmail.com
Global Business and Investment Info Databank - www.ibpus.com

Travel Inside (Swiss trade magazine for tourism) http://www.travelinside.ch

For additional analytical, business and investment opportunities information,
please contact Global Investment & Business Center, USA
at (703) 370-8082. Fax: (703) 370-8083. E-mail: ibpusa3@gmail.com
Global Business and Investment Info Databank - www.ibpus.com

AGRICULTURAL SECTORS

CONSUMER ORIENTED PRODUCTS

Given Swiss generally high income and refined consumer tastes and preferences, it is not surprising that consumer-oriented products are the leading category of U.S. exports. In addition, given Swiss support programs for home-grown products and the relative distance of the United States compared to other suppliers, specialty U.S. products or those without local or nearby competition are the most successful. Notable agricultural products meeting these criteria include wine, essential oils, nuts, asparagus, fresh grapefruit, processed fruit & vegetables, certain seafood and high-quality beef. Total Swiss imports of consumer oriented food products from the United States in 2011 were valued over USD 145 million, a 15 percent increase from 2010.

NUTS:

Tree nuts, mainly almonds and walnuts, are a top Swiss agricultural import from the United States. The U.S. is the top supplier of shelled almonds and walnuts to the Swiss market. Swiss imports of all types of nuts are consistently strong, with the United States supplying a fifth of the USD 177 million worth of total imports of tree nuts for 2011.

WINE:

U.S. wines continue to show a strong shelf presence in Swiss retail outlets against tough world and local competition and there is good demand for higher quality wines in the restaurant and hotel sector. Distribution of U.S. wines is relatively well established throughout Switzerland. Swiss imports of U.S. wines were valued at approximately USD 35 million in 2011.

ESSENTIAL OILS:

Swiss imports of U.S. essential oils, based on citrus, peppermint and other raw materials and valued at over USD 27 million, were among the top U.S. agricultural products imported into Switzerland in 2011. The United States, with 20 percent of total market share, is the third largest supplier of these products to the Swiss market after France and Germany.

FRESH ASPARAGUS:

Despite challenges from France, Spain, Peru, and Germany, U.S. fresh asparagus exports to Switzerland continue to hold the top market position because of the Swiss preference for larger-stalked, tender asparagus. Swiss imports of U.S. fresh asparagus were valued at USD 12 million in 2011. A tariff-rate quota may be applied to imports between May 1 and June 15 each year, but otherwise imports come in at zero duty.

BEEF:

Switzerland continues to be an attractive market for small amounts of U.S. high quality beef, which enters under a special tariff quota of 1,200 metric tons. The demand for high quality beef is especially strong in the HRI sector, particularly to supply upper end resorts during the winter sports season. Swiss Beef imports from the United States totaled approximately 560 tons in 2011 and valued at USD 18 million, a 35 percent increase from 2010.

For additional analytical, business and investment opportunities information, please contact Global Investment & Business Center, USA at (703) 370-8082. Fax: (703) 370-8083. E-mail: ibpusa3@gmail.com Global Business and Investment Info Databank - www.ibpus.com

SEAFOOD:

Switzerland represents a healthy market for a range of U.S. fish and seafood products, with imports attaining over USD 16 million in value in 2011. The main products imported from the United States are frozen salmon, lobsters and scallops. The U.S. is the top supplier of frozen salmon to the Swiss market.

OPPORTUNITIES:

Vitafoods International 2014 Trade Show, 5/6/2014 to 5/8/2014, Europe's leading nutraceutical and dietary supplement exhibition, Palexpo Center, Geneva, Switzerland

Website: http://www.vitafoods.eu.com/

TRADE REGULATIONS, CUSTOMS AND STANDARDS

IMPORT TARIFFS

Swiss duties are generally "specific" rather than "ad valorem". Duty varies according to the item imported, and the Swiss customs tariff uses the Harmonized System (HS) for the classification of goods. Customs duties are levied per 100 kilograms of gross weight, unless some other method of calculation is specified in the tariff (e.g. per unit, per meter, per liter). The gross dutiable weight includes the actual weight of the goods and their packaging, including the weight of any fixing material and supports on which the goods are placed. More information can be found on the homepage of the Swiss Customs Office .

Although Switzerland has one of the highest applied average MFN tariff rates for agricultural products (almost 30%), its tariff rates for non-agricultural or manufactured exports are quite low, in fact one of the lowest (at roughly 2% or half the average U.S. rates). Hence, with some exceptions, import tariffs for U.S. exporters of manufactured goods to Switzerland tend to be negligible.

VALUE ADDED TAX

Imported goods and services are also subject to a Swiss value added tax (VAT). The standard VAT rate is 8.0%, although there is a reduced rate of 2.4% for certain goods and services, including the following: foodstuffs; agricultural products (meats, cereals, plants, seed and flowers); medicine and drugs; newspapers; magazines; books and other printed materials; and radio and TV services. Domestically produced goods are subject to the same VAT rates.

The VAT is levied at the border and is prepaid by the customs broker/freight forwarder, who then invoices it to the importer or end-user. The VAT is assessed based upon the value of the imported commodities, including customs duties, insurance and transportation costs (cif) and any other taxes. Customs clearance and related activities are typically handled by international freight forwarding companies on behalf of Swiss

customs. The average handling fee per shipment, exclusive of duty rates transportation costs, etc.) ranges between USD 150 and USD 250.

A U.S. exporter selling services for more than SFr. 75,000 into Switzerland is liable to pay VAT of 8.0% and should register with the Swiss Federal Tax Administration:

For additional analytical, business and investment opportunities information,
please contact Global Investment & Business Center, USA
at (703) 370-8082. Fax: (703) 370-8083. E-mail: ibpusa3@gmail.com
Global Business and Investment Info Databank - www.ibpus.com

Swiss Federal Tax Administration

Main Division of the Value Added Tax
Schwarztorstrasse 50
3003 Bern
Tel. +41-31 322 21 11, Fax. +41-31 325 71 38
www.estv.admin.ch

TRADE BARRIERS

Switzerland generally meets its commitments under WTO and bilateral agreements. However, due to significant tariff and quota barriers for many agricultural products, combined with a restrictive approval process for biotech products, labeling for meat produced with hormones and antibiotics and general consumer rejection of biotech products, US market opportunities in Switzerland are limited for these products.

Switzerland has a strict regulatory regime for agricultural biotechnology products. In order for biotech food or animal feed products to be imported and sold on the Swiss market, they must undergo a lengthy approval process. In addition, labeling is required for products containing biotech ingredients or derived from such ingredients. Recently, Switzerland further tightened labeling rules so that even so-called "second-generation" products derived from a biotech derivative (such as corn syrup produced from starch made from biotech corn) must also be labeled as biotech. The Swiss rules on approval and labeling roughly parallel those of the European Union. In addition, a referendum vote has established a moratorium on planting of biotech crops and production of biotech animals in Switzerland. This moratorium went into effect on November 27, 2005, and will be in force for five years, but does not apply to imports of biotech food or feed.

A continuing obstacle to certain U.S. exporters, particularly those of high value products, is the food retailing system. Two retail giants Migros and Coop, accounting for nearly 70% of grocery sales, dominate the food retail market. U.S. exporters are disadvantaged by this system because the two food chains emphasize their own store brand products and favor products from their own processing plants. They are devoted primarily to in-house brands, followed by international brands. Another barrier for U.S. brands represented by these major retail chains is their policy not to sell genetically modified (GMO) foods.

Over the past few years, Switzerland has taken steps to remove barriers to competition in its automotive, electricity, telecommunications, and postal sectors. The Swiss automotive market was liberalized in 2005, giving consumers greater choice in purchases of new automobiles and parts and giving independent car dealerships the right to sell, service and repair vehicles without violating warranty rules. Postage services are liberalized with the exception of the Swiss Postal Service's monopoly for shipments (letters/parcels) weighing less than 100 grams (one-tenth of a kilo).

The new Federal Electricity Supply Act that went into effective January 1, 2008, will partially open the Swiss electricity market for competition as of January 1, 2009, when customers with an annual electricity consumption of 100,000 kWh will be able to choose their suppliers. Industry analysts foresee increasingly challenging market conditions for Swiss electricity companies over the next few years; however, most are already prepared for price competition and will have time to adjust to new market conditions. As electricity is a product that is very difficult to differentiate, pricing is expected to remain key in an increasingly competitive market environment. With environmental concerns growing in importance, the longer term may well see the emergence of more eco-labels in the Swiss electricity market.

For additional analytical, business and investment opportunities information,
please contact Global Investment & Business Center, USA
at (703) 370-8082. Fax: (703) 370-8083. E-mail: ibpusa3@gmail.com
Global Business and Investment Info Databank - www.ibpus.com

An amendment to the Telecommunications Act was implemented in April 2007 that encourages competition in the fixed telephony market and provides for unbundling of the local loop, known as "opening of the last mile". As a result, telecommunications service providers have the right to access Swisscom's infrastructure and services in relation to the following: fully unbundled access to the local loop, fast bit stream (data stream) access, billing for the connection to the fixed network, interconnection, leased lines, and access to cables. The amendment to the Telecommunications Act follows the main principles of EC law with one exception—the Swiss regulatory authority (Comcom) does not impose specific obligations on service providers unless one party to an agreement requests intervention.

Alternative service providers have started to take advantage of the market liberalization. In fall 2007, Sunrise Communications installed its first shared local exchange station with Swisscom. Sunrise plans to build a nationwide fixed network; it installed equipment in 120 local exchanges in 2008 and plans to roll out its network to 80% of Swiss households by 2010.

In January 2008, Swisscom challenged Comcom's ruling of November 2007 that upheld Bit stream access for alternative suppliers. Ultimately, Swisscom was ordered to offer broadband internet access at cost oriented prices over a limited period (4 years as opposed to the 6 years that were originally proposed). This is because Swisscom is not willing to pay R&D alone endlessly, and it agrees to provide its infrastructure, for only a limited period, to enable other providers to install their own channels.

IMPORT REQUIREMENTS AND DOCUMENTATION

All imported goods must be presented to the appropriate Customs office and declared for clearance. Goods imported into Switzerland must be declared within the following time limits from arrival in the country by various means of transportation: road, 24 hours; river, 48 hours; rail, 7 days; and air, 7 days. The importer may examine goods before submitting them for clearance. For Swiss Customs purposes, an ordinary commercial invoice in duplicate or triplicate is considered sufficient documentation. The invoice should contain the following details: description of the products and packaging, gross and net weight of each package, quantity (in metric terms), country of origin, and CIF value to the Swiss border. As Swiss duties are specific, indication of value is required only for statistical purposes. No consular or other stamp is required.

For practical purposes, almost all commercial shipments are handled by forwarding companies, which, in most cases, also are legally empowered to act as Customs agents. They handle the Customs clearance, including the VAT and any applicable duties. The

Customs agent pays the VAT, duties and other fees on behalf of the importer and then invoices the total cost as well as a service fee to the importer. Shipments sent by courier are handled in the same manner.

Swiss importers are able to counsel suppliers with information on Swiss requirements to facilitate documentation on the Swiss side. A certificate of origin is not normally required unless preferential duty rates are requested; however, one may be required for health reasons (meats and plants) or for reasons of quality control as with appellation wine.

Special health certificates, stamped by the competent authorities of the country of origin, are required for animals and animal products (including fish and bees). Official plant health certificates of the country of origin must accompany shipments of some vegetables, fresh fruits, and wild plants. Switzerland is gradually aligning its import requirements for agricultural products with those of the European Union.

For additional analytical, business and investment opportunities information,
please contact Global Investment & Business Center, USA
at (703) 370-8082. Fax: (703) 370-8083. E-mail: ibpusa3@gmail.com
Global Business and Investment Info Databank - www.ibpus.com

As of January 1, 2009 Switzerland has implemented a common veterinary space with the European Union (EU). After undergoing inspection at an EU border inspection post (BIP) or the airports in Zurich or Geneva, animals and meat products may circulate freely within the EU and Switzerland. As the Swiss airports are not equipped to handle large animals, live horses and other hoofed animals must enter the common veterinary space through an EU BIP. Animals and meat products which have not undergone prior inspection at an EU BIP may only be imported into Switzerland through the airport in Zurich or Geneva. Hormone-treated beef may only be imported through Zurich and Geneva airports and must not be re-exported.

For live animals or animal products shipped into Switzerland by land or river, the complete border veterinary inspection takes place at the first point of entry into the EU. The importer must check with the relevant EU BIP to find out the requirements regarding the time limits for declaration of lots and required documents. The import certificates are the same as those required for direct importation into Switzerland. The importation of live hoofed animals, poultry, waterfowls and rates must continue to be declared in advance to the competent cantonal veterinary service 6 days before arrival.

For more information, please consult the websites below.

Federal Office for Agriculture , www.bwl.admin.ch
Swiss Federal Veterinary Office , www.bvet.admin.ch

Import licenses are required only for a limited number of products. These generally fall into the two categories of measures to protect local agriculture production and measures of state control. To protect the agriculture sector and to maintain a degree of independence from external supplies, Switzerland imposes quantitative restrictions on agricultural imports. Products under these restrictions include cattle, meat, milk and dairy products, indigenous fresh fruit and vegetables, seasonal cut flowers, cereals and forage products, wine and grape juice.

More information is available through the Federal Office of Agriculture.

Federal Office for Agriculture , www.bag.admin.ch

Products subject to a quota require import licenses, which are granted only to importers based in Switzerland. Most quotas vary from year to year according to the size of harvests, volume of stocks and market requirements. Import licenses are also required

for certain products not subject to quotas, but which are covered by special regulations concerned with public health, plant health, quarantine (plants), veterinary regulations; regulations concerning the protection of endangered species, safety measures, price control (for certain textile products); and measures for the protection of the Swiss economy and public morality.

More detailed information on import requirements is available from the Swiss Customs Office at www.ezv.admin.ch .

SWISS EXPORT CONTROLS

The Government of Switzerland regulates the export, import, and transit of goods usable for civilian and military purposes and is an active member of all major export control regimes, including the Wassenaar Arrangement (WA), the Missile Technology Control Regime (MTCR), the Nuclear Supplier Group (NSG), the Australia Group (AG) and the Chemical Weapons Convention (CWC).

For additional analytical, business and investment opportunities information,
please contact Global Investment & Business Center, USA
at (703) 370-8082. Fax: (703) 370-8083. E-mail: ibpusa3@gmail.com
Global Business and Investment Info Databank - www.ibpus.com

The Office of Export Controls and Sanctions within the State Secretariat for Economic Affairs (SECO) http://www.seco.admin.ch/index.html?lang=en is responsible for implementation of Swiss commitments pursuant to the multilateral export control regimes. SECO can deny an export license if there is reason to assume that goods proposed for export would be used for the development, production, or use of biological or chemical weapons; serve for the development, production, or use of nuclear weapons or of an unmanned missile for the delivery of nuclear, biological or chemical weapons or the proliferation of such weapons; or contribute to the conventional armaments of a state, which, by its behavior, endangers regional or global security.

As a UN member, Switzerland follows UN provisions for export licensing controls. In certain cases, where there is a high likelihood of diversion of goods to WMD or missile uses, the Government of Switzerland applies the "catch-all" provisions of its export control law to deny the export of goods not specifically included on any export control list.

The Government of Switzerland cooperates with the U.S. and other governments to avoid the diversion of Swiss exports for use in weapons of mass destruction (WMD) or missile uses. An export control dialogue is part of the U.S.-Swiss Joint Economic Commission (JEC). These meetings have served to move forward discussions on ways to strengthen the Wassenaar Agreement and other WMD control systems.

TEMPORARY ENTRY

Imported goods that are destined for re-export may be cleared on the basis of a "Begleitschein" or "free-pass" certificate. The importer must apply for the certificate from the Customs Administration and provide surety for the Customs charges applicable to the imported goods. The certificate must be presented to Customs within the stipulated time with the goods in unchanged condition for re-export.

Goods transiting Switzerland must be declared for clearance at the point-of-entry Customs office and be covered by a national or international transit document (bond

note, TIR carnet, T1/T2 dispatch declaration, or international waybill). These goods must be re-exported intact within the designated time limit. No transit duties or fees are levied.

A transit permit is required only for narcotic drugs, armaments, nuclear fuels, and nuclear fuel residues. In the case of direct transit by rail, the railway authorities guarantee duties and taxes. The issuing authority is the guarantor of road transit covered by a TIR carnet. A surety or financial deposit is required for transit covered by a bond note or transit through the EU covered by a T1/T2 dispatch declaration.

Goods temporarily imported or exported for processing or repair may be eligible for a reduction in duty or duty-free treatment granted on the basis of the economic interests of Swiss industry. Authorization is granted only to residents who do the processing or repair themselves or who commission a third party. Authorization is for particular goods that are to undergo specified processing. Special conditions may be imposed for Customs handling and supervision.

Goods for display at public exhibitions are eligible for free passage (Freipass) through Swiss customs. Certification from the trade fair authorities that the goods are entering Switzerland for the exhibition is usually required. Exhibition goods must be re-exported within a month of the end of the exhibition. If the goods are sold to a Swiss resident off the exhibition floor, the buyer incurs a liability for the customs charges. Almost all fairgrounds have a Customs office on site.

For additional analytical, business and investment opportunities information, please contact Global Investment & Business Center, USA at (703) 370-8082. Fax: (703) 370-8083. E-mail: ibpusa3@gmail.com Global Business and Investment Info Databank - www.ibpus.com

LABELING AND MARKING REQUIREMENTS

Swiss labeling requirements apply mostly to food products. False descriptions are strictly prohibited. As a rule, the label or packaging for consumer goods must indicate the specific name of the product (in French, German or Italian), metric measure, sales price, unit price, weight of each component in the case of mixed products, and ingredients and additives in decreasing order of weight. Consumer goods must be marked with the country of manufacture prior to sale. Packaged goods must also indicate the quality of purity, the ingredients and the net weight of measure of the contents. All particulars of weight and measurements must comply with the regulations of the Federal Measurement Office (Eidgenossisches Amt für Messwesen).

The Foodstuffs Ordinance specifies additional information that must be provided in the case of certain products, including the name of the manufacturer or distributor, country of origin of the product, and 'use by' date. Many distributors provide additional information on their labels, such as the 'EAN code' for computerized data retrieval, and/or the nutritional or energy value of the product.

Switzerland's food law generally conforms with European Union food law. According to Swiss regulators, all standards are equal to or less strict than EU standards with the exception of standards for aflatoxins, microtoxins, and certain pesticides. Standards address acceptable levels of pesticides in water for drinking and food processing. The regulations cover all food products as well as tobacco and packaging and labeling standards.

For safety, health, environmental and consumer protection, as well as for compliance with international and national standards, certain products are subject to further regulations.

Medicines, cosmetics, cleaning agents, electrical appliances, measuring and weighing devices, heating systems, pressure vessels and motorcycles that are imported into and marketed in Switzerland are subject to additional regulations concerning safety, labeling, and packaging.

PROHIBITED AND RESTRICTED IMPORTS

The Swiss method of controlling unwanted imports is through the imposition of restrictions, quotas and other rules and regulations as noted previously in this chapter.

CUSTOMS REGULATIONS AND CONTACT INFORMATION

Imported goods from the United States are subject to regular Swiss Customs duties at the time of importation. See also the sub-heading Import Tariffs.

Federal Customs Administration
Monbijoustrasse 40
3003 Bern
Tel. +41-31 322 65 11, Fax. +41-31 322 78 72
www.ezv.admin.ch

For additional analytical, business and investment opportunities information,
please contact Global Investment & Business Center, USA
at (703) 370-8082. Fax: (703) 370-8083. E-mail: ibpusa3@gmail.com
Global Business and Investment Info Databank - www.ibpus.com

EXPORT-IMPORT AND TRADE STANDARDS

Over 50% of Switzerland's GDP is dependent on foreign trade, and the country plays an active international role in helping to reduce or eliminate relevant hurdles, particularly non-tariff barriers (NTB), with the exception of agricultural products. As a member of CEN (European agency for standards), Switzerland adopts any new European standards in reconciliation with any conflicting national standards. Switzerland applies "Harmonized European Standards" pertaining to health, safety and environmental criteria. All products covered by those standards must carry the CE label as a sign of compliance in all EU countries. However, Switzerland does not require the CE label on products for domestic (Swiss) use. Swiss manufacturers, if qualified, may use CE labels on their products.

All standards organizations in Switzerland are under the umbrella of SNV, the Schweizerische Normen Vereinigung or Swiss Standards Association. SNV provides local manufacturers with guidance on worldwide standards, serves as the link to relevant European (CEN) and international organizations (ISO), and is responsible for introducing the Swiss position at conferences and meetings.

STANDARDS ORGANIZATIONS

Major organizations/agencies with programs to propose and/or implement standards:
1. SNV – Schweizerische Normen Vereinigung
Bürglistrasse 29, CH-8400 Winterthur, Switzerland
Phone +41 52 224 5454; Fax +41 52 224 5474; www.snv.ch

Association serving as the national umbrella for all Swiss organizations interested in standards. Provides guidance on new standards. Publishes new standards in its "SNV Bulletin" (instead of a "National Gazette")

2. Electrosuisse, SEV Verband für Elektro- Energie- und Informationstechnik
Luppmenstrasse 1, CH-8320 Fehraltdorf, Switzerland
Phone +41 1 956 1111; Fax +41 1 956 1122; www.electrosuisse.ch
Sector covered: electrical safety standards, electromagnetic emissions
3. SIA, Schweiz. Ingenieur- & Architektenverein
Selnaustrasse 16, CH-8001 Zürich, Switzerland
Phone +41 1 283 1515; Fax +41 1 20-1 6335; www.sia.ch

Sector covered: building standards (above and underground construction, cultural aspects, environmental criteria, insulation, air-cond/heating/safety)

4. VSS, Schweiz. Verband der Strassen- und Verkehrsfachleute
Sihlquai 255, CH-8005 Zürich, Switzerland
Phone +41 1 269 4020; Fax +41 1 252 3130; www.vss.ch
Sector covered: traffic safety, planning of public and private sector transportation networks, energy efficiency, signaling, safety in tunnels, financing

5. SVGW, Schweiz. Verein des Gas- und Wasserfaches
Grütlistrasse 44, CH-8002 Zürich, Switzerland
Phone: +41 1 288 3333; Fax +41 1 202 1633; www.svgw.ch
Sector covered: quality standards of processes and equipment for drinking water and natural gas

6. VSA, Verband Schweiz. Abwasser- und Gewässerschutzfachleute

Europastrasse 3, P.O. Box, CH-8152 Glattbrugg, Switzerland
Phone +41 43 343 7070; Fax +41 1 241 61 29; www.vsa.ch
Sector covered: sewage treatment and water pollution control

7. BAFU, Bundesamt für Umwelt
Papiermühlestrasse 172, CH-3003 Bern-Ittigen, Switzerland
Phone: +41 31 322 9311; Fax +41 31 322 9981; www.bafu.admin.ch

8. ASUT, Swiss Telecommunication Association
Klösterlistutz 8, CH-3013 Bern, Switzerland
Phone +41 31 560 66 66; +41 31 560 66 67; www.asut.ch
Sector covered: Communications equipment

9. BAKOM, Swiss Federal Office for Communications
Zukunftstrasse 44, P.O. Box 332, CH-2501 Biel, Switzerland
Phone +41 32 327 5511; Fax +41 32 5555
Sector covered: telecommunications incl. radio and TV; www.bakom.admin.ch

10. Swissmem, ASM Verband Schweiz. Arbeitgeber der Maschinenindustrie
Kirchenweg 4, P.O. Box, CH-8032 Zürich, Switzerland
Phone +41 44 384 4111; Fax +41 44 384 4242; www.swissmem.ch
Sector covered: industrial machinery such as machine tools, textile machines, packaging
machine, power generating and distribution equipment etc.

11. Interpharma, Verband forschender Pharmafirmen in der Schweiz
Petersgraben 35, P.O. Box CH-4003 Basel, Switzerland
Phone +41 61 264 3400; Fax: +41 61 264 3435; www.interpharma.ch
Secor covered: manufacturers of pharmaceuticals with own research departments

12. SWISSMEDIC, Swiss Agency for Therapeutic Products
Hallerstrasse 7, CH-3000 Bern 9, Switzerland
Phone +41 31 322 0211; Fax +41 31 322 0212; www.swissmedic.ch
Sector covered: Swiss government agency comparable to the U.S. FDA

13. SUVA, Schweiz. Unfallversicherungsanstalt
Fluhmattstrasse 1, CH-6002 Luzern, Switzerland
Phone +41 41 419 5111; Fax +41 41 419 5828; www.suva.ch
Sector covered: occupational safety, agency comparable to U.S. OSHA

14. BAG – Swiss Public Health Agency (FOPH)
Schwarztorstrasse 96, CH-3003 Bern, Switzerland
Phone: +41 31 322 2111; Fax +41 31 323 3772; www.bag.admin.ch
Sector covered: public health

CONFORMITY ASSESSMENT

Conformity assessment is controlled by a multitude of laboratories and companies that must be accredited by a Swiss Government Agency known as "SAS" (Schweizerische Akkreditierungsstelle). This agency is comparable to the U.S. NIST and includes its own extensive testing laboratories. It is the sole authority that provides relevant laboratories and companies with the accreditation to certify products in specific areas according to

For additional analytical, business and investment opportunities information,
please contact Global Investment & Business Center, USA
at (703) 370-8082. Fax: (703) 370-8083. E-mail: ibpusa3@gmail.com
Global Business and Investment Info Databank - www.ibpus.com

ISO/EC 17000 and series EN 45000. The accreditation procedure is a complex process that includes the physical inspection of the laboratories and equipment, the staffing, and a determination of the organization's level of independence and possible conflicts of interest.

Swiss Federal Office for Metrology and Accreditation Lindenweg 50, CH-3003 Bern-Wabern, Switzerland Phone: +41 31 323 3511; Fax +41 31 323 3510; www.sas.ch

PRODUCT CERTIFICATION

Product certification is covered by laboratories and companies licensed or accredited by SAS. All relevant laboratories and companies are listed by sector on the SAS website www.sas.ch (in English).

Underwriter Laboratories (UL) maintains its own Swiss office in Schwerzenbach as follows:

UL International (Schweiz) AG (Mr. Martin Fies, GM) Ringstrasse 1, CH-8604 Schwerzenbach, Switzerland Phone: +41 43 355 4020; Fax +41 43 355 4039; http://www.ul-europe.com

ACCREDITATION

The accreditation of relevant laboratories is controlled exclusively by the Swiss Government Agency SAS (see above). www.sas.ch

PUBLICATION OF TECHNICAL REGULATIONS

SNV (see above) publishes all new norms in its "SNV Bulletin" in a dedicated section called "SWITEC". Nearly all new standards published in the SNV Bulletin are standards that have been processed and approved first by CEN.

LABELING AND MARKING

Generally, labeling and marking requirements follow EU regulations (CE labeling). However, Switzerland does not require the CE label on products intended solely for domestic (Swiss) use. http://www.newapproach.org/

TRADE AGREEMENTS

Switzerland, Liechtenstein, Iceland, and Norway are members of the European Free Trade Association (EFTA). EFTA members maintain their own external tariffs, although tariff duties on trade in industrial products among member countries have been eliminated. Although not a member of the European Union (EU), Switzerland has bilateral agreements with the EU that guarantee many of the same economic

advantages and lowered barriers to trade that EU members enjoy. Preferential or duty-free rates apply to goods imported from the EU-EFTA free trade area when an importer makes a request on the import declaration and produces a certificate of origin. The Swiss also accord tariff preferences under the GSP to developing countries.

The United States and Switzerland have strong bilateral ties. Switzerland is a key supporter of the United States on a number of political and economic issues, particularly matters within the World Trade Organization. Geneva is host to the WTO, several UN agencies, and other international bodies. In 2006, the United States and Switzerland formed the "Trade and Investment Cooperation Forum" in order to address and achieve progress in trade topics of mutual interest.

WEB RESOURCES

Swiss Customs Tariff http://xtares.admin.ch/
Swiss Federal Customs Administration http://www.ezv.admin.ch/
State Secretariat for Economic Affairs http://www.seco.admin.ch
Swiss Federal Office for Metrology http://www.metas.ch/
Underwriters Laboratories Europe http://ul-certification.com/
Schweizerische Normenvereinigung (SNV) http://www.snv.ch/
European Committee for Standardization (CEN) http://www.cen.eu/
International Organization for Standardization (ISO) www.iso.org
European Committee for Electrotechnical Standardization (CENELEC) http://www.cenelec.eu/

TRADE AND PROJECT FINANCING

METHODS OF PAYMENT

Export financing is primarily conducted through commercial sources. Payment terms are arranged with the bank or financing institution.

BANKING SYSTEM

Switzerland is one of the world's foremost banking and financial centers with over 290 bank headquarters. The banking network is highly developed, and Swiss banks are among the world's leaders in specialized fields such as private banking and asset management. The total assets of the Swiss banking system at the end of 2012 amounted to USD 6.8 trillion (Swiss francs 6.4 trillion) including assets managed by Swiss banks abroad. The physical presence of U.S. and other foreign entities in Switzerland is vital to successful financial service trade and continues to play an important role in the competitiveness of financial services. Banking in Switzerland is extremely diverse. Although it is based on the principle of universal banking, several bank groups are now fully or partially specialized.

Established in 1907, the Swiss National Bank (SNB) has executive offices in Bern and Zurich and branch offices in six other cities. More than one-half of its share capital is held by the cantons, the cantonal banks and other public bodies; Swiss citizens own the remaining shares. Although the Federal Government is not a shareholder, it has statutory power to appoint the majority of the Bank Council members as well as the three members of the Governing Board and their deputies. As the SNB fulfills a public task, it is administered with the cooperation and under supervision of the Confederation.

The SNB conducts the country's monetary policy as an independent central bank. Its primary goal is to ensure price stability, while taking due account of economic developments. It determines and implements monetary and credit policy, has the exclusive right to issue or withdraw bank notes and coins, and serves as a clearing-house for inter-bank transfers. Furthermore, it has an arrangement with the Principality of Liechtenstein to permit the use of the Swiss Franc as the country's currency, and the SNB clears Liechtenstein's transactions.

The SNB Bank Council oversees and controls the conduct of business by the SNB. It consists of 11 members. The Federal Council (Switzerland's executive body of 7 ministers, including the President of the Confederation) appoints six members, including the SNB president and vice president. The Shareholders appoint the remaining five members. The SNB's managing and executive body is the Governing Board, which is responsible for the monetary policy, asset investment strategy and international monetary cooperation. The Enlarged Governing Board consists of the three members of the Governing Board and their deputies. It is responsible for strategic and operational management. Upon the recommendation of the Bank Council, the Federal Council appoints the members of the Governing Board and their deputies.

The object of the new Financial Market Supervisory Authority (FINMA), which entered into full force on January 1, 2009, is to group together under one authority the government supervision of banks, insurance companies, stock exchanges and securities dealers as well as other financial intermediaries in Switzerland. FINMA is a merger of the Federal Office of Private Insurance (FOPI), the Swiss Federal Banking Commission (SFBC) and the Anti-Money Laundering Control Authority. The aim of FINMA is to protect creditors, investors, insured persons and to ensure the general functioning of the financial markets in accordance with financial market legislation. It thus helps reinforce Switzerland's image and competitiveness as a financial center.

Financial Services, such as portfolio management and financial counseling, can be freely offered under the law of contracts. However, the provisions of criminal law on money laundering and the Federal Money-laundering Act are binding for all providers of financial services.

The "Federal Law on Combating Money Laundering in the Financial Sector" took effect in 1998 and strengthened due diligence obligations on the part of banks and other financial intermediaries. Officials believe this legislation puts Switzerland among the leading countries in terms of establishing a legal framework with which to effectively combat money laundering.

The following is information on the key players of the Swiss banking sector:

UBS AG and Credit Suisse: The two largest banks, UBS AG and the Credit Suisse Group, together account for over 50% of the balance sheet total of all banks in Switzerland. They are universal banks engaged in all types of banking business.

Cantonal banks: Cantonal banks are defined as banks with a statutory basis under cantonal law, with the canton holding a minimum of one-third of the banks' capital and voting rights. With the revised Banking Law of October 1, 1999, the state guarantee is no longer a constitutive characteristic of cantonal banks. The 24 cantonal banks are engaged in all banking businesses with an emphasis on lending and deposits.

The Raiffeisen Group: The Raiffeisen Group consists of affiliated independent banks with strong local roots and organized along cooperative lines. The Raiffeisen banks have the highest number of branches in Switzerland and are affiliated with the Swiss Union of Raiffeisen Banks. In recent years, Raiffeisen has positioned and established itself as the third largest bank group in Switzerland. Raiffeisen meanwhile counts 3 million Swiss citizens among its customers. Of these, some 1.4 million are members of the cooperative and hence co-owners of their Raiffeisen bank.

Private Banks: The 10 private banks include individually owned firms, collectives, and limited partnerships. Private bankers are subject to unlimited subsidiary liability with their personal assets. Their field of activity is asset management, chiefly for private clients.

Foreign banks: The approximately 140 foreign banks in Switzerland have a majority shareholder domiciled abroad. All foreign banks in Switzerland are subject to the same laws and supervision as banks whose majority shareholder is Swiss.

For additional analytical, business and investment opportunities information, please contact Global Investment & Business Center, USA at (703) 370-8082. Fax: (703) 370-8083. E-mail: ibpusa3@gmail.com
Global Business and Investment Info Databank - www.ibpus.com

Commercial & Investment banks: As a rule, the commercial banks are universal banks for which mortgage investments play a significant role, in addition to commercial loans.

Consumer credit institutes: Consumer credit institutes specialize in small loans to private individuals and industry.

Post Finance: The activities of Post Finance are run by the governmental postal service and include payments, investments, savings, mortgages, loans, provident and retirement planning. It has no banking license and must outsource some of its services such as mortgages, pensions, mutual funds, etc. More than 2 million private customers use postal accounts and the PostFinance Card. In 2013 customer deposits amounted to USD 119 billion (Swiss francs 112 billion).

SIX Interbank Clearing, a subsidiary of SIX Group, operates the SIC and euroSIC interbank payment systems. These systems allow participating financial institutions to securely make cashless payments in Swiss Francs and Euro in real time between themselves. The SIC system processes interbank payments in francs on behalf of and under the supervision of the Swiss National Bank. In association with SECB Swiss Euro Clearing Bank, SIX Interbank Clearing provides the processing of Euro transactions through the euroSIC system on behalf of the Swiss financial center. Both interbank systems provide financial institutions within Switzerland and beyond its borders with efficient access to national and international payment traffic.

SIX Group, which emerged from the merger of the SWX Group, SIS Group and Telekurs Group at the beginning of 1988, is owned by its users (150 banks of various sizes and orientation). As one of Europe's leading securities exchange and financial market infrastructure operators, SIX Group offers first-rate services that address all aspects of Swiss and cross boarder securities trading as well as the admission of securities to trading. The company's other business fields focus on rendering cost effective and efficient services in the areas of clearing, settlement, securities safekeeping and administration, as well as supplying international financial information for investment advisors, portfolio managers, financial analysts and administrators of securities transactions. In addition, its services in the area of payment transactions cover the acceptance and processing of payments made with credit, debit and customer cards, as well as the handling of interbank transfers and e-invoices.

Eurex: Eurex is one of the world's leading derivates exchanges and is jointly operated by the German Futures and Options Exchange, Deutsche Börse AG, and SIX Swiss Exchange. Eurex offers a broad range of international benchmark products and operates the most liquid fixed income markets, featuring open and low-cost electronic access. With market participants connected from 700 locations worldwide, trading volume at Eurex exceeds 1.5 billion contracts annually.

FOREIGN-EXCHANGE CONTROLS

The Swiss franc is freely convertible. With the exception of certain regulations applicable to banks and finance companies, there are no exchange controls. The SNB has

authority to introduce measures concerning minimum reserve requirements, foreign currency position, foreign source funds and a calendar for public issues of bonds and shares. However, these measures are intended for use only to counter exceptional circumstances, such as massive speculation resulting in overvaluation of the Swiss currency leading to significant problems for the Swiss export industry. Bank accounts may be maintained in local or foreign currencies either within or outside Switzerland without restriction. There is no distinction between resident and nonresident accounts.

Repatriation of capital, loans, dividends, interest, royalties, service fees and branch office profits can be transacted without limitation through any bank. Export proceeds may be disposed of freely. Leading and lagging of import and export payments is allowed; there are no limitations and no requirement for prior authorization. Netting of trade-related payments and financial transactions is also allowed without prior authorization.

U.S. BANKS AND LOCAL CORRESPONDENT BANKS

Bank Morgan Stanley, Ltd.
Bahnhofstrasse 92
CH-8021 Zurich, Switzerland
Tel: (41-44) 220 91 11, Fax: (41-44) 220 98 00
http://www.morganstanley.com

Citibank (Switzerland) AG
Bleicherweg 10
CH-8021 Zurich, Switzerland
Tel: (41-58) 750 70 00, Fax: (41-58) 750 72 92
http://www.citigroup.com

GE Money Bank AG
Bändliweg 20
CH-8048 Zurich, Switzerland
Tel: (41-44) 439 81 11, Fax: (41-44) 439 84 04
http://www.gemoneybank.ch

Goldman Sachs Bank AG
Münsterhof 4
CH-8001 Zurich, Switzerland
Tel: (41-44) 224 10 00, Fax: (41-44) 224 10 50
http://www.goldman-sachs.ch

J.P. Morgan (Suisse) SA
Rue de Confederation 8
CH-1211 Geneva 11, Switzerland
Tel: (41-22) 744 19 00, Fax: (41-22) 744 19 10
http://www.jpmorgan.com

Merrill Lynch Bank (Suisse) SA
Rte. de Florrissant 13
CH-1211 Geneva 3, Switzerland
Tel: (41-22) 703 17 17, Fax: (41-22) 703 17 27
http://www.mlbs.ch

Standard Chartered Bank (Switzerland) SA.
Rue du Rhone 50
CH-1211 Geneva 3, Switzerland
Tel: (41-22) 319 08 08, Fax: (41-22) 311 22 88
http://www.standardchartered.com

PROJECT FINANCING

For additional analytical, business and investment opportunities information, please contact Global Investment & Business Center, USA at (703) 370-8082. Fax: (703) 370-8083. E-mail: ibpusa3@gmail.com
Global Business and Investment Info Databank - www.ibpus.com

Generally speaking, there is no special financing available for projects in Switzerland. The federal government may grant long-term loans at preferential interest rates for a limited category of projects in designated regions, primarily in remote, mountainous areas, that are threatened with economic decline. Cantonal and communal governments offer a wider variety of incentives, including financing, for investment projects in their respective areas. Most cantons maintain economic development agencies, some even with offices or representatives abroad, for the purpose of dealing with projects and investments.

WEB RESOURCES

Swiss National Bank (SNB) http://www.snb.ch
Swiss Financial Market Supervisory Authority (FINMASA) http://www.finma.ch
Swiss Bankers Association http://www.swissbanking.org
Association of Foreign Banks in Switzerland http://www.foreignbanks.ch
SIX Interbank Clearing http://www.six.ch
SIX Group http://www.six-group.com

IMPORTANT BUSINESS CONTACTS

U.S. Embassy Bern:

Ambassador: Ms. Suzan LeVine
Charge Deputy Chief of Mission: Mr. Jeffrey Cellars
Economic/Commercial Officer: Mr. Jeremy Beer
Political/Economic Section Counselor Mr. Thomas Kelsey
Political Officer: Ms. Rachael Doherty
Consular Services: Mr. Timothy Buckley
Consular – American Citizen Services: Ms. Burret Travis
Consular Services – Visa Mr. Jonathan Koehler
Public Affairs Officer: Mr. Stephanie Morimura
International Mail Address: U.S. Pouch Address:
Sulgeneckstrasse 19 American Embassy Bern
P.O. Box U.S. Department of State
CH-3001 Bern, Switzerland 5110 Bern Place
Tel. +41 31 357 70 11 Washington, DC 20521-5110
Fax +41 31 357 73 36

Chambers of Commerce:
Swiss-American Chamber of Commerce
http://www.amcham.ch/

Chambers of Commerce and Industry of Switzerland http://www.cci.ch/en/map.htm

Swiss Trade or Industry Associations:

The following lists trade associations most relevant to U.S. companies pursuing business in Switzerland. For a complete listing of associations, please consult the Publicus 2011 "Schweizer Jahrbuch des öffentlichen Lebens", published by Schwabe & Co. AG Verlag, P.O. Box 832, CH-4132 Muttenz 1, Switzerland; Tel. (+41-61) 467-8509; Fax (+41-61) 467-8586, www.publicus.ch

Autogewerbe-Verband der Schweiz (AGVS) (Swiss Motor Trade and Repair Association), www.agvs.ch

Economiesuisse (Swiss Federation of Commerce and Industry), www.economiesuisse.ch

Swissmem (Machine- Electro- and Metal Industry / MEM Industry), www.swissmem.ch

VSMWH (Machine & Tool Traders Association), www.vsmwh.ch

Electrosuisse (Association for Electrical Engineering, Power & Information Technologies)

Swiss Standards Association , www.sev.ch

Switzerland Global Enterprise (Swiss Office for Trade Promotion), www.switzerland-ge.com

VSIG Swiss Federation of Importers & Wholesalers, www.vsig.ch

Swiss Technology Network (Electronics, Automation Eqp. & Computer Manuf. & Distributor Association), www.swisst.net

ASUT (Swiss Telecommunications Users Assn.), www.asut.ch

SWICO (Swiss Assn. For Information, Communication, Organizational Technology), www.swico.ch

FASMED (Swiss Medical Device Technology Assn.), www.fasmed.ch

SIA (Society for Engineers and Architects), www.sia.ch

Swiss Textile Federation , www.tvs.ch

Swiss Society of Chemical Industries , www.sgci.ch

Swiss Banking Association , www.swissbanking.org/en/home.htm

Swiss Hotel Association , www.swisshotels.ch

Federation of the Swiss Watch Industry (FH) , www.fhs.ch

Swiss Exchange SWX , www.swx.com/index_en.html

SWISS GOVERNMENT AGENCIES:

The following list of Swiss government agencies may be of relevance to U.S. companies doing business in and with Switzerland. The "Eidgenössischer Staatskalender", published by Bundesamt fuer Bauten und Logistik, Eidg. Drucksachen- und Materialzentrale (Federal Printing Office), CH-3000 Bern, Switzerland, Tel. (+41-31) 325 50 50, Fax (+41-31) 325 50 58, www.admin.ch/edmz provides a comprehensive listing of Swiss government departments and officials. Another source of information is www.admin.ch

Federal Department of Home Affairs:

Federal Office for Statistics , www.bfs.admin.ch

Federal Office for Public Health , www.bag.admin.ch

Federal Department of Justice and Police: www.ejpd.admin.ch

Federal Office of Metrology and Accreditation , www.metas.ch

Federal Office for Intellectual Property , www.ige.ch

Federal Department of Economic Affairs:

State Secretariat for Economic Affairs (SECO) , www.seco.admin.ch

Federal Office for Professional Education and Technology http://www.sbfi.admin.ch/

Federal Department of Defense, Protection of the Population and Sport:

Defense Procurement Agency (Armasuisse) , www.armasuisse.ch

Federal Department of Finance:

Federal Customs Administration , www.zoll.admin.ch

Federal Department of Environment, Transport, Energy and Communications:

Federal Office for Civil Aviation , www.aviation.admin.ch

Federal Office for the Environment, Forestry and the Landscape , www.buwal.ch

Federal Office for Communications , www.bakom.ch

Quasi-Public Organization: SwissPost , www.swisspost.ch

SWISS MARKET RESEARCH FIRMS:

Following are some of the major Swiss companies performing market research as well as polling. The U.S. Company must solicit terms and fees. The U.S. Embassy cannot recommend one firm over another.

A.C. Nielsen , www.acnielsen.ch
IHA-GFK , www.ihagfk.ch
Trimedia Group , www.trimedia.ch
Link Institute , www.link.ch
Demoscope , www.demoscope.ch
ISOPUBLIC , www.isopublic .ch

SWISS COMMERCIAL BANKS:

Following are the head offices of the two largest commercial banks in Switzerland. Each has numerous branches throughout the country. For additional information on these and other banks, please consult the Swiss Financial Yearbook, published by Elvetica Edizioni SA, P.O. Box 134,

For additional analytical, business and investment opportunities information,
please contact Global Investment & Business Center, USA
at (703) 370-8082. Fax: (703) 370-8083. E-mail: ibpusa3@gmail.com
Global Business and Investment Info Databank - www.ibpus.com

Via Vela 6a CH-6834 Morbio-Inferiore, Switzerland; Tel: (+41-91) 683 50 56; Fax: (+41-91) 683 76 05.

UBS AG , www.ubs.com

Credit Suisse Group , www.credit-suisse.com

U.S.-Based Multipliers Relevant for Switzerland:

The Swiss-American Chamber of Commerce, in addition to its head office in Zurich (see Chamber heading above), maintains offices in six U.S. locations:

Swiss-American Chamber of Commerce US locations http://www.amcham.ch/about_us/

Swiss-American Chamber of Commerce
San Francisco Chapter
P.O. Box 26007
San Francisco, CA 94126-6007
Phone: +1 (415) 433-6679
E-Mail: sanfrancisco@amcham.ch
www: http://www.saccsf.com
Facebook:
http://www.facebook.com/pages/Swiss-American-Chamber-of-Commerce-San-Francisco/187635394616556?sk=wall

SWITZERLAND OFFSHORE PROFILE

There are two main types of companies, the company limited by shares–AG/SA–requires the minimum amount of CHF 100,000 of which 20% of the registered share capital but at least CHF 50,000 must be paid up before incorporation. The partnership limited by quota-parts – GmbH/Sarl – is an association whose capital of at least CHF 20,000 of which at least 50% must be paid before incorporation is divided into quota-parts where quotaholders state how much of a share they take in the company.

ADVANTAGES	Highly respected, confidential, good for holding companies
DISADVANTAGES	Large amount of paid up capital required. Civil code, rather than Common Law legal base
CORPORATE LEGISLATION SOURCE	Swiss Code of Obligations
COMPANY STATUS	Aktiengesellschaft-AG or Societe anonyme-SA-public stock corporation / Gesellschaft mit beschrankter Haftung-GmbH or Societe a responsabilite limitee-Sarl public limited company
USUAL MINIMUM CAPITAL	AG/SA-CHF 100,000 of which at least 20% but no less than CHF 50,000 must be paid up before incorporation. GmbH/Sarl-CHF 20,000 of which 50%

	must be paid up before incorporation
COMPANY NAME	Any name not already registered may be chosen. Names such as Switzerland, International etc are subject to certain conditions. If a proper name is used for an AG/SA the name must end in AG/SA
TIME TAKEN TO INCORPORATE	2 – 4 weeks
ARE SHELF COMPANIES AVAILABLE	Available but very rarely used
CAPITAL DUTY	1% as of CHF 250,000
MINIMUM NUMBER OF SHAREHOLDERS	AG/SA-Three. GmbH/Sarl-No shareholders as such as the company is not permitted to issue shares in the sense of securities. It has a register of its quotaholders and their part of the capital; at least two quotaholders
ARE BEARER SHARES / SHARES OF NO PAR VALUE POSSIBLE?	AG / SA - Yes / No GmbH / Sarl - No / No
DIRECTORS: MINIMUM NUMBER / CORPORATE DIRECTORS ALLOWED / LOCATION	AG/SA-One / No / At least one director must be a Swiss resident and the majority of board members must be Swiss nationals residing in Switzerland. GmbH/Sarl-One / No / At least one director must be a Swiss resident
SECRETARY: MANDATORY / CORPORATE SECRETARY ALLOWED / LOCATION	No / No / Anywhere in Switzerland
IS THERE A REQUIREMENT FOR A REGISTERED OFFICE / REGISTERED AGENT	Yes / Individual directors (AG/SA) respectively associates (GmbH/Sarl) in principle represent the company
IS THERE A REQUIREMENT BY THE AUTHORITIES PRIOR TO INCORPORATION OR PRIOR TO TAX STATUS BEING GRANTED	Confirmation of paid in capital. Declaration from the Directors that the company's capital has not been paid for by a contribution in kind
INFORMATION AVAILABLE ON PUBLIC FILE	Registered Office / Share Capital details / Directors / Auditors / Articles of Association
DOCUMENTS TO BE KEPT AT REGISTERED OFFICE	None need be kept there
CORPORATE BOOKS AND SEAL	Not in common law sense
ACCOUNTS REQUIRED / FILED	Yes / Only in connection with tax return
ANNUAL RETURN REQUIRED	Yes

WHERE ARE MEETINGS TO BE HELD	No restriction
ANNUAL FEES PAYABLE TO THE GOVERNMENT: TAX / ANNUAL RETURN FILING FEE	Federal taxes of around 10%, cantonel taxes vary with cantons and in function of company's activity (15 – 32%)
ARE THERE ANY EXCHANGE CONTROLS	No
DOUBLE TAX TREATIES	Many including Australia, Austria, Belgium, Canada, Denmark, Finland, France, Germany, Great Britain, Greece, Hungary, Ireland, Italy, Japan, Luxembourg, Netherlands, Norway, Portugal, Russia, Singapore, South Africa, Spain, Sweden and the USA

The creation of co-ordination and service centres in Switzerland offers an interesting opportunity to foreign companies and entrepreneurs whose aim is to set up cost effective and tax efficient corporate structures.

SWITZERLAND AS THE IDEAL LOCATION TO SAFEGUARD YOUR COMPANY'S FUTURE

Switzerland, being located at the heart of the European market, offers outstanding telecommunication and financial services, professional multilingual personnel, high efficiency of public administration and simplified bureaucracy, a moderate tax system, and a stable legal and social environment. In addition to the background of efficient organisation present in Switzerland, which is facilitated by the above mentioned conditions, limited fiscal costs provide an additional advantage especially in an international context. The final economic net result after taxes is indeed relevant and important for both entrepreneurs and investors alike.

Fidinam's support
Fidinam assists its client companies in a preliminary evaluation, planning and the setting up of businesses as well as the provision of co-ordination and service centres in the Canton of Ticino (and other Swiss Cantons). A complete service is offered which includes the implementation of all necessary procedural requirements for their fulfilment.

PRINCIPAL ADVANTAGES OF THE CANTON OF TICINO FOR THE LOCATION OF BUSINESS CENTRES AND OF CO-ORDINATION AND SERVICE CENTRES

Business centres
Business centres generally provide a platform for companies operating at an international level to merge in a single operational centre the following main activities:

- the sale and purchase of goods, services and general investment goods

- the co-ordination purchase of raw materials and semi-manufactured goods

- the co-ordination of sales direct to final customers or to local sales agents in international markets

- customers assistance and back-up

* factoring and other financial activities

* market research, promotional activities, organisation of agencies and sales representative networks.

Taxation

The type of activity described above, which should be mainly managed and controlled by non-residents generating no substantial income on Swiss territory, may be conducted through a Swiss joint stock company or through a permanent establishment (branch) of a foreign company situated in Switzerland.

Canton Ticino tax law contains provisions which offer advantageous fiscal treatment to permanent establishments (branches of foreign companies). In particular, branches of foreign companies enjoy a privileged fiscal burden ranging between 6,5% and 10% on their realised gross profits. It should be understood that these commercial entities must be economically sound, carry out a real commercial activity and have adequate operational premises.

Co-ordination and infra-group service centres

The function and main use of these centres is to create an infra-group service unit to support several subsidiaries of an international holding group; mainly in the following fields:

* treasury and financial management

* monitoring and control of group companies

* centralisation of various preliminary, auxiliary and supporting group activities such as marketing, advertising, quality control and reporting.

Taxation

The choice of locating an entity in the Canton of Ticino makes available a particular and efficient tax regime for certain services and co-ordination activities directed mainly at companies forming part of a large holding group.

In the Canton of Ticino, service and co-ordination companies are taxed according to the circular letter of the Federal Tax Administration dated September 17th, 1997. The minimum assessable base is calculated according to an amount equal to at least 5% of the total costs incurred locally (10% if it is a Swiss branch of a foreign company).

Summary and conclusion

The globalisation of markets requires broader diversification, both geographically and functionally, of all operational units of a business activity (managing unit, R&D unit, business centres, production centres, financial centres, etc.). Switzerland, due to its location at the centre of Europe and more particularly the Canton of Ticino, offers in terms of an international framework the advantages of one of the best operational and fiscal environments. This is subject to the conditions that such centres are economically sound, carry out a real commercial activity and have adequate operational premises.

CONTACTS

Lic. oec. publ. **CHRISTIAN BALLABIO**
TEL.: +41 91 9731 393
e-mail: christian.ballabio@fidinam.ch

Lic. oec. HEC **GIORGIO CROTTA**
TEL.: +41 91 9731 367
e-mail: giorgio.crotta@fidinam.ch

Lic. rer. pol. **ALBERTO GENOVESI**
TEL.: +41 91 9731 388
e-mail: alberto.genovesi@fidinam.ch

LEGAL FRAMEWORK AND OPERATIONS

This is a non-exhaustive list of some of the main Swiss statutes affecting low-tax status and non-resident business. The statutes are listed in alphabetical order – click on the statute for a fuller description of the statute or the legal regime it forms part of.

Banking Law 1934 (as amended) 1999
Federal Act on International Mutual Assistance in Criminal Matters 1997\
Law On Investment Funds 1994

Money Laundering Act 1997
Stock Exchange Law
Swiss Civil Code 1907

BANKING LAW

The Swiss banking sector is regulated by the Federal Banking Commission (FBC) under the Banking Law of 1934, as amended most recently in 1999. Banking is defined to include all deposit-taking activity, in whatever corporate format, but does not include the issuance of bonds or securities trading. The offices, branches, agencies and permanent representatives of foreign banks are covered by the law.

Banks are licensed by the FBC. The main conditions for the granting of a license are as follows:

- If the banking activity is to be on any significant scale, the management and supervisory functions of the bank must be separated;
- The bank must conform with currently applicable minimum capital requirements, as set by the Federal Council;
- Officers must have good antecedents;
- Persons having 10% or more of the bank's capital (a 'qualified participation') must guarantee that they will not influence the bank in any negative way;
- The bank (and the persons concerned) must notify the FBC of any change in a qualified participation;
- Corporate documents (statutes etc) must be lodged with the FBC, and any changes notified;
- Establishment of a foreign subsidiary or branch must be notified.

Banks with a controlling foreign shareholding must conform additionally to the following requirements:

- The home country of the controlling shareholder must guarantee reciprocity;
- The name of the bank must not indicate Swiss control;
- If the foreign owner is a group, it is likely that the FBC will require consolidated supervision;

- The foreign owner must keep the FBC fully informed about its activities; in particular, changes in 'qualified participations' may lead to a demand for a new license.

The FBC applies world-standard equity, capital and liquidity rules to banks that it supervises. There are compulsory reserve requirements for banks which solicit deposits from the public, but these do not apply to private banks which avoid public solicitation of clients.

Banks licensed by the FBC must report both to the FBC and to the Swiss National Bank, and the latter has considerable reserve powers under the Banking Law. Reports submitted are however to be kept secret.

The Banking Law imposes strict secrecy on Swiss banks, but the Money Laundering Law 1998 (MLL) responded to increasing international concern by clarifying the circumstances under which banks should breach secrecy.

Under the MLL financial intermediaries were placed under a legal duty to report suspicious transactions and to retain clients' funds for a period of 5 days so as to give the authorities time to seize the assets should circumstances warrant such a response. Banks can be fined up to US$7m for non compliance with the money-laundering regulations. Other regulations include the requirement that customers be identified by way of adequate documentation, that staff be trained in money laundering detection techniques and that internal money laundering units be set up within institutions. Within 6 months of the law being passed US$124m of assets were seized.

See Other International Agreements for details of the regulations under which the Swiss authorities grant administrative and judicial assistance to foreign investigators.

In April 2002 the Federal Banking Commission announced that it wanted to introduce provisions to make information exchange with foreign securities regulators easier in order to prevent the misuse of the Swiss banking sector.

The banking watchdog made the announcement at a press conference in Bern, explaining to reporters that the recommendations had come about partly as the result of international pressure from the OECD, the EU, and the International Commission of Securities Commissions. The federal regulator revealed that it would be sending its proposals to Finance Minister Kaspar Villiger, the government, and parliament for consideration.

Director of the Banking Commission, Daniel Zuberbuhler, explained that although banking secrecy is an integral part of the country's financial sector, certain provisions can be overly restrictive when dealing with international securities regulators:

'Our legal provisions are too narrow and make it very complicated and recently as we've seen in the case of the Federal Supreme Court impossible even to grant information to the United States Securities and Exchanges Commission, which is clearly not what the legislator had intended.'

Although in various ways the Swiss authorities have attempted to fall into line with the international campaign against money-laundering, they have not seriously dented the principle of banking secrecy. For instance, they refused to sign the OECD's declaration concerning 'Unfair Tax Competition' in late 1999, and in 2000, while they signed the OECD's 'Information Exchange' declaration, they stated that they considered they already conformed to its standards.

In mid-2001 the Swiss parliament decided to form a new central authority to combat financial crime in the country. The decision arose from concerns raised over just how efficient the system is regarding money laundering controls.

In the three years since Switzerland implemented its anti-money laundering legislation, not one single case headed by the federal authorities had been successfully prosecuted. However, cantonal prosecutors acting on their own authority had secured 213 convictions.

The Money Laundering Control Authority (MLCA) had been dogged by controversy with its director, Niklaus Huber handing in his resignation after bemoaning a lack of support from the Swiss finance ministry. His departure did not help to quash rumours, rife at the time, that the MLCA was under-staffed and under-funded.

And the MLCA branch which is the first port of call for the banking industry when reporting suspicious transactions, the Money Laundering Reporting Office (MLRO), had not been free from difficulties either. In the previous year, four employees had resigned including senior official, Daniel Thelesklaf, who declared that he had not been awarded the necessary authority to deal effectively with financial criminal activities.

But Judith Voney, Mr Thelesklaf's replacement, told the local press that the office was indeed making headway. She said: 'We are investigating suspicious cases and the fact that we can forward them to the investigating authorities is a success in itself.'

James Nason of the Swiss Bankers Association informed Swissinfo that the MLRO had mastered its brief. 'The Office only sets the ball rolling,' he said, 'then they hand [cases] over to the cantonal authorities.'

Ultimately, the inconsistency of the system across the cantons is unhelpful to implementation of the law; so parliament has decided to try a different tack by removing the responsibility for prosecuting cases from the cantons and giving it instead to the new central authority which will also be responsible for notifying and investigating cases.

The new authority, to be located in Bern, is currently training its staff in Lucerne and it is expected to employ around 450 staff in total.

In addition to the forming of the new body, Judith Voney has confirmed that a new law is due to be enforced next year that will further centralise Switzerland's attempts to effectively tackle money laundering, organised crime and corruption. 'Under the new law, the Federal Police Office will receive the mandate to investigate cases with an international dimension. This will allow experts with specialist know-how to be more efficient in their investigations,' she said.

In December, 2002, the Swiss Bankers Association issued new guidelines designed to separate research and banking activities in the country's financial institutions. The SBA said:

'The Board of Directors of the Swiss Bankers Association (SBA) has passed binding guidelines concerning the independence of financial analysis with a view to further strengthening the good reputation of Switzerland as a banking and financial centre. In particular, the SBA wants to ensure that financial analysis in Switzerland continues to remain independent and credible.'

The new rules proposed by the Swiss Bankers Association stipulate the establishment of so-called 'Chinese Walls' between a financial institute's research department and its other business areas, prohibit analysts from investing in firms or financial instruments which they assess or play a part in assessing, and ensure that analysts are not recompensed according to the success of specific transactions, making the possibility of biased analysis less likely.

INVESTMENT FUNDS LAW

Investment funds in Switzerland are authorised and supervised by the Federal Banking Commission (FBC) under the Federal Law on Investment Funds 1994.

The law applies only to Collective Investment Funds, and to foreign investment funds whatever their corporate basis; however, the FBC will only authorise a foreign fund if it is licensed at home under an acceptable regulatory regime (reciprocity provisions).

Swiss funds formed as companies under the Swiss Civil Code remain subject to pre-existing legislation, but the previous fund management legislation was repealed, so that they are very limited in scope.

The new Law contains rules governing the establishment of a Collective Investment Fund, and recognises three types of Fund:

- Securities Funds, which may only invest in securities issued on a large scale and which are publicly-traded on a stock exchange or equivalent; there are limitations on stock-lending, short-selling etc; interestingly, the wording accommodates any type of investment behaviour which the EU may in future permit to Collective Investment Funds;
- Real Estate Funds, which may invest in real property at home and abroad, and may own controlling interests in real estate companies; there are extensive prudential conditions in the Law;
- 'Other' Funds, which covers riskier types of investment including commodity funds, derivative (hedge) funds and funds of funds; managers are required to draw the attention of investors to the risks.

Funds authorised under the Law are subject to extensive reporting requirements both to the FBC and to the Swiss National Bank. Annual audits are compulsory for all categories of fund.

The Law permits the formation of in-house, limited-membership funds, which may not be marketed to the public but which in other respects are covered by the Law.

The Law requires the separation of Fund Management and Custody. The Fund Manager must be a limited company exclusively devoted to fund management with registered office and principal place of administration in Switzerland; there are other conditions dealing with professional qualifications etc. The FBC authorises Fund Managers and exercises continuing supervision. They have statutory duties towards investors.

Custody must be exercised by a bank within the meaning of the Federal Banking Law. The Custodian has a statutory duty towards the investors, including the exercise of a supervisory role in relation to the Fund Manager.

It is possible for Fund Manager and Custodian to be separate ('independent') entities within a group.

Sanctions for misbehaviour under the Law are quite severe.

ENTRY AND RESIDENCE

Entry into Switzerland, residence in Switzerland, Swiss naturalization and the right to work or purchase property in the country are all inextricably interlinked and so are all dealt with together.

Entry for a short period of time: For nationals of most countries visa-free entry is permitted for a period of up to 90 days after which time the visitor must leave the country.

Obtaining Residence in Switzerland: The available types of permit are the '120-day' permit, the class A, B or C permits, the fiscal deal permit and the political refugee permit. The class A permit (for 'blue-collar' workers) and the political refugee permit are not described further here. Permits other than the '120-day' variety are subject to a quota system. However, agreements with the EU are gradually putting EU freedom-of-movement rules into place which will eventually allow EU citizens to by-pass the quota permit system altogether.

The '120-Day' Permit: This permit allows a managerial or specialist worker to work in a specified position for up to 120 days in a particular year; rotation among a number of individuals is not allowed.

The Class B permit: The class B permit is the most commonly issued permit and gives the right to live and work in Switzerland. It is the permit of choice for professional and managerial people, self employed individuals who wish to start their own company in Switzerland, and people who wish to reside in Switzerland and are wealthy enough to live off their own resources (but see the Fiscal Deal Permit below). The Class B permit has the following characteristics:

- It is usually granted for a period of up to one year at a time;
- If the permit is for work purposes then the applicant must have a job to go to in Switzerland;
- The granting of his permit must not have the effect of depriving a Swiss national of employment. Since many trades in Switzerland are protected by guilds which prohibit the recruitment of foreign workers an application for a class B permit is not always successful;
- The class B permit allows the applicant to bring his wife and children into the country but not his extended family;
- The application is not prejudiced by inability to speak the official languages of Switzerland;
- It takes about 3 months to obtain a Class B permit.

In May 2001, the Swiss government said it would not award extra work permits for information technology specialists, rejecting calls for 10,000 special work permits to be set aside for computer experts, which some members of parliament claimed would encourage the creation of new companies in Switzerland. Under the proposal, the permits would have been handled by the federal government, rather than the cantons, which are normally responsible for issuing work permits. The government says statistical evidence shows that Switzerland does not have a shortage of computer specialists.

The Class C permit: The class C permit is a longer-term residency permit which gives the applicant almost the same rights as Swiss citizens and allows the applicant to buy real estate in Switzerland. To obtain a class C permit one must have had a class B permit for between 5 and 10 years depending on country of origin. The class C permit is the last step before applying for Swiss citizenship. It is subject to the same conditions as the class B permit.

The 'Fiscal Deal' Permit: This is a variant of the class B permit and is primarily for wealthy individuals who wish to live in Switzerland off income earned outside Switzerland (e.g. international tennis players and formula 1 drivers) but who have no need or desire to work in the country. To obtain a fiscal deal permit the applicant needs a certified net wealth of at least 2m Swiss Francs and must be willing to spend at least 180 days a year in the country. The fiscal deal permit allows the applicant to pay considerably less tax than a Swiss national of his income bracket would normally pay since the assessment to tax is not based on the applicant's real income but rather on a much lower notional amount.

For further information see lump sum assessment method in our personal income tax section. The amount of tax payable by the holder of such a permit is a matter of personal negotiation with the canton in which the applicant resides. Switzerland is already a low tax country by OECD standards and the 'fiscal deal' results in extremely low levels of taxation. It takes about 3 months to obtain a fiscal deal permit.

Obtaining Swiss nationality: It goes without saying that Swiss nationals do not need permits to reside, work or purchase property in Switzerland. Obtaining Swiss nationality or citizenship is a long-drawn-out process involving procedures at federal, canton and communal levels. In order to obtain Swiss citizenship an applicant who is not the offspring of a Swiss national must satisfy the following criteria:

- There is an examination in Swiss history and culture;
- The applicant must have lived in the country for several years with a class B (or 'fiscal deal') permit;
- The applicant must then obtain a class C permit and continue to live in Switzerland for several more years.

Purchasing Real Estate in Switzerland: Since 1960 there have been restrictions on the purchase of real estate by non-Swiss nationals which although substantially relaxed in recent years are still draconian by OECD standards.

3 situations apply:

- Foreigners who have acquired a class C permit can buy vacation properties in designated areas.
- Foreigners who are not deemed resident in Switzerland under Swiss law can only purchase tax-exempt apartment blocks tied to below-market rentals for a period of 20 years. Such purchases require official permission. After 20 years they may raise the rents on the blocks purchased.
- The acquisition of premises for business purposes is unrestricted and although permission is required it is normally granted.

The purchase of real estate is conducted by a notary public who will not allow the transaction to proceed unless it is permitted by the law. The purchaser's details will be entered in the property owners' registry after the Government issues a notice of confirmation that the transaction is legal.

THE SWX SWISS EXCHANGE

The Swiss stock exchange (SWX) was formed in 1995 by a merger between the country's three existing exchanges in Geneva, Basle and Zurich.

SWX is now the world's sixth largest securities exchange, and the third largest in Europe. It lists more than 3,500 securities, and has 60 members, 15 of whom are foreign.

The Exchange is governed by the Swiss Stock Exchange and Securities Trading Act of 1995, which includes listing requirements and continuing obligations for listed companies.

SWX has a highly-integrated electronic trading platform. It has also been innovative in product terms, launching the electronic SWX repo market in 1999, and a high-growth market called SWX New Market in the same year which has already seen a number of successful high-tech listings. Eurex, the first transnational derivatives exchange, is a joint venture between SWX and Deutsche Borse AG. SWX is also a partner in STOXX.

Stocks, bonds and warrants are traded on the SWX Swiss Exchange. Since July 1998, SWX has also provided facilities for electronic trading in Eurobonds. Latterly, it has introduced Exchange Traded Funds (ETFs). One of the best-known SWX products is the SwissIndex family of securities market indicators. It comprises the Swiss Market Index (SMI), which is made up of the most important Swiss stocks and represents 80% of total market capitalization in Switzerland; the broader-based Swiss Performance Index (SPI), which covers all Swiss stocks (including those of Liechtenstein); and the Swiss Bond Index (SBI), which measures the performance of CHF bonds with a minimum life of one year. A separate index is published for investment companies.

After years of planning, SWX finally committed itself to a virtual future in June 2001 when its alliance with Tradepoint culminated in the launching of the virt-x pan-European electronic stock market on June 25th. The joint venture between Tradepoint, a consortium of leading international investment banks, and the Swiss exchange SWX (which stopped separate dealing in Swiss blue-chip equities) lists the top stocks from most of Europe's largest bourses on a single screen, operates with a counterparty facility provided by the London Clearing House, offers a seamless back office with clearing through Euroclear and has a single rulebook for all stocks regardless of listing location. The exchange operates under UK regulatory standards.

Virt-x offers full dealing services in all the main index stocks in France, German and Italy as well as the FTSE Eurotop 300, Stoxx and MCI indices which cover smaller European markets as well. The consortium controlling Tradepoint includes Instinet, the financial markets arm of Reuters, the investment banks ABN Amro, Credit Suisse First Boston, Deutsche Bank, Dresdner Kleinwort Benson, JP Morgan, Merrill Lynch, Morgan Stanley Dean Witter and UBS Warburg, the fund manager American Century, and Archipelago, an electronic trading system.

After one year of operation, Virt-x had to report in June 2002 that it had not yet succeeded in attracting significantly more trading than it acquired with SWX itself.

INVESTMENTS BY FOREIGNERS

There are no controls on inward investment, or on the repatriation of profits or capital on disinvestment, other than applicable taxes (see Direct Corporate Taxation). The Swiss authorities have a 'laissez-faire' attitude towards investment, but the other side of that coin is that there is relatively little official support for investment, at least at Federal level. However, the Government does support infrastructural investment (tourist facilities, communications and training facilities) with subsidised loans up to 25% of a financing package. There are also a few traditional, mainly rural, industries in long-term decline in which the Government offers rather more generous financial support.

The picture is quite different at cantonal level, where a wide variety of investment supports is available. The cantons frequently compete vigorously to secure attractive projects, and the terms of incoming investment are extremely negotiable in many cases. The types of support available include assistance or subsidy with land or premises, waiving of work permit requirements, tax holidays up to 10 years, cheap energy and training subsidies. Some cantons have designated industrial zones which have some or all of the listed privileges.

Although most cantons are 'open to offer', some in particular are more open than others: Fribourg, Grisons, Lucerne, Schwyz, Untervalden, Uri, Valais and Vaud, all of which are predominantly agricultural areas, are thought to be particularly keen on attracting inward investment.

DISTRIBUTION OF FOREIGN INVESTMENT FUNDS

According to the Federal Law on Investment Funds of March 18 1994, the distribution of foreign funds in Switzerland is prohibited unless (i) the foreign funds have been authorized by the Swiss Federal Banking Commission (SFBC) and (ii) the representatives/distributors are agreed upon by the SFBC.

Definitions

An 'investment fund' under Swiss law is

> "*constituted of assets contributed by investors based on public advertising for the purpose of common investment, and is managed by the fund manager for the account of the investors, normally according to the principle of an adequate diversification of risks*"(Article 2(1)).

Advertising is regarded as 'public', regardless of its form, if it is not addressed to a narrowly defined and limited group of persons (Article 2(2)). According to SFBC practice, a 'limited group of persons' means no more than 20 potential investors.

The Law on Investment Funds identifies the following funds as foreign investment funds subject to regulation on the distribution of units in Switzerland:

- any funds, generated on the basis of a collective investment contract or another contract with similar effects, which are administered by a management company with its registered offices and administrative headquarters outside Switzerland (Article 44(1) a);

- any foreign company which has a corporate purpose of collective investment activity with a right of redemption available to the investor (Article 44(1) b); and

- any foreign funds or foreign companies which are regulated in terms of investments by their home country legislation on investment funds (Article 44(2)).

Authorization

This broad Swiss definition of 'investment fund' covers open-ended investment funds registered abroad.

With respect to closed-end funds, the SFBC has ruled that these fall within the scope of the Law on Investment Funds if they are regulated in their home jurisdiction (Article 44(2)). However, authorization will only be granted if this supervision is comparable to Swiss standards. If it is insufficient (eg, Bermuda), then no authorization may be obtained.

In cases where no supervision exists (eg, Bahamas, British Virgin Islands, Cayman Islands), Article 44(2) does not apply, and thus such funds would not be subject to authorization. However, this rather illogical result, which is contrary to the Law on Investment Funds's basic purpose of protecting investors (Article 1), has led the SFBC to state that even if they are not regulated in their home jurisdiction, closed-end funds could nonetheless fall within the scope of the Law on Investment Funds if investors are not in a position to protect their interests themselves (Article 3(4)).

Closed-end funds which are not subject to licensing requirements in Switzerland may not be distributed in Switzerland under the label, denomination or name 'fund', or under a similar label, denomination or name (Article 5, LIF).

Proposal and Distribution

Pursuant to Article 45, a person must apply for an authorization to act as a representative or distributor of a foreign fund in Switzerland if (i) the person "proposes and/or distributes" units of a foreign investment fund in Switzerland, and (ii) the proposal or distribution of units in Switzerland is done "on a professional basis".

These conditions are explained in a circular which the Secretariat of the SFBC issued in June 1995.

The concept of 'proposal and/or distribution' is broadly construed, in order to cover any professional contact with interested investors in Switzerland. The SFBC circular specifies that a proposal and/or distribution can occur in Switzerland even where the targeted investors belong to a limited and specific circle, and regardless of the scope of distribution. In this respect, the Law on Investment Funds differs from the previous legal regime, in that the 1971 Ordinance on Foreign Investment Funds was based on the criterion of a 'call to the public', that is, public solicitation, which allowed some flexibility with respect to Swiss licensing requirements when dealing with a limited number of so-called 'sophisticated investors'.

The activity is carried out 'on a professional basis' if the person earns direct or indirect remuneration from it.

The SFBC has admitted that a strict interpretation of these criteria would produce inappropriate results. The circular describes situations in which the SFBC has confirmed the need to obtain a licence. It also mentions situations in which licensing is not normally required. The criteria which the SFBC applies in its analysis include the following:

- if the client takes the initiative to buy fund units himself;

- the existence of a discretionary investment mandate for the Swiss portfolio manager who buys units for his client;

- the intensity of sales, that is, whether occasional or repeated; and

- direct promotion in Switzerland.

However, there still is a large grey area outside the typical situations set forth in the circular. The SFBC suggests that cases which fall within this grey area should be submitted to it for a ruling. If a situation fits exactly the criteria described in the circular, then an advance ruling is not necessary, since the projected activity is not subject to licensing.

Exemption

As an exemption to Swiss fund licensing requirements, the distribution of foreign funds targeting Swiss-based institutional investors (eg, banks, insurance companies and pension funds) is authorized without obtaining a licence from the SFBC, but no public solicitation is permitted (Article 2(4) of the Ordinance on Investment Funds of October 19 1994, as amended). This means that no more than 20 Swiss-based institutional investors may be invited to invest in the foreign investment fund concerned.

Finally, the SFBC has stated that an investment company may seek potential investors in Switzerland through public solicitation in order to increase its share capital, as long as the following conditions are met:

- The company is not subject to supervision as an investment fund in the country of its incorporation;

- The shareholders have voting rights and other shareholder rights comparable to those of a Swiss company's shareholders; and

- The company does not refer to the label, denomination or name 'investment fund', or use equivalent or analogous wording, either in its materials or its communications with prospective Swiss investors.

COMPANIES

Switzerland is a 'code' country, and business entities are governed by the Civil Code. As in all civil law jurisdictions, formation and administration of companies tends to be considerably more bureaucratic than in common law jurisdictions. Although the Civil Code is at Federal Level, businesses are domiciled in a particular canton. Each canton maintains a Commercial Register (Registre de Commerce), and the mandatory entries in the Register of subscribers, directors, capital structure etc have strict legal force. The Register is a public document.

The forms of business entity with legal personality are the Stock Corporation and its variants (dealt with below), the Limited Liability Company (Societe a Responsabilite Limite), and the Limited Partnership (Societe en Commandite). These last two are not much used by foreign investors. General Partnerships (Societe en Nom Collectif) and Sole Proprietorships (Raison de Commerce) are also possible.

THE STOCK CORPORATION

The Stock Corporation ("Societe Anonyme" or "Aktiengesellschaft") is the form almost universally used by foreign investors and has the following characteristics:

- The minimum number of subscribers is 3;
- Nominee shareholders and nominee subscribers are permitted;

- The minimum authorized share capital is 100,000 Swiss Francs of which either 20% or 50,000 Swiss Francs (which ever is the greater) must be paid up by way of a deposit of funds in a bank account; the bank will not relinquish control over these funds until the company registration certificate has been issued;
- Share capital cannot be increased by more than 50% of the authorized capital at any one time;
- Shares can be ordinary shares, preference shares, voting shares or non voting shares and can be issued at a premium; bearer shares are permitted;
- A majority of directors must be Swiss nationals and must be domiciled in the country;
- All directors must be shareholders whether they are the beneficial owners of those shares or hold as nominees (the holding of one share as a nominee is sufficient to meet this requirement);
- The company must have an auditor and a registered office;
- A person whose name appears in the articles of association signs on behalf of the company.

A company must have an auditor, and accounts must be filed each year with the Companies Registration Office. Small companies can prepare abbreviated accounts which do not have to include the level of turnover.

THE HOLDING COMPANY

The 'Holding' Company is a Stock Corporation with a particular tax status (see Offshore Legal and Tax Regimes). Holding companies benefit from reductions in corporate income tax and capital gains at federal and cantonal levels, and from a reduction in net worth tax at cantonal level.

For federal tax purposes a company is defined as a holding company if it holds either a minimum of 20% of the share capital of another corporate entity or if the value of its shareholding in the other corporate entity has a market value of at least 2m Swiss Francs (known as a "participating shareholding"). The reduction in the level of corporate income payable tax depends on the ratio of earnings from "participating shareholding" to total profit generated.

Although the definition of a holding company varies among cantons, broadly speaking a corporate entity is a holding company for cantonal corporate income tax purposes so long as it either:

- derives 51%-66% of its income from dividends remitted by the subsidiary; or
- holds 51%-66% of the subsidiary's shares.

THE DOMICILIARY COMPANY

Domiciliary Companies are Stock Corporations that are both foreign-controlled and managed from abroad, have a registered office in Switzerland (i.e. at a lawyer's premises) but have neither a physical presence nor staff in Switzerland. They must carry out most if not all of their business abroad and receive only foreign source income . The use of domiciliary companies can result in savings in corporate income tax levied on income and capital gains and net worth tax. See Offshore Legal and Tax Regimes.

THE AUXILIARY COMPANY

An Auxiliary Company is essentially a Domiciliary Company which in addition may carry out a certain proportion of its business in Switzerland. Auxiliary Companies are possible in only seven cantons, and do not benefit at federal level. Treatment varies according to canton, but in most cases an auxiliary company may have Swiss offices and staff and be in receipt of Swiss income (which is taxed at normal rates). Most income though must be from a foreign source. See Offshore Legal and Tax Regimes.

THE SERVICE COMPANY

Service Companies are Stock Corporations whose sole activity is the provision of technical, management, marketing, publicity, financial and administrative assistance to foreign companies which are part of a group of which the service company is a member. Service companies may not in general derive income from third parties (i.e. companies outside their corporate group). Service company status is obtained by way of an advance cantonal tax ruling (there is no benefit at federal level). See Offshore Legal and Tax Regimes.

BACK TO TOP

THE MIXED COMPANY

Mixed Companies are Stock Corporations which have the characteristics of both domiciliary companies and holding companies but which do not qualify as either. There is no benefit at federal level, but at cantonal and municipal level there are corporate income tax benefits if the mixed company meets the following conditions:

- the company is foreign controlled;
- a minimum of 80% of its total income comes from foreign sources;
- the company has close relationships to foreign entities

OFFSHORE TAXES

The term 'offshore' is not used in Swiss legislation or in describing company forms. However, there are a number of specialised forms of the basic Stock Corporation which offer tax-privileged treatment equivalent to that obtainable in offshore jurisdictions.

FORMS OF TAX-PRIVILEGED OPERATION

Tax-privileged operations may take place within the following forms, all of which are variants of the basic Stock Corporation:

- Holding Company
- Domiciliary Company
- Auxiliary Company
- Service Company
- Mixed Company

TAX TREATMENT OF OFFSHORE OPERATIONS

See Domestic Corporate Taxes for the general principles of Swiss corporate taxation, which also apply to offshore entities except as indicated below.

HOLDING COMPANIES:

For federal tax purposes a company is defined as a holding company if it holds either a minimum of 20% of the share capital of another corporate entity or if the value of its shareholding in the other corporate entity has a market value of at least 2m Swiss Francs (known as a "participating shareholding").

Although the definition of a holding company varies among cantons a corporate entity is a holding company for cantonal corporate income tax purposes so long as it either

- derives at least 51%-66% of its income from dividends remitted by the subsidiary; or
- holds at least 51%-66% of the subsidiary's shares.

Generally speaking foreign dividends remitted to a Swiss company and any capital gains realized by a Swiss company on the sale of shares in a foreign entity in which it holds a stake are taxable in Switzerland unless they are remitted to a company which by Swiss fiscal law is defined as a Swiss "holding" company.

Swiss holding companies enjoy the following relief from corporate income tax:

- At federal level a holding company pays a reduced level of corporate income tax on any dividend income received from the subsidiary or the company in which it holds a "participating shareholding". The reduction in the level of corporate income tax payable depends on the ratio of earnings from "participating shareholding" to total profit generated.
- At cantonal or municipal level no corporate income tax is payable on income represented by dividends so long the corporate entity meets the cantonal definition of a holding company.

Furthermore holding companies which hold a minimum of 20% of the share capital of a subsidiary pay reduced corporation tax on any capital gains made on the sale of that shareholding so long as

- the shareholding was held for at least one year and was purchased after 1st January 1998; or
- the shareholding was purchased before 1st January 1997 and will be disposed of after 1st January 2007.

Fribourg is currently considered the best canton in which to locate a holding company for corporate income tax purposes.

DOMICILIARY COMPANIES:

Domiciliary companies are companies that:

- are both foreign-controlled and managed from abroad;

For additional analytical, business and investment opportunities information,
please contact Global Investment & Business Center, USA
at (703) 370-8082. Fax: (703) 370-8083. E-mail: ibpusa3@gmail.com
Global Business and Investment Info Databank - www.ibpus.com

- have a registered office in Switzerland (i.e. at a lawyer's premises);
- have neither a physical presence nor staff in Switzerland;
- carry out most if not all of their business abroad;
- receive only foreign source income.

Domiciliary companies enjoy the following relief from corporate income tax:

- At a federal level there are no tax advantages in terms of corporate income tax payable on income and gains;
- At a cantonal and municipal level the corporate income tax rate may be substantially reduced or even reduced to zero; taxes levied by the cantons are calculated according to a formula which relates the company's paid up share capital and reserves to profit.

AUXILIARY COMPANIES:

An auxiliary company is essentially a domiciliary company which in addition may carry out a certain proportion of its business in Switzerland. Auxiliary companies can exist in only seven cantons. An auxiliary company may:

- have Swiss offices and staff;
- be in receipt of Swiss income (which is taxed at normal rates) though most of its income must be from a foreign source.

Auxiliary companies enjoy the following relief from corporate income tax:

- At a federal level no exemptions are granted on corporate income tax;
- At a cantonal and municipal level the level of corporate income tax payable on income and capital gains varies among the 7 cantons who give favorable treatment. However, in general Swiss-sourced income is taxed at 5% whereas foreign-sourced income is tax exempt. The tax concessions can vary and an advance tax ruling should be sought.

SERVICE COMPANIES:

Service companies are companies whose sole activity is the provision of technical, management, marketing, publicity, financial and administrative assistance to foreign companies which are part of a group of which the service company is a member.

Service companies may not in general derive income from third parties (i.e. companies outside their corporate group). Service company status is obtained by way of an advance tax ruling.

Service companies enjoy the following relief from corporate income tax:

- At a federal level relief is not available on corporate income tax payable;
- At a cantonal and communal level corporate income tax rates will be adjusted depending on the international orientation of the services provided. There are a number of ways of calculating annual taxable profit for cantonal and municipal purposes but generally speaking annual taxable profit will be the equivalent of 8.5% of the payroll or 5%-20% of overheads (unless overheads are very low in which case a higher percentage rate will be used).

For additional analytical, business and investment opportunities information,
please contact Global Investment & Business Center, USA
at (703) 370-8082. Fax: (703) 370-8083. E-mail: ibpusa3@gmail.com
Global Business and Investment Info Databank - www.ibpus.com

MIXED COMPANIES:

Mixed companies are companies which have the characteristics of both domiciliary companies and holding companies but which do not qualify as either. A mixed company gets the following relief from corporate income tax:

- At federal level no relief is granted;
- At a cantonal and municipal level a mixed company may pay reduced tax or be totally exempt if it meets the following conditions:
    - it is foreign controlled;
    - a minimum of 80% of its total income comes from foreign sources;
    - the company has close relationships to foreign entities.

TAXATION OF FOREIGN EMPLOYEES OF TAX-PRIVILEGED OPERATIONS

There are no special rules applying to the foreign or Swiss employees of tax-privileged operations. The various exemptions from income tax described above do not apply to employees: any business employing and paying people in Switzerland will have to follow the normal rules for the taxation of individuals.

See Domestic Personal Taxes for the general principles of individual taxation of individuals in Switzerland.

A person is deemed resident in Switzerland if:

- He has Swiss employment (to work in Switzerland a non-national needs a work permit - limited work permits of 90-120 days can be granted and where granted lead to limited taxation);
- He carries on a business in Switzerland; or
- He lives in Switzerland for not less 180 days in any one year. If however he remains in the same abode the time required to be a resident for tax purposes drops to 90 days.

EXCHANGE CONTROLS

Switzerland has no exchange controls.

ACTIVITIES OF TAX-PRIVILEGED OPERATIONS

The various tax-privileged forms described above are all subject to limitations on their activities or structures as set out. In approximate terms:

- Holding Companies must derive most of their income from subsidiaries;
- Domiciliary Companies must have only the smallest toe-hold in Switzerland;
- Auxiliary Companies (in 7 cantons only) may have some local activity;
- Service Companies must be active only within their own groups; and
- Mixed Companies combine Domiciliary and Service Company restrictions.

See above for further details.

EMPLOYMENT AND RESIDENCE

There are no special privileges for the employees of non-resident or tax-privileged entities in Switzerland. Entry into Switzerland, residence in Switzerland and the right to work or purchase property in the country are all inextricably interlinked.

Obtaining Residence in Switzerland: The available types of permit are the '120-day' permit, the class A, B or C permits, the fiscal deal permit and the political refugee permit. The class A permit (for 'blue-collar' workers) and the political refugee permit are not described further here. Permits other than the '120-day' variety are subject to a quota system. However, agreements with the EU are gradually putting EU freedom-of-movement rules into place which will eventually allow EU citizens to by-pass the quota permit system altogether.

The '120-Day' Permit: This permit allows a managerial or specialist worker to work in a specified position for up to 120 days in a particular year; rotation among a number of individuals is not allowed.

The Class B permit: The class B permit is the most commonly issued permit and gives the right to live and work in Switzerland. It is the permit of choice for professional and managerial people, self employed individuals who wish to start their own company in Switzerland, people who wish to reside in Switzerland and are wealthy enough to live off their own resources (but see the Fiscal Deal Permit below). The Class B permit has the following characteristics:

- It is usually granted for a period of up to one year at a time;
- If the permit is for work purposes then the applicant must have a job to go to in Switzerland;
- The granting of his permit must not have the effect of depriving a Swiss national of employment. Since many trades in Switzerland are protected by guilds which prohibit the recruitment of foreign workers an application for a class B permit is not always successful;
- The class B permit allows the applicant to bring his wife and children into the country but not his extended family;
- The application is not prejudiced by inability to speak the official languages of Switzerland;
- It takes about 3 months to obtain a Class B permit.

The Class C permit: The class C permit is a longer-term residency permit which gives the applicant almost the same rights as Swiss citizens and allows the applicant to buy real estate in Switzerland. To obtain a class C permit one must have had a class B permit for between 5 and 10 years depending on country of origin. The class C permit is the last step before applying for Swiss citizenship. It is subject to the same conditions as the class B permit.

The 'Fiscal Deal' Permit: This is a variant of the class B permit and is primarily for wealthy individuals who wish to live in Switzerland off income earned outside Switzerland (e.g. international tennis players and formula 1 drivers) but who have no need or desire to work in the country. To obtain a fiscal deal permit the applicant needs a certified net wealth of at least 2m Swiss Francs and must be willing to spend at least 180 days a year in the country. The fiscal deal permit allows the applicant to pay considerably less tax than a Swiss national of his income bracket would normally pay since the assessment to tax is not based on the applicants real income but rather on a much lower notional amount.

For further information see lump sum assessment method in our personal income tax section. The amount of tax payable by the holder of such a permit is a matter of personal negotiation with the canton in which the applicant resides. Switzerland is already a low tax country by OECD standards and the 'fiscal deal' results in extremely low levels of taxation. It takes about 3 months to obtain a fiscal deal permit.

DOUBLE-TAX TREATIES

Switzerland has Double Taxation Treaties with 52 other countries. The general effect of the treaties for non-residents from treaty countries is that they can obtain a partial or total refund of tax withheld by the Swiss paying agent. Although the full amount of withholding tax is deducted at source the difference can be re-claimed by the non resident from the Swiss tax authorities. Where there is no double taxation treaty in place withholding taxes deducted in the foreign jurisdiction on remittances paid to a Swiss entity give rise to a tax credit in Switzerland.

No withholding tax is levied on royalties paid to foreign beneficiaries. Profits repatriated abroad by the Swiss branch of a foreign company do not attract withholding taxes irrespective of any double taxation treaty.

Treaty abuse: A repayment of withholding taxes under the terms of a treaty will be denied where there has been "abuse". Abuse occurs when a foreign-controlled legal entity which is resident in Switzerland fails one of the 4 following tests:

- The entity must have a reasonable debt/equity ratio (generally the total of all interest-bearing loans should not exceed 6 times the company's equity);
- The entity must not pay excessive interest rates on debt (for the purposes of this test the accepted rate varies from time to time);
- The entity must not pay more than 50% of its income as management fees, interest or royalties to non residents;
- The entity must distribute at least 25% of the income which could be distributed as dividend.

Where any one of the 4 tests are failed the portion of withholding tax deducted and which is deemed refundable under the terms of the treaty is not refunded.

Additionally, treaty provisions do not apply to dividends, interest or royalties paid by a Swiss entity to a German, Italian, French or Belgian entity if the Swiss entity is wholly or partly exempt from cantonal tax under the tax incentives applicable to specific types of company (i.e. domiciliary, holding, auxiliary, mixed and service companies). See Offshore Legal and Tax Regime.

The following countries have double-tax treaties with Switzerland:

• Albania	• Latvia
• Armenia	• Lithuania
• Australia	• Luxembourg
• Austria	• Macedonia
• Azerbaijan	• Malaysia
• Belgium	• Moldova
• Belarus	• Netherlands
• Bulgaria	• New Zealand
• Canada	• Norway
• CIS (ex-USSR)	• Poland
• Denmark	• Portugal
• Egypt	• Romania

• Estonia	• Russia
• Federal Rep. of Germany	• Singapore
• Finland	• South Africa
• France	• South Korea
• Georgia	• Spain
• Greece	• Sri Lanka
• Hungary	• Sweden
• Iceland	• Tajikistan
• Indonesia	• Trinidad & Tobago
• Ireland	• Turkmenistan
• Italy	• Ukraine
• Japan	• United Kingdom
• Kazakhstan	• United States
• Kirghistan	• Uzbekistan

Switzerland has an impending tax treaty protocol with India. The Swiss-Indian protocol aims at improving the competitiveness of Indian enterprises doing business in Switzerland. The new provisions apply to Swiss withholding taxes levied on or after 1 January 2001 and to Indian withholding taxes levied on or after 1 April 2001.

TABLE OF TREATY RATES

The rates shown are those of withholding taxes applied to payments made by Swiss entities or persons to non-resident entities or persons; a zero rate applies to royalties. Although Switzerland recognises the member states of the CIS as successor states to the USSR, and therefore applies its USSR Double Tax Treaty to them, they are not included in the table because the USSR treaty does not contain concessionary rates of withholding tax for dividends or interest.

Country	Dividends, %	Interest, %
	Paid from Switzerland	Paid from Switzerland
Australia	15	10
Austria	5	5
Belgium	10/15 (Note 1)	10
Bulgaria	5/15 (Note 1)	10
Canada	15	15
China	10	10
Denmark	nil	nil
Egypt	5/15 (Note 1)	15
Finland	5/10 (Note 2)	nil
France	5 (Note 3)	10
Germany	10/30 (Note 4)	nil
Greece	5	10
Hungary	10	10
Iceland	5/15 (Note 1)	nil
Indonesia	10/15 (Note 1)	10
Ireland	nil/10 (Note 1)	nil
Italy	15	12.5

For additional analytical, business and investment opportunities information, please contact Global Investment & Business Center, USA at (703) 370-8082. Fax: (703) 370-8083. E-mail: ibpusa3@gmail.com Global Business and Investment Info Databank - www.ibpus.com

Japan	10/15 (Note 1)	10
Luxembourg	nil/15 (Note 1)	10
Malaysia	5/15 (Note 1)	10
Netherlands	nil/15 (Note 1)	5
New Zealand	15	10
Norway	10/15 (Note1)	nil
Pakistan	15/35 (Note 5)	15/35 (Note 6)
Poland	5/15 (Note1)	10
Portugal	10/15 (Note1)	10
Singapore	10/15 (Note 1)	10
South Africa	7.5	35
South Korea	10/15 (Note 1)	10
Spain	10/15 (Note 1)	10
Sri Lanka	10/15 (Note 1)	10
Sweden	nil/15 (Note 7)	5
Trinidad & Tobago	10?20 (Note 8)	10
UK	5/15 (Note 1)	nil
USA	5/15 (Note 1)	5

Notes:

(1)   The higher rate applies if the payment is received by a company holding directly less than 25% of the capital of the Swiss paying company

(2)	5% if the recipient is a company
(3)	Only 20% is refunded (making the effective rate 15%) if non residents of France have substantial interests in the recipient company, if the recipient company controls at least 20% of the Swiss company and if the shares of either company are neither quoted at a stock exchange nor traded over the counter
(4)	The 30% rate applies to dividends from jouissance rights, participating loans and silent participations. Withholding tax shall not exceed the tax chargeable on the profits out of which the dividends are paid.
(5)	The lower rate applies if the recipient is a company which owns at least one third of the voting stock in the Swiss company
(6)	If the recipient is an individual no refund of the Swiss 35% withholding tax is granted
(7)	The zero rate applies where the payer is a corporate shareholder which has a participation of at least 25% for a continuous period of at least 2 years immediately preceding the distribution. 5% applies where the participation requirement is satisfied but not for the requisite period and 15% is the rate for smaller holdings
(8)	The lower rate applies if the recipient is a company which controls directly or indirectly at least 10% of the voting power in the Swiss paying corporation

OTHER INTERNATIONAL AGREEMENTS

Switzerland has passed its own mutual assistance law, and is also a party to a number of international mutual assistance treaties, some multilateral and some bilateral, including the following:

- The European Convention on Mutual Assistance in Criminal Matters, 1959;
- Treaty on Mutual Assistance in Criminal Matters with the USA, 1973;
- The Federal Act on International Mutual Assistance in Criminal Matters, 1983, as amended in 1997;
- The European Convention on Laundering, Search, Seizure and Confiscation of the Proceeds of Crime, 1993.

The Federal Act, particularly since the 1997 amendments, enables the transmission of documents and information abroad for the purposes of criminal proceedings. From the point of view of banking secrecy the following can be said about the current situation:

- According to a recent decision of the Federal Supreme Court the transmission of such information requires the permission of the Swiss police authorities who must inform the customer about the order and give him a right to appeal;
- It is not permitted to forward information on persons who are not the subject matter of the investigation;
- Information will not be given if
  o The foreign authorities might use the information for purposes other than those for which it was requested;
  o The offence alleged is not equally punishable in Switzerland;
  o The requesting state does not offer Switzerland reciprocal treatment in these matters;
  o The offence is related to tax, politics or military matters.

The Swiss authorities now grant administrative assistance as well as judicial assistance. Administrative assistance is regulator to regulator contact as opposed to judicial assistance which takes place between judicial authorities within the scope of civil or criminal legal proceedings.

The Swiss Federal Banking Commission which regulates banks, mutual funds, stock exchanges and security dealers is the regulator charged with rendering administrative assistance. A number of conditions attach to the granting of administrative assistance by the Swiss Federal Banking Commission namely:

- The foreign authority must be recognized by the Commission as a supervisory authority authorized to request administrative assistance;
- The foreign authority may only use the information for the purposes of direct supervision of the institution concerned;
- The foreign authority must be bound by official or professional secrecy;
- The foreign body can only re-transmit the information under very restrictive circumstances. This is called the principle of specificity and means that information that was given for the purposes of a criminal offence such as drug dealing cannot be used in proceedings for tax evasion. In practice the foreign authority must confirm that it will not so transmit the information unless required to do so by a competent court against whose decision it will appeal. Since the grant of assistance by the commission is discretionary if specificity cannot or was not guaranteed future assistance may be denied though in practice the commission is always eager to be seeing to play its part;
- If the information requested gives the name of a client he must be notitfied and given time to contest the decision;

- There is a right of appeal to the Federal Supreme Court.

Banking secrecy in Switzerland is evidently under threat from the international crusade currently being waged, overtly against money-laundering, but with a sub-agenda of fiscal harmonisation and information exchange. Switzerland is holding fast so far against the tide, but may have to give way in the future to a certain amount of information exchange. Along with Luxembourg, Switzerland refused to sign the OECD's declaration in late 1999 against 'unfair tax competition'. It did sign the unanimous OECD declaration in April 2000 on information exchange and banking secrecy, but stated immediately afterwards that in its opinion it already conformed to the necessary standards.

However, the task of enforcing regulation in the non-banking sector is proving to be an uphill struggle for the new Money Laundering Control Authority. According to the Swiss Money Laundering Reporting Office's latest annual report, of the 311 reports of suspicious transactions, only 75 came from the country's 7,000 non-bank financial intermediaries. Of those 75, very few have resulted in prosecution, according to Swiss officials.

In addition to dealing with the passive resistance of the non-banking sector and staffing shortages at the Money Laundering Control Authority, its chief Dina Balleyguier also faces the challenge of deciding if any other sectors should be brought, doubtless unwillingly, under the umbrella of greater supervision and reporting.

'There are about 10...open-ended questions,' she explained in November 2001: 'One is whether commodities traders must have a license with us; another is whether asset traders with one-man offshore companies should be included. Another is whether someone doing asset management for their family should be included. It's very complicated.'

The Swiss government is also considering extending existing money laundering laws to cover art and jewellery trading companies. Following the introduction of enhanced legislation on traditional financial institutions and banks in Switzerland, laundering funds through non-traditional channels such as art dealers, jewellery traders, and money changers has become an increasing problem for the authorities.

Although Swiss-based asset managers are already overseen by the country's anti-money laundering unit, the goverment has also announced that is considering whether the sector should be put under the authority of the Swiss Federal Banking Commission, which oversees banks, brokers, and investment funds.

Below is a joint response, from The Swiss Federal Banking Commission and the National Bank, to the members of the Financial Stability Forum who complained about the Switzerland's inclusion on an OECD list issued in May of countries whose financial systems posed a risk to global stability.

To All Members of the FSF Berne/Zurich,
5 September 2000
Financial Stability Forum -
List of "Offshore Financial Centres" (OFC)

Dear Mr . . . Mrs

In May 2000, the Financial Stability Forum (FSF) published a list of "Offshore Financial Centres" (OFC) defined with respect to their compliance with international standards in the financial area. This list also includes Switzerland.

Switzerland is an international financial centre with a significant amount of business with non-residents. The same applies to other countries like the USA and the UK. However, it is incorrect to intermingle the typical features of international financial centres, such as the importance of financial business with non-residents, with the characteristics of "Offshore Financial Centres" as established by the OFC working group of the FSF itself (page 9, table 2 of the report). In fact, none of these characteristics apply to Switzerland. In our country:

-Business and investment income is taxed at rates close to the average of OECD countries. The overall tax burden of 33.8% in Switzerland (total tax revenue as % of GDP) is above the OECD average and higher than in the United States (29.7%), Japan (28.8%) or Australia (29.8%).

-A withholding tax of 35% applies to all interest and dividend payments of Swiss issuers or debtors, irrespective of the domicile of the recipient. The incorporation regime follows international standards. In particular, there is no regulatory or supervisory distinction between onshore/offshore or resident/non-resident activities. In Switzerland, there are neither offshore-licences nor is there preferential treatment for offshore activities. No shell-branches or brass-plate banks are admitted.

-The supervisory regime for financial services is in line with international standards and G10 standards in particular.

-Regulation does not offer the possibility to create trusts.

-Financial institutions without physical presence in Switzerland can not be licensed by the Swiss Federal Banking Commission (SFBC) and, therefore, can not lawfully operate as such from Switzerland.

 Swiss supervisors have full access to all files and privacy protection for bank customer information is no obstacle to international mutual assistance in criminal matters such as money laundering, corruption, insider trading or tax fraud.

-The volume of non-resident business does not "substantially exceed" the volume of domestic business despite the fact that, in general, the share of international transactions tends to be higher in smaller countries than in larger economies. In terms of funds under management, the share of domestic and foreign securities holders is about equal.

-The financial sector accounts for 11% of GDP.

The FSF argues that many supervisory and regulatory authorities of major financial centres referred to Switzerland as an OFC. This is certainly not an acceptable reason for placing Switzerland on the Forum's list. We urge you to take into due consideration that Switzerland is a G10-member with a regulatory and supervisory regime that is in compliance with international standards. Therefore, it is not understandable why Switzerland should be assessed as an OFC.

Yours faithfully
Swiss Federal Banking Commission
Dr Kurt Hauri Chairman

Swiss National Bank
Dr Hans Meyer Chairman of the Governing Board.

In 2001 the European Union began negotiations with Switzerland to attempt to gain agreement to the information-sharing required as part of the EU's withholding tax directive and without which it will not be effective.

Switzerland has been politely helpful, offering to extend its 35% withholding tax on resident savings income to non-resident account holders, and to distribute much of the tax collected among EU member states, but the government is adamant that it will not shift on the issue of banking secrecy. The Finance Minister, Kaspar Villiger confirms this, commenting frequently that: 'Banking secrecy is not negotiable'.

Jean-Baptiste Zufferey, a Swiss tax expert and professor at the University of Fribourg expresses the situation more bluntly: 'It's not because we fear banks would lose business, but most Swiss people have an attachment to the idea that a human being is entitled to financial privacy. It is the problem of foreign countries if they cannot tax their citizens. We in Switzerland don't have to help other countries do their job.'

This poses a serious problem for the EU - not just because the alpine jurisdiction is home an estimated one third of the world's offshore wealth, but because other countries, in particular Luxembourg and Austria, have said that they will refuse to back information exchange plans if Switzerland does not participate. The EU had set the end of 2002 as the deadline for final adoption of its information exchange plans, but Luxembourg's refusal to accept the Swiss compromise position as acceptable meant that negotiations are set to continue into 2003.

For additional analytical, business and investment opportunities information, please contact Global Investment & Business Center, USA at (703) 370-8082. Fax: (703) 370-8083. E-mail: ibpusa3@gmail.com Global Business and Investment Info Databank - www.ibpus.com

OFFSHORE SERVICE PROVIDERS

LAW FIRMS

▶ Brunschwig Wittmer

| 10 Cours de Rive, P O Box 3054, CH-1211
Geneva 3, Switzerland | Telephone
+41 22 817 4000 | Fax
+41 22 817 4001 |

▶ Jawer SA

| Route de Pré-Bois 20, ICC Building, P O Box
1918 Geneva 15 Airport, CH 1215, Switzerland | Telephone
+41 22 710 9900 | Fax
+41 22 710 9999 |

▶ Manal Consultance AG

| Lavaterstrasse 67, Zurich 8002, Switzerland | Telephone
+41 1 201 3832 | Fax
+41 1 201 3834 |

▶ Rickenbach & Partner

| Schlossbergstrasse 22
CH-8702 Zollikon-Zurich, Switzerland | Telephone
+41 1 391 4477 | Fax
+41 1 391 7735 |

COMPANY FORMATION AND SHIP REGISTRATION

▶ AAMIL

| 8 Place du Bourg-de-Four, P O Box 3627, CH
1211 Geneva 3, Switzerland | Telephone
+41 22 818 6100 | Fax
+41 22 818 6101 |

▶ ABN AMRO Trust Company (Suisse) SA

| Rue du Rhone 80, P O Box 3768, CH-1204
Geneva, Switzerland | Telephone
+41 22 310 8319 | Fax
+41 22 310 8321 |

▶ CITCO (Suisse) SA

| Haus Zum Schwert, Weinplatz 10
8001 Zurich, Switzerland | Telephone
+41 1 226 8210 | Fax
+41 1 226 8220 |

▶ Credit Suisse Trust

| Bleicherweg 33, P O Box 656, 8027 Zurich 2, Switzerland | Telephone
+41 1 204 2828 | Fax
+41 1 204 2929 |

▶ Experta -BIL

| 65 rue du Rhone, P O Box 3038, 1211 Geneva 3 | Telephone
+41 22 787 5858 | Fax
+41 22 787 5868 |

Switzerland

▶ Ilex Trust Services SA

6 Pl des Eaux-Vives, P O Box 3338 CH-1211 Geneva 3, Switzerland	Telephone +41 22 849 8340	Fax +41 22 786 1846

▶ Morgan & Morgan Corporation Services SA

63 rue de Lausanne, P O Box 2565 CH-1211 Geneva 2, Switzerland	Telephone +41 22 738 0630	Fax +41 22 738 7321

▶ Multifiduciaire Geneve SA

1 Carrefour de Rive, Case Postale CH-1204 Geneva 3, Switzerland	Telephone +41 22 786 2650	Fax +41 22 786 5890

▶ Radcliffes Trustee Company Limited

12 rue de l'Arquebuse CH-1204 Geneva, Switzerland	Telephone +41 22 807 2000	Fax +41 22 807 2005

▶ Thalmann Consulta Services SA

Place Issac Mercier No 3, P O Box 2257 CH- 1211 Geneva 1, Switzerland	Telephone +41 22 732 4588	Fax +41 22 732 2927

▶ Von Sury Trust Limited

Spalentorweg 20, P O Box 109 CH-4009 Basel, Switzerland	Telephone +41 61 269 2020	Fax +41 61 269 2000

TRUST MANAGEMENT

▶ AAMIL

8 Place du Bourg-de Four, P O Box 3627, CH- 1211 Geneva 3, Switzerland	Telephone +41 22 818 6100	Fax +41 22 818 6101

▶ ABN AMRO Trust Company (Suisse) SA

Rue du Rhone 80, P O Box 3768, CH-1204 Geneva, Switzerland	Telephone +41 22 310 8319	Fax +41 22 310 8321

▶ Ansbacher (Switzerland) Ltd

Mühlebachstrasse 54, CH-8032 Zurich, Switzerland	Telephone +41 1 252 1155	Fax +41 1 251 4581

▶ Bank Julius Baer & Co Ltd

P O Box, CH-8010 Zurich, Switzerland	Telephone + 41 1 228 5111	Fax +41 1 211 2560

▶ Bittiner Whitehouse & Cie S.A.

PO Box 5132, CH-1211, Geneva 11 Switzerland	Telephone + 41 22 328 8390	Fax +41 22 328 6485

▶ CITCO (Suisse) SA

Haus Zum Schwert, Weinplatz 10 8001 Zurich, Switzerland	Telephone + 41 1 226 8210	Fax +41 1 226 8220

▶ Coutts & Co (Trustees) SA

13 Quai de l'ille, Case postale 5511 CH-1211 Geneva 11, Switzerland	Telephone +41 22 319 0101	Fax +41 22 319 0102

▶ Credit Suisse Trust

Bleicherweg 33, P O Box 656, 8027 Zurich 2, Switzerland	Telephone +41 1 204 2828	Fax +41 1 204 2929

▶ EPS Finance Ltd

Bahnhofstr 46, Postfach, Zurich 8021, Switzerland	Telephone +41 1 212 7474	Fax +41 1 212 7484

▶ Experta -BIL

65 rue du Rhone, P O Box 3038, 1211 Geneva 3 Switzerland	Telephone +41 22 787 5858	Fax +41 22 787 5868

▶ Ilex Trust Services SA

6 Pl des Eaux-Vives, P O Box 3338 CH-1211 Geneva 3, Switzerland	Telephone +41 22 849 8340	Fax +41 22 786 1846

▶ Intertrust Management SA

16 Rue de la Pélisserie, CH-1211 Geneva Switzerland	Telephone +41 22 317 8000	Fax +41 22 317 8011

▶ MeesPierson (Suisse) SA

Route de Malagnou 6, P O Box 140,	Telephone	Fax

For additional analytical, business and investment opportunities information, please contact Global Investment & Business Center, USA at (703) 370-8082. Fax: (703) 370-8083. E-mail: ibpusa3@gmail.com Global Business and Investment Info Databank - www.ibpus.com

CH-1211 Geneva 17, Switzerland	+41 22 839 4400	+41 22 839 4434

▶ MeesPierson Trust (Schweiz)AG

Alpenstrasse 15, P O Box 4620 CH-6304 Zug, Switzerland	Telephone +41 41 726 8200	Fax +41 41 726 8250

▶ New World Trust Corporation

16 rue de la Pelisserie, CP 3501 CH-1211 Geneva 3, Switzerland	Telephone +41 22 317 7373	Fax +41 22 317 7383

▶ Radcliffes Trustee Company Limited

12 rue de l'Arquebuse CH-1204 Geneva, Switzerland	Telephone +41 22 807 2000	Fax +41 22 807 2005

▶ Rathbone Trust Company SA

P O Box 2049, 1 Place de Saint-Gervaise CH- 1211 Geneva 1, Switzerland	Telephone +41 22 909 8900	Fax +41 22 909 8939

▶ RNB Trust Company AG

Rue du Rhone 92, Case Postale 3580 CH-1211 Geneva 3, Switzerland	Telephone +41 1 22 705 5705	Fax +41 22 705 5755

▶ Societe Financiere de l'Etoile

2 boulevard Jaques-Dalcroze, CH-1204 Geneva Switzerland	Telephone +41 22 318 4830	Fax +41 22 310 1592

▶ Thalmann Consulta Services SA

Place Issac Mercier No 3, P O Box 2257 CH- 1211 Geneva 1, Switzerland	Telephone +41 22 732 4588	Fax +41 22 732 2927

▶ Trident Corporate Services SA

Zunikerstrasse 18, P O Box 85 8702 Zollikon- Zurich, Switzerland	Telephone +41 1 392 0350	Fax +41 1 392 0355

▶ Valmet

1 Rue des Moulins, P O Box 5740 CH-1211 Geneva 11, Switzerland	Telephone +41 22 819 9000	Fax +41 22 819 9090

For additional analytical, business and investment opportunities information,
please contact Global Investment & Business Center, USA
at (703) 370-8082. Fax: (703) 370-8083. E-mail: ibpusa3@gmail.com
Global Business and Investment Info Databank - www.ibpus.com

▶ Von Sury Trust Limited

Spalentorweg 20, P O Box 109 CH-4009 Basel, Switzerland	Telephone +41 61 269 2020	Fax +41 61 269 2000

BANKING SERVICES AND ASSET MANAGEMENT

▶ Bank Julius Baer & Co Ltd

P O Box, CH-8010 Zurich, Switzerland	Telephone +41 1 228 5111	Fax +41 1 211 2560

▶ Bank Sarasin & Co

Elisabethenstrasse 62, CH-4002 Basel, Switzerland	Telephone +41 61 277 7777	Fax +41 61 277 7730

▶ Bank von Ernst & Cie AG

Marktgasse 63/61, CH-3001 Bern, Switzerland	Telephone +41 31 329 1111	Fax +41 31 311 6391

▶ Coutts & Co (Trustees) SA

13 Quai de l'ille, Case postale 5511 CH-1211 Geneva 11, Switzerland	Telephone +41 22 319 0101	Fax +41 22 319 0102

▶ EFG Private Bank SA

Bahnhofstrasse 16, P O Box 5216, 8022 Zurich Switzerland	Telephone +41 1 226 1717	Fax +41 1 226 1726

▶ Experta -BIL

65 rue du Rhone, P O Box 3038, 1211 Geneva 3 Switzerland	Telephone + 41 22 787 5858	Fax +41 22 787 5868

▶ IAM - Investment Asset Management SA

15 Rue de la Confederation, CP 3788 1211 Geneva 3, Switzerland	Telephone +41 22 818 3640	Fax +41 22 310 5557

▶ MeesPierson (Suisse) SA

Route de Malagnou 6, P O Box 140, CH-1211 Geneva 17, Switzerland	Telephone +41 22 839 4400	Fax +41 22 839 4434

▶ Societe Financiere de l'Etoile

2 boulevard Jaques-Dalcroze, CH-	Telephone	Fax

| 1204 Geneva Switzerland | +41 22 318 4830 | +41 22 310 1592 |

▶ Thalmann Consulta Services SA

| Place Issac Mercier No 3, P O Box 2257 CH- 1211 Geneva 1, Switzerland | Telephone +41 22 732 4588 | Fax +41 22 732 2927 |

▶ Treuco Treuhand-Gesellschaft

| Claridenstrasse 25, P O Box 562 Zurich 8027, Switzerland | Telephone +41 1 289 2525 | Fax +41 1 289 2550 |

▶ Union Bancaire Privee

| 96-98 rue du Rhone, CH-1204 Geneva, Switzerland | Telephone +41 22 819 2111 | Fax +41 22 819 2200 |

ISP HOSTING AND E-COMMERCE SERVICE PROVIDERS

▶ Sellys

| 28, Rue du Marche 1204 Geneva, Switzerland | Telephone +41 22 8173 767 | Fax +41 22 8173 768 |

SWISS COMPANY BY FOREIGN NATIONALS

Increasingly, therefore want to entrepreneurs with foreign nationality in Switzerland to operate independently. On the following pages you will find the conditions for personal and company formation as well as the main information about the companies located in Switzerland. On the following pages you will find the conditions for personal and company information as well as the main information about the companies located in Switzerland.

In Switzerland, for the admission of foreign workers a dual system. In Switzerland, for the admission of foreign workers a dual system employed workers from the EU / EFTA may differ from the free movement of persons to benefit. Employed workers from the EU / EFTA may differ from the free movement of persons to benefit.

For all other states are only a limited amount of well-qualified admitted. For all other states are only a limited amount of well-qualified admitted.
All citizens of EU / EFTA - still with the exception of Romania and Bulgaria - have in principle the right to freely in Switzerland to live and work. All citizens of EU / EFTA - still with the exception of Romania and Bulgaria - have in principle the right to freely in Switzerland to live and work. That is, they can also self-employed. That is, they can also self-employed.

Further information can be found in the sub-heading "Persons from the EU-/EFTA-Raum».
Further information can be found in the sub-heading "Persons from the EU-/EFTA-Raum».

Persons from the EU-/EFTA-Raum Persons from the EU-/EFTA-Raum

-- ----------------------------

Entrepreneurs from countries which are not from the EU / EFTA region originate in Switzerland, and self-employed want to be in Switzerland prevailing labor market demands (ANAG guidelines) requirements. Entrepreneurs from countries which are not from the EU / EFTA region originate in Switzerland, and self-employed want to be in Switzerland prevailing labor market demands (ANAG guidelines) requirements.

Further information can be found in the sub-heading "people from third countries." Further information can be found in the sub-heading "people from third countries."
Persons from third persons from third countries

Cross-border commuters from EU / EFTA in Switzerland can start a business and be self-employed. Cross-border commuter from EU / EFTA in Switzerland can start a business and be self-employed. For them, the same conditions as for EU-/EFTA-Staatsbürgerinnen and citizens. For them, the same conditions as for EU-/EFTA-Staatsbürgerinnen and citizens.

On third-country nationals, a frontier permit be granted only if such a right of permanent residence in a neighboring country of Switzerland and also have at least 6 months in a foreign border zone resident. On third-country nationals, a frontier permit be granted only if such a right of permanent residence in a Neighboring country of Switzerland and also have at least 6 months in a foreign border zone resident. Based on the free movement of these cross-border commuters a week at their residence abroad to return. Based on the free movement of these cross-border commuter a week at their residence abroad to return.

Requirements for person
Cross-border commuters from EU-EFTA States cross-border commuter from EU-EFTA

Cross-border commuters in Switzerland can start a business and be self employed. Cross-border commuter in Switzerland can start a business and be self-employed. The Swiss authorities must demonstrate that a self-employed in Switzerland may be exercised. The Swiss authorities must demonstrate that a self-employed in Switzerland may be exercised. This can be done through the submission of relevant documents such as business firms, in the commercial application, opening an office or workshop, the establishment of the firm, accounting, etc. happen. This can be done through the submission of relevant documents such as business firms, in the commercial application, opening an office or workshop, the establishment of the firm, accounting, etc. happen. Accurate information about the requested evidence obtained from the cantonal migration offices. Accurate information about the requested evidence obtained from the cantonal migration offices.

After providing proof that the independence can succeed, a cross-border commuter permit G EG / EFTA for 5 years. After providing proof that the independence can succeed, a cross-border commuter permit G EG / EFTA for 5 years. In addition, the procedure is similar to that of the persons from EU / EFTA countries living in Switzerland. In addition, the procedure is similar to that of the persons from EU / EFTA countries living in Switzerland.

Most cross-border commuters who work in Switzerland, are members of EU and EFTA states and therefore fall under the personal scope of freedom of movement agreement. Most cross-border commuter who work in Switzerland, are members of EU and EFTA states and therefore fall under the personal scope of freedom of movement agreement.

Previously existing conditions as a Voraufenthalt six months in the border region are foreign to these people disappeared. Previously existing conditions as a Voraufenthalt six months in the border region are foreign to these people disappeared. Also, the full professional and geographical mobility. So, the full professional and geographical mobility. Place, occupation, work can be freely changed. Place, occupation, work can be freely changed. There must be no longer a day, but only once a week at the residence abroad will be returned. There must be no longer a day, but only once a week at the residence abroad will be returned.

For the 8 Central and Eastern European EU Member States, which at 2004 on the EU joined, apply until May 2011, the labor market restrictions on workers. For the 8 Central and Eastern European EU Member States, which at 2004 on the EU joined, apply until May 2011, the labor market restrictions on workers. This is in advance of national priority and the control of wages and working conditions. This is in advance of national priority and the control of wages and working conditions. The national priority is the statutory scheme that foreigners from the countries concerned in Switzerland only have a work permit if the job does not already included in the Swiss labor market integrated person can be found. The national priority is the statutory scheme that foreigners from the countries concerned in Switzerland only have a work permit if the job does not already included in the Swiss labor market integrated person can be found. Frontier workers from these countries are still at the border zones bound a certain Voraufenthalt is not necessary. Frontier workers from these countries are still at the border zones bound a certain Voraufenthalt is not necessary.

Frontier workers from third countries (Nicht-EU-/EFTA-Staaten) Frontier workers from third countries (Nicht-EU-/EFTA-Staaten)

On third-country nationals, a frontier permit be granted only if such a right of permanent residence in a neighboring country of Switzerland and also have at least 6 months in a foreign border zone resident. On third-country nationals, a frontier permit be granted only if such a right of permanent residence in a Neighboring country of Switzerland and also have at least 6 months in a foreign border zone resident. Based on the free movement of persons must be cross-border commuters a week at their residence abroad to return. Based on the free movement of persons must be cross-border commuter a week at their residence abroad to return.

Otherwise similar to the procedure for acquiring their own frontier than the persons from third countries with residence in Switzerland. Otherwise similar to the procedure for acquiring their own frontier than the persons from third countries with residence in Switzerland.
Requirements for Company Formation Requirements for Company Formation
The following nationality, residence rules and requirements apply to the following formation of a nationality, residence rules and requirements apply to the formation of a
Single Company Individual Company
The sole proprietorship is the sole property of the company's owner. The sole proprietorship is the sole property of the company's owner. Accordingly, the labor requirements of the person. Accordingly, the labor requirements of the person. In principle, to work in Switzerland, a residence and work permits are available. In principle, to work in Switzerland, a residence and work permits are available.

Collective and Collective and commandite commandite
The collective and limited partnerships are considered primarily as a small, highly personal form of enterprise. The collective and limited partnerships are considered primarily as a small, highly personal form of enterprise. The partnership is the involvement of external not actively involved in the management investors. The partnership is the involvement of external not actively involved in the management investors. Accordingly, the natural persons for the labor provisions of the person with a valid residence and work permit. Accordingly, the natural persons for the labor provisions of the person with a valid residence and work permit.

Limited liability company (GmbH) Limited liability company (GmbH)
The limited liability company (GmbH) as a legal person must be at least represented by a person, should be able to reside in Switzerland. The limited liability company (GmbH) as a legal person must be at least represented by a person, should be able to reside in Switzerland. This may be the CEO or a director. This may be the CEO or a director. Accordingly, this person must have these people for Switzerland valid residence and work permit have. Accordingly, this person must have for Switzerland thesepeoplecomedy valid residence and work permit have.

Aktiengesellschaft (AG) Aktiengesellschaft (AG)
In stock, as a legal person must be a representative of the AG authorized person residing in Switzerland. In stock, as a legal person must be a representative of the AG authorized person residing in Switzerland. Accordingly, this person must be one for the valid Switzerland residence and work permit have. Accordingly, this person must be one for the valid Switzerland residence and work permit have.
Siting Siting
Companies have widely differing demands on their ideal company headquarters. Companies have widely differing demands on their ideal company headquarters. To ease the burden of choice, it makes sense to evaluate potential business locations after ten to twenty fundamental criteria. To ease the burden of choice, it makes sense to evaluate potential business locations after ten to twenty fundamental criteria.

Critical factors in the choice of location are critical factors in site selection are:
Amount of corporate taxes and any tax breaks amount of corporate taxes and any tax relief

Regular contact and exchange with universities and research institutions Regular contact and exchange with universities and research institutions

Importance and value of traffic connections (road, air, rail) Importance and value of traffic connections (road, air, rail)

Number and frequency of travel abroad by plane number and frequency of foreign travel by plane

Importance of customer and / or suppliers near Importance of customer and / or suppliers close

Needs of space / area, eg for a production facility Needs of space / area, eg for a production plant

Budget for the budget office for office space

Standard office equipment, standard office equipment

Distance between home and work Distance between home and work

Parking needs parking needs

Rural region or urban environment, urban or rural region environment
(Source: www.greaterzuricharea.ch) (Source: www.greaterzuricharea.ch)
Land Purchase Land Purchase
Frontier may, in Switzerland, both secondary as well as real estate, the practice is intended to buy. Frontier may, in Switzerland, both secondary as well as real estate, the practice is intended to buy. They have the same rights as Swiss citizens (national treatment). They have the same rights as Swiss citizens (national treatment). With Frontier may also permit an apartment in

Switzerland buy. With Frontier may also permit an apartment in Switzerland buy. If a frontier to Switzerland, he bought the property does not sell. If a frontier to Switzerland, he bought the property does not sell.

In connection with property and land purchases / sales tax due the following: In connection with property and land purchases / sales tax due the following:
Land-tax profit: 0.3 to 3 ‰ land-tax profit: 0.3 to 3 ‰

Change hands for real estate tax (depending on the Canton partially removed): 1-3% change hands for real estate tax (depending on the Canton partially removed): 1-3%
Taxes for individuals tax for natural persons
Income taxes in Switzerland, both by the federal government (federal tax), as well as by the cantons and municipalities (state and municipal taxes) will be charged. Income taxes in Switzerland, both by the federal government (federal tax), as well as by the Cantons and municipalities (state and municipal taxes) will be charged. Since each of the 26 cantons has its own tax laws, the tax burden in the individual cantons. Since each of the 26 Cantons has its own tax laws, the tax burden in the individual Cantons. In principle, taxpayers an annual tax return form. In principle, taxpayers an annual tax return form Based on this, the tax factors (income and assets) is determined and the taxes set. Based on this, the tax factors (income and assets) is determined and the taxes set.

Foreign workers, the foreign police establishment permit C do not possess, in Switzerland, however, tax domicile or residence, for their income from salaried employment tax credits at the source subject, ie the taxes from the employer directly deducted from the salary (tax). Foreign workers, the foreign policy establishment permit C do not possess, in Switzerland, however, tax domicile or residence, for their income from Salaried employment tax credits at the source subject, ie the taxes from the employer directly deducted from the salary (tax) . The tax is normally paid. The tax is normally paid.

According to tax law (Section 94) shall be persons without a residence permit for income from self-employed pay no tax. According to tax law (Section 94) shall be persons without a residence permit for income from self-employed pay no income tax are using this tax to be declared, so as for an established alien or a Swiss citizen (see the Federal Law on Direct Federal Tax , Part Four: taxes for natural persons and legal entities). This means income tax return to declare, that is established like an alien or a Swiss citizen (see the Federal Law on Direct Federal Tax, Part Four: taxes for natural persons and legal entities).

The avoidance of international double taxation is by inter-governmental agreements. The avoidance of international double taxation is by inter-governmental agreements. Switzerland has almost 100 countries, including almost all Western industrialized countries, such an agreement. Switzerland has almost 100 countries, including almost all Western industrialized countries, such an agreement. Country-specific details from the respective apparent agreement (see the double taxation law and overview of double taxation agreements). Country-specific details from the respective apparent agreement (see the double taxation law and overview of double taxation agreements).

Corporate Taxes Corporate Taxes
Companies are at their place of value creation, ie at the company headquarters or at the place of economic activity. In comparison, corporate taxes are low in Switzerland. In the country of the tax as a percentage of company profits, Switzerland, with an average of 21.3% (as of 2006) to Rank 2 behind Ireland (12.5%) and Sweden (28%). Companies are at their place of value creation, ie at the company headquarters or at the place of economic activities. In comparison, corporate taxes are low in Switzerland. In the country of the tax as a percentage of company profits, Switzerland, with an average of 21.3% (as of 2006) to Rank 2 behind Ireland (12.5%) and Sweden (28%). The

For additional analytical, business and investment opportunities information,
please contact Global Investment & Business Center, USA
at (703) 370-8082. Fax: (703) 370-8083. E-mail: ibpusa3@gmail.com
Global Business and Investment Info Databank - www.ibpus.com

total tax burden including the benefits for social security is less than 30% of gross domestic product (GDP). The total tax burden including the benefits for social security is less than 30% of gross domestic product (GDP).

The federal tax is a flat rate, the cantonal tax rates vary according to location and partly to the amount of capital or profit. The federal tax is a flat rate, the cantonal tax rates vary according to location and partly to the amount of capital or profit. The regular tax rate on the direct federal tax is 8.5%. The regular tax rate on the direct federal tax is 8.5%. Since the taxes on the profit after taxes are calculated, results in an effective tax rate of 7.83%. Since the taxes on the profit after taxes are calculated, results in an effective tax rate of 7.83%.

The current rates are moving in the following sizes (appr. data): The current rates are moving in the following sizes (appr. data):
Direct federal taxes on income 7.83% (effective rate) Direct federal taxes on income 7.83% (effective rate)

Cantonal and communal income tax: 8-17% Cantonal and Communal income tax: 8-17%

Cantonal and communal capital tax: 0.08 to 0.25% Cantonal and communal capital tax: 0.08 to 0.25%
That makes for a regular company tax burden of total 16 to 25%. That makes for a regular company tax burden of total 16 to 25%.
Tax optimization Tax optimization
Tax optimization, companies can significantly lower rates of up to less than 10% realized. Tax optimization, companies can significantly lower rates of up to 10% less than realized. According to position the cantonal economic development organizations and also try new tax benefits to businesses in their area offering. According to position the cantonal economic development organizations and also try new tax benefits to businesses in their area offering. This allows companies such as from the tax authorities a binding preliminary decision on the effective tax received (Tax Ruling). This allows companies such as from the tax authorities a binding preliminary decision on the effective tax received (Tax Ruling). Tax exemption is also depending on the location and type of activity for a limited period. Tax exemption is also depending on the location and type of activity for a limited period. Focal point in any case, the cantonal economic development agencies. Focal point in any case, the cantonal economic development agencies.

Corporate taxes are depending on the chosen form of operation in varying degrees affect. Corporate taxes are depending on the chosen form of operation in varying degrees affect. Characteristic are Characteristic are the
Operating companies

Holding Companies Holding Companies

Swiss branches of a company based abroad. Swiss branches of a company based abroad.

The Economic Development organization Greater Zurich Area is an excellent example of possible tax optimization models for three models: the economic development organization Greater Zurich Area is an excellent example of possible tax optimization models for three models:
Mixed Company (company coordinates its activities in Switzerland and is mainly abroad) Mixed Company (company coordinates its activities in Switzerland and is mainly abroad)

Principal company (business risks, assets and decision-makers in Switzerland) Principal company (business risks, assets and decision-makers in Switzerland)

Holding company (company holds majority stakes) holding company (company holds a majority

shareholding)
VAT VAT
Switzerland has by far the lowest VAT in Europe. Switzerland has by far the lowest VAT in
Europe. The normal rate is 7.6%. The normal rate is 7.6%. Hotels will be 3.5%, goods of daily
needs with only 2.4% tax. Hotels will be 3.5%, goods of daily needs with only 2.4% tax Other
goods and services such as health care and education, are exempt from VAT. Other goods and
services such as healthcare and education, are exempt from VAT.
Framework conditions
Switzerland Switzerland as a location as a location
Geographic and economic factors influence the choice of location for a corporate relocation
considerably. Geographic and economic factors influence the choice of location for a corporate
relocation considerably. The geostrategic position of Switzerland and its federal structure made
the country a meeting place of different cultures and languages. The geostrategic position of
Switzerland and its federal structure made the country a meeting place of different cultures and
languages. Long-term, stable decision-making, liberal legislation, protection of free competition
and cooperative authorities encourage the establishment of companies or operations and
research facilities. Long-term, stable decision-making, liberal legislation, protection of free
competition and cooperative authorities encourage the establishment of companies or operations
and research facilities.

Switzerland is in the international comparison a leading space. Switzerland is in the international
comparison a leading space. It is one of the countries with the longest working hours, the majority
of valid patents per capita, the highest per capita spending for Science, Research and Education
and the largest foreign share of the gross domestic product. It is one of the countries with the
longest working hours, the majority of valid patents per capita, the highest per capita spending for
Science, Research and Education and the largest foreign share of the gross domestic product.

Economy Economy
The Swiss economy owes its high level of development of both the industriousness and ingenuity
of their population as well as the close relations with foreign countries. The Swiss economy owes
its high level of development of both the Ingenuity and industriousness of its people as well as the
close relations with foreign countries. The competitive pressure, political stability, sound public
finances, low capital costs and high purchasing power stability to ensure present and future
growth. The competitive pressure, political stability, sound public finances, low capital costs and
high purchasing power stability to ensure present and future growth.

High gross domestic product: The Swiss economy is most competitive in the world (ranked 1) and
is among the most globalized countries (rank 2). High gross domestic product: The Swiss
economy is most competitive in the world (ranked 1) and is among the most globalized countries
(rank 2). The gross domestic product (GDP) per capita is one of approximately CHF 61'000 .-
(U.S. $ 49'000 .-) are among the highest in the world. The gross domestic product (GDP) per
capita is one of approximately CHF 61'000 .- (U.S. $ 49'000 .-) are among the highest in the
world.

Depth unemployment rate - high employment rate: Switzerland has 57% with one of the highest
employment rates in the world. Depth unemployment rate - high employment rate: Switzerland
has 57% with one of the highest employment rates in the world. The unemployment rate is
among the lowest in Europe. The unemployment rate is among the lowest in Europe.

Strong Swiss franc: Switzerland is not a member of the EU and has its own stable currency, the
Swiss franc (CHF). Strong Swiss franc: Switzerland is not a member of the EU and has its own
stable currency, the Swiss franc (CHF). The euro is widely accepted as payment. The euro is

For additional analytical, business and investment opportunities information,
please contact Global Investment & Business Center, USA
at (703) 370-8082. Fax: (703) 370-8083. E-mail: ibpusa3@gmail.com
Global Business and Investment Info Databank - www.ibpus.com

widely accepted as payment.

Strong service sector and new technologies: The most important economic sector in Switzerland is the service sector. Strong service sector and new technologies: The most important economic sector in Switzerland is the service sector. Almost three-quarters of all employees in services generate 70% of GDP. Almost three-quarters of all employees in services generate 70% of GDP. An important pillar in the service sector is the financial center of Zurich. An important pillar in the service sector is the financial center of Zurich.

Approximately one third of the population works in trade and industry, which together account for nearly one quarter of the GDP. Approximately one third of the population works in trade and industry, which together account for nearly one quarter of the GDP. Especially in the medical and biotechnology, micro-, nano-and high-tech industry and in telecommunications technology (ICT) are the major educational inputs of the Federal universities, polytechnics, and the combination of school and teaching profession to bear. Especially in the medical and biotechnology, micro-, nano-and high-tech industry and in telecommunications technology (ICT) are the major educational inputs of the Federal universities, polytechnics, and the combination of school and teaching professionals to bear.

Agriculture has only marginal economic importance. Agriculture has only marginal economic importance. However, it is important for Switzerland because it helps to preserve the natural landscape and rural structures beyond the metropolitan areas to be preserved. However, it is important for Switzerland because it helps to preserve the natural landscape and rural structures beyond the metropolitan areas to be preserved.

Foreign trade: Switzerland is the world's goods exports to No.21 Foreign trade: Switzerland is the world's goods exports to No.21 in 2005 the Swiss exports to CHF 158 billion, while imports amounted to CHF 155 billion. In 2005 the Swiss exports to CHF 158 billion, while imports amounted to CHF 155 billion. Four-fifths of all imported goods and almost two thirds of exports of Switzerland is in the trade with the EU. Four-fifth of all imported goods and almost two-thirds of exports of Switzerland is in the trade with the EU. Germany is traditionally the most important customer and also the largest supplier of Switzerland. Germany is traditionally the most important customer and also the largest supplier of Switzerland.

Access to 500 million consumers in the markets of the EU and the EFTA countries is close and good co-operation ensured. Access to 500 million consumers in the markets of the EU and the EFTA countries is close and good co-operation ensured. Besides free trade agreements with nearly 100 countries, Switzerland has the WTO Agreement on Government Procurement signed. Besides free trade agreements with nearly 100 countries, Switzerland has the WTO Agreement on Government Procurement signed. Thus, Switzerland, the main markets by entities of government in the EU, U.S., Canada, Japan, Korea, Norway and Israel. Thus, Switzerland, the main markets by entities of government in the EU, U.S., Canada, Japan, Korea, Norway and Israel.

Infrastructure Infrastructure
The infrastructure of Switzerland is among the world's most developed and reliable. The infrastructure of Switzerland is among the world's most developed and reliable. A highly developed IT infrastructure and advanced technological tools offer optimum conditions for the development of new technologies. A highly developed IT infrastructure and advanced technological tools offer optimum conditions for the development of new technologies. On the property are sufficient supply of land and buildings for economic activities. On the property are

For additional analytical, business and investment opportunities information, please contact Global Investment & Business Center, USA at (703) 370-8082. Fax: (703) 370-8083. E-mail: ibpusa3@gmail.com Global Business and Investment Info Databank - www.ibpus.com

sufficient supply of land and buildings for economic activities. The restriction of land ownership by foreign nationals in recent years largely eased. The restriction of land ownership by foreign nationals in recent years largely eased.

Laboratory workers
Well-trained workforce is a prerequisite for any successful business. Well-trained workforce is a prerequisite for any successful business. The overall productivity of the Swiss economy is in a global comparison ranks 5th The overall productivity of the Swiss economy is in a global comparison ranks 5th, the workforce is motivated and strikes are virtually unknown. The workers are highly motivated and strikes are virtually unknown. Although salaries seem relatively high, the total labor costs significantly lower than in competing countries. Although salaries seem relatively high, the total labor costs significantly lower than in competing countries. Non-wage costs and social costs are low. Non-wage costs and social costs are low.

Market Market
From Switzerland can be both the Swiss and the European market is an ideal process. From Switzerland can be both the Swiss and the European market is an ideal process. A branch in Switzerland will grant access to a domestic market of 7 million consumers with the highest purchasing power. A branch in Switzerland wants to grant access to a domestic market of 7 million consumers with the highest purchasing power. But the European market (500 million consumers) can be from Switzerland ideally open and edit. But the European market (500 million consumers) can be from Switzerland ideally open and edit this reason, many international companies of various industries for their main office, foreign branch or service center to Switzerland. That's why many international companies of various industries for their main office, foreign branch or service center to Switzerland.

PERSONS FROM THE EU-/EFTA

How can a person from the EU-/EFTA-Raum in Switzerland set up a business? Below the main legal requirements, background information and tips for foreign entrepreneurs who EU-/EFTA-Raum from the stem. Below the main legal requirements, background information and tips for foreign entrepreneurs who come from the EU-/EFTA-Raum.

Requirements Requirements for person to person
All citizens of EU / EFTA - still with the exception of Romania and Bulgaria - have in principle the right to freely in Switzerland to live and work. All citizens of EU / EFTA - still with the exception of Romania and Bulgaria - have in principle the right to freely in Switzerland to live and work. That is, they can also self-employed. That is, they can also self-employed.

According to the Free Movement of Persons Agreement may be an independent contractor without a permanent residence permit (C permit) to act. According to the Free Movement Of Persons Agreement may be an independent contractor without a permanent residence permit (C permit) to act. The 5-year-old B-Aufenthaltsbewilligung enough to do so. The 5-year-old B-Aufenthaltsbewilligung enough to do so. When logging in Switzerland, but he planned his own business can. When logging in Switzerland, but he planned his own business can. This can, for example, with the dissolved VAT registration number, an entry in a professional register, the registration with a social security than self-employed respondents, a business plan, the accounting numbers or the entry in the Commercial happen. This can, for example, with the Dissolved VAT registration number, an entry in a professional register, the registration with a social security than self-employed respondents, a business plan, the accounting numbers or the entry in the Commercial happen. Accurate information about the requested evidence obtained from the cantonal migration offices. Accurate information about the requested evidence obtained from the cantonal migration offices.

A residence permit B EC / EFTA for self-employment, in a first step for 5 years and includes the

For additional analytical, business and investment opportunities information, please contact Global Investment & Business Center, USA at (703) 370-8082. Fax: (703) 370-8083. E-mail: ibpusa3@gmail.com Global Business and Investment Info Databank - www.ibpus.com

full geographical and occupational mobility. A residence permit B EC / EFTA for self-employment, in a first step for 5 years and includes the full geographical and occupational mobility. EU companies can Mende in Switzerland both their residence and workplace as well as change their profession. EU companies can Mende in Switzerland both their residence and workplace as well as change their profession.

Similarly, a change from dependent to self-activity is possible. Similarly, a change from dependent to self-activity is possible. Before 31 Before May 31, 2007 this was still a new residence permit is necessary. May 2007 was for a new residence permit is necessary. Today, the same permit to be maintained. Today, the same permit to be maintained.

If the motion fails to independence and the Mende of corporate welfare is dependent, is also deprived of the right of residence. If the motion fails to independence and the Mende of corporate welfare is dependent, is also deprived of the right of residence. Obviously you can but then someone a job as a salaried employee search. Obviously you can but then someone a job as a Salaried Employees search.

Furthermore, a change from independence to the general grant employees must be persons from the 2004 Eastern Europe which joined EU member states (Hungary, Poland, Czech Republic, Slovakia, Estonia, Latvia, Lithuania and Slovenia). Furthermore, a change from independence to the general grant employees must be persons from the 2004 Eastern Europe which joined EU member states (Hungary, Poland, Czech Republic, Slovakia, Estonia, Latvia, Lithuania and Slovenia). These rules apply until 2011. These rules apply until the 2011th

The would-be self-employed entrepreneurs will be free, in which division he wants to be active. The would-be self-employed entrepreneurs will be free, in which division he wants to be active. The only restriction there is regarding the regulated professions. The only restriction there is regarding the regulated professions.
Requirement for firms founded Founded on the condition
The following nationality, residence rules and requirements apply to entrepreneurs from the EU / EFTA region establishing a The following nationality, rooidonoo rules and requirements apply to entrepreneurs from the EU / EFTA region establishing an
Single Company Individual Company
The sole proprietorship is the sole property of the company's owner. The sole proprietorship is the sole property of the company's owner. Accordingly, the labor requirements of the person. Accordingly, the labor requirements of the person. In principle, to work in Switzerland, a residence and work permits are available. In principle, to work in Switzerland, a residence and work permits are available.

Collective and Collective and commandite commandite
The collective and limited partnerships are considered primarily as a small, highly personal form of enterprise. The collective and limited partnerships are considered primarily as a small, highly personal form of enterprise. The partnership is the involvement of external not actively involved in the management investors. The partnership is the involvement of external not actively involved in the management investors. Accordingly, the natural persons for the labor provisions of the person with a valid residence and work permit. Accordingly, the natural persons for the labor provisions of the person with a valid residence and work permit.

Limited liability company (GmbH) Limited liability company (GmbH)
The limited liability company (GmbH) as a legal person must be at least represented by a person that can be domiciled in Switzerland. The limited liability company (GmbH) as a legal person must be at least represented by a person that can be domiciled in Switzerland. This may be the CEO

or a director. This may be the CEO or a director. Accordingly, this person must be one for the valid Switzerland residence and work permit have. Accordingly, this person must be one for the valid Switzerland residence and work permit have.

Aktiengesellschaft (AG) Aktiengesellschaft (AG)
In stock, as a legal person must be a representative of the AG authorized person residing in Switzerland. In stock, as a legal person must be a representative of the AG authorized person residing in Switzerland. Accordingly, this person must be one for the valid Switzerland residence and work permit have. Accordingly, this person must be one for the valid Switzerland residence and work permit have.
Siting Siting
Companies have widely differing demands on their ideal company headquarters. Companies have widely differing demands on their ideal company headquarters. To ease the burden of choice, it makes sense to evaluate potential business locations after ten to twenty fundamental criteria. To ease the burden of choice, it makes sense to evaluate potential business locations after ten to twenty fundamental criteria.

Critical factors in the choice of location are critical factors in site selection are:
Amount of corporate taxes and any tax breaks amount of corporate taxes and any tax relief

Regular contact and exchange with universities and research institutions Regular contact and exchange with universities and research institutions

Importance and value of traffic connections (road, air, rail) Importance and value of traffic connections (road, air, rail)

Number and frequency of travel abroad by plane number and frequency of foreign travel by plane

Importance of customer and / or suppliers near Importance of customer and / or suppliers close

Needs of space / area, eg for a production facility Needs of space / area, eg for a production plant

Budget for the budget office for office space

Standard office equipment, standard office equipment

Distance between home and work Distance between home and work

Parking needs parking needs

Rural region or urban environment, urban or rural region environment
(Source: www.greaterzuricharea.ch) (Source: www.greaterzuricharea.ch)
Land Purchase Land Purchase
For EU citizens, resident in Switzerland are considered the acquisition of property for the same rights as Swiss citizens (national treatment). For EU citizens, resident in Switzerland are considered the acquisition of property for the same rights as Swiss citizens (national treatment). EU-Swiss entrepreneur and principal residence permit abroad at the property purchase only the same rights as Swiss, if the Property of the profession serves. EU-Swiss entrepreneur and principal residence permit abroad at the property purchase only the same rights as Swiss, if the Property of the profession serves. Permit are secondary and vacation homes. Permit are secondary and vacation homes. Someone leaves, Switzerland, has acquired property not be sold again. Someone leaves, Switzerland, has acquired property not be sold again.

The land acquisition for the exercise of an economic activity by a foreign company according to Lex Koller possible without a permit. The land acquisition for the exercise of an economic activity by a foreign company according to Lex Koller possible without a permit. It may, however, in principle, that is, with few exceptions, no miterworben homes, or be built. It may, however, in principle, that is, with few exceptions, no miterworben homes, or be built.

In connection with property and land purchases / sales tax due the following: In connection with property and land purchases / sales tax due the following:
Land-tax profit: 0.3 to 3 ‰ land-tax profit: 0.3 to 3 ‰

Change hands for real estate tax (depending on the Canton partially removed): 1-3% change hands for real estate tax (depending on the Canton partially removed): 1-3%
Taxes for individuals tax for natural persons
Income taxes in Switzerland, both by the federal government (federal tax), as well as by the cantons and municipalities (state and municipal taxes) will be charged. Income taxes in Switzerland, both by the federal government (federal tax), as well as by the Cantons and municipalities (state and municipal taxes) will be charged. Since each of the 26 cantons has its own tax laws, the tax burden in the individual cantons. Since each of the 26 Cantons has its own tax laws, the tax burden in the individual Cantons. In principle, taxpayers an annual tax return form. In principle, taxpayers an annual tax return form Based on this, the tax factors (income and assets) is determined and the taxes set. Based on this, the tax factors (income and assets) is determined and the taxes set.

Foreign workers, the foreign police establishment permit C do not possess, in Switzerland, however, tax domicile or residence, for their income from salaried employment tax credits at the source subject, ie the taxes from the employer directly deducted from the salary (tax). Foreign workers, the foreign policy establishment permit C do not possess, in Switzerland, however, tax domicile or residence, for their Salaried income from employment tax credits at the source subject, ie the taxes from the employer directly deducted from the salary (tax) . The tax liability is usually covered. The tax is normally paid.

According to tax law (Section 94) shall be persons without a residence permit for income from self-employment tax does not. According to tax law (Section 94) shall be persons without a permit residence for income from self-employment tax does not. This means income tax return to declare, that is like an established alien or a Swiss citizen (see the Federal Law on Direct Federal Tax, Part Four: taxes for natural persons and legal entities). This means income tax return to declare, that is established like an alien or a Swiss citizen (see the Federal Law on Direct Federal Tax, Part Four: taxes for natural persons and legal entities).

The avoidance of international double taxation is by inter-governmental agreements. The avoidance of international double taxation is by inter-governmental agreements. Switzerland has almost 100 countries, including almost all Western industrialized countries, such an agreement. Switzerland has almost 100 countries, including almost all Western industrialized countries, such an agreement. Country-specific details from the respective apparent agreement (see the double taxation law and overview of double taxation agreements). Country-specific details from the respective apparent agreement (see the double taxation law and overview of double taxation agreements).

Corporate Taxes Corporate Taxes
Companies are at their place of value creation, ie at the company headquarters or at the place of economic activity. Companies are at their place of value creation, ie at the company headquarters or at the place of economic activity. In comparison, corporate taxes are low in Switzerland. In comparison, corporate taxes are low in Switzerland. In the country of the tax as a percentage of

company profits, Switzerland, with an average of 21.3% (as of 2006) to Rank 2 behind Ireland (12.5%) and Sweden (28%). In the country of the tax as a percentage of company profits, Switzerland, with an average of 21.3% (as of 2006) to Rank 2 behind Ireland (12.5%) and Sweden (28%). The total tax burden including the benefits for social security is less than 30 percent of gross domestic product (GDP). The total tax burden including the benefits for social security is less than 30 percent of gross domestic product (GDP).

The federal tax is a flat rate, the cantonal tax rates vary according to location and partly to the amount of capital or profit. The federal tax is a flat rate, the cantonal tax rates vary according to location and partly to the amount of capital or profit. The regular tax rate on the direct federal tax is 8.5%. The regular tax rate on the direct federal tax is 8.5%. Since the taxes on the profit after taxes are calculated, results in an effective tax rate of 7.83%. Since the taxes on the profit after taxes are calculated, results in an effective tax rate of 7.83%.

The current rates are moving in the following sizes (approximate): The current rates are moving in the following sizes (approximate):
Direct federal taxes on income 7.83% (effective rate) Direct federal taxes on income 7.83% (effective rate)

Cantonal and communal income tax: 8-17% Cantonal and Communal income tax: 8-17%

Cantonal and communal capital tax: 0.08 to 0.25% Cantonal and communal capital tax: 0.08 to 0.25%

That makes for a regular company tax burden of total 16 to 25%. That makes for a regular company tax burden of total 16 to 25%.
Tax optimization Tax optimization
Tax optimization, companies can significantly lower rates of up to less than 10% realized. Tax optimization, companies can significantly lower rates of up to 10% less than realized. According to position the cantonal economic development organizations and also try new tax benefits to businesses in their area offering. According to position the cantonal economic development organizations and also try new tax benefits to businesses in their area offering. This allows companies such as from the tax authorities a binding preliminary decision on the effective tax received (Tax Ruling). This allows companies such as from the tax authorities a binding preliminary decision on the effective tax received (Tax Ruling). Tax exemption is also depending on the location and type of activity for a limited period. Tax exemption is also depending on the location and type of activity for a limited period. Focal point in any case, the cantonal economic development agencies. Focal point in any case, the cantonal economic development agencies.

Corporate taxes are depending on the chosen form of operation in varying degrees affect. Corporate taxes are depending on the chosen form of operation in varying degrees affect. Characteristic are Characteristic are the
Companies, operating,

Holding Companies, Holding Companies

Swiss branches of a company based abroad. Swiss branches of a company based abroad.

The Economic Development organization Greater Zurich Area is an excellent example of possible tax optimization models for three models: the economic development organization Greater Zurich Area is an excellent example of possible tax optimization models for three models:
Mixed Company (company coordinates its activities in Switzerland and is mainly abroad) Mixed Company (company coordinates its activities in Switzerland and is mainly abroad)

For additional analytical, business and investment opportunities information,
please contact Global Investment & Business Center, USA
at (703) 370-8082. Fax: (703) 370-8083. E-mail: ibpusa3@gmail.com
Global Business and Investment Info Databank - www.ibpus.com

Principal company (business risks, assets and decision-makers in Switzerland) Principal company (business risks, assets and decision-makers in Switzerland)

Holding company (company holds majority stakes) holding company (company holds a majority shareholding)

VAT VAT

Switzerland has the lowest VAT in Europe. Switzerland has the lowest VAT in Europe. The normal rate is 7.6%. The normal rate is 7.6%. Hotels will be 3.5%, goods of daily needs only 2.4%. Hotels will be 3.5%, goods of daily needs only 2.4%. Other goods and services such as health care and education, are exempt from VAT. Other goods and services such as healthcare and education, are exempt from VAT.

Framework conditions

Switzerland Switzerland as a location as a location

Geographic and economic factors influence the choice of location for a corporate relocation considerably. Geographic and economic factors influence the choice of location for a corporate relocation considerably. The geostrategic position of Switzerland and its federal structure made the country a meeting place of different cultures and languages. The geostrategic position of Switzerland and its federal structure made the country a meeting place of different cultures and languages. Long-term, stable decision-making, liberal legislation, protection of free competition and cooperative authorities encourage the establishment of companies or operations and research facilities. Long-term, stable decision-making, liberal legislation, protection of free competition and cooperative authorities encourage the establishment of companies or operations and research facilities.

Switzerland is in the international comparison a leading space. Switzerland is in the international comparison a leading space. She is one of the countries with the longest working hours, the majority of valid patents per capita, the highest per capita spending for Science, Research and Education and the largest foreign share of the gross domestic product. It is one of the countries with the longest working hours, the majority of valid patents per capita, the highest per capita spending for Science, Research and Education and the largest foreign share of the gross domestic product.

Economy Economy

The Swiss economy owes its high level of development of both the industriousness and ingenuity of their population as well as the close relations with foreign countries. The Swiss economy owes its high level of development of both the industriousness and Ingenuity of their population as well as the close relations with foreign countries. The competitive pressure, political stability, sound public finances, low capital costs and high purchasing power stability to ensure present and future growth. The competitive pressure, political stability, sound public finances, low capital costs and high purchasing power stability to ensure present and future growth.

High gross domestic product: The Swiss economy is most competitive in the world (ranked 1) and is among the most globalized countries (rank 2). High gross domestic product: The Swiss economy is most competitive in the world (ranked 1) and is among the most globalized countries (rank 2). The gross domestic product (GDP) per capita is one of approximately CHF 61'000 .- (U.S. $ 49'000 .-) are among the highest in the world. The gross domestic product (GDP) per capita is one of approximately CHF 61'000 .- (U.S. $ 49'000 .-) are among the highest in the world.

Depth unemployment rate - high employment rate: Switzerland has 57% with one of the highest

For additional analytical, business and investment opportunities information,
please contact Global Investment & Business Center, USA
at (703) 370-8082. Fax: (703) 370-8083. E-mail: ibpusa3@gmail.com
Global Business and Investment Info Databank - www.ibpus.com

employment rates in the world. Depth unemployment rate - high employment rate: Switzerland has 57% with one of the highest employment rates in the world. The unemployment rate, with 3.1% to the lowest in Europe. The unemployment rate, with 3.1% to the lowest in Europe.

Strong Swiss franc: Switzerland is not a member of the EU and has its own stable currency, the Swiss franc (CHF). Strong Swiss franc: Switzerland is not a member of the EU and has its own stable currency, the Swiss franc (CHF). The euro is widely accepted as payment. The euro is widely accepted as payment.

Strong service sector and new technologies: The most important economic sector in Switzerland is the service sector. Strong service sector and new technologies: The most important economic sector in Switzerland is the service sector. Almost three-quarters of all employees in services generate 70% of GDP. Almost three-quarters of all employees in services generate 70% of GDP. An important pillar in the service sector is the financial center of Zurich. An important pillar in the service sector is the financial center of Zurich.

Approximately one third of the population works in trade and industry, which together account for nearly one quarter of the GDP. Approximately one third of the population works in trade and industry, which together account for nearly one quarter of the GDP. Especially in the medical and biotechnology, micro-, nano-and high-tech industry and in telecommunications technology (ICT) are the major educational inputs of the Federal universities, polytechnics, and the combination of school and teaching profession to bear. Especially in the medical and biotechnology, micro-, nano-and high-tech industry and in telecommunications technology (ICT) are the major educational inputs of the Federal universities, polytechnics, and the combination of school and teaching professionals to bear.

Agriculture has only marginal economic importance. Agriculture has only marginal economic importance. However, it is important for Switzerland because it helps to preserve the natural landscape and rural structures beyond the metropolitan areas to be preserved. However, it is important for Switzerland because it helps to preserve the natural landscape and rural structures beyond the metropolitan areas to be preserved.

Foreign trade: Switzerland is the world's goods exports to No.21 Foreign trade: Switzerland is the world's goods exports to No.21 in 2005 the Swiss exports to CHF 158 billion, while imports amounted to CHF 155 billion. In 2005 the Swiss exports to CHF 158 billion, while imports amounted to CHF 155 billion. Four-fifths of all imported goods and almost two-thirds of exports of Switzerland is in the trade with the EU. Four-fifth of all imported goods and almost two-thirds of exports of Switzerland is in the trade with the EU. Germany is traditionally the most important customer and also the largest supplier of Switzerland. Germany is traditionally the most important customer and also the largest supplier of Switzerland.

Access to 500 million consumers in the markets of the EU and the EFTA countries is close and good co-operation ensured. Access to 500 million consumers in the markets of the EU and the EFTA countries is close and good co-operation ensured. Besides free trade agreements with nearly 100 countries, Switzerland has the WTO Agreement on Government Procurement signed. Besides free trade agreements with nearly 100 countries, Switzerland has the WTO Agreement on Government Procurement signed. Thus, Switzerland, the main markets by entities of government in the EU, U.S., Canada, Japan, Korea, Norway and Israel. Thus, Switzerland, the main markets by entities of government in the EU, U.S., Canada, Japan, Korea, Norway and Israel.

For additional analytical, business and investment opportunities information,
please contact Global Investment & Business Center, USA
at (703) 370-8082. Fax: (703) 370-8083. E-mail: ibpusa3@gmail.com
Global Business and Investment Info Databank - www.ibpus.com

Infrastructure Infrastructure
The infrastructure of Switzerland is among the world's most developed and reliable. The infrastructure of Switzerland is among the world's most developed and reliable. A highly developed IT infrastructure and advanced technological tools offer optimum conditions for the development of new technologies. A highly developed IT infrastructure and advanced technological tools offer optimum conditions for the development of new technologies.
On the property are sufficient supply of land and buildings for economic activities. On the property are sufficient supply of land and buildings for economic activities. The restriction of land ownership by foreign nationals in recent years largely eased. The restriction of land ownership by foreign nationals in recent years largely eased.

Laboratory workers
Well-trained workforce is a prerequisite for any successful business. Well-trained workforce is a prerequisite for any successful business. The overall productivity of the Swiss economy is in a global comparison ranks 5th The overall productivity of the Swiss economy is in a global comparison ranks 5th, the workforce is motivated and strikes are virtually unknown. The workers are highly motivated and strikes are virtually unknown.
Although salaries seem relatively high, the total labor costs significantly lower than in competing countries. Although salaries seem relatively high, the total labor costs significantly lower than in competing countries. Non-wage costs and social costs are low. Non-wage costs and social costs are low.

Market Market
From Switzerland can be both the Swiss and the European market is an ideal process. From Switzerland can be both the Swiss and the European market is an ideal process. A branch in Switzerland will grant access to a domestic market of 7 million consumers with the highest purchasing power. A branch in Switzerland wants to grant access to a domestic market of 7 million consumers with the highest purchasing power. But the European market (500 million consumers) can be from Switzerland ideally open and edit. But the European market (500 million consumers) can be from Switzerland ideally open and edit this reason, many international companies of various industries for their main office, foreign branch or service center to Switzerland. That's why many international companies of various industries for their main office, foreign branch or service center to Switzerland.

PERSONS FROM THIRD COUNTRIES

Requirements for person
Persons from third countries which do not originate from the EU-/EFTA-Raum and Switzerland operate independently, they must in Switzerland prevailing labor market demands (ANAG guidelines) requirements. Persons from third countries which do not originate from the EU-/EFTA-Raum and Switzerland operate independently, they must in Switzerland prevailing labor market demands (ANAG guidelines) requirements.

Legal right to exercise an independent activity, only the holder of a C-card (permanent residence permits for third country nationals), or the spouse of C Ausweisinhabenden, respectively, of Swiss citizens. Legal right to exercise an independent activity, only the holder of a C-card (permanent residence permits for third country nationals), or the spouse of Ausweisinhabenden C, respectively, of Swiss citizens.

All other persons have no legal right to self-employment activities. All other persons have no legal right to self-employment activities. You must be at the respective cantonal authorities make a request. You must be at the respective cantonal authorities make a request. Crucial in assessing the credible evidence that the company has a "lasting positive impact on the Swiss economy" can perceive. Crucial in assessing the credible evidence that the company has a "lasting positive impact on the Swiss economy" can perceive. Similarly, companies Mende their business idea prior to the possible relocation to Switzerland have advanced. Similarly, companies Mende their business idea prior to the possible relocation to Switzerland have advanced. A convincing business plan offers the best foundation for successful testing procedures. A convincing business plan offers the best foundation for successful testing procedures.

If the application of the cantonal authorities acknowledged, the company Mende a short residence permit (Permit L). If the application of the cantonal authorities acknowledged, the company Mende short a residence permit (Permit L). This is - if there is still spare capacity in the quota for annual and short-term residents (BVO-quota) - usually limited to one year and may, exceptionally, a maximum of 12 months. This is - if there is still spare capacity in the quota for annual and short-term residents (BVO-quota) - usually limited to one year and may, exceptionally, a maximum of 12 months. For a possible extension after this 12, or 24 months, a new labor market test by the authority. For a possible extension after this 12, or 24 months, a new labor market test by the authority. Is this a positive, can then possibly a new authorization issued. Is this a positive, can then possibly a new authorization issued. However, there is no right to claim part of the request set ends. However, there is no right to claim part of the request set ends.
Requirements for Company Formation Requirements for Company Formation
The following nationality, residence rules and requirements apply to non-entrepreneurs from establishing a The following nationality, residence rules and requirements apply to non-entrepreneurs from establishing an
Single Company Individual Company
The sole proprietorship is the sole property of the company's owner. The sole proprietorship is the sole property of the company's owner. Accordingly, the labor requirements of the person. Accordingly, the labor requirements of the person. In principle, to work in Switzerland, a residence and work permits are available. In principle, to work in Switzerland, a residence and work permits are available.

Collective and Collective and commandite commandite
The collective and limited partnerships are considered primarily as a small, highly personal form of enterprise. The collective and limited partnerships are considered primarily as a small, highly personal form of enterprise. The partnership is the involvement of external not actively involved in the management investors. The partnership is the involvement of external not actively involved in the management investors. Accordingly, the natural persons for the labor provisions of the person with a valid residence and work permit. Accordingly, the natural persons for the labor provisions of the person with a valid residence and work permit.

Limited liability company (GmbH) Limited liability company (GmbH)
The limited liability company (GmbH) as a legal person must be at least represented by a person that can be domiciled in Switzerland. The limited liability company (GmbH) as a legal person must be at least represented by a person that can be domiciled in Switzerland. This may be the CEO or a director. This may be the CEO or a director. Accordingly, this person must have these people for Switzerland valid residence and work permit have. Accordingly, this person must have for Switzerland thesepeoplecomedy valid residence and work permit have.

Aktiengesellschaft (AG) Aktiengesellschaft (AG)
In stock, as a legal person must be a representative of the AG authorized person residing in Switzerland. In stock, as a legal person must be a representative of the AG authorized person residing in Switzerland. Accordingly, this person must be one for the valid Switzerland residence

and work permit have. Accordingly, this person must be one for the valid Switzerland residence and work permit have.
Siting Siting
Companies have widely differing demands on their ideal company headquarters. Companies have widely differing demands on their ideal company headquarters. To ease the burden of choice, it makes sense to evaluate potential business locations after ten to twenty fundamental criteria. To ease the burden of choice, it makes sense to evaluate potential business locations after ten to twenty fundamental criteria.

Critical factors in the choice of location are critical factors in site selection are:
Amount of corporate taxes and any tax breaks amount of corporate taxes and any tax relief

Regular contact and exchange with universities and research institutions Regular contact and exchange with universities and research institutions

Importance and value of traffic connections (road, air, rail) Importance and value of traffic connections (road, air, rail)

Number and frequency of travel abroad by plane number and frequency of foreign travel by plane

Importance of customer and / or suppliers near Importance of customer and / or suppliers close

Needs of space / area, eg for a production facility Needs of space / area, eg for a production plant

Budget for the budget office for office space

Standard office equipment, standard office equipment

Distance between home and work Distance between home and work

Parking needs parking needs

Rural region or urban environment, urban or rural region environment
(Source: www.greaterz0richarea.ch) (Source: www.greaterzuricharea.ch)
Land Purchase Land Purchase
Will an entrepreneur from a third country in Switzerland or buy real estate, he needs a valid residence permit and C must actually live in Switzerland. Will to entrepreneur from a third country in Switzerland or buy real estate, he needs a valid residence permit and C must actually live in Switzerland. This also applies if the spouse of the acquisition ends Swiss citizens. This therefore applies if the spouse of the acquisition ends Swiss citizens.

If these conditions apply to the acquisition of real estate the same rights as Swiss citizens (national treatment), or for EU-EFTA citizens. If these conditions apply to the acquisition of real estate the same rights as Swiss citizens (national treatment), or for EU-EFTA citizens.

In connection with property and land purchases / sales tax due the following: In connection with property and land purchases / sales tax due the following:
Land-tax profit: 0.3 to 3 ‰ land-tax profit: 0.3 to 3 ‰

Change hands for real estate tax (depending on the Canton partially removed): 1-3% change hands for real estate tax (depending on the Canton partially removed): 1-3%
Taxes for individuals tax for natural persons
Income taxes in Switzerland, both by the federal government (federal tax), as well as by the cantons and municipalities (state and municipal taxes) will be charged. Income taxes in

Switzerland, both by the federal government (federal tax), as well as by the Cantons and municipalities (state and municipal taxes) will be charged. Since each of the 26 cantons has its own tax laws, the tax burden in the individual cantons. Since each of the 26 Cantons has its own tax laws, the tax burden in the individual Cantons. In principle, taxpayers an annual tax return form. In principle, taxpayers an annual tax return form Based on this, the tax factors (income and assets) is determined and the taxes set. Based on this, the tax factors (income and assets) is determined and the taxes set.

Foreign workers, the foreign police establishment permit C do not possess, in Switzerland, however, tax domicile or residence, for their income from salaried employment tax credits at the source subject, ie the taxes from the employer directly deducted from the salary (tax). Foreign workers, the foreign policy establishment permit C do not possess, in Switzerland, however, tax domicile or residence, for their income from Salaried employment tax credits at the source subject, ie the taxes from the employer directly deducted from the salary (tax) . The tax is normally paid. The tax is normally paid.

According to tax law (Section 94) shall be persons without a residence permit for income from self-employed pay no tax. According to tax law (Section 94) shall be persons without a residence permit for income from self-employed pay no income tax are using this tax to be declared, so as for an established alien or a Swiss citizen (see the Federal Law on Direct Federal Tax , Part Four: taxes for natural persons and legal entities). This means income tax return to declare, that is established like an alien or a Swiss citizen (see the Federal Law on Direct Federal Tax, Part Four: taxes for natural persons and legal entities).

The avoidance of international double taxation is by inter-governmental agreements. The avoidance of international double taxation is by inter-governmental agreements. Switzerland has almost 100 countries, including almost all Western industrialized countries, such an agreement. Switzerland has almost 100 countries, including almost all Western industrialized countries, such an agreement. Country-specific details from the respective apparent agreement (see the double taxation law and overview of double taxation agreements). Country-specific details from the respective apparent agreement (see the double taxation law and overview of double taxation agreements).
Corporate Taxes Corporate Taxes
Companies are at their place of value creation, ie at the company headquarters or at the place of economic activity. Companies are at their place of value creation, ie at the company headquarters or at the place of economic activity. In comparison, corporate taxes are low in Switzerland. In the country of the tax as a percentage of company profits, Switzerland, with an average of 21.3% (as of 2006) to Rank 2 behind Ireland (12.5%) and Sweden (28%). In comparison, corporate taxes are low in Switzerland. In the country of the tax as a percentage of company profits, Switzerland, with an average of 21.3% (as of 2006) to Rank 2 behind Ireland (12.5%) and Sweden (28%). The total tax burden including the benefits for social security is less than 30% of gross domestic product (GDP). The total tax burden including the benefits for social security is less than 30% of gross domestic product (GDP).

The federal tax is a flat rate, the cantonal tax rates vary according to location and partly to the amount of capital or profit. The federal tax is a flat rate, the cantonal tax rates vary according to location and partly to the amount of capital or profit. The regular tax rate on the direct federal tax is 8.5%. The regular tax rate on the direct federal tax is 8.5%. Since the taxes on the profit after taxes are calculated, results in an effective tax rate of 7.83%. Since the taxes on the profit after taxes are calculated, results in an effective tax rate of 7.83%.

The current rates are moving in the following sizes (appr. data): The current rates are moving in the following sizes (appr. data):
Direct federal taxes on income 7.83% (effective rate) Direct federal taxes on income 7.83%

(effective rate)

Cantonal and communal income tax: 8-17% Cantonal and Communal income tax: 8-17%

Cantonal and communal capital tax: 0.08 to 0.25% Cantonal and communal capital tax: 0.08 to 0.25%
That makes for a regular company tax burden of total 16 to 25%. That makes for a regular company tax burden of total 16 to 25%.
Tax optimization Tax optimization
Tax optimization, companies can significantly lower rates of up to less than 10% realized. Tax optimization, companies can significantly lower rates of up to 10% less than realized. According to position the cantonal economic development organizations and also try new tax benefits to businesses in their area offering. According to position the cantonal economic development organizations and also try new tax benefits to businesses in their area offering. This allows companies such as from the tax authorities a binding preliminary decision on the effective tax received (Tax Ruling). This allows companies such as from the tax authorities a binding preliminary decision on the effective tax received (Tax Ruling). Tax exemption is also depending on the location and type of activity for a limited period. Tax exemption is also depending on the location and type of activity for a limited period. Focal point in any case, the cantonal economic development agencies. Focal point in any case, the cantonal economic development agencies.

Corporate taxes are depending on the chosen form of operation in varying degrees affect. Corporate taxes are depending on the chosen form of operation in varying degrees affect. Characteristic are Characteristic are the
Companies, operating,

Holding Companies, Holding Companies

Swiss branches of a company based abroad. Swiss branches of a company based abroad.

The Economic Development organization Greater Zurich Area is an excellent example of possible tax optimization models for three models: the economic development organization Greater Zurich Area is an excellent example of possible tax optimization models for three models:
Mixed Company (company coordinates its activities in Switzerland and is mainly abroad) Mixed Company (company coordinates its activities in Switzerland and is mainly abroad)

Principal company (business risks, assets and decision-makers in Switzerland) Principal company (business risks, assets and decision-makers in Switzerland)

Holding company (company holds majority stakes) holding company (company holds a majority shareholding)
VAT VAT
Switzerland has by far the lowest VAT in Europe. Switzerland has by far the lowest VAT in Europe. The normal rate is 7.6%. The normal rate is 7.6%. Hotels will be 3.5%, goods of daily needs with only 2.4% tax. Hotels will be 3.5%, goods of daily needs with only 2.4% tax Other goods and services such as health care and education, are exempt from VAT. Other goods and services such as healthcare and education, are exempt from VAT.
Framework conditions
Switzerland Switzerland as a location as a location
Geographic and economic factors influence the choice of location for a corporate relocation considerably. Geographic and economic factors influence the choice of location for a corporate relocation considerably. The geostrategic position of Switzerland and its federal structure made the country a meeting place of different cultures and languages. The geostrategic position of Switzerland and its federal structure made the country a meeting place of different cultures and

For additional analytical, business and investment opportunities information,
please contact Global Investment & Business Center, USA
at (703) 370-8082. Fax: (703) 370-8083. E-mail: ibpusa3@gmail.com
Global Business and Investment Info Databank - www.ibpus.com

languages. Long-term, stable decision-making, liberal legislation, protection of free competition and cooperative authorities encourage the establishment of companies or operations and research facilities. Long-term, stable decision-making, liberal legislation, protection of free competition and cooperative authorities encourage the establishment of companies or operations and research facilities.

Switzerland is in the international comparison a leading space. Switzerland is in the international comparison a leading space. It is one of the countries with the longest working hours, the majority of valid patents per capita, the highest per capita spending for Science, Research and Education and the largest foreign share of the gross domestic product. It is one of the countries with the longest working hours, the majority of valid patents per capita, the highest per capita spending for Science, Research and Education and the largest foreign share of the gross domestic product.

Economy Economy
The Swiss economy owes its high level of development of both the industriousness and ingenuity of their population as well as the close relations with foreign countries. The Swiss economy owes its high level of development of both the industriousness and Ingenuity of their population as well as the close relations with foreign countries. The competitive pressure, political stability, sound public finances, low capital costs and high purchasing power stability to ensure present and future growth. The competitive pressure, political stability, sound public finances, low capital costs and high purchasing power stability to ensure present and future growth.
High gross domestic product: The Swiss economy is most competitive in the world (ranked 1) and is among the most globalized countries (rank 2). High gross domestic product: The Swiss economy is most competitive in the world (ranked 1) and is among the most globalized countries (rank 2). The gross domestic product per capita is one of approximately CHF 61'000 .- (U.S. $ 49'000 .-) are among the highest in the world. The gross domestic product per capita is one of approximately CHF 61'000 .- (U.S. $ 49'000 .-) are among the highest in the world.

Depth unemployment rate - high employment rate: Switzerland has 57% with one of the highest employment rates in the world. Depth unemployment rate - high employment rate: Switzerland has 57% with one of the highest employment rates in the world. The unemployment rate, with 3.1% to the lowest in Europe. The unemployment rate, with 3.1% to the lowest in Europe.

Strong Swiss franc: Switzerland is not a member of the EU and has its own stable currency, the Swiss franc (CHF). Strong Swiss franc: Switzerland is not a member of the EU and has its own stable currency, the Swiss franc (CHF). The euro is widely accepted as payment. The euro is widely accepted as payment.

Strong service sector and new technologies: The most important economic sector in Switzerland is the service sector. Strong service sector and new technologies: The most important economic sector in Switzerland is the service sector. Almost three-quarters of all employees in services generate 70% of GDP. Almost three-quarters of all employees in services generate 70% of GDP. An important pillar in the service sector is the financial center of Zurich. An important pillar in the service sector is the financial center of Zurich.
Approximately one third of the population works in trade and industry, which together account for nearly one quarter of the GDP. Approximately one third of the population works in trade and industry, which together account for nearly one quarter of the GDP. Especially in the medical and biotechnology, micro-, nano-and high-tech industry and in telecommunications technology (ICT) are the major educational inputs of the Federal universities, polytechnics, and the combination of school and teaching profession to bear. Especially in the medical and biotechnology, micro-, nano-and high-tech industry and in telecommunications technology (ICT) are the major

For additional analytical, business and investment opportunities information, please contact Global Investment & Business Center, USA at (703) 370-8082. Fax: (703) 370-8083. E-mail: ibpusa3@gmail.com
Global Business and Investment Info Databank - www.ibpus.com

educational inputs of the Federal universities, polytechnics, and the combination of school and teaching professionals to bear.

Agriculture has only marginal economic importance. Agriculture has only marginal economic importance. However, it is important for Switzerland because it helps to preserve the natural landscape and rural structures beyond the metropolitan areas to be preserved. However, it is important for Switzerland because it helps to preserve the natural landscape and rural structures beyond the metropolitan areas to be preserved.

Foreign trade: Switzerland is the world's goods exports to No.21 Foreign trade: Switzerland is the world's goods exports to No.21 in 2005 the Swiss exports to CHF 158 billion, while imports amounted to CHF 155 billion. In 2005 the Swiss exports to CHF 158 billion, while imports amounted to CHF 155 billion. Four-fifths of all imported goods and almost two-thirds of exports of Switzerland is in the trade with the EU. Four-fifth of all imported goods and almost two-thirds of exports of Switzerland is in the trade with the EU. Germany is traditionally the most important customer and also the largest supplier of Switzerland. Germany is traditionally the most important customer and also the largest supplier of Switzerland.

Access to 500 million consumers in the markets of the EU and the EFTA countries is close and good co-operation ensured. Access to 500 million consumers in the markets of the EU and the EFTA countries is close and good co-operation ensured. Besides free trade agreements with nearly 100 countries, Switzerland has the WTO Agreement on Government Procurement signed. Besides free trade agreements with nearly 100 countries, Switzerland has the WTO Agreement on Government Procurement signed. Thus, Switzerland, the main markets by entities of government in the EU, U.S., Canada, Japan, Korea, Norway and Israel. Thus, Switzerland, the main markets by entities of government in the EU, U.S., Canada, Japan, Korea, Norway and Israel.

Infrastructure Infrastructure
The infrastructure of Switzerland is among the world's most developed and reliable. The Infrastructure of Switzerland is among the world's most developed and reliable. A highly developed IT infrastructure and advanced technological tools offer optimum conditions for the development of new technologies. A highly developed IT infrastructure and advanced technological tools offer optimum conditions for the development of new technologies.
On the property are sufficient supply of land and buildings for economic activities. On the property are sufficient supply of land and buildings for economic activities. The restriction of land ownership by foreign nationals in recent years largely eased. The restriction of land ownership by foreign nationals in recent years largely eased.

Laboratory workers
Well-trained workforce is a prerequisite for any successful business. Well-trained workforce is a prerequisite for any successful business. The overall productivity of the Swiss economy is in a global comparison ranks 5th The overall productivity of the Swiss economy is in a global comparison ranks 5th, the workforce is motivated and strikes are virtually unknown. The workers are highly motivated and strikes are virtually unknown. Although salaries seem relatively high, the total labor costs significantly lower than in competing countries. Although salaries seem relatively high, the total labor costs significantly lower than in competing countries. Non-wage costs and social costs are low. Non-wage costs and social costs are low.

Market Market
From Switzerland can be both the Swiss and the European market is an ideal process. From

Switzerland can be both the Swiss and the European market is an ideal process. A branch in Switzerland will grant access to a domestic market of 7 million consumers with the highest purchasing power. A branch in Switzerland wants to grant access to a domestic market of 7 million consumers with the highest purchasing power. But the European market (500 million consumers) can be from Switzerland ideally open and edit. But the European market (500 million consumers) can be from Switzerland ideally open and edit this reason, many international companies of various industries for their main office, foreign branch or service center to Switzerland. That's why many international companies of various industries for their main office, foreign branch or service center to Switzerland.

VENTURE CAPITAL STRUCTURES

Venture capital and private equity is generally felt to be a good thing in Europe. It has a positive effect on economic generation, employment and cross border activity. The private equity industry remains largely dominated by the US (almost 70 per cent of money invested). But, over the last five years, Europe has seen a tremendous increase in private equity firms and investments made in private and start-up companies.

Switzerland has been among the top continental European countries with growth rates of more than 100 per cent in 1999 and 2000. The number of start-ups is booming and the Swiss Federal Institutes of Technology of Lausanne and Zurich have generated more than 70 start-ups over the last few years.

In addition, there have been many success stories, including IPOs. Several major consulting firms, as well as Swiss banks, business schools and even large companies have set up programmes and incubators to help and participate in promising young companies. An entrepreneurial mindset is spreading among young people, tentatively supported by specific local authority initiatives, such as tax holidays for start-ups. These recent developments are positioning Switzerland as a land for great opportunities despite the recent major falls on international stock exchanges.

A private equity investment vehicle is an instrument for enabling pooled investments by a number of investors in equity and equity-related securities in private companies. The vehicle can take the form either of a company or of a similar arrangement such as a limited partnership, or, as in some countries, an investment fund. The management of the vehicle can either be conducted by the vehicle itself or, as is increasingly common, by a separate management company or manager providing services to the vehicle.

The main issue with such a private equity vehicle is to avoid the additional layer of taxation that would apply to investments in a structure subject to usual income taxes that in turn invested in target companies. Tax would arise both on the sale by the vehicle of its interest in the investee companies and again on the distribution of those gains to investors or, if there is capital gains tax, on the sale by investors of their interest in the vehicle. The distribution of sale proceeds from individual investments during the life of the vehicle are treated as a dividend rather than a partial realisation of capital, which converts a capital gain from the sale of an investment into dividend income. Some institutional investors may find this advantageous. But a general principle in structuring private equity vehicles is that most investors will be best served by a tax-neutral structure under which they will be no worse off than they would have been by investing directly into the investee companies.

BASIC STRUCTURES

The principal structures that may be used for private equity investment vehicles in Switzerland are as follows:

Investment fund/investment foundation
The Swiss Investment Fund Act regulates the activities of Swiss investment funds - open-ended contractual structures managed in Switzerland - and of foreign investment funds that distribute in a professional manner their shares or units in Switzerland. Swiss investment funds may only be set up after the Federal Bank Commission (FBC) has approved the fund regulations established by the fund management and the depository bank. In addition, the Swiss fund manager has to obtain an authorisation from the FBC. Investment foundations are also regulated and supervised by a governmental authority.

As seen above, Swiss investment funds and investment foundations are highly regulated. Both vehicles offer low flexibility for private equity purposes. There are many compulsory investment restrictions, too. In particular, by law, investors in an investment fund must be entitled to make at least quarterly redemptions. Finally, Swiss law does not permit these vehicles to be structured to allow the classic draw down procedures. Swiss management and control are required and, more importantly, for Swiss investment funds, there might be high tax on the management's carried interest when compared to a manager's position in an offshore jurisdiction.

The quarterly redemptions and the heavy regulations make Swiss investment funds and investment foundations inappropriate for investing in private equity because it is only worthwhile on a mid to long-term basis.

Joint stock company ('*Société Anonyme*', '*Aktiengesellschaft*')
Swiss joint stock companies have been used in the past for private equity purposes. Ordinarily, a standard Swiss holding company is set up as a two-layer structure with a wholly-owned offshore subsidiary holding company. The Swiss company collects funds by issuing shares to the public and the investments in the targeted private equity investments are then made through the offshore intermediary holding company. Companies structured in this way have been listed on the Swiss Exchange SWX in the Investment companies segment.

The advantages are:

- The company is governed by the well established provisions of the Swiss Code of Obligations (SCO) and is therefore in a well known legal environment

- The company's shares can be listed. This is essential for liquidity to offset the rigidities deriving from the Swiss corporate law

This structure is not subject to FBC supervision or any other regulatory supervision, unlike the investment funds mentioned above
But there are disadvantages:

- Most importantly, share capital increases have to be made in compliance with the cumbersome procedures set out in the SCO. This makes it difficult for investors to respond quickly to draw downs that the managers request to meet underlying investments on a case-by-case basis

- A Swiss company cannot be structured in a way that allows a redemption of shares or that grants its shareholders redemption rights

- Swiss corporate law allows for the creation of authorised share capital. However, this is limited by time (two years) and by amount, (no more than half the existing share capital)

- Swiss law provides for some shareholders' rights. This is certainly an interesting safeguard for investors but is not necessarily attractive for investment vehicle managers who like to have as much control and flexibility as possible. This problem is however largely avoided through the two-layer structure.

Under current Swiss law, the Swiss holding company is exempt from cantonal and communal income tax. At the direct Swiss federal tax level, the Swiss holding company qualifies for participation exemption in respect of dividends received from its (offshore) subsidiary, so it is practically free of tax. The same applies to a dividend paid when an offshore subsidiary is in liquidation. The Swiss holding company is subject to a relatively insignificant capital tax on the cantonal and communal level, as well as the direct tax at federal level. The taxation of income, capital gains and net wealth (capital) of the shareholders of the Swiss holding company is subject to the laws and practice in Switzerland or the jurisdiction in which holders are resident or otherwise subject to tax.

Any potential liquidation surplus, consisting of the difference between the Swiss holding company's nominal share capital and the net asset value of the investment portfolio, will be subject to income tax for Swiss residents holding the shares in their private (as opposed to commercial) fortune in Switzerland. For corporate investors and individuals holding the shares in their commercial fortune, the difference between the shares, book-value and the liquidation proceeds will be subject to tax. Under certain conditions, corporate investors can benefit from participation exemption.

Normally, Swiss investment companies do not have a policy of paying out dividends but instead re-investing any realised cash from these investments. However, under present Swiss law, any distributions made by the Swiss holding company are subject to the Swiss withholding tax at a rate of 35 per cent. The Swiss holding company is required to withhold tax at this rate from any dividend payments it makes to a shareholder. The Swiss resident holder and beneficial owner of these shares may, if declared, qualify for a full refund of the Swiss withholding tax from such dividends. A holder and beneficial owner of shares that is not a resident of Switzerland, but a resident of a country that maintains a double taxation treaty with Switzerland may qualify for a full or a partial refund of the Swiss withholding tax. Most investment companies are listed on the stock exchange and, as a consequence, shares in that company would be sold by the shareholders. Such sale by a Swiss individual is free from capital gains tax.

Some improvements have been recently made to make these companies more attractive for investments in private equity. The Act on Venture Capital Companies came into effect on 1 May 2000. Although this new law does not yet completely satisfy the private equity industry, it does provide a few noteworthy improvements, mainly by introducing tax relief to some extent for venture capital companies and business angels.

Swiss limited partnership ('Société en commandite', 'Kommanditgesellschaft')
The Swiss limited partnership of Articles 594 et seq. SCO is the Swiss equivalent of a Delaware limited liability company. There is a general partner/limited partner structure with a general partner fully liable for all the partnership's liabilities and limited partners liable just for their respective interests in the partnership. This would be a perfect vehicle for private equity investments.

However, there is a major obstacle. By law, the general partner must be an individual. Given the highly risky nature of private equity investments, no individual would want to assume such risks.

For this reason, an amendment has recently been proposed to Art. 594 para.2 SCO to allow general parties to be legal entities or commercial companies.

However, the Delaware LLC has not so far developed as the favourite investment vehicle for private equity investments in Switzerland. The foreign, UK-type limited partnership has.

Foreign limited partnership

The limited partnership provides investors with the tax transparency and limited liability that they need. Plus, it is subject to fewer investment restrictions and other regulations than most other private equity vehicles in Europe.

The partnership is not a taxable entity in its chosen jurisdiction. If a limited partner is not resident in that jurisdiction, any income derived from the partnership's international operations and any interest the limited partner receives is not regarded as arising or accruing from a source in the partnership's jurisdiction. In addition, no inheritance, capital gains, gifts, turnover or sales taxes are levied in the chosen jurisdiction in connection with the acquisition, holding or disposal of interests and no stamp duty or similar taxation is levied on the issue or redemption of partnership interests. However, interests in the partnership are not freely transferable and no secondary market for such interests exists.

The set-up is usually as follows: the partnership is organised as a closed-end limited partnership. The general partner is often a company limited by shares incorporated in the same jurisdiction. The general partner has full control over the business affairs of the partnership, including overall management responsibility for the partnership's investments and will be entitled to the carried interest. The adviser to the general partner may be a Swiss company limited by shares.

An industry advisory group - consisting of experienced business advisors who have substantial experience and an extensive network in the targeted sectors and countries in which the partnership may invest - assists the advisor and general partner in various activities. Sometimes, the structure is completed by a strategy investment committee consisting of limited partners. This committee reviews the partnership's overall strategy and make recommendations to avoid or resolve conflict of interest situations.

These limited partnerships are not subject to any supervision in their country of jurisdiction nor in Switzerland. They do not fall within the scope of the Swiss Investment Fund Act's anti-abuse provisions, as long as the limited partners have certain control rights over the general partner.

COMMERCIAL REGISTER

The Commercial Register is public, managed by the Cantons database. It contains the essential information about the "under a commercial nature led 'businesses. It contains the essential information about the" under a commercial nature led' businesses.

In Commercial, the most important business information, a company registered. In Commercial, the most important business information, a company registered. The Commercial, the legal relationships of public companies and thus transparent. The Commercial, the legal relationships of public companies and thus transparent. It promotes legal certainty in commercial transactions. It promotes legal certainty in commercial transactions.

Registration according to the law are all commercial, manufacturing and other commercial species after discontinued businesses. Registration according to the law are all commercial, manufacturing and other commercial species after discontinued businesses. The concept of the industry is very broad and refers to not only craft a typical operation, but separate, permanent acquisition based on economic activity. The concept of the industry is very broad and refers to not only craft a typical operation, but separate, permanent acquisition based on economic activity. Must be named in the Commercial Register: Must be named in the Commercial Register:

● individual firms from CHF 100'000 .- annual sales ● individual firms from CHF 100'000 .- Annual Turnover
Collective societies ● ● Collective Societies
● ● commandite commandite
● ● limited liability limited liability
● ● Kommanditaktiengesellschaft Kommanditaktiengesellschaft
● Limited Liability Companies Limited Liability Companies ●
● ● Co-operatives Co-operatives
● clubs, after which a commercial nature run industrial ● clubs operate, after which a commercial nature run commercial operating
● Foundations (without families and religious foundations) ● Foundations (without families and religious foundations)
● branches of foreign companies and Swiss ● branches of foreign companies and Swiss
Some traders, such as agents, brokers or trustees have registration, even if it is CHF 100'000 .- annual sales do not reach. Some traders, such as agents, brokers or trustees have registration, even if it is CHF 100'000 .- annual sales do not reach.
An entry contains, among other things: An entry contains, among other things:

● Name (company) ● Name (Company)
● Year ● Founded in
● Purpose of the seat and seat ● company and nature of the company
● the names of shareholders, administrators, business leaders, drawing entitled ● the names of shareholders, administrators, business leaders, drawing entitled
● ● capital ratios capital ratios
● auditors (if any) ● auditors (if any)
The federal government is the ultimate supervision and maintains a central register. The federal government is the ultimate supervision and maintains a central register. This is updated daily and is the central company index Zefix accessible. This is updated daily and is the central company index Zefix accessible. The driving of the trade is up to the cantons. The driving of the trade is up to the Cantons. They must have at least have a trade in the cantons of BE and VS will register as district led. They must have at least have a trade in the Canton of BE and VS will register as district led

Currently, one in Switzerland 31 commercial registries. Currently, one in Switzerland 31 commercial registries. With them, you can register for a fee request extracts and thus relatively well-founded on a specific company information. With them, you can register for a fee request extracts and thus relatively well-founded on a specific company information. The extracts are also available on the Internet. The extracts are also available on the Internet. Detailed instructions can be found at the Federal Office of Justice. Detailed instructions can be found at the Federal Office of Justice.
Paid entries in the commercial are also in the Swiss Official Gazette. Paid entries in the commercial are also in the Swiss Official Gazette. The main data of the registered firms can also be found in the Swiss Ragionenbuch. The main data of the registered firms can also be found in the Swiss Ragionenbuch.
Costs of the Commercial Record Costs Of The Commercial Record

Swiss Official Gazette of Commerce (external link, new window) Swiss Official Gazette of Commerce (external link, new window)

Caution: As Neuunternehmerin or new companies are often contacted by private registries.

Caution: As Neuunternehmerin or new companies are often contacted by private registries. Such a record is in any case voluntary. Such a record is in any case voluntary. Remember that such an entry but usually nothing more than costs. Remember that such an entry but usually nothing more than costs.

Registration: Beware of riding Registration: Beware of riding

Duties ... Duties ...

If your company in the Commercial Register must be, then you are the accounting requirements (art. 957 CO). If your company in the Commercial Register must be, then you are the accounting requirements (art. 957 CO). This obliges you to correct and seamless accounting (Art. 958 OR) with this oblige you to correct and seamless accounting (Art. 958 OR) with

- Inventory and receipt record store opening ● Inventory and receipt record store opening
- income at each end of the year ● income at each end of the year
- ● Annual Balance Sheet
- Annual Report (required for AGs, for all legal persons GmbH) ● Annual Report (required for AGs, for all persons legally GmbH)

These documents, you must keep at least 10 years (art. 962 CO). These documents, you must keep at least 10 years (art. 962 CO).

With the entry into the commercial register under your company operating in bankruptcy Article 39 para 1 SchKG). With the entry into the commercial register under your company operating in bankruptcy Article 39 para 1 SchKG). This means that a single creditor can bring with its request that the entire property in a bankruptcy estate reached, giving all creditors in proportion to their claims to operate. This means that a single creditor can bring with its request that the entire property in a bankruptcy estate reached, giving all creditors in proportion to their claims to operate. This means nothing else than the total liquidation of the company. This means nothing else than the total liquidation of the company.

... and rights ... and Rights

The advantages of a commercial register entry should outweigh the obligations. The advantages of a commercial register entry should outweigh the obligations. So is the name of the company (the Company) protected. So is the name of the company (the Company) protected. This protection is limited: This protection is limited:

Individual companies, collective, and partnerships with people names on the place of establishment, individual companies, collective, and partnerships with people names on the place of establishment;

AGs and limited liability on the whole of Switzerland. AGs and limited liability on the whole of Switzerland.

Attention: competition law can, under certain circumstances, a conflict between a legally protected trademark and a registered company later revealed. Attention: competition law can, under certain circumstances, a conflict between a legally protected trademark and a registered company later revealed. To avoid this, should mark the register of the Swiss Federal Institute of Intellectual Property to check whether identical or similar trademarks registered. To avoid this, should mark the register of the Swiss Federal Institute of Intellectual Property to check whether identical or similar trademarks registered.

Schweizerisches Schutzrechtstregister (Swissreg) (external link, new window) Swiss Schutzrechtstregister (Swissreg) (external link, new window)

The Commercial Registry are also business partners insight into the legal situation of the company. The Commercial Registry are also business partners insight into the legal situation of the company. It may therefore indicate that, in operation under the law a certain order and rules overview. It may therefore indicate that, in operation under the law a certain order and rules overview. In addition, increases the entrepreneur with an entry his credit because the creditors in

For additional analytical, business and investment opportunities information, please contact Global Investment & Business Center, USA at (703) 370-8082. Fax: (703) 370-8083. E-mail: ibpusa3@gmail.com Global Business and Investment Info Databank - www.ibpus.com

the event of bankruptcy are more protected. In addition, increases the entrepreneur with his entry to credit because the creditors in the event of bankruptcy are more protected.

PROS AND CONS OF PARTNERSHIPS AND CORPORATIONS

In Switzerland, private companies are typically for very small ratios. But the corporation (joint stock and limited liability company) is used by many businesses. But the corporation (joint stock and limited liability company) is used by many businesses.

Benefits of partnership to limited liability benefits of partnership to corporation
The incorporation procedure is simpler and cheaper. The incorporation procedure is simpler and cheaper. There are few formal rules. There are few formal rules. The shareholders can be the role of the institutions themselves take over. The shareholders can be the role of the institutions themselves take over.

The economic double taxation of profits in Switzerland can be avoided (at the joint stock company is the profit taxed twice: first at the level of society itself, secondly as a dividend to the shareholder). The economic double taxation of profits in Switzerland can be avoided (at the joint stock company is the profit taxed twice: first at the level of society itself, secondly as a dividend to the shareholder).

Partnerships are well suited for small businesses. Partnerships are well suited for small businesses.
Disadvantages partnership to corporation Disadvantages partnership to corporation
The partners have unlimited liability. The partners have unlimited liability.

Property shares are heavier transferable. Heavier Property shares are transferable.

Dar-call entry in the commercial register of shareholders is necessary (lack of anonymity). Dar-call entry in the commercial register of shareholders is necessary (lack of anonymity).

Difficult access to capital. Difficult access to capital.

Partnership is social insurance. Partnership is social insurance.

Corporations are suitable for capital companies, where the investment of the shareholders a greater role and its liability should be limited. Corporations are suitable for capital companies, where the investment of the shareholders a greater role and its liability should be limited. Comparing the advantages and disadvantages between the two forms of society:

For additional analytical, business and investment opportunities information,
please contact Global Investment & Business Center, USA
at (703) 370-8082. Fax: (703) 370-8083. E-mail: ibpusa3@gmail.com
Global Business and Investment Info Databank - www.ibpus.com

SWISS CORPORATE LAW BASICS

TYPES OF COMPANY

STOCK CORPORATION (SA)

This type of company is often used by foreign investors. There should be at least 3 subscribers, where nominee shareholders and nominee subscribers are allowed. The minimum authorized share capital should be 100,000 CHF. Share capital cannot be increased by more than 50% at one time. Shares can be ordinary, preference, voting or non-voting. Bearer shares are permitted. A majority of directors should be Swiss nationals and should reside within the jurisdiction. There should be a registered office and audited accounts, which must be filed with the Companies Register annually.

HOLDING COMPANY

This is a Stock Corporation with a particular tax status. This type of company benefits from reduced income tax and capital gains tax at federal and cantonal levels. For federal level a holding company is any entity which holds at least 20% of shares of another corporate entity or the holding values of shares are evaluated at least at 2m CHF at a market price. The definition of a holding company may differ within the cantons, but generally, a holding company is regarded as such by a canton in case it derives 51%-66% of its income from dividends remitted by a subsidiary or it holds 51%-66% of its shares.

DOMICILIARY COMPANY

These companies are Stock Corporations which are managed from a foreign country and are controlled by foreign persons, which however has a registered office in Switzerland, without having physical presence or staff within the jurisdiction. A business activity must be conducted abroad, from which such a company's income is derived. This type of company has favourable corporate and capital gains taxation regimes.

AUXILIARY COMPANY

It is a Domiciliary Company, which, in addition to its business conducted in foreign countries, can also have some business activities in Switzerland. This type of company is possible to incorporate and manage only in seven cantons, and it does not have any privileges at federal level. Even though the major part of such a company's income must derive from foreign source, Swiss offices and staff may be established and held in Switzerland.

MIXED COMPANY

This type of company combines characteristics of a Holding and a Domiciliary companies. There are no tax advantages at federal level, but a favourable taxation is applied at cantonal and municipal levels, in case the following conditions are satisfied: the company is controlled by foreign persons, the company has close relations/cooperation with foreign entities, at least 80% of its income derives from activities/sources conducted/held abroad.

SERVICE COMPANY

It is a Stock Corporation the only activity of which is provision of technical services, management, marketing, publicity, financial and administrative services provision to foreign companies. A Service Company may not usually derive income from companies outside their corporate group. A Service Company does not have any tax advantages at federal level, and the status of a Service Company is obtained in a canton.

BRANCH

A branch of a foreign company or a company from another canton must be registered in a chosen canton, where the branch needs to be established. A nominated Swiss resident must be a branch representative. All the incomes derived from activities conducted in Switzerland are taxed as local companies at federal and cantonal levels, as if they were resident corporations. No withholding tax is levied on transfers of a branch to its parent company abroad.

GENERAL PARTNERSHIP

Two or more partners join in one enterprise and have joint and several unlimited liability for a partnership's obligations. A partnership contract must be submitted to the Commercial Register.

LIMITED PARTNERSHIP

A minimum of one general partner and a minimum of one limited partner form a limited partnership. General partner is fully liable for partnership's obligations, but a limited partner is liable only up to the amount invested. Only private persons can become general partners, while corporate entities can become limited partners.

LIMITED LIABILITY COMPANY

Registered capital must be at least 20,000 CHF and must not exceed 2,000,000 CHF. This type of company is a mix between a corporation and a partnership. The name of the company must be registered in the Commercial Register. Issue of bearer shares is not allowed. At least one of the directors must be resident in Switzerland. Auditors are not obligatory.

SOLE PROPRIETORSHIP

Registration with Commercial Register of a Sole proprietorship – a private person resident of Switzerland who conducts its own business at its own expense, occurs only when the annual turnover reaches 100,000 CHF. A proprietor has unlimited liability for such a structure's obligations.

Partnerships				
		Simple Company	SS	CO 530 ss
		The General Partnership (quasi-personality)	SNC	CO 552 ss
		The limited partnership (quasi-personality)	SC	CO 594 ss
	Corporations (legal personality)			
		Company limited by shares	SC per share	CO 764 ss
		The Limited Liability Company	Sàrl	CO 772 ss

	The Company anomyme		SA	620 ff
Company with caratéristique of partnerships and capital				
	Cooperative Society		SCoop	CO 828 ss
Other organizations				
	The Association			CCS 60 ss
	Foundation			CCS 80 ss

PARTNERSHIPS

SIMPLE COMPANY

Simple societies - Art. 530-551 CO

Definition	1. The company is a contract by which two or more persons agree to combine their efforts and resources to achieve a common goal. 2. The Company is a company within the meaning of this title, if it does not offer the distinctive characteristics of other companies regulated by law.
Founders	Two or more natural or legal persons.
Foundation	By contract. (The written form is not required)
Company name	Has no name.
Commercial register	No registration required, except an association for profit.
Capital	Freely established. Equal contributions unless otherwise provided by contract.
Stocks	Freely established.
Management	By all associated sets unless otherwise provided in the contract or social decisions confident either one or more of them or to others.
Distribution of profit	With equal shares unless otherwise provided by contract.
Subject to taxation	Each partner
Liability for debts	Each partner directly (no social wealth), personally, unlimited and supportively.

THE GENERAL PARTNERSHIP (QUASI-PERSONALITY)

Partnership - Art. 552-593 CO

Companies carrying on business	1. The partnership is the contract that two or more natural persons, without a name and without limiting their liability to creditors of the company, to commercially exploit a mill or exercise any other form of commercial industry . 2. The members of society are required to be registered in the commercial register.
Founders	Several individuals, minimum 2 persons with physical

Foundation	By partnership agreement, no form is specified.
Company name	Name of all the partners or at least one of the partners with the addition indicating the existence of a company (eg & Co).
Commercial register	Registration is required. Subject registration: art. 554 CO
Capital	Contributions and amounts determined freely. Equal contributions unless otherwise specified in the contract. May change at any time.
Stocks	Made freely.
Management	According to contract. If nothing: all equal partners. Law related to profits, interest and fees on invested capital for work.
Right to vote	Defined in the contract. According to the rules of the single company.
Honorary	Yes, according to convention considered a debt of the company, a burden.
Interest	4% default, CO 558
Distribution of profit	According contract or equally. But the distribution of profits can be made when potential losses are mopped and inputs are restored. In case of loss, distribution equally unless otherwise agreed.
Subject to taxation	Generally each partner for him.
Liability for debts	1) Fortune company 2) All partners personally, unlimited and supportively.

THE LIMITED PARTNERSHIP (QUASI-PERSONALITY)

Limited partnership-Art. 594-619 CO

Companies carrying on business	1. The Partnership is one contract two or more persons under a name, to trade, use a mill or exercise commercial form any other industry where at least one partner is fully liable and one or more other, called sponsors are required only up to a certain contribution, called sponsorship. 2. The partners may be only physical persons;sponsors, however, may also be legal persons and corporations. 3. Members of the company are required to be registered in the commercial register.
Founders	Two or more natural or legal persons: Partner (Associate) = person = unlimited liability only individuals. Sponsor = Limited = natural or legal persons responsible.
Foundation	By partnership agreement, no form is specified.
Company name	Name of all the partners or at least one of the partners with the addition indicating the existence of a company (eg & Co).
Commercial register	Yes, CO 594
Capital	Contributions and amounts determined freely.
Stocks	Made freely.

For additional analytical, business and investment opportunities information,
please contact Global Investment & Business Center, USA
at (703) 370-8082. Fax: (703) 370-8083. E-mail: ibpusa3@gmail.com
Global Business and Investment Info Databank - www.ibpus.com

Management	Fully liable partner.
Right to vote	Partner: Decision Management each associated without the help of others. Sponsor: Can oppose ordinary societal decision.
Honorary	GP: Yes Sponsor: not available except.
Interest	GP: Yes, 4% default 598, 558, CO Sponsor: yes, 4% default 598, 558 CO can not be taken if sponsorship reduced.
Distribution of profit	Partner: according to the partnership agreement or equally. Sponsors: fixed by contract or by discretion of the judge. Earnings distributed if any losses were blotted and contributions restored.
Subject to taxation	Generally, each partner for him.
Liability for debts	Capital of the company. Sponsored: personal, joint and unlimited. Sponsor: up to partnership registered in the commercial register.

CORPORATIONS (LEGAL PERSONALITY)

COMPANY LIMITED BY SHARES

THE LIMITED LIABILITY COMPANY

Limited liability company (old law) - Art. 772-827 ACO

Definition	1. The limited liability company is one form two or more persons or companies trading under a business name and whose capital is determined in advance (social capital).2. Each shareholder participates in the share capital without its share (share) has the character of an action. It meets the commitments of the company beyond its share, but not more than up to the registered capital, in the cases determined by law. Moreover, it can not be held to benefits other than those provided by the statutes. 3. The company can be founded to commercially exploit a mill or exercise any other form of commercial industry, or to achieve other economic goals.
Founders	At least two natural or legal persons.
Bodies	Meeting of shareholders.
Foundation	By act passed in authentic form.
Company name	Free choice as to the SA mentioning Sàrl.
Commercial register	Sign constitutive. Subject registration: art. CO 781.
Input / output	Difficult in principle, 3/4 partners representing three quarters of the share capital for

For additional analytical, business and investment opportunities information,
please contact Global Investment & Business Center, USA
at (703) 370-8082. Fax: (703) 370-8083. E-mail: ibpusa3@gmail.com
Global Business and Investment Info Databank - www.ibpus.com

	approval.
Capital	Minimum share capital of CHF 20'000. - And a maximum of CHF 2 million francs paid up to at least 50%. The amount of shares of the various partners may be different, but must be of CHF 1'000. - Or at least a multiple of CHF 1'000. - A shareholder can own more than one share. The partner must at the foundation of society, releasing its 50 per cent or more by payment in cash or in-kind contributions.
Stocks	By law, allocation of at least 5% of the profit for the year to the general reserve until it reaches 20% of paid up share capital.
Management	According to the law by all the partners or by the articles by certain shareholders (associates manager) or by third parties.
Right to vote	Unless the articles, voting rights in proportion to the value of their own, each CHF 1000 entitling to one vote provision. However, the right to vote can not be removed by the statutes.
Distribution of profit	According to the statutes and the law. Distribution of profits only after allocation to legal and statutory reserves.
Subject to taxation	Society. The distribution of income are taxed as income to the recipients.
Liability for debts	Wealth of society. Insofar as social capital is not fully paid each partner responds to the amount not paid.

THE COMPANY ANOMYME

Limited company - Art. 620-763 CO

Definition	1. The corporation is one formed under a name whose share capital is determined in advance, divided into shares, and whose debts are guaranteed by the Company's assets. 2. Shareholders are held as statutory benefits and are not personally liable for corporate debts. 3. The corporation may be based also to pursue a goal that is not economic in nature.
Founders	At least 3 natural or legal persons.
Bodies	General Assembly, Board of Directors, auditors.
Foundation	By deed including decisions and statutes.
Company name	Fancy name, designation or name of person thing. (If the name of a person therein, the designation SA must be perforated)
Commercial register	Sign constitutive. Subject registration: art. CO 641.
Input / output	In principle easy. (Except for nameplates and related actions)
Capital	100,000 francs at least, released at 20% but at least up to 50,000 francs. No maximum capital. capital is divided into shares. The value of the minimal action is 1 Swiss centime.
Stocks	By law, allocation of at least 5% of the profit for the year to the general reserve until it reaches 20% of paid up share capital.
Management	By the Board with the possibility to delegate to third parties on the basis of a settlement organization. (Elected by the General Assembly)
Right to vote	According to number of shares. (Possibly depending privileges)

Distribution of profit	According to the statutes and the law. The dividend distribution is possible only after allocation to legal and statutory reserves.
Subject to taxation	Society. Dividends are taxed as income to the beneficiaries.
Liability for debts	Capital and reserves. Obligation to pay for shares subscribed partially release or unreleased.

COMPANY WITH PARTNERSHIPS AND CAPITAL

COOPERATIVE SOCIETY

Cooperative Society - Art. 828-926 CO

Cooperative Corporation Law of Obligations	1. The cooperative society that formed individuals or commercial companies with a variable number, corporately organized, and continues primarily to promote or ensure, through common action, the economic interests of its members determined. 2. The formation of cooperative societies in capital determined in advance is prohibited.
Founders	At least seven individuals or corporations people.
Foundation	Status in writing and adoption of the constitution by the founders, no deed necessary.
Company name	In choice as to SA: Invented name, designation or name of person thing.
Commercial register	Sign constitutive. Subject registration: art. 836 CO
Input / output	In principle easy: Anyone who wants to acquire a partner must submit a written statement. (Art. 840 CO) administration decides on the admission of new members, unless the articles do not have an input statement is sufficient, or do not require a decision of the general meeting. All member has the right to leave the company as long as the dissolution has not been decided. (Art. 842 CO)
Optional Capital	If a key is created, each cooperator must have a share. Capital can not be determined in advance.
Stocks	In some cases determined by law (art. 860 and 861 CO).
Management	By a three-member administration at least.
Distribution of profit	According to the law no. Profits are allocated to the assets of the company. The statutes may provide a distribution of profits.
Subject to taxation	Society. Profit distributions are taxed as income to the recipients.

OTHER ORGANIZATIONS

THE ASSOCIATION

Associations - Art. 60-79 CCS

Constitution Corporate Organization	Political associations, religious, scientific, artistic, charitable, recreational or others who do not have an economic purpose as soon as they acquire the personality expressed in their statutes will be held corporately.

Founders	Two or more natural or legal persons
Foundation	By written constitution
Company name	Has no name
Commercial register	No registration required, except in the case of a partnership profit
Capital	Freely determined. Membership fee to cover the liabilities
Stocks	Freely established
Management	By management
Distribution of profit	No. Revenues are attributed to the assets of the Association
Subject to taxation	The association. Membership dues are generally exempt
Liability for debts	According to statutory provisions. No provision statuary members respond equally

INCORPORATION IN SWITZERLAND: PRACTICAL INFORMATION AND REGULATIONS

INCORPORATING BASICS

German	French	Italian	Notes
AG (Aktiengesellschaft)	SA (Société anonyme)	SA (Società anonima)	≈ PLC (UK) or Inc. (US). Min. share capital CHF 100,000. Bearer or registered shares, of a par value of min. CHF 0.01 each. Details of shareholders generally not publicly available (except for main shareholders and management shares of publicly listed companies).
GmbH (Gesellschaft mit beschränkter Haftung)	Sàrl (Société à responsabilité limitée)	Sagl (Società a garanzia limitata)	≈ Ltd. (UK), LLC (US). Min. capital CHF 20,000. Registered shares only, of a par value of min. CHF 100 each. Name, address and share of each owner (and any changes) publicly recorded in the Official Register of Commerce (http://zefix.admin.ch/).

The Aktiengesellschaft is a legal entity with a firm name of its own and whose capital is divided into shares. The shareholders have no liability for the company's debts beyond their capital subscriptions. No governmental certificate or permit is needed for its formation or for the issue of shares. The company may perform any lawful activity, enter into contracts, transact business, and sue or be sued in its own name.

The share capital must be a minimum of SFr. 50,000 of which at least SFr. 20,000 or 20%, whichever is greater, must be paid in cash or in kind at the time of incorporation. Contributions in kind must be clearly defined in the corporate statutes.

The par value of each share must be at least SFr. 100 and may be issued in either registered or bearer form. The capital structure of an Aktiengesellschaft is not limited to one class of stock. It may have a combination of bearer and registered shares, preferred shares and shares of different par values but with equal voting rights. Bearer shares and shares with preferential voting rights must be fully paid in when issued. Shares only partly paid in must be in registered form but may be converted into bearer shares when fully paid.

At least three founders are necessary who subscribe the entire share capital and who adopt the articles of incorporation, representing in one integrated document the incorporation data and the statutes. The founders may be natural persons or legal entities acting through representatives. Neither Swiss nationality nor residence is required.

The articles of incorporation must be drawn up in the form of a notarial deed and must contain:

(i) the name and domicile of the company;
(ii) the purpose of the company (a brief listing of the main activities is sufficient.
The company may perform all business activities incidental to its purpose clause.
The ultra vires doctrine is of very limited significance for Swiss companies. The
case-by-case enumeration of business activity or of legal acts the company may

For additional analytical, business and investment opportunities information,
please contact Global Investment & Business Center, USA
at (703) 370-8082. Fax: (703) 370-8083. E-mail: ibpusa3@gmail.com
Global Business and Investment Info Databank - www.ibpus.com

perform is, therefore, unnecessary);
(iii)the amount of the share capital and the par value of individual shares, type of shares, and (when appropriate) the number of registered and bearer shares;
(iv) the value of capital contributions in kind, if any, the consideration in shares given in exchange and the name of the contributor;
(v) any special benefits received by the founders;
(vi) the number of shares required to be deposited by each member of the board of directors as security;
(vii)the bodies which are to manage and to audit the company and the manner in which the company is to be represented;
(viii) method of giving notice of the general meeting of the shareholders and a description of the shareholders' voting rights; and
(ix) the manner in which the company publishes its official notices.

Clauses regulating the following matters are only valid if they appear in the articles of incorporation:

(i) deviations from the normal legal provisions concerning changes of the articles of incorporation, particularly with respect to expansion or restriction of the purpose of the company, increases or reductions in the capital stock and changes of the normal legal provisions concerning a merger;
(ii) clauses concerning the sharing of the board of directors in the net profits of the company;
(iii)payment of interest out of capital stock during construction periods;
(iv) limitation of the duration of the company;
(v) fixing of the amount to be paid in on shares if higher than the legal minimum;
(vi) rules concerning penalties in case the subscribed capital is not paid in within the stated time;
(vii)the possibility to convert registered shares into bearer shares and vice-versa;
(viii) the prohibition of, or restrictions on the transfer of registered shares;
(ix) clauses concerning the issue of preferred shares, profit sharing certificates and founders' shares;
(x) restrictions on voting rights and the rights of a stockholder to appoint a proxy, as well as restrictions on the issue of voting shares;
(xi) clauses whereby the general meeting of stockholders may pass certain resolutions only with a qualified majority in addition to the cases provided for by law;
(xii)the power of the board of directors to delegate its authority to individual members of the board or to third persons; and
(xiii) clauses concerning the organization, rights and duties of the auditors, if such rules exceed the requirements established by law.

Subsequent to the subscription of the shares and the adoption of the articles of incorporation, the company must be registered in the Register of Commerce of the canton of its domicile. The company comes into legal existence only upon such registration.

The company is registered under a firm name. It may be a coined name, an abbreviation, or the family name of a shareholder. If the family name is used, it must include the words Aktiengesellschaft or societ, anonyme or their abbreviations AG or SA. Designations of objects without additions are not allowed. The use of national or territorial designations is also not permitted unless specifically approved. The principle of authenticity demands that everything contained in the firm name must accord with the facts. The principle of discernibility requires that the firm name of a new company be clearly discernible from those firms already in existence in

For additional analytical, business and investment opportunities information, please contact Global Investment & Business Center, USA at (703) 370-8082. Fax: (703) 370-8083. E-mail: ibpusa3@gmail.com
Global Business and Investment Info Databank - www.ibpus.com

Switzerland. Once the name of a company has been approved and entered in the Register of Commerce, it cannot be used by any other company.

An ordinary general meeting of the shareholders must be held annually within six months after the close of the financial year of the company. The shareholders' meeting is the supreme authority of the company. It has the following specific powers: to amend the statutes, to appoint and remove directors and auditors, to approve the balance sheet, the profit and loss statement as well as the business report to be presented by the board of directors, to discharge the directors for their conduct of the company's business, to determine the allocation of the net profit and, in particular, to declare dividends.

Extraordinary shareholders' meetings must be held at the request of the directors, auditors or shareholders representing at least 10% of the share capital.

The board of directors is elected by and is directly responsible to the shareholders. Directors are legally responsible for the proper conduct of the business of the company, in accordance with the statutes with the law. The directors must be shareholders and are required to deposit with the company the number of (qualifying) shares stipulated in the statutes (at least one) as security for the proper performance of their duties.

The board of directors may participate in the day-to-day management of the company, or it may delegate such duties to one of its members (the managing director) or to third parties (managers) and confine itself to a supervisory role. In any case, they are responsible for the annual profit and loss statement as well as the annual accounts. Managers of an "Aktiengesellschaft" are comparable to the officers of a U.S. corporation. There are no nationality requirements with respect to managers. They are appointed and removed by the board of directors which also determines the scope of their authorities.

At least one director is required, but there is no maximum limit. The board of directors must consist of a majority of Swiss citizens residing in Switzerland. In case of a one-man board, the sole director must also meet these requirements.

Legal entities or partnerships cannot become directors although their representatives are eligible.

Statutory auditors are appointed by the shareholders' meeting. Professional qualifications are not mandatory for an auditor. Although he may be a shareholder, the auditor may not be a director or an employee of the company.

Independent accountants are mandatory for companies that have a share capital of SFr. 5,000,000 or more, or have bonds or debentures outstanding, or invite the public to entrust money to them. The independent accountant is appointed by the board of directors; if the statutory auditors meet the requirement of an independent accountant, they can act in this capacity and are normally appointed. The independent accountants must render a detailed report to the board of directors, and the statutory auditors on the results of their examination; this report is not available to the shareholders.

SWISS INCORPORATION: SWISS COMPANY FORMATION REQUIREMENTS

Legal form: There are two forms of companies in Switzerland most commonly used by foreign investors: Aktiengesellschaft-AG or Societe anonyme-SA-public stock corporation and Gesellschaft mit beschrankter Haftung-GmbH or Societe a responsabilite limitee-Sarl private limited liability company.

For additional analytical, business and investment opportunities information,
please contact Global Investment & Business Center, USA
at (703) 370-8082. Fax: (703) 370-8083. E-mail: ibpusa3@gmail.com
Global Business and Investment Info Databank - www.ibpus.com

Company name: Any name not already registered may be chosen. Names such as Switzerland, International, European, etc. are subject to certain conditions. Name must end with suffix AG/SA or GmbH/SARL depending on the type of the company.

Usual minimum capital: AG/SA - CHF 100,000. A minimum of 20% of the nominal value of the share capital or CHF 50,000 (whichever is higher) should be paid in cash or in kind. The share capital is transferred to a blocked account at a Swiss bank to be held in the name of the company until the company is registered. GmbH/Sarl-CHF 20,000 of which 50% must be paid up before incorporation.

Formation procedure: An organizational meeting of the shareholders is held during which the founders adopt the bylaws, subscribe to all the initial shares, elect the members of the initial board of directors and the auditors, and have the minutes of the meeting notarized. The company must be registered in the Commercial Register at the site of its headquarters. The headquarters site should also be specified in the bylaws. A registration application must be prepared and signed by all board members and signatories and sent to the Commercial Register together with the notarized minutes of the founders' meeting and additional required information. This information includes the corporation's legal address, a statement of acceptance of office and duties by the board members and auditors, disclosure of the nature of the initial capital contribution of the founders (whether in cash or in kind), major assets to be acquired and a statement of non-violation of the Statute on Acquisition of Real Estate by Foreigners. The corporation becomes a legal entity when it is entered in the Commercial Register.

Minimum number of shareholders: AG/SA - the company must have at least three shareholders (who may act in a fiduciary capacity), but this requirement has no practical consequences after the formation of the corporation. Shares may be issued in the shareholder's name (registered shares) or to the bearer (bearer shares), which should be wholly paid. A AG/SA company can issue both types. Par value of each share must be at least CHF 10. Although each share is allowed one vote, the bylaws can establish that the right is not accorded proportionally to the par value. The par value of other shares may not exceed ten times the par value of shares granting privileged voting rights. Swiss corporate law also provides for other equity instruments, such as participation certificates, which are similar to shares but lack voting rights. Within the limits allowed by law, a company may restrict the transferability of its registered shares.

GmbH/Sarl has no shareholders as such, as the company is not permitted to issue shares in the sense of securities. It has a register of its quota holders and their part of the capital; at least two quota holders must be registered.

Minimum number of directors: AG/SA minimum one director is required. Corporate bodies are not permitted. At least one director must be a Swiss resident and the majority of board members must be Swiss nationals residing in Switzerland. GmbH/Sarl - minimum one director is required. At least one director must be a Swiss resident.

Taxation: Switzerland is divided into 26 cantons, and each canton has its' own tax system. In general, in Switzerland there is a three-level tax system: 1) At a federal level - the federal profit tax (3.63 % - 9.8 %) and taxes to export of the capital (35 %); 2) On canton level - the basic profit tax (20 % - 35 %); 3) Communes assess incomes, basically in percentage terms from canton taxes. Depending on a kind of carried out activity, such as the company (holding, administrative and another) and canton where the company is registered, are applied various rates of taxes to incomes.

Registered address: All companies registered in Switzerland must have registered address in Switzerland.

Annual reporting and audits: All Swiss companies must be audited annually. Elected by the shareholders' meeting, the auditors can either be an independent person or a company and must be domiciled in Switzerland. The auditors, which should be independent of the company, examine the books and the annual financial statements in order to submit their report at the shareholders' meeting. Accounts must be filed each year with the Companies Registration Office.

Time needed for formation: usually 2-4 weeks.

Incorporating in Switzerland is relatively easier than in any other countries in Europe but it still requires a considerable amount of time, money and effort. As there are two types of companies you can incorporate in Switzerland, there are a few differences in the procedures and requirements of each.

Swiss GmbH

Swiss GmbH is a Limited Liability Company primarily undertaken by small businesses because of lower costs in registration requirements and capital investment. Incorporation fee of a Limited Liability Company is estimated at CHF 7,500 (Swiss Francs) or roughly USD5,700. The capital investment should remain at CHF 20.000 (roughly 12,320 in Euro). In excess of this amount, your company will already be considered as a corporation and as such should be registered under Swiss AG. There should be at least two partners to form a Swiss GmbH; and at least one director is a local resident.

Swiss AG

Swiss AG is a Corporation where much stricter requirements are necessary to be able to incorporate this kind of company. A capital investment of 100, 000 Swiss Francs is required; half of which should be paid up front upon application. A minimum of three shareholders is required but unlike in the Swiss GmbH, shareholders in a Swiss AG remain anonymous. And unlike with the Swiss Limited Liability Company, the majority of the company's directors should be local residents.

Regular requirements for both are the payment of stamp duties, registration for taxes and enrollment for Social Security. Taxes differ from one Canton to the next and are also dependent on applicable federal taxation regulations. Compared to other offshore destinations, incorporating in Switzerland may appear to be a bit more exacting but its reputation is held in the highest regard. It has the most sophisticated and elaborate infrastructure that offshore companies are sure to benefit from.

COMPANY NAME CLEARANCE

Company name clearance is advisable but not obligatory.

Following notorisation of documents, the name must be entered in the commercial registry of the appropriate Canton.

DEPOSITING SHARE CAPITAL

CHF 20,000 CHF is placed in a bank during the incorporation and the notary needs to see the certificate of deposit.

Once the company is registered, this money is free to be used.

NOTARIAL WORK

Draft the Articles of Association in the presence of a notary public

The notary public notarises the personal and corporate signatures on the application form and authenticates the articles of association and the public deed of incorporation.

The Stamps Declaration Form and Lax Friedrich declaration Form are necessary documents for incorporation.

OTHER PROCESSES

Three more processes are done, before the company is ready to trade:

- Presenting documents to the Commercial Registry
- Payment of stamp duty
- Registry with the tax and social security authorities

SWISS OFFSHORE COMPANY FORMATION INFORMATION

Switzerland is often regarded as an offshore company location along with many other offshore jurisdictions. However unlike other "brass plate" jurisdictions it enjoys relatively low tax rates, a reputation for quality and security and is enviably located in the heart of Europe and, whilst not a member of the EU, enjoys many bilateral treaties with the EU as well as an extensive range of International Double Tax Treaties.

Many International Companies and Entrepreneurs decide to incorporate in Switzerland for these reasons and in some cases decide to take up the option of personal residency.

Below is some useful information relating to Swiss Offshore Company Formation, types of business organisation, share capital structures, corporate taxation, company formation procedures and documentation, and incorporation costs.

FORMS OF BUSINESS ORGANIZATION FOR OFFSHORE OPERATIONS

Swiss Corporation (Aktiengesellschaft (AG))	Company with predetermined capital divided into bearer or registered shares. Shareholders liability limited to nominal capital invested in shares.
Limited Liability Company (Gesellschaft mit beschränkter Haftung (GmbH))	Company with limited capital divided into quotas. Any change or transfer of quotas requires amendment of statutes.
General Partnership (Kollektivgesellschaft)	Partnership of two or more individuals in which partners have unlimited liability.
Limited Partnership (Kommanditgesellschaft)	Partnership of two or more persons or companies. One or more have unlimited liability while other partners may have limited liability.
Simple Partnership (Einfache Gesellschaft)	Contractual relationship between two or more individuals or companies relating to a specific project.
Cooperative (Genossenschaft)	Union of min seven persons (with no upper limit) organised as an entity mainly by agricultural and/or large retail organisations.

For additional analytical, business and investment opportunities information,
please contact Global Investment & Business Center, USA
at (703) 370-8082. Fax: (703) 370-8083. E-mail: ibpusa3@gmail.com
Global Business and Investment Info Databank - www.ibpus.com

| Branch | Locally registered branch office of Foreign Corporation. |
| Sole Proprietorship | Individual trade |

TYPES OF SHARE CAPITAL AND SHARE CLASSES

Minimum Share Capital	For a Swiss Corporation (AG) the minimum capital is CHF 100'000 of which min CHF 50'000 must be paid-in. For a Limited Liability Company (GmbH) the minimum capital requirement is CHF 20'000.
Denomination	Minimum par value for an AG is CHF 0.01 per share. For a GmbH the min quotas are CHF 100.00 or multiples thereof.
Registered Shares	Registered Shares may be issues provided that 20% of the capital has been subscribed subject to a minimum of CHF 50'000. For an AG shareholders identity is not recorded in the Commercial Registry.
Bearer Shares	Bearer Shares may be issues only if fully paid up and not subject to any transfer restriction.
Dual-Class Common Stock	Shares may be issued with differing voting power and par values. Voting shares must be in Registered form.
Non-Voting Shares (Participation certificates)	Swiss Corporations may issue Non-Voting Shares which convey rights etc. but do not permit the holders to vote at shareholders meetings.
Non-Equity Shares	Swiss Corporations may issue these shares, which have no par value or voting rights - but may confer on the holder certain rights to liquidation proceeds or rights to subscribe to new Shares.

CORPORATE TAXES FOR ZUG COMPANIES

Tax Description	Swiss Activities	International Activities
Federal Corporate Income Taxes	8.5%	8.5%
Canton/Municipal Corporate Income Taxes	3% on profits up to CHF 100'000 6.25% on profits over CHF 100'000 (6% in 2013 and 5.75% in 2014)	There are a variety of tax privileged companies, which may benefit from 0% tax on foreign profits. e.g. Holding Companies Management Companies Mixed Companies Principal Companies
Cantonal/Municipal Capital & Reserves Tax	0.5%	Reduced to 0.075% for tax privileged companies.
Withholding Taxes	35% Dividends and Bond Interest 0% on Royalties, Licenses and Similar Fees Dependent on Double tax treaties.	Shares may be issued with differing voting power and par values. Voting shares must be in Registered form.
VAT	8.0% Standard Rate 2.5% for goods covering basic needs	Swiss VAT not chargeable on services performed outside Switzerland or goods exported

For additional analytical, business and investment opportunities information,
please contact Global Investment & Business Center, USA
at (703) 370-8082. Fax: (703) 370-8083. E-mail: ibpusa3@gmail.com
Global Business and Investment Info Databank - www.ibpus.com

	3.6% for accommodation related services.	outside Switzerland.
Capital Gains	Capital Gain is generally recognized as income for Federal and Cantonal tax purposes. Investments in CH - Normal Income tax rates apply or exempt.	Investments where over 10% (or CHF 2 Mio) voting rights held and held for more than one year are exempt from CH tax-
Capital Gains on Real Estate	Real Estate in CH - 5%-60%	Gains on Foreign Real Estate exempt from CH tax.
Dividend Income	0% or partially exempt provided more than 20% or CHF 2 Million equity holding.	0% or partially exempt provided more than 10% or CHF 1 Million equity holding.
Foreign Income	Not taxed incl. Real Estate Income	Not taxed incl. Real Estate Income

COMPANY INCORPORATION PROCEDURES

Core Incorporation Tasks	
Company Name	Agree and check availability with Swiss Commercial Registry
Prepare founding documents	Articles of Association etc.
Payment of capital	Swiss Bank Account
Founding of Company	Deed of incorporation with Notary Public
Commercial Registry	Publication in Official Gazette of Canton

DOCUMENTATION REQUIRED FOR INCORPORATION OF A SWISS COMPANY

Core Incorporation Tasks	
Company Name	Confirm availability with Swiss Commercial Registry
Articles of Association	Draft and agree
Corporate Information	Company Name Registered Office and address Capital Structure Founders Details & Signatory Powers Board of Directors & Signatory Powers Statutory Auditors (if required) Officers & Signatory Powers
Auditor Acceptance Letter	Auditor appointed must confirm acceptance in writing (if required)
Confirmation of paid in Capital	Must be in blocked account at Swiss Bank
Power of Attorney	To represent founders in incorporation matters
Founder's delcaration	
Qualifying shares declaration	
Proxy Agreement	If to be incorporated in absence of founders
Statutes	Draft and agree
Shareholder's Agreement	Draft and agree if applicable
Form 3 Stamp Duty on new shares	1% only if value greater than CHF 1'000'000
Shareholder Register	Make entries/issue certificates

Commercial Registry Submission	New company details to be submitted to Commercial Registry
Entry in Commercial Register	Official Publication of incorporation
VAT Registration	If Applicable

STARTING BUSINESS IN SWITZERLAND

MARKET OVERVIEW

Switzerland's population of 7.8 million is affluent and cosmopolitan
GDP of about USD 594 billion; forecast growth of 1.3% for 2012
In 2011 total exports from the U.S. to Switzerland amounted to USD 24.5 billion.
U.S.-Swiss trade generally stable despite financial and economic crisis;
World-class infrastructure, business-friendly legal and regulatory environment
Highly educated, reliable, and flexible work force
Consumer and producer of high quality, value-added industrial/consumer goods
Manufacturing sector is highly automated and efficient
Strong market demand for U.S. components and production systems
Strong demand for high quality products with competitive prices
Highest per capita IT spending in the world
Multilingual/multicultural European test market and business environment
Many U.S. firms with European and regional headquarters in Switzerland

US EXPORTS TO SWITZERLAND BY CATEGORY (USD)

Product Category	2009	2010	2011
910-Waste and Scrap	3,263,911,178	5,081,031,521	7,275,778,906
331-Primary Metal Mfg.	3,419,361,668	4,695,976,230	5,419,312,479
325-Chemicals	3,152,409,386	2,805,982,509	3,110,705,019
*339-Miscellaneous Manufactured Commodities	2,185,913,741	2,386,292,425	2,750,573,637
All Others	5,482,813,896	5,718,051,011	5,896,367,969
Total exports	17,504,409,869	20,687,333,696	24,452,738,010

Source: International Trade Administration (ITA) 2011 Exports to Switzerland of NAICS (North American Industry Classification System), total all merchandise

*339-Miscellaneous Manufactured Commodities include: Medical and Dental Equipment and Supplies, Jewelry and Silverware, Sporting and Athletic Goods, Toys and Games, Office Supplies (except Paper), Pens and Pencils, Marking Devices, Signs, Gasket, Packing and Sealing Devices, Musical Instruments, Brooms, Brushes, Mops, Burial Caskets, all other miscellaneous manufacturing.

US Exports to Switzerland 2011 by Category – All Others

Item	Amount

920 --Used or Second☐Hand Merchandise	1,853,019,669
334 --Computer and Electronics Products	1,080,906,780
336 -- Transportation Equipment	718,739,307
990 -- Special Classification Provisions, Nesoi	595,853,570
333 -- Machinery, except Electrical	461,518,095
332 --Fabricated Metal Products, Nesoi	240,919,423
111 --Agricultural Products	237,203,705
324 --Petroleum & Coal Products	173,931,542
335 --Electrical Equipment, Appliances & Components	128,659,126
326 --Plastics & Rubber Products	77,726,961
311 --Food Manufacturers	60,387,186
327 -- Nonmetallic Mineral Products	52,276,931
312 -- Beverages & Tobacco Products	42,202,923
322 --Paper	41,345,392
323 --Printed Matter and Related Products, Nesoi	28,362,408

315 --Apparel Manufacturing Products	22,191,362
212 -- Minerals & Ores	17,966,686
313 --Textiles & Fabrics	13,447,175
316 -- Leather & Allied Products	13,280,687
337 --Furniture & Fixtures	11,243,520
314 --Textile Mills Products	6,504,704
114 -- Fish, Fresh/Chilled/Frozen & Other Marine Products	6,068,441
511 --Newspaper, Books & Other Published Matter, Nesoi	3,931,273
113 --Forestry Products, Nesoi	3,517,634
321 --WoodProducts, Wood Prodts	2857405,,
112 --Other Animals	2,285,577
211 --Oil & Gas	20,487
Total	5,896,367,969

MARKET CHALLENGES

Market is sophisticated, quality-conscious, high tech and competitive

An epicenter of European and global competition

While EU-type regulations and standards exist in general, there are significant exceptions

Unique Swiss requirements for , pharmaceuticals, cosmetics, detergents, and chemicals

MARKET OPPORTUNITIES

Products with relatively advanced technologies are best prospects

Switzerland is strategically placed as a gateway to EU markets

For additional analytical, business and investment opportunities information,
please contact Global Investment & Business Center, USA
at (703) 370-8082. Fax: (703) 370-8083. E-mail: ibpusa3@gmail.com
Global Business and Investment Info Databank - www.ibpus.com

Ideal test market for introduction of new high tech and consumer products

Excellent platform for marketing into Europe, Middle East and Africa

High concentration of computer/Internet usage per capita

Sophisticated market for U.S. devices

Switzerland is becoming a European center for commercial aviation business

Fast growing demand for highly sophisticated security equipment/systems

One of world's top countries for R&D

Excellent opportunities for partnerships in biotech, nanotech, and renewable energies, especially solar

Venture capital funds largest in Europe, opportunities for U.S. exporters in third country markets with Swiss financing

MARKET ENTRY STRATEGY

Express commitment to the market and establish long term relationships

Work directly with Swiss importers/distributors for maximum market penetration

Be prepared to meet customer's needs and willing to sell in small volumes

Offer high quality and environmentally friendly products

Enter the market early to gain and maintain competitive edge

Evaluate carefully prospective partner's technical qualifications and ability to cover the German, French and Italian regions

SWISS BUSINESS REGISTRATION PROCEDURE

No.	Procedure	Time to Complete	Associated Costs
1	Place the paid-up capital in an escrow account with a bank The capital is released by the bank upon completing the registration procedure at the Commercial Registry. Bank fees range from CHF 200 to CHF 2,000. A minimum bank fee of CHF 200 is charged for transferring capital from the escrow account to the company account after the company registration.	1 day	no charge
2	Draft the articles of association in the presence of a notary public, who notarizes the personal and corporate signatures on the application form and authenticate the articles of association and the public deed of incorporation. All signatures on the company registration application form have to	7 days	0.1% of capital, minimum CHF 500, maximum CHF 5,000 + CHF 100 (for 5 signatures)

No.	Procedure	Time to Complete	Associated Costs
	be legalized (CHF 20 per personal or corporate signature). The Stampa Declaration Form (a negative declaration on investments in kind or chattels or founders' privileges, which is compulsory as documentary evidence) and the Lex Friedrich Declaration Form (a permit for foreigners to acquire real estate) must be signed and handed to the Register of Commerce. The filing of both declaration forms is obligatory for all company incorporation applicants, irrespective of nationality. The name check is not mandatory but is recommended. The fee is CHF 50. Along with the request for name check, required for incorporation and available on the Internet are the public deed, the application form, the Stampa Declaration Form, and the Lex Friedrich Declaration Form.		
3	File the deed certifying the articles of association to the local commercial register to obtain a legal entity If by express mail, registration takes 3 to 5 days, and if by regular mail, about 7 days. The fee ranges from CHF 600 (for capital of CHF 20,000) to a maximum of CHF 10,000. In 5–9 days, the Registry publishes the date of the statutes and all names of shareholders in the Swiss Commercial Gazette; the announcement fee is included in the registration fee. Entry in the Commercial Register protects the company's trade name and gives it a legal personality. Required documents also include the Stampa Declaration Form and Lex Friedrich Declaration Form (described in Procedure 1), as well as automatic registration for income tax payment.	7 days	CHF 600+ 0.02% of capital exceeding CHF 200,000 up to a maximum of CHF 10,000
4	Pay stamp tax at post office or bank after receiving an assessment by mail An application can be filed with the Federal Tax Administration after incorporating the company with the Commercial Registry. Because not every company is subject to tax, a procedure exists to determine whether the company is subject to the tax.	1 day	1% capital with the first CHF 1,000,000 exempt
5	Register for VAT An application for VAT registration can be filed with the Federal Tax Administration only after incorporating the company with the Commercial Registry. Because not every company is subject to VAT, a procedure exists to determine whether the company is subject to this tax.	1 day, within 30 days after being subject to VAT	no charge
6	Enroll employees in the social insurance system (federal and cantonal authorities) After the company has registered with the Commercial Registry, the cantonal social security office (Ausgleichskasse) will send the employer an application for registering employees in the social insurance system, which includes retirement and survivors' insurance benefits (AHV), disability insurance (IV), occupational accident insurance (UVG), and retirement pension (BVG). In practice, more applicants are using application forms in Internet.	1 day	no charge

DIRECT INVESTMENT: PRACTICAL INFORMATION

Swiss law does not distinguish between Swiss-owned and foreign-owned business entities. There are, in principle, neither registration nor local agent requirements.

For additional analytical, business and investment opportunities information, please contact Global Investment & Business Center, USA at (703) 370-8082. Fax: (703) 370-8083. E-mail: ibpusa3@gmail.com Global Business and Investment Info Databank - www.ibpus.com

Investments by foreigners may be made through the purchase of stock or assets of an existing company, by establishing a branch or subsidiary, or also by entering into a joint venture or partnership with a Swiss company. It cannot be said that one form is generally preferred over another.

The forms of Swiss business entities are:

- sole proprietorship (Einzelfirma, raison de commerce);
- corporation (Aktiengesellschaft, soci,t, anonyme);
- limited liability company (Gesellschaft mit beschr„nkter Haftung, soci,t, … responsabilit, limit,e);
- partnership limited by shares (Kommanditaktiengesellschaft, soci,t, en commandite); and
- unlimited partnership (Kollektivgesellschaft, soci,t, en nom collectif).

The corporation, the limited liability company, and the partnership limited by shares have a separate legal personality independent of the management or the shareholders. The corporation is by far the most common form of legal organization in Switzerland (see Section XII below).

All companies must, as a rule, be entered into the Register of Commerce. Entry into this register has, in some cases, a constitutive effect. An Aktiengesellschaft, for instance, comes into legal existence only upon its registration. The purpose of such registration is to make public all Swiss companies and the Swiss branches of foreign companies engaged in business in Switzerland, and to prove information about their legal status. The entry is comprised of the name of the company, its domicile, capitalization, nominal value of the shares, members of the board of directors, officers, signing powers, etc. The Register of Commerce is open to the public. In addition, most entries are published in summarized form in the Swiss Journal of Commerce.

PURCHASE BY FOREIGN CORPORATION OF BUSINESS IN SWITZERLAND

Swiss law does not prohibit foreign corporations from acquiring local companies. Foreign corporations can also acquire all of the assets of local companies. Notwithstanding the foregoing, two limitations (apart from the acquisition of real estate as mentioned in chapter IV. A, above) have to be mentioned.

The acquisition of a substantial part (i.e., a controlling influence) of a Swiss bank requires a license from the Swiss Banking Commission. Such license is subject to the following conditions:

- The country of residence of the foreign bank or the foreign controlling corporate or individual shareholder has to grant reciprocity;
- The chosen name of the foreign controlled Swiss bank shall in no way indicate or suggest that the bank is Swiss controlled; and
- The Swiss National Bank must confirm having received from the bank the necessary undertaking that it will adhere to the credit and monetary policy of Switzerland.

A Swiss bank is deemed to be foreign-controlled within the meaning of the Banking Act if foreigners own a direct or indirect interest exceeding 50% of the share capital or the voting rights of the bank or if they own a controlling interest in some other manner. The term foreigner includes individual persons who are neither Swiss nationals nor have the permit to permanently reside in Switzerland as well as corporate persons and partnerships incorporated abroad or, if incorporated in Switzerland, controlled by foreign individuals.

The other limitation which has to be mentioned stems from the fact that many Swiss corporations have issued registered shares. This possibility, permitted by the Code of Obligations, makes it possible to more or less freely restrict share ownership and to give authority and discretion to the board of directors to accept or reject applications of new shareholders for registration. Since only holders of shares that are actually registered in the stockregister are recognized, the board of directors may virtually control registered share ownership if the board of directors is given the necessary authority by the corporate articles. Over the years, this mechanism has been used to protect Swiss corporations from acquisition by foreigners. Originally, however, during and after the war, it was used to prove, particularly to the U.S. government, that a particular Swiss corporation was not "enemy held".

Switzerland also has antitrust laws, but they are by far not as stringent as those of the major European countries or of the EC. In particular, they do not contain any absolute figures or limitations, but rather refer to the aggregate effect ("on balance") of monopolies and restrictive trade practices.

BRANCHES

The branch office of a foreign company must be registered in the canton in which it is located in the same way as the branch office of a Swiss firm. An authorized representative residing in Switzerland must be appointed.

A branch office must use the same company name as that of its head office, but must make it clear in its name that it is only a branch office.

As far as registration is concerned, there is no difference between a trading and a non-trading branch office. A branch office does not have to publish its annual financial statement. However, due to the fact that a branch office always constitutes a permanent establishment for direct tax purposes, the foreign company is required to disclose certain financial information with respect to its branch office to the Swiss tax authorities.

Under the Swiss-American income tax treaty of 1951, an American enterprise doing business in Switzerland may be subject to taxation by Switzerland on such industrial and commercial profits allocable to its permanent establishment in Switzerland. Attributed to the branch office are the profits which it might be expected to earn if it were an independent enterprise engaged in the same or similar activities under the same or similar conditions and dealing at arm's length with the American headquarters.

In the determination of the taxable income of the branch office, all expenses which are reasonably applicable to it may be deducted, including executive and general administrative expenses. In practice, the branch office will either be taxed on the basis of its own profit and loss account, if applicable, or on the basis of a deemed net profit which represents a certain percentage of its annual running expenses (e.g., 10%). There is no withholding tax on the transfer of branch profits to the foreign company's headquarters.

EXCHANGE CONTROLS

Currency matters are normally delegated by the federal government to the Swiss National Bank. The Swiss franc is freely convertible into any other currency.

For additional analytical, business and investment opportunities information,
please contact Global Investment & Business Center, USA
at (703) 370-8082. Fax: (703) 370-8083. E-mail: ibpusa3@gmail.com
Global Business and Investment Info Databank - www.ibpus.com

TAX SYSTEM

DIRECT TAXES

As a result of Switzerland's confederate structure, direct taxes are levied simultaneously by three different authorities, viz. the federal government, the cantons, and the communities. While the Swiss federal tax laws apply throughout Switzerland, cantonal tax laws governing the taxes of the cantons and communities are only valid within their respective territories. This reflects the territorial concept to which Switzerland adheres in its taxation policy, including that of international taxation (unless varied by treaty).

The federal, as well as the cantonal tax laws are administered by the cantonal tax administrations. The federal authorities exercise a supervisory function and may reject a cantonal decision so far as the federal tax is concerned.

Federal tax is uniform throughout the country. The federal income tax rates are usually lower than the cantonal rates which vary from canton to canton. Subject to tax are corporations and similar business entities organized in Switzerland, as well as entities incorporated abroad doing business through a branch or other permanent establishment in Switzerland (see Section XI). The federal income tax rate on net profits of corporations is based on the ratio between taxable income and equity, starting at 3.63% and rising to a maximum of 9.8% of the taxable income, which maximum is arrived at if the income is more than 23.15% of the equity.

The federal capital tax rate for corporations is 0.0825%. Taxable capital is considered the shareholders' equity as shown in the books (paid-in capital, legal reserves and other retained earnings) and those "silent" reserves that have been taxed as income.

Swiss resident individuals are liable to the federal direct tax on their worldwide income. Non-resident individuals deriving Swiss-source business income through a permanent establishment or fixed place of business in Switzerland are taxed on such income. The applicable tax rates vary depending on the income level. As from January 1, 1991, the maximum rate of 11.5% will apply to taxable income of at least SFr. 501,700 for single taxpayers and of at least SFr. 595,200 for married taxpayers.

Each of the twenty-six cantons has its own tax law for direct taxation and more or less different rules for determining the taxable income or net wealth of individuals as well as corporate taxable income or capital. The local tax rates vary widely. The communities generally levy their tax as a percentage of the taxes imposed by the cantons in which they are located. Each community is, within certain limits of the cantonal law, free to set its tax multiplier.

B. INDIRECT TAXES

The main indirect taxes in Switzerland are the tax on turnover of goods (which might soon be replaced by a value-added tax), the stamp duties on securities, and the anticipatory tax (withholding tax) on corporate profit distributions and interest payments from Swiss bank accounts and bonds. All these indirect taxes are within the exclusive competence of the federal government.

Subject to the turnover tax are domestic deliveries of goods by wholesalers and imports. The tax is levied on net sales proceeds at the rate of 6.2% for deliveries to end-users and 9.3% for deliveries to retailers.

For additional analytical, business and investment opportunities information, please contact Global Investment & Business Center, USA at (703) 370-8082. Fax: (703) 370-8083. E-mail: ibpusa3@gmail.com Global Business and Investment Info Databank - www.ibpus.com

A stamp duty is levied on the issuance of corporate shares and other contributions to corporate capital at the rate of 3% of the net amount received by the corporation. Stamp duties are also levied on the turnover of Swiss and foreign securities at the rate of 0.15% and 0.3%, respectively, if a Swiss securities broker is involved as a party or intermediary to the transaction.

The anticipatory tax must be withheld at source by the debtor of the taxable dividend or interest payment and be submitted to the federal tax administration. The tax rate is 35%. Recipients who are residents of Switzerland are entitled to a full refund of the anticipatory tax provided they duly report the full dividend or interest as income. Non-resident (individual or corporate) recipients may only claim a tax refund to the extent provided for by an applicable Swiss international double taxation treaty.

LABOR

In comparison with other European countries, Switzerland regulates relatively few areas of the contractual relationship between employers and employees. The result is a system of labor law which is readily comprehensible and generally more favorable to the employer than the labor law in many other jurisdictions.

Generally, no specific form is required for a contract of employment. The contract of employment has to be in writing only where it relates to certain particular categories of employees, e.g., apprentices, travelling salesmen and workers employed at home, or where other particular circumstances exist, e.g., the contract provides for overtime other than as determined by law. Non-competition agreements need also to be in writing.

With certain exceptions, the maximum working hours for industrial, technical and office workers and other white-collar employees (including shop personnel) are 45 hours a week. For other workers, the maximum hours are 50 hours a week. The maximum weekly working hours may be exceeded under certain exceptional circumstances in accordance with prescribed limitations on hours and pay for overtime. Certain rules apply only to women. Exceptions are permitted only under very specific circumstances.

Generally, regular day time work must not begin before 5:00 a.m. in the summer or 6:00 a.m. in the winter and must not continue beyond 8:00 p.m. Minimum breaks or rest times are also provided for by the law. Other than in exceptional circumstances, work at night and on Sundays is not permitted.

Persons not subject to the foregoing restrictions include, among others, managerial employees and employees active in scientific or independent artistic pursuits.

Employers must give employees one day off every week, usually Sunday. Other arrangements for days off may be made with the employee's consent. Further, employers must give employees at least four weeks annual vacation. For employees under the age of twenty, the minimum is five weeks annual vacation. A minimum of two weeks annual vacation must be taken by the employee at one time. While the employment relation lasts, mandatory vacation time must not be replaced by monetary compensation.

There are no paternity rights granted by Swiss law in relation to employment. Swiss law does, however, recognize differences between the types of labor which men and women are able to perform, and recognizes the special cases of pregnant women, those in childbirth and nursing mothers. For example, a pregnant woman or nursing mother may not be required to do work which is a hardship for her. Except with her consent, a pregnant woman may not work beyond normal working hours. She may take time off or discontinue work upon giving notice of her wish to do so and without regard to the regular minimum periods of notice. In addition, an employer is prohibited from giving notice of termination to a pregnant employee up to sixteen weeks after the birth of her child.

Any such notice given within this period is void. A woman is not permitted to work during the eight week period after the birth of her child. If she wishes, however, this period may be reduced to six weeks provided her doctor confirms that she is able to return to work. A nursing mother may only begin work, with her consent, eight weeks after the birth of her child. An employer must give a nursing mother the necessary free time to nurse her child while at work. In order to ensure proper rest before and after childbirth, Swiss law also requires that the time allocated for a female employee's vacation must not be shortened if she was not present at work for a total of up to two months due to pregnancy and childbirth. A woman unable to work because of pregnancy and childbirth is entitled to compensation for a limited period if she has been employed for more than three months.

The limited period is generally three weeks at full pay during the first year of service. After that it increases proportionately in accordance with the length of employment and other special circumstances. More compensation may be agreed upon between the parties, or may be determined by a standard provision contract or a collective bargaining agreement.

An employee and employer may enter into a non-competition agreement which requires the employee to refrain from engaging in any competitive activity after termination of the employment relationship, in particular neither to operate a business for his own account which competes with the employer's business, nor to work for or participate in such a business. However, the prohibition against competition is only binding if the employment relationship gives the employee access to customer information or to manufacturing or business secrets and if the use of such knowledge could significantly damage the employer. The prohibition must be reasonably limited in terms of place, time, and subject in order to preclude an unreasonable impairment of the employee's economic prospects. It may exceed three years only under special circumstances.

If an employment contract has no specific term, either the employee or the employer may give notice of termination. Legal notice periods are of one to three months depending on the length of the employment relationship.

At any time during a probationary period, either the employee or the employer may give notice of termination with a notice period of seven days.

The employer may not give notice of termination in any of the following four situations:

> - during compulsory military or civil defense service, women's military service or Red Cross service, and if such service continues for more than twelve days, during the four weeks before the beginning and the four weeks after the end of such service;
> - in case of full or part-time absence from work due to illness or accident, as long as the employee is not at fault for such illness or accident, in the first year of employment during thirty, from the second to the fifth year of employment during ninety and from the sixth year of employment during 180 days of such absence;
> - during pregnancy and sixteen weeks after employee has given birth; or
> - during a foreign relief service in which an employee serves with the consent of the employer and which has been ordered by the competent federal authorities.

An employer or employee may terminate the contract of employment without notice when he has "cause." A party is considered to have cause when the circumstances are such that the party can no longer be expected to continue the employment relationship with loyalty and trust. Whether or not cause exists is a decision made largely at the judge's discretion.

An employee with twenty or more years of service and at least 50 years of age is entitled to receive from the employer special compensation on his termination. The amount of the special compensation may be determined by written agreement, by the terms of a standard provision contract, or by a collective bargaining agreement; but the amount may not be less than the compensation which the employee would receive for two months work. If the amount of the special compensation is not determined, a judge must determine the amount, taking into consideration all the circumstances; but the amount may not be more than the compensation which the employee would receive for eight months work. The special compensation need not be paid to the extent that the employee receives a payment from a social insurance institution, which is the result of the employer's prior contribution to that institution. Similarly, the employer is not required to pay any special compensation if he guarantees the employee's required future social insurance payments or if he arranges to have a third party provide such a guarantee.

COMPANY DISSOLUTION

Once an insolvent company has been declared bankrupt by the court, the bankruptcy office draws up an inventory and publishes the bankruptcy. It orders all creditors and debtors to file their claims and debts. The estate is administrated by the bankruptcy office, which may be replaced by one or more persons elected by the creditors.

The creditors may also elect a committee of creditors to supervise the administrators and to authorize them to take certain important measures. For such elections and other urgent matters, meetings of creditors are held. The administrators must establish a schedule of creditors. Thereafter, a second creditors meeting passes on all matters, including realization of assets by public auction or private sale. After distribution of the proceeds, the bankruptcy court receives a final accounting and declares the bankruptcy closed. Every creditor receives a "certificate of loss" for the unpaid balance of his claim.

The bankruptcy court may order summary proceedings if the assets found do not warrant the expenses of ordinary proceedings. The bankruptcy office then proceeds to the liquidation without the participation of the creditors. Any creditor can demand ordinary proceedings by advancing the costs.

If no assets are found, the bankruptcy court also orders the bankruptcy closed, but no "certificate of loss" is issued. During a two year period thereafter, any creditor can institute execution of seizure against the debtor.

Composition is also known in Swiss law. Basically, there are three types of it: stay of payment during a certain time period; payment of a percentage on all non-privileged debts; and abandonment of all or part of the debtor's assets to creditors. Composition is possible for any debtor, even after execution proceedings have started. Except in cases of a bankruptcy already declared, the debtor must apply for a stay of payment with the "composition authority", submitting a statement of assets and liabilities and a draft composition plan. If the authority grants the composition, a commissioner is appointed. The debtor can, under supervision of the commissioner, dispose of his property but not sell or encumber it. If the composition liquidation is confirmed, a creditors' meeting elects the liquidators and a committee of creditors to supervise

For additional analytical, business and investment opportunities information,
please contact Global Investment & Business Center, USA
at (703) 370-8082. Fax: (703) 370-8083. E-mail: ibpusa3@gmail.com
Global Business and Investment Info Databank - www.ibpus.com

the liquidators. The realization of the assets and the distribution of the proceeds to the creditors is similar to bankruptcy proceedings.

Special regulations apply to banks, hotels, farms and some other businesses.

Under chapter 11 of the Private International Law Statute, a foreign bankruptcy decree issued in the country of the debtor's domicile will be recognized in Switzerland upon application by the foreign trustee in bankruptcy or by one of the creditors, if (a) the decree is enforceable in the country where it was rendered, (b) the recognition is not against Swiss public policy and, (c) the country issuing the decree grants reciprocity.

An application for recognition of a foreign bankruptcy decree must be filed with the court where the assets are located in Switzerland. If assets are located in several places, jurisdiction lays with the court where the application was first filed.

As soon as a motion to recognize a foreign bankruptcy decree has been made, the court may, upon petition, order conservatory measures. Actions in attachment that are pending or have become pending during the recognition proceedings are suspended until the proceedings are concluded.

The judgment on the recognition of the foreign bankruptcy decree is published in Switzerland. The recognition is officially communicated to the office of execution, the office of bankruptcy, the office for land registration, the office for commercial registration at the location of the assets and, depending on the case, to the office of industrial property. The same applies for closing, suspension and cancellation of the proceedings.

Unless otherwise provided, with respect to the assets in Switzerland, the recognition of a foreign bankruptcy decree has the effects of bankruptcy set forth under Swiss Law.

INTERNATIONAL RELATIONSHIPS

INTERNATIONAL CONVENTIONS

Switzerland is not a member of the United Nations, but it belongs to important UN sub-organizations such as UNCTAD and hosts the United Nations in Geneva. As Switzerland is highly dependent on free international trade, bilateral agreements or multinational conventions have been concluded with nearly all countries involved in international trade.

Switzerland has a crucial interest in protecting free international trade. To promote this international trade policy, Switzerland has been, since 1966, a member of the General Agreement on Tariff and Trade (GATT) and, since 1963, a member of the OECD. Switzerland is a member of the European Free Trade Association (EFTA) and, in 1972, concluded a Free Trade Agreement with the European Economic Community (EEC), which provides for the free exchange of goods between the members of the EFTA and the EEC.

The UN Convention on Contracts for the International Sale of Goods of 1980 is expected to come into force in Switzerland in 1991.

With its more important trading partners, Switzerland has concluded "double taxation treaties." Between the United States and Switzerland, two double taxation treaties have been concluded:

one to avoid double taxation on income and the other to avoid double taxation on inheritance. Both were concluded in 1951.

The Swiss Federal Council has recently submitted a bill to Parliament for ratification of the Convention on Jurisdiction and the Enforcement of Judgments in Civil and Commercial Matters, signed in Lugano, Switzerland, on September 16, 1988. The Lugano Convention, which would heavily influence Swiss procedural law, is presently expected to be ratified by Switzerland early in 1991.

BILATERAL TREATIES WITH THE U.S.

Numerous treaties between the United States and Switzerland are particularly noteworthy in the context of this guide:

1. Convention of friendship, commerce and extradition of November 25, 1850.

The convention stipulates the principle that the citizens of the two Contracting States shall be admitted and treated upon a footing of reciprocal equality in the two countries, where such admissions and treatment shall not conflict with the constitutional and legal provisions of the Contracting Parties.

2. Treaty on mutual assistance in criminal matters of May 25, 1973.

The treaty provides for assistance in criminal investigations with respect to certain offenses, the punishment of which falls within the jurisdiction of the judicial authorities of the requesting Country. The assistance to be granted includes ascertaining the whereabouts of persons, taking the testimony or statements of persons, effecting the production of documents, the service of judicial documents and the authentication of documents. The treaty does not apply to investigations concerning political and military offenses. Also excluded are the enforcement of cartel or antitrust law, as well as the prosecution of tax violations. Political, antitrust and fiscal offenses fall under the treaty if the investigation is directed against a person connected with organized crime.

3. Treaty on social security of July 18, 1979, with supplementary agreement of June1, 1988.

The treaty applies to Swiss and U.S. federal old-age, survivors and disability insurance for citizens of the two countries, refugees and stateless persons residing in either country, and other persons with respect to rights derived from persons in the above groups. The treaty provides for equality of treatment of the citizens of the two countries under the social security law of both countries.

4. Treaty for the avoidance of double taxation with respect to taxes on income of May 24, 1951.

This treaty covers, in the case of the United States, the federal income taxes, including surtaxes and excess profits taxes, and, in the case of Switzerland, the federal, cantonal and community taxes on income and any other income or profits tax of a substantially similar character imposed by one of the countries.

5. Treaty for the avoidance of double taxation with respect to taxes on estates and inheritances of July 9, 1951.

The treaty refers to taxes asserted upon death; in the case of the United States, to the federal estate tax, and in the case of Switzerland, to the estate and inheritance taxes imposed by the cantons and any political subdivision thereof.

There is no convention between the United States and Switzerland on service abroad, or on the taking of depositions in civil and commercial matters.

DISPUTE RESOLUTION

ARBITRATION PRACTICE

Arbitration is widely used in Switzerland, especially in international commercial litigation. Residence of one of the parties or a special link with Swiss law is not required. Parties often insist on the seat of the arbitration court being on neutral ground.

The procedure of international arbitration in Switzerland is not necessarily conducted in one of Switzerland's official languages. Quite often arbitration cases are conducted in English. The parties can agree upon the procedural rules applicable in the arbitration case. The Zurich, Geneva, and Basel chambers of commerce and even the Swiss-American Chamber of Commerce have adopted arbitration rules which the parties may agree to apply. For arbitration in Switzerland, the parties may, of course, also agree on the rules of the International Chamber of Commerce (ICC) in Paris or other (e.g., UNCITRAL) rules.

The Zurich Chamber of Commerce recommends the following arbitration clauses:

1. Clause providing for appointment of all three arbitrators by the Zurich Chamber of Commerce:

All disputes arising out of or in connection with the present agreement, including disputes on its conclusion, binding effect, amendment and termination, shall be resolved, to the exclusion of the ordinary courts by an Arbitral Tribunal (or a three-person arbitral tribunal/a sole arbitrator) in accordance with the International Arbitration Rules of the Zurich Chamber of Commerce. (Optional: The decision of the Arbitral Tribunal shall be final, and the parties waive all challenge of the award in accordance with Art. 192, Private International Law Statute.)

2. Clause providing for the appointment of one arbitrator each by the parties:

All disputes arising out of or in connection with the present agreement, including disputes on its conclusion, binding effect, amendment and termination, shall be resolved, to the exclusion of the ordinary courts by a three-person Arbitral Tribunal in accordance with the International Arbitration Rules of the Zurich Chamber of Commerce. If there are not more than two parties involved in the procedure, each party nominates an arbitrator. (Optional: The decision of the Arbitral Tribunal shall be final, and the parties waive all challenge of the award in accordance with Art. 192, Private International Law Statute.)

The recognition and enforcement of foreign arbitration awards in Switzerland is governed by the New York Convention on the Recognition and Enforcement of Foreign Arbitral Awards of June 10, 1958. Likewise, an award rendered by an arbitral tribunal with seat in Switzerland is enforceable in almost any country.

The provisions of Switzerland's Private International Law Statute of December 18, 1987, apply to all international arbitrations, i.e., to arbitrations where the seat of the arbitral tribunal is in

Switzerland and where, at the time of the conclusion of the arbitration agreement, at least one of the parties had neither its domicile nor its habitual residence in Switzerland. The following is a brief synopsis of the international arbitration rules.

The arbitration agreement must be made in writing, by telegram, telex, telecopier or any other means of communication which permits it to be evidenced by a text. Furthermore, an arbitration agreement is valid if it conforms either to the law chosen by the parties, or to the law governing the subject matter of the dispute, in particular the main contract, or to Swiss law.

The arbitrators shall be appointed, removed or replaced in accordance with the agreement of the parties. In the absence of such agreement, the judge where the tribunal has its seat may be seized with the question; he then shall apply, by analogy, the provisions of cantonal law on appointment, removal or replacement of arbitrators. The parties may, directly or by reference to rules of arbitration, determine the arbitral procedure; they may also submit the arbitral procedure to a procedural law of their choice. If the parties have not determined the procedure, the arbitral tribunal shall determine it to the extent necessary, either directly or by reference to a statute or to rules of arbitration.

Regardless of the procedure chosen, the arbitral tribunal shall have to guarantee equal treatment of the parties and the right of both parties to be heard in adversarial proceedings.

A plea of lack of jurisdiction must be raised prior to any defense on the merits. The arbitral tribunal may then decide on its own jurisdiction by preliminary award.

The arbitral tribunal shall decide the case according to the rules of law agreed upon by the parties or, in the absence of a choice of law, by applying the rules of law with which the dispute has the closest connection. The parties may also authorize the arbitral tribunal to decide the case ex aequo et bono.

The award is final from its notification and may only be challenged:

- when the sole arbitrator was not properly appointed or when the arbitral tribunal was not properly constituted;
- when the arbitral tribunal wrongly accepted or declined jurisdiction;
- when the arbitral tribunal's decision went beyond the questions submitted to it, or failed to decide one of the items in the claim;
- when the principle of equality of the parties or the right of the parties to be heard was breached; and
- when the award is contrary to public policy.

If none of the parties have their domicile, their habitual residence, or a business establishment in Switzerland, they may, by an express statement in the arbitration agreement or by a subsequent written agreement, waive fully the action for annulment, or they may limit it to one or several of the grounds listed in Art. 190, subsection 2. If the parties have waived fully the action for annulment and if the award is to be enforced in Switzerland, the New York Convention of June 10, 1958 on the Recognition and Enforcement of Foreign Arbitral Awards applies by analogy.

TRADE REGULATIONS AND STANDARDS[2]

TRADE BARRIERS, INCLUDING TARIFFS AND NON-TARIFF BARRIERS

---

[2] Based on the materials of the US State Department and the US Department of Cemmerce

With the possible exception of agricultural products, Swiss barriers to trade are more an annoyance than a major roadblock. Concerns for exporters include:

Agricultural Products: Until July 1, 1995, Switzerland's highly subsidized agricultural sector operated behind a variety of import restrictions -- licensing, quotas, supplementary import charges, variable levies, conditional import rules, import calendars, and the like. Prices of most agricultural imports were raised to domestic levels by variable import duties and specific non-tariff requirements on importers of agricultural products. A wide variety of U.S. agricultural products felt the effects of these barriers.

According to Organization for Economic Cooperation and Development (OECD) estimates, these policies resulted in Switzerland having one of the most highly protected agricultural sectors in the world. While Swiss consumers have one of the highest levels of per capita expenditures for food, totaling over $4,000 per year, and Switzerland imports about $6 billion of agricultural products per year, structural impediments in the Swiss market and high tariffs restrict imports. As a result, Switzerland poses particular challenges to U.S. agricultural exporters, exemplified by the fact that currently less than 5 percent of agricultural imports are shipped from the United States.

In recent years, Swiss agricultural policy has been reformed in order to be consistent with international (WTO) commitments. Most non-tariff measures have been converted into tariffs, export subsidies continue to be reduced, and domestic support payments have been de-linked from production. With greater transparency on the import regimes, U.S. exporters of agricultural products may have new market opportunities as a result of these changes.

Food Retailing System: A continuing obstacle to U.S. exporters, particularly those of high value products, is the food retailing system. The retail market is dominated by two retail giants who account for nearly half of grocery sales. U.S. exporters are disadvantaged by this system because the two food chain stores emphasize their own store brand products and favor products from their own processing plants. They are devoted primarily to in-house brands, followed by international brands to which they have exclusive marketing rights in Switzerland.

SWISS CARTELS

Cartels in Switzerland used to be the subject of critical comments at regular intervals by the OECD. Indeed, cartels had been playing a significant anti-competitive role until the introduction of the new Swiss Cartel Law in June 1995. The law aimed, in particular, at breaking up so-called hard cartels which included price fixing and/or territorial and quantity allocations. WEKO (Wettbewerbskommission), a special 14 member commission, was established to enforce the new law. Many well known cartels, as a result, have disappeared. Prominent examples are the so-called "beer cartel," the "tobacco cartel," or the "chocolate cartel."

Companies in the pharmaceutical and fossil fuel industries also have been scrutinized as well as legal and medical services. Consumer organizations have shown, however, that there is still a long way to go. The Swiss Federal Government, as a result and in connection with a proposed revision of the existing antitrust legislation, is planning to toughen the anti-cartel law. The new law will give WEKO more power and allow sanctions as of the first offense. Previously, sanctions could be applied only if caught a second time. Fines can now be as high as 10 percent of a company's total revenues in the past three years.

In addition, all industry lobbyists will be removed from WEKO which will be reduced to seven members. WEKO also will be permitted to call witnesses and to conduct searches. The revised law, in spite of considerable opposition, is expected to be put into effect as of spring, 2002. This will bring Swiss anti-cartel legislation to the same level as that applied by the EU.

Agricultural products are similarly affected by cartel practices. The marketing of many domestic farm products, and of competing imports, is controlled by cartel-like organizations of producers, wholesalers, processors, and retailers. Prior to Switzerland's implementation of its Uruguay Round commitments in 1995, these organizations were frequently behind non-tariff import restrictions, with government support. These groups will continue to play an important role in formulating import policy.

Complaints regarding the system come primarily from consumer groups because once a producer or exporter (through a distributor) joins a cartel, the protection afforded is appealing. The new Swiss Cartel Law entered into force on July 1, 1996, and aims (per legal measures patterned on European Union competition policy) to stop anti-competitive practices on the part of "hard cartels". The so-called "soft cartels," however, may continue to enjoy dominant market share as long as they do not indulge in abusive practices such as price fixing or territorial or quantity allocation.

CUSTOMS REGULATIONS

Imported goods from the United States are subject to regular Swiss customs duties at the time of their importation. There is no specific free trade agreement between Switzerland and the USA.

TARIFF RATES

Generally speaking, Swiss duties are "specific" rather than "ad valorem". The customs duty varies according to the item imported; the Swiss customs tariff uses the Harmonized System (HS) for the classification of goods. Customs duties are levied per 100 kilograms of gross weight, unless some other method of calculation is specified in the tariff (e.g. per unit, per meter, per liter). The gross dutiable weight includes the actual weight of the goods and their packaging, including the weight of any fixing material and supports on which the goods are placed.

- Custom Broker's Fees

These are subject to negotiation but some typical fees are listed below:

- Arrival costs (when shipped by air) SF 4.00/100 kg gross (for unloading aircraft payable to airport administration)

- Costs for customs clearance, if picked up at customs:

- 20 kg SF 80.00
20 - 50 kg 89.00
50 - 100 kg 98.00
100 - 200 kg 107.00
200 - 300 kg 116.00
900 - 1000 kg 179.00
over 1000 kg
for every add.
100 kg + 5.50

For additional analytical, business and investment opportunities information,
please contact Global Investment & Business Center, USA
at (703) 370-8082. Fax: (703) 370-8083. E-mail: ibpusa3@gmail.com
Global Business and Investment Info Databank - www.ibpus.com

If items are not picked up at customs (and are forwarded by the broker), there is an additional 1 SF per parcel or a minimum of SF 10 per shipment.

- Truck deliveries: depending on weight and distance

(e.g. up to 20 kg within a distance of 20 km costs SF 34.50)

These are the usual costs which are invoiced by the customs broker. Additional costs will arise if the customs broker advances funds, to be reimbursed by the recipient including the following:

- for freight charges: additional 2 % or min. SF 5.00
- for customs duties: additional 2 % or min. SF 5.00
- for VAT: 0.5 % or min. SF 2.00

Fees for special services if applicable:

- precious metal control per shipment SF 39.00
- veterinarian inspection per shipment SF 39.00
- plant inspection per shipment SF 39.00
- weight control per 100 kg SF 03.40
- inspection of dangerous shipments SF 34.00

- Extra time charges (applicable for special shipments which require a considerable amount of time for inspection, unloading, unpacking, weight control etc.)
minimum SF 39.00
1 man/hour SF 78.00
1 man/1/2 hour SF 39.00

- Definite clearance after provisional clearance:

(goods which are subject to further customs procedures before the customs charges can be determined are given provisional clearance) per document SF 37.00

GELEITSCHEIN (FREE-PASS CERTIFICATE)

Goods which are to be re-exported or transported to another customs office or a customs warehouse may be cleared on the basis of a "Geleitschein" or free-pass certificate.

minimum SF 10.00
maximum SF 100.0

- Prolongation of free-passes: per document SF 70.00
- Precious shipments extra charge 100 %
- Clearance outside customs opening hours
extra charge 100 %
- Clearance on Sundays or public holidays
extra charge 200 %

The above fees are based on one major customs broker in Switzerland, however, these prices may vary from broker to broker.

For additional analytical, business and investment opportunities information,
please contact Global Investment & Business Center, USA
at (703) 370-8082. Fax: (703) 370-8083. E-mail: ibpusa3@gmail.com
Global Business and Investment Info Databank - www.ibpus.com

IMPORT TAXES

- Import Taxes Including Value Added Taxes, Purchase Taxes, Uplifts and Surcharges, and Provincial Taxes

VALUE ADDED TAX

Imported goods and services are also subject to a VAT. The standard VAT rate is 7.6 percent, although there is a reduced rate of 2.3 percent for certain goods and services, such as foodstuffs, agricultural products (meats, cereals, plants, seed and flowers), medicine and drugs, newspapers, magazines, books and other printed materials as well as on services of radio and TV companies. Domestically produced goods pay the same rates.

The VAT will be levied at the border and is usually prepaid by the customs broker/freight forwarder who maintains an account with the Swiss Customs Administration (Oberzolldirektion). Some important Swiss importers maintain their own account.

EXCISE TAXES

Excise taxes are charged on certain goods such as cigarettes and spirits. There are also some special charges for "storage" in the case of various feeds and grains.

More information about excise taxes can be obtained from:
For the importation of spirits:

Federal Administration of Alcohol
Länggasstrasse 31
CH-3005 Bern, Switzerland
Tel. (41-31) 309 12 11
Fax. (41-31) 309 15 00
For the importation of wine as well as other agricultural products:

Federal Office of External Economic Affairs
Division Import-Export
Zieglerstrasse 30
CH-3000 Bern, Switzerland
Tel. (41-31) 322 23 61
Fax. (41-31) 322 78 55

QUOTAS

The allocation of import quotas for agricultural products varies from product to product, while some import quotas are auctioned, others are coupled with a domestic purchase requirement.

Environmental Taxes: Environmental taxes on imported items are collected by the importer/distributor on behalf of the competent government agencies and are known as "prepaid elimination fees". All environmental taxes are included in the final retail prices and, as a result, are borne by the consumers. Environmental taxes are used, in particular, to cover recycling costs and are presently applied on:

- cars SF 40.00 per unit
- bottles and cans depending on the material (aluminum, recyclable pet-labeled, glass etc.)
- Office and consumer electronics (based upon a voluntary industry agreement with SWICO (Schweizerischer Wirtschaftsverband der Informations-, Kommunikations- und Organisationstechnik)
Badenerstrasse 356
CH-8040 Zurich, Switzerland
Tel: (41-1) 492 48 48
Fax: (41-1) 492 35 09

- Batteries depending on type and weight (a voluntary industry agreement was replaced by a federal decree as of January 1999).
- VOC (Volatile Organic Compounds) SF 3.00 per kilogram (the goal being to eliminate VOC's wherever possible).

For further information on environmental taxes, please contact:

Bundesamt für Umwelt
Wald & Landschaft (Environmental Protection Agency)
Papiermühlestrasse 172
CH-3063 Ittigen/Bern, Switzerland
Tel: (41-31) 322 93 11
Fax: (41-31) 322 79 58

IMPORT LICENSE REQUIREMENTS

Import licenses are required only for a limited number of products. These generally fall into two categories -- measures to protect local agriculture production, and measures of state control. To protect the agriculture sector and to maintain a degree of independence in case external supplies get cut off, Switzerland imposes quantitative restrictions on agricultural imports. Products under these restrictions include cattle, meat, milk and dairy products, indigenous fresh fruit and vegetables, seasonal cut flowers, cereals and forage products, wine and grape juice.

Products subject to a quota may not be imported without import licenses, which are granted only to importers based in Switzerland. Most quotas vary from year to year according to the size of harvests, volume of stocks and market requirements.

Import licenses are also required for certain products not subject to quotas, but which are covered by special regulations concerned with public health, plant health, quarantine (plants), veterinary regulations and regulations concerning the protection of species, safety measures, price control (for certain textile products), and measures for the protection of the Swiss economy and public morality. Such import licenses are again issued only to persons and firms domiciled in Switzerland.

TEMPORARY GOODS ENTRY REQUIREMENTS

Goods imported from abroad which are to be re-exported or transported to another customs office or a customs warehouse may be cleared on the basis of a "Begleitschein" or free-pass certificate. The importer must apply for the certificate from the Customs Administration and provide security for the customs charges applicable to the imported goods. The certificate must be presented to customs within the stipulated time, together with the goods in unchanged condition for re-export.

Goods transiting Switzerland must be declared for clearance at the point-of-entry customs office, covered by a national or international transit document (bond note, TIR carnet, T1/T2 dispatch declaration, or international waybill). These goods must be re-exported intact within the designated time limit. No transit duties or fees are levied.

A transit permit is required only for narcotic drugs, armaments, and nuclear fuels and their residues. In the case of direct transit by rail, duties and taxes are guaranteed by the railway authorities. The issuing authority is the guarantor of road transit covered by a TIR carnet. A surety or financial deposit is required for transit covered by a bond note or transit through the EU covered by a T1/T2 dispatch declaration.

Goods temporarily imported or exported for processing or repair may be eligible for customs favored treatment. Reduction in duty or duty-free treatment can be granted when justified by economic interests of Swiss industry. Authorization is granted only to residents who do the processing or repair themselves, or commission a third party. Authorization is for particular goods that are to undergo specified processing. Special conditions may be imposed for customs handling and supervision.

Goods for display at public exhibitions are eligible for free passage (Freipass) through Swiss customs. Certification from the trade fair authorities that the goods are entering Switzerland for the exhibition, is usually required. Exhibition goods must be re-exported within a month of the end of the exhibition. If the goods are sold to a Swiss resident off the exhibition floor, the buyer incurs a liability for the customs charges. Almost all fairgrounds have a customs office on site and charges can be easily handled.

SPECIAL IMPORT/EXPORT REQUIREMENTS AND CERTIFICATIONS

All imported or exported goods must be presented to the appropriate customs office and declared for clearance. Goods imported into Switzerland must be declared to customs within the following time limits from arrival in the country: by road, 24 hours; river, 48 hours; rail, 7 days; and by air, 7 days. The importer may examine goods before submitting them for clearance. For Swiss customs purposes, an ordinary commercial invoice in duplicate or triplicate is considered sufficient documentation. The invoice should contain the following details: description of the products and packaging, gross and net weight of each package, quantity (in metric terms), country of origin, and value CIF (cost, insurance and freight) to the Swiss border. As Swiss duties are specific, indication of value is required only for statistical purposes. No consular or other stamp is required.

A certificate of origin is not normally required. An exception is if preferential duty rates are requested. Additionally, a certificate of origin may be required for health reasons (meats and plants) or for reasons of quality control (appellation wine).

Special health certificates, stamped by the competent authorities of the country of origin, are required for the import of horses, bovine animals, farm animals, certain domestic animals, bees and eggs for hatching, as well as for meat, game, seafood, beeswax and comb honey. Shipments of some vegetables, fresh fruits and wild plants must be accompanied by official plant health certificates of the country of origin.

Swiss importers are normally cooperative in informing the exporter of Swiss requirements, and in assisting in meeting those requirements from the Swiss side.

LABELING REQUIREMENTS

Swiss labeling requirements apply mostly to food products. False descriptions are strictly prohibited. As a rule, the label or packaging for sale to consumers must indicate the specific name of the product (in French, German or Italian), metric measure, sales price and unit price, weight of each component in the case of mixed products, and ingredients and additives in decreasing order of weight. All particulars of weight and measurements must comply with the regulations of the Federal Measurement Office (Eidg. Amt fuer Messwesen).

The Foodstuffs Ordinance specifies additional information that must be provided in the case of certain products, such as the name of the manufacturer or distributor, country of origin of the product, and 'use by' date. A growing number of distributors prefer to provide additional information on their labels, such as the 'EAN code' for computerized data retrieval, and/or the nutritional or energy value of the product.

Switzerland's food law is in general conformity with European Union food law. According to Swiss regulators, all standards are equal to or less strict than EU standards, except for aflatoxins, microtoxins, and certain pesticides such as the level of pesticides in water for drinking and food processing. The regulations cover all food products as well as tobacco and packaging and labeling standards.

TESTING AND CERTIFICATION

Switzerland imposes technical standards and testing and labeling requirements for certain products; Swiss electrical safety standards (SEV-Standards) require that electrical equipment be tested before it can be marketed; tests may be costly and time-consuming. In most cases, procedures can be simplified for those manufacturers whose equipment has already been cleared in another country participating in the CENELEC (European Committee for Electro-technical Standardization) Certification Agreement (CCA).

Other certifying requirements apply to drugs (prescription and over-the-counter), which must receive approval from the inter-cantonal drug commission. Imported products must also be labeled in all three official languages (German, French, and Italian). As of October 1, 1995, individuals living in Switzerland have been able to import one US-made car of a single model type per year for personal use only, with (in most cases) only minor modifications, testing, and specifications requirements. An information sheet on the procedures is available from the Embassy's Commercial Section.

PROHIBITED IMPORTS

Strictly speaking, there are no prohibited imports in licit, commercial trade with Switzerland. The Swiss method of controlling unwanted imports is through the imposition of restrictions, quotas and other rules and regulations such as detailed in other parts of this section.

- Warranty and Non-warranty Repairs

In general, warranty of one year is offered for the following products:

- Electrical household goods (except spare parts)
- Electrical consumer goods (except spare parts)

For additional analytical, business and investment opportunities information,
please contact Global Investment & Business Center, USA
at (703) 370-8082. Fax: (703) 370-8083. E-mail: ibpusa3@gmail.com
Global Business and Investment Info Databank - www.ibpus.com

Televisions, PCs, refrigerators generally have a warranty of 2 to 3 years depending upon agreement. The same applies to automobiles. Spare parts are always excluded.

Non-warranty products are: toys, food and clothing.

EXPORT CONTROLS

The Government of Switzerland regulates the export, import, and transit of goods usable for civilian and military purposes and is an active member of all major export control regimes, including the Wassenaar Arrangement (WA), the Missile Technology Control Regime (MTCR), the Nuclear Supplier Group (NSG), the Australia Group (AG) and the Chemical Weapons Convention (CWC).

The Office of Export Controls and Sanctions within the Swiss Secretariat for Economic Affairs (SECO) is responsible for implementation of Swiss commitments pursuant to the multilateral export control regimes and can deny an export license if there is reason to assume that goods proposed for export would:
a. be used for the development, production, or use of biological or chemical weapons;
b. serve for the development, production, or use of nuclear weapons or of an unmanned missile for the delivery of nuclear, biological or chemical weapons or the proliferation of such weapons; or
c. contribute to the conventional armaments of a state which, by its behavior endangers regional or global security.

Although Switzerland is not a UN member, it regularly adopts UN sanctions and denies export licenses if the UN, or states participating, together with Switzerland, in international export control measures, forbid the export of such goods. In certain cases, where there is a high likelihood of diversion of goods to WMD or missile uses, the Government of Switzerland applies the "catch-all" provisions of its export control law to deny export of goods not specifically included on any export control list.

The Government of Switzerland regularly cooperates with the U.S. and other governments to avoid the diversion of Swiss exports to WMD or missile uses and has taken steps to tighten its export controls in recent years. The U.S. and Swiss Governments have recently discussed the need to improve mechanisms for minimizing the risk that Swiss firms might be used as intermediaries for illicit transactions with entities of proliferation-risk and to strengthen Swiss monitoring and enforcement of export regulations. Accordingly, the Governments of Switzerland and the U.S. have recently initiated an export control dialogue as part of the U.S.-Swiss Joint Economic Commission (JEC). The first meeting of the U.S.-Swiss Export Control Dialogue will take place in Washington, D.C. in July 2001.

More detailed information about specific Swiss export control regulations is available on-line at: www.seco.admin.ch.

STANDARDS

The umbrella organization for Swiss standards is the Schweizerische Normen-Vereinigung (SNV, or Swiss Standards Association), a private, nonprofit association under Swiss law which groups Swiss governmental and private agencies and firms for the purpose of developing industrial standards and technical regulations. Certification rests with a variety of governmental and private agencies such as the Swiss Association of Machinery Manufacturers (VSM), Swiss Association of Electrical Apparatus Manufacturers (SEV), Federal Health Office, and the PTT. (See Appendix E for addresses.)

For additional analytical, business and investment opportunities information,
please contact Global Investment & Business Center, USA
at (703) 370-8082. Fax: (703) 370-8083. E-mail: ibpusa3@gmail.com
Global Business and Investment Info Databank - www.ibpus.com

The SNV is in turn a member of the International Standards Organization (ISO) in Geneva, in which some 2,000 industry associations worldwide participate in the establishment of a system of quality management and recommendations. In its Series 9000, ISO has issued recommendations aiming at introducing some 20 issues in basic processes dealing with quality testing and management for manufactured products.

Swiss industry is increasingly adopting ISO 9000 standards. More Swiss producers are seeking certification, even though Swiss certification according to ISO standards is not yet recognized by the European Union. To overcome this, Swiss exporters are turning to agents or their own subsidiaries in the EU to obtain equivalent certification under the EN 29000 series of European Quality Management Standards, or double certification through an international network of private quality management associations.

Swiss industries incorporating U.S. components in their end products, especially in machinery and instrumentation (key Swiss export commodities), increasingly specify ISO 9000 standards for imports. Under the EN 29000 directives issued by the EU, the equivalent ISO 9000 series of norms are becoming a sales factor in the EU, and in Switzerland, even when not explicitly stated.

In the service sector, the Swiss banking industry and financial institutions are gradually looking at ISO's Series 9001 recommendations, which deal with product or service development and design, as well as with training. The ISO Series 9001-9003 recommend specific approaches and processes in systematic quality control. 9003 concentrates on end testing. Among the 1,000 Swiss organizations which have been certified so far, two banking giants, Union Bank of Switzerland and Swiss Bank Corporation, were the first to seek certification under the 9001 series.

An increasing number of Swiss and other European (particularly German and Scandinavian) manufacturing companies are seeking environmental certification according to ISO 14001 standards as a complement to ISO 9000. An unexpected benefit of the environmental ISO 14001 certification process is the uncovering and elimination of waste in manufacturing, procurement, storage and waste management (recycling). ISO 14001 certification also covers compliance with the growing number of environmental standards and greatly facilitates the introduction of new-to-market products.

However, and at least as important as the above mentioned regulatory aspects, the resulting certification can be used in novel marketing techniques. Leading marketing specialists have found ISO 14001 to be an effective marketing tool, particularly in environmentally conscious and sensitive markets like Switzerland, Germany or the Scandinavian countries. The two main Swiss supermarket chains COOP and MIGROS, for example, have introduced a whole range of products manufactured by means of environmentally "friendly" processes and materials. Although somewhat more expensive, these product groups are the fastest growing. This trend, which is still in its beginning phase, is expected to take on significant dimensions in the years to come.

American manufacturers and exporters should be aware of this development and may wish to consider (while preparing for ISO 9000 certification) combining it with ISO 14001 certification (which may result in considerable cost savings).

Swiss industry, trade and quality management associations, as well as official agencies such as the Swiss Federal Testing Agency EMPA recommend or conduct audits. Switzerland is also represented within the private European Organization for Testing and Certification Group (EOTC). A system of joint audits offering reciprocal treatment has been introduced between participating quality control associations in different European countries under the so-called E-Q-NET (European Network for Quality System, Assessment and Certification). In addition,

For additional analytical, business and investment opportunities information,
please contact Global Investment & Business Center, USA
at (703) 370-8082. Fax: (703) 370-8083. E-mail: ibpusa3@gmail.com
Global Business and Investment Info Databank - www.ibpus.com

reciprocity for quality management certification is on the agenda of negotiations between the government of Switzerland and the EU.

FREE TRADE ZONES/WAREHOUSES

There are no free trade zones per se in Switzerland, but there are four ways of maintaining goods not cleared through customs -- free ports, federal bonded warehouses, private bonded warehouses, and in transit in the Rhine River port of Basel. Free ports are considered extraterritorial, and goods may be stored indefinitely without customs inspection. Goods may be unpacked and repacked, as well as undergo certain processing such as analysis, sorting, mixing and sampling. Major processing resulting in changes of tariff classification may be undertaken only with customs authorization. One or more free ports exist in or near virtually every major city around the country.

Federal bonded warehouses, considered to be on Swiss customs territory, are subject to stricter regulations. Goods stored are under customs control, involving registration of arrivals and departures. Storage may not exceed five years, and only processing essential for the preservation of the goods may be undertaken. There are some dozen federal bonded warehouses.

Private bonded warehouses are operated by companies to store goods not cleared for free circulation through customs. Only wholesale traded goods are generally accepted. An import license or customs clearance note must be shown when goods covered by import restrictions or quotas are imported and cleared through customs for storage in a private bonded warehouse. Clearance for private storage is on the basis of a bond note, testifying to a cash deposit or bond to cover eventual customs charges.

The Rhine River port of Basel has transit warehouses for grain and similar goods for mass consumption; storage time is unlimited. Similar goods imported by ship in quantities of at least 12 tons may be stored for up to two years. Liquid fuels in transit are also stored.

MEMBERSHIP IN FREE TRADE ASSOCIATIONS

Switzerland is a member of the European Free Trade Area. EFTA members (currently Iceland, Liechtenstein, Norway, and Switzerland) maintain their own external tariffs, although tariff duties on trade in industrial products among member countries have been eliminated. EFTA countries have free trade agreements with the European Union, Romania, Poland, Czech Republic, Slovakia, Hungary, Bulgaria, Estonia, Lithuania, Israel and Turkey, (and soon Canada) providing duty-free trade in industrial goods and certain farm and fisheries products. Additional such agreements are foreseen for Slovenia, Albania, Macedonia, Egypt, Malta, Morocco, Tunisia, Cyprus, the Palestinian Authority, Jordan and Lebanon. Preferential or duty-free rates apply to goods imported from the EU-EFTA free trade area when an importer makes a request on the import declaration and produces a certificate of origin. The Swiss also accord tariff preferences under the GSP to developing countries.

In December 1992, the Swiss population voted against joining the European Economic Area (EEA), whose aim is to achieve more complete economic integration between EU and EFTA members. The reasons for the rejection were many and varied, but the opposition was successful in casting the vote as a proxy decision on future EU membership and instinctive fears of abandoning neutrality, ceding sovereignty to Brussels, and an unwanted influx of foreigners prevailed. Nonetheless, a referendum seeking to force the Swiss government to retract the country's application for EU membership was rejected in May, 1997. The Government has been making a concerted effort to bring Swiss laws and regulations into line with those of the EU, and Switzerland recently concluded a package of seven sectoral agreements with the EU, known as "the Bilaterals" which will afford Switzerland many of the economic advantages that joining the EEA would have. The Bilaterals must still be ratified by all EU member states, thus entry into force isn't likely until 2001. While Swiss EU membership is the government's stated goal and opinion polls indicate that the population is gradually warming to the idea, any decision to join is likely still a number of years away.

IMPORTANT LAWS AND REGULATIONS AFFICTING BUSINESS ACTIVITY

TITLE: SPECIFIC LEGAL PROVISIONS FOR THE REGISTRATION

1. CHAPTER: INDIVIDUAL COMPANY

Article 36 Registration mandatory and voluntary registration

1 natural persons running a commercial after commercial nature run and operate for one year Roheinnahmen of at least 100 000 francs (annual sales) to achieve, are committed to their individual businesses in the Commercial Register to leave. 1 Natural persons running a commercial after commercial nature run and operate for one year at least Roheinnahmen of 100 000 francs (annual sales) to achieve, are committed to their individual businesses in the Commercial Register to leave. Belong to a person several individual companies, it is their aggregate turnover. Belong to a person several individual companies, it is their aggregate turnover.

2 The obligation to register arises when reliable figures on the annual turnover is available. 2 The obligation to register arises when reliable figures on the annual turnover is available.

3 A requirement for registration under other regulations are reserved. 3 A requirement for registration under other regulations are reserved.

4 Individuals who operate a business and not on the registration are obliged to have the right to their individual businesses to register. 4 Individuals who operate a business and not on the registration are obliged to have the right to their individual businesses to register.

Article 37 application and supporting documents With the application for registration of a single company documents must be filed only if: With the application for registration of a single company documents must be filed only if:

a. the facts do not indicate in the registration position;
b. this is due to other regulations..
Article 38 Content of the entry
For individual companies must be registered in the commercial: For individual companies must be registered in the Commercial Register:

a. the name and identification number;
b. the seat and the right of domicile;
c. the legal status, legal;
d. the purpose;
e. the owner or proprietor of the sole proprietorship;
f. representing the people.

2. CHAPTER: COLLECTIVE AND COMMANDITE

Article **40** application and supporting documents

ith the application for registration of a collective or limited evidence need only be filed if:

a.; the facts do not indicate in the registration position;
b. this is due to other regulations.

Article **41** Contents of the entry

[1] Collective societies must be registered in the commercial:

a.
b. the seat and the right of domicile;
c. legal;
d. the date of commencement of the company;
e. the purpose;
f. fthe partners and shareholders;
g. For partnerships must be entered in the Commercial Register:
a.; the name and identification number;
b. the seat and the right of domicile;
c. legal;
d. the date of commencement of the company;
e. the purpose;
f. the unlimited liability of shareholders and shareholders' (complementary and complementary);
g. the limited liability shareholders and shareholders (Kommanditärinnen and Kommanditäre) having regard to the amount of their respective Kommanditsumme;
h. wholly or partly in kind will be done: its purpose and value;
i.. representing the people.
[3] For group companies or partnerships, under which no commercial nature run commercial operation, the date of commencement of the Company the date of the registration days to register.

Article **42** resolution and disposition

If a collective or limited for the purpose of winding up dissolved, the partners and shareholders' resolution for entry in the Commercial Register (Article 574 paragraph 2 SCO).

[2] With the application for dissolution must be no further evidence can be submitted. Reserved for the deposit of the signatures of Liquidatorinnen or liquidators who are not shareholders.

[3] In the case of the dissolution of society must be entered in the Commercial Register:

  a.; the fact that the company has been dissolved;
  b. the company with the additional liquidation;
  c.. Liquidatorinnen and the liquidators.
Upon completion of the liquidation, the liquidators Liquidatorinnen and the deletion of the Company to register (Art. 589 CO).

Together with the deletion, the deletion reason in the Commercial registered.

CHAPTER: STOCK

SECTION: FOUNDATION

Article **43** application and supporting documents

[1] With the registration of the founding of a joint stock company for registration shall be the Commercial the following documents submitted:

For additional analytical, business and investment opportunities information,
please contact Global Investment & Business Center, USA
at (703) 370-8082. Fax: (703) 370-8083. E-mail: ibpusa3@gmail.com
Global Business and Investment Info Databank - www.ibpus.com

a. the official record of the instrument;

b. the statutes;

c. a proof that the members of the Board of Directors have adopted their choice;

d. where applicable, proof that the statutory auditor has approved their choice;

e. the minutes of the Board on its constitution, concerning the rules of the Presidency and on the issue of the drawing power;

f. in cash, a certificate from the show, in which bank deposits are deposited, unless the banking institution in the public deed is not mentioned;

g. in the case of Article 117, paragraph 3: the declaration of domicile of the owner or home owner that he or she have a right of domicile at the place of its headquarters granted;

h. the declaration of the Founders of that no other kind, Sachübernahmen, clearing facts or special benefits exist, as in the above documents.

[2] For information already in the instrument can be seen, and no additional proof is required.

[3] of kind, Sachübernahmen intended Sachübernahmen, clearing facts or specific benefits, it must also be submitted the following documents:

a. the contracts with the cash necessary supplements;

b. the Sachübernahmeverträge with the necessary supplements;

c. by all the founders and founding founders signed report;

d. Revisors. the unconditional test confirmation of a state regulated audit firm, an accredited expert revision, revision of approved experts, an approved Auditor or by an approved auditor.

Article **44** instrument

The official record of the instrument must contain:

a. persons information on the founders and creators, and, where appropriate, to their representatives;

b. the declaration of the Founders of a joint stock company to establish;

c. the confirmation of the Founders of that statute shall apply;

d. the explanation of each founder and each founder of the subscription of shares, indicating the number, nominal value, type, category and issue price and the unconditional commitment to the issue amount corresponding to deposit;

e. the fact that the members of the Board of Directors were elected and the relevant personal details;

f. the fact that the auditor was elected, or the waiver of a revision;

g. the determination of the Founders of that:

1. valid for all the shares are subscribed,

2. the promised deposit the total amount is equivalent

the legal and statutory requirements for the performance of the deposits are met;

h. the citation of all the evidence and the confirmation of Urkundsperson that the documents and their founders and the founders have existed;

i.. the signatures of the founders and founders.

IMPORTANT COMPANY LAW DEVELOPMENTS

A major reform of Swiss company law took place in 1992, when the partially revised Corporation Law (part of the Swiss Federal Code of Obligations) was enacted. While not influenced by the British Cadbury Report issued in the same year, the revised law substantially overhauled the corporate governance triad of board-management-shareholders. The revised law establishes the inalienable core powers of the board of directors and specifies its non-transferable duties. It also clarifies the role and function of management, the shareholders' meeting and the auditors. More recent statutes in the field of securities regulation have an additional impact on the development of corporate governance standards for public companies.

The introduction of two new sets of corporate governance rules in 2002 marked a milestone in the development of corporate governance principles in Switzerland.

The Directive on Information relating to Corporate Governance, issued by the SWX Swiss Exchange, came into force on July 1 2002 and aims to enhance corporate transparency. To this end, the directive requires Swiss listed issuers to disclose in their annual reports important information on the management and control mechanisms at the highest corporate level. While information on remuneration is compulsory, other broad categories of information – such as group and capital structure, board of directors, auditors, shareholder participation rights, change of control or defence measures, and information policy – may be dealt with in accordance with the 'comply or explain' principle: if the issuer decides not to disclose certain information, it must explain why. The SWX directive is thus an efficient tool which increases the transparency of the corporate governance mechanisms of Swiss issuers and the Swiss corporate governance system in general.

The Swiss Code of Best Practice for Corporate Governance was issued by economiesuisse, the federation of Swiss businesses from all sectors of the economy, on March 25 2002. It sets corporate governance standards which have the character of non-binding recommendations. The code primarily addresses Swiss public companies, but also serves as a guideline for non-listed Swiss companies and organisations of economic significance. It integrates and reflects various provisions of Swiss legislation which deal with corporate governance aspects. It also seeks to embody the high standards of corporate practice already observed by many companies in Switzerland. The code is of particular assistance to foreign investors who wish to have a better understanding of corporate governance in the Swiss context. In developing the new code, the expert panel which drafted its provisions drew on current international models, particularly those in use in the United Kingdom and other countries.

Forces for reform

The new corporate governance rules were adopted following several prominent cases of managerial misconduct and mismanagement which caused a public outcry. These included the excessive remuneration of board members and management at collapsed Swissair, excessive pension benefits at ABB and alleged misuse of corporate funds at Rentenanstalt/Swiss Life. An extensive public debate on board accountability and liability, excessive management compensation and shareholder control began as a result and remains ongoing.

Shareholders' rights

The Corporation Law affords several fundamental, non-transferable powers to the shareholders' meeting. In particular, shareholders may vote on:

• the appointment and removal of directors and statutory auditors;

• the approval or rejection of the annual business report;

• the setting of dividends; and

• any amendment to the articles of association, including changes in the share capital.

In addition, shareholders may bring actions against the company in order to protect their rights, or against liable directors or officers in case of non-compliance with their statutory duties.

Right to call meetings and propose resolutions

A shareholders' meeting is called by the board of directors or, in extraordinary situations, by the auditors. However, one or more shareholders whose holding or combined holdings represent at least 10 per cent of the share capital may request that a shareholders' meeting be called. Shareholders whose combined holdings represent at least 10 per cent of the share capital or an aggregate par value of at least CHF1 million (whichever is lower) may propose resolutions for adoption at the meeting.

Institutional investors as shareholders

Traditionally, shareholder democracy, supported by rules on proxy voting, has not been pursued vigorously. However, judging from the many hotly debated shareholders' meetings in recent years, shareholder activism appears to be on the rise as, for various reasons, an increasing number of institutional investors and some minority shareholders' groups have started shareholder motions. While some Swiss pension funds have mandated active corporate governance players, such as the ethosfund, to represent their votes and question management at shareholders' meetings, the majority still do not seek an active role in the exercise of their shareholder rights.

MANAGEMENT STRUCTURE AND THE ROLE OF DIRECTORS

Nomination, removal and election

The shareholders' meeting elects each member of the board of directors, mostly upon nomination and motion by the incumbent board, but sometimes upon counter-motion of the shareholders. The shareholders' meeting may also remove directors and auditors, provided the matter has been timely included on the agenda.

Qualifications and term of office

Directors must be individuals and either shareholders or representatives of shareholding entities. Under current law the majority of the board members must be of Swiss nationality and must reside in Switzerland, although the nationality requirement is expected to be abolished in the near future. Exemptions from the nationality requirement already exist for citizens of EU and European Free Trade Agreement countries. In the absence of other provisions in the articles of association, the board members are elected for a term of office of three years and re-election is permitted.

Directors' duties

The board of directors is responsible for managing and representing the company, and can be described as the ultimate executive body of the company. In general, the board is authorised to decide all matters that are not reserved to the general shareholders' meeting or to the auditors. The directors, and any officers to whom the company's day-to-day management has been delegated, must carry out their duties with due care and maintain the company's interests in good faith.

Two provisions of the Federal Code of Obligations form the backbone of a system which can be read as a short manual for the board on good governance. Article 715a acknowledges that timely and appropriate information from management is crucial to the effective discharge of the board's duties, and thus grants individual board members the right to comprehensive information and inspection of company documents. Article 716a provides the following checklist of fundamental matters which are specifically reserved to the board of directors:

- the duty to determine the overall corporate strategy and to allocate corporate resources accordingly (strategic governance);

- the duty to set up and structure a sound system of internal control;

- the duty to appoint and monitor management;

- the duty to define the fundamental organisational structure; and

- the duty to prepare for the shareholders' meeting.

These board responsibilities are non-transferable and are firmly embedded within a statutory corporate framework which – while far from resembling a Delaware-type of legislative model – may be characterised as liberal and quite flexible relative to other European corporate laws.

Generally, the day-to-day management is delegated to the executive body of the management. The executive body may be structured in accordance with organisational models common in or legally required by other jurisdictions. Such models range from the German dual board system, with two strictly separate executive bodies, to the Anglo-American unitary board system, which integrates executive and non-executive board members, to the French '*président-directeur général*' (PDG) system, which essentially centres around the almost omnipotent PDG.

Directors' liability

Liability may arise out of statute, contract or tort. Statutory liability applies whenever a duty under corporate law has been violated. Directors may also be subject to criminal prosecution in case of misappropriation of corporate funds or exploitation of insider information.

Corporate liability actions may be brought by:

- the company;

- the shareholders (either directly or through a derivative action brought on behalf of the company if a shareholder has suffered indirect damage to the value of his shares as a result of the damage suffered by the company); or

- the company's creditors in case of its bankruptcy.

Class actions as envisaged under US law do not exist under Swiss law.

The board members, *de facto* directors (ie, persons not formally appointed as directors who effectively behave as directors and significantly influence the decision-making process) and members of the top tier of management are jointly and severally liable for damages caused by any intentional or negligent breach of their duties.

For additional analytical, business and investment opportunities information, please contact Global Investment & Business Center, USA at (703) 370-8082. Fax: (703) 370-8083. E-mail: ibpusa3@gmail.com Global Business and Investment Info Databank - www.ibpus.com

An action by shareholders against the board or management may be combined with the special audit procedure (*Sonderpruefung*). A shareholder may request a special audit which will have access to inside information not disclosed to the public. Upon approval by the shareholders' meeting or by a judge, the special audit is carried out by an independent auditor who acts as an intermediary between the shareholders and the company.

Directors' and officers' liability (D&O) insurance is purchased by virtually all public companies in Switzerland. D&O policies are generally claims-made policies with single-year policy periods.

Committees of the board

With regards to the structure of the board of directors, the Code of Best Practice for Corporate Governance proposes that an audit committee, a remuneration committee and a nomination committee be established. Depending on their tasks, these committees are subject to specific criteria with respect to independence and must be established accordingly. However, these are merely 'soft' law provisions, and due to the inalienable rights of the board, such committees merely have a decision-shaping, rather than decision-taking, role.

Remuneration

According to the SWX directive, it is mandatory to provide information on the total remuneration paid and shares and loans granted both to directors and to management. With regards to the board member with the largest total compensation package, the compensation, shareholdings and any loans must be disclosed individually, although the director's identity need not be made known.

Disclosure

Increasing expectations of accountability and transparency have led to the introduction of new securities regulations in recent years.

In addition to the Swiss Corporation Law amendments, the Swiss Federal Stock Exchange Act contains provisions which aim to establish an efficient and more transparent market for corporate control. There is a duty to disclose immediately direct or indirect shareholdings in Swiss public companies when the shareholder passes certain voting right thresholds (5, 10, 20, 33.3, 50 and 66.6 per cent). In addition, the Corporation Law requires listed companies to include in the attachment to the annual balance sheet a list of significant shareholders (ie, those whose participations exceed 5 per cent of the voting rights).

Where a shareholding exceeds 33.3 per cent of the voting rights of the target company, unless the articles of association provide otherwise, the shareholder has a far-reaching obligation to make a public offer to all shareholders. In a takeover situation, both the bidder and the board of the target company must abide by certain rules, including the continuing disclosure of shareholdings, to ensure a fair and transparent takeover process and to protect the interests of the non-bidding minority shareholders.

Furthermore, *ad hoc* publicity rules of the SWX require that listed companies inform all investors immediately and simultaneously of share price-sensitive information. The moment of publication should be such as to allow market participants sufficient time to process the notification.

ACCOUNTS AND AUDITS

For additional analytical, business and investment opportunities information,
please contact Global Investment & Business Center, USA
at (703) 370-8082. Fax: (703) 370-8083. E-mail: ibpusa3@gmail.com
Global Business and Investment Info Databank - www.ibpus.com

Accounts

While the Corporation Law only provides for annual reporting in compliance with the broad principles of the statutory Swiss generally accepted accounting principles, the reporting duties included in the SWX Listing Rules require publication of an annual report and a semi-annual interim report based on much more sophisticated accounting standards.

As of 2005, all companies listed in the main segment of the SWX will be required to comply with international financial reporting standards or US generally accepted accounting principles.

Auditors

The shareholders' meeting elects and re-elects the auditors, usually for a term of one year. The Corporation Law states that auditors must have the "necessary" qualifications to perform their duties in auditing the company's financial statements, but must meet higher professional standards in certain cases – for example if the company has bonds outstanding or if its shares are listed on a stock exchange.

The auditors are liable to the company itself, to any shareholder and to any creditor for damages caused by wilful or negligent breach of their duties.

Enforcement

Case law shows that the number of liability claims against directors and officers is on the increase. Liability claims have become almost routine in bankruptcies, but are still rare where the company is not over-indebted. However, judging by the number of reported court decisions, relatively few actions for liability are successful. Many proceedings are settled at some point prior to judgment, especially with D&O liability insurers. Nevertheless, the right to bring an action against the directors and officers is still a threatening weapon in the hands of shareholders with substantial means

Corporate social responsibility

The principle of corporate responsibility and sustainability has begun to form an integral part of the long-term business strategies of many Swiss multinational players. Such companies acknowledge the importance of sustainable value for shareholders, clients and employees, and at the same time the importance of preserving the environment and contributing to the development of the communities in which their business is located. In general, such endeavours are set out in the annual business report.

Sarbanes-Oxley

The Sarbanes-Oxley Act applies to any Swiss company whose securities are registered with the US Securities and Exchange Commission and are listed on a US stock exchange (also where listed as a dual listing or in the form of American depositary receipts). In particular, Sarbanes-Oxley imposes duties on the board and management such as the appointment of an independent audit committee, which deals with the appointment, remuneration and supervision of the auditors. Sarbanes-Oxley further encompasses, among other things, the duty of the chief executive officer and the chief financial officer to issue periodic reports to the SEC, and introduces certain duties for in-house and outside counsel.

For additional analytical, business and investment opportunities information, please contact Global Investment & Business Center, USA at (703) 370-8082. Fax: (703) 370-8083. E-mail: ibpusa3@gmail.com Global Business and Investment Info Databank - www.ibpus.com

Sarbanes-Oxley has also influenced the draft Swiss Federal Law on Admission and Oversight of Auditors. The draft sets out new and more stringent requirements on the professional qualifications and independence of auditors. Importantly, it establishes a public oversight board which will implement a system for the admission of auditors, and requires that listed companies be constantly supervised.

Recent developments

A partial revision of the Federal Code of Obligations aims to improve transparency in relation to the remuneration of directors and officers of public companies. It provides that the aggregate and individual remuneration of directors, as well as their shares in the company, must be published. For officers, the aggregate amount of remuneration and the highest individual remuneration are also subject to publication. Further issues addressed are the review by external auditors and sanctions for non-compliance with these requirements.

In addition, following a number of parliamentary motions, the Federal Department of Justice appointed a Corporate Governance Working Group, tasked with evaluating whether Swiss law is in conformity with accepted corporate governance rules. In September 2003 the working group produced its final report. Its recommendations will be submitted to interested groups before being discussed by Parliament. The report encompasses a variety of proposals on corporate governance matters for listed and non-listed companies.

Finally, in October 2003 the Admissions Board of the SWX adopted rules on the disclosure of management transactions, subject to approval by the Swiss Federal Banking Commission expected in 2004. Directors and officers must disclose their transactions in financial instruments of the company in which they serve, and must indicate their position, but not their name. Transactions carried out directly or indirectly which exceed CHF100,000 must be reported within four exchange days.

MODERNIZING COMPANY LAW

FEDERAL COUNCIL OPENS COMMITTEE HEARINGS ON REVISION OF COMPANY AND ACCOUNTING LEGISLATION

Press Release, FDJP, 05.12.2005

Bern, 05.12.2005. Swiss company law is to be comprehensively modernized and brought into line with the needs of the economy. Corporate governance, in particular, is to be improved, new rules on capital structures and accounting and reporting requirements will be introduced, and the provisions governing annual general meetings will be updated. With this purpose in mind, on Friday the Federal Council opened committee hearings on the revision of company and accounting legislation.

Corporate governance is intended to achieve a balance between the various governing and executive bodies of a company, sufficient transparency with regard to internal company procedures, and a secure legal position for the shareholders. The initial draft bill specifically strengthens the position of shareholders as the owners of the company. Their rights to information are set out in clearer terms, and in the case of private limited companies, they will be given the right to information on the remuneration packages paid to top management. Furthermore, the thresholds for the exercise of a variety of shareholders' rights – such as special audits and the rights to convene meetings and have items included on the agenda – are to be lowered. Legal proceedings concerning the reimbursement of unjustified payments will be improved. In addition, the right of banks to exercise the voting rights attached to stock they hold in

For additional analytical, business and investment opportunities information, please contact Global Investment & Business Center, USA at (703) 370-8082. Fax: (703) 370-8083. E-mail: ibpusa3@gmail.com Global Business and Investment Info Databank - www.ibpus.com

safekeeping, as well as the practice of shareholders being represented at annual general meetings by the company's own governing and executive bodies, will be abolished. In future, it will be possible to appoint only independent persons as proxies.

More flexible capital structure

A second area of revision concerns the rules governing *capital structures*, which will take account of changing needs. The procedure for increasing and reducing share capital will be made more flexible. By adopting a "capital band", the annual general meeting will be able to authorize the board of directors to increase or reduce share capital as it wishes within a given bandwidth. The present requirement for a certain minimum par value will also be relaxed, meaning that a company can lower the par value of its stock as close to zero as it wishes. The importance of bearer shares has declined steadily in recent years. They are therefore to be abolished, in line with the international trend. It will still be possible to issue bearer participation certificates, however. Furthermore, the present rules restricting participation capital to twice the level of share capital will cease to apply.
The regulations governing the holding of annual general meetings are another area that will be revised. In the future, companies will be able to use electronic tools when preparing for and holding their annual general meetings. The bill also contains rules on holding annual general meetings at several venues and abroad.

Accounting and reporting legislation to be standardized

The initial draft also provides for a comprehensive revision of Switzerland's outdated *accounting and reporting legislation*. It will create standard rules for all forms of company, although requirements will differ depending on the economic significance of the company in question. The new rules will not impact on the amount of tax paid by the corporate sector and thus abide by the principle of authoritative law. Under certain circumstances, a company may have to produce an additional set of financial statements in accordance with recognized accounting and reporting requirements. This will significantly improve transparency and better protect those with minority holdings.

REFORM OF SWISS COMPANY LAW APPROVED IN PRINCIPLE

SWISS FEDERAL COUNCIL NOTES RESULTS OF CONSULTATION PROCESS

Press Release, FDJP, 14.02.2007

Berne. The reform of Swiss company and accounting law met with general approval during the statutory consultation process. However, a number of proposals aroused controversy. On Wednesday, the Federal Council noted the results of the consultation and gave the FDJP the task of formulating an Opinion by the end of the year.

The overwhelming majority of the over 100 participants in the consultation process approved the preliminary draft prepared by the Federal Department of Justice and Police (FDJP) as a whole, endorsing the need for legislative action. However, the bill, the aim of which is to modernize company law and adapt it to the country's economic needs, will have to be revised to take account of the views expressed.

The proposals to improve corporate governance were particularly controversial. On the one hand, the new measures aimed at achieving a balance between the governing and executive bodies of a company, making internal company procedures properly transparent and securing the position of shareholders as the owners of the company were welcomed. On the other hand, however, the

For additional analytical, business and investment opportunities information, please contact Global Investment & Business Center, USA at (703) 370-8082. Fax: (703) 370-8083. E-mail: ibpusa3@gmail.com Global Business and Investment Info Databank - www.ibpus.com

extension of shareholders' rights and the reorganization of the way institutional voting rights are represented met with some opposition. The provisions concerning the disclosure of senior management pay and the annual election of the Board of Directors were also the subject of dispute. The proposal to limit auditors' liability likewise came in for some criticism.

Bearer shares retained

The new measures relating to capital structures also met with broad approval. In particular, the introduction of the "capital band" was generally welcomed. The capital band enables a company to increase and reduce its share capital within a specific range by following a simplified procedure. By contrast, the abolition of bearer shares came in for some fierce criticism. Business associations in particular are keen to retain bearer shares as they believe this would preserve the room for manoeuvre currently enjoyed by companies when designing their capital structures. In view of this powerful resistance, the Federal Council decided not to abolish bearer shares as part of the current company law reform.

The proposals to modernize annual general meetings also received a positive response. The use of electronic media in the preparation and holding of annual general meetings was considered an important contribution to updating Swiss company law.

Relationship to tax law revised

The complete overhaul of Switzerland's very outdated accounting and reporting legislation was generally given a positive reception. The main issue to arise was the revision of the proposed relationship with tax law. The preliminary bill stated that depreciation, writedowns and provisions must be reversed in a company's balance sheet if they are not accepted by the tax authorities. Many of the participants in the consultation process resolutely rejected this proposal on the grounds that it would be inappropriate for tax law to be the deciding factor in respect of balance sheets, which are governed by commercial law. They proposed publishing the amount of any set-off in an appendix to the annual accounts rather than including set-offs in the balance sheet. The Federal Council endorsed this proposal as it achieves the desired transparency in financial statements.

COMPANY LAW TO BE MODERNIZED

FEDERAL COUNCIL ADOPTS OPINION ON REVISION OF JOINT-STOCK COMPANY AND ACCOUNTING LEGISLATION

Press Release, FDJP, 21.12.2007

Bern. By revising joint-stock company and accounting legislation, the Federal Council wishes to modernize the law in these areas and bring it in to line with the needs of the economy. It adopted its Opinion and the draft legislation on Friday. The bill improves corporate governance, gives companies more scope with regard to their capital structures, permits annual general meetings to be held by electronic means, and replaces outdated accounting legislation.

One aim of the draft legislation is to improve corporate governance. Specifically, it lends greater weight to the position of shareholders as the company's owners. It sets out rights to information more clearly, and creates a right to written information in the case of privately held companies. Furthermore, the bill lowers the thresholds for exercising a variety of shareholder rights, such as calling a general meeting, and improves the legal framework for actions to reclaim unjustified payments.

In the future, the members of the board of directors will have to stand for election by the annual general meeting each year. This will permit shareholders to show what they think of the board's performance and the payments that its members have received. The revised law also creates a shareholder's right to information about the compensation paid to the top managers of privately-held joint-stock companies. Unlike public companies, these corporations are not obliged to disclose such payments in the notes to their financial statements.

Banks' voting rights originating from the securities they hold in safekeeping, as well as the possibility of shareholder representation by an officer of the company, have been abolished. In the future, proxies will have to be independent persons.

More flexible capital structures

A second area of revision concerns the rules on capital structures, which will be made more flexible to give companies greater scope. By adopting a "capital band", the annual general meeting will be able to authorize the board of directors to increase or reduce share capital as it wishes within a given bandwidth. The statutory minimum par value for shares will also be abolished, allowing companies to split their shares as they wish. Furthermore, in the case of listed non-voting stock, the present rules restricting non-voting capital to twice the level of share capital will cease to apply. By contrast, in response to criticism at the committee hearing stage, the Federal Council has decided not to abolish bearer shares.

Modernization of the annual general meeting

The draft legislation creates a legal foundation for the use of electronic means of communication in preparing and staging of the annual general meeting. This will allow costs to be reduced and active shareholder participation to be encouraged. The new law also provides for an annual general meeting to be held at several venues simultaneously, or abroad. An exclusively electronic or virtual AGM can be held if all shareholders agree.

Comprehensive revision of accounting legislation

Finally, the bill replaces Switzerland's outdated accounting legislation, creating standard rules for all forms of company. Requirements will nonetheless differ depending on the economic significance of the company in question. The general provisions reflect current bookkeeping and accounting practices at a well-run SME, while large companies and groups of companies are subject to stricter rules. Under certain circumstances, in the interests of the capital market or to protect persons with minority holdings, closing statements will have to be drawn up according to a set of private rules to give a true and fair presentation of the company's actual financial circumstances.

The new accounting legislation will not impact on taxes. Although accounting entries that are not recognized for tax purposes must still be disclosed, companies may decide themselves whether to state only the total in the notes to the annual financial statements, or to include the figure in the statements themselves.

APPROPRIATE RESPONSE TO EXCESSIVE MANAGEMENT SALARIES

FEDERAL COUNCIL PASSES INDIRECT COUNTER-PROPOSAL TO THE POPULAR INITIATIVE "AGAINST FAT-CAT SALARIES"

Press Release, FDJP, 05.12.2008

Bern. In the light of the current financial crisis, the Federal Council has extended the ongoing revision of company and accounting law in Switzerland to give greater protection

For additional analytical, business and investment opportunities information, please contact Global Investment & Business Center, USA at (703) 370-8082. Fax: (703) 370-8083. E-mail: ibpusa3@gmail.com Global Business and Investment Info Databank - www.ibpus.com

to shareholders' assets. In its Opinion, passed on Friday, it recommends that the Swiss parliament pass the Council's moderate yet more comprehensive bill as an indirect counter-proposal to the Swiss federal popular initiative "Against fat-cat salaries". The Federal Council believes that accepting the initiative into law would reduce the appeal of Switzerland as a business location.

The popular initiative "Against fat-cat salaries", bearing 114,260 valid signatures, was submitted to the Federal Chancellery on 26 February 2008. By improving corporate governance, its initiators aim to put a stop to what they believe are excessive pay packages for the top management of exchange-listed companies. Specifically, the initiative proposes that the annual general meeting should vote on the total pay awarded to the board of directors, executive board and advisory board, and that directors, the chairman and the compensation committee should be elected on an annual basis. Golden parachutes, golden handshakes and bonuses would all be outlawed.

Concerns already addressed

The Federal Council Opinion offers a reminder that the need to improve corporate governance was one of the factors that prompted the ongoing revision of company and accounting law. The revision will institute changes that will result in balance between the various governing and executive bodies in a company, create sufficient transparency in the pay packages awarded to top managers, as well as in internal processes, and instigate measures to secure the position of shareholders as the company's owners. Compared with the initiative, the proposed revision is more comprehensive and essentially covers all joint-stock companies under Swiss law – not just those whose equities are listed on a stock exchange.

Additional provisions

The Federal Council has also extended its bill to give greater protection to shareholders' assets. The experience of recent months and years has shown that pay policy in the corporate sector cannot continue to be self-regulated. The additional provisions of the bill would therefore mean, specifically, that the fees paid to the directors of exchange-listed companies would have to be approved on an annual basis by the company's annual general meeting. The bill would also make it easier to enforce claims for the reimbursement of unjustified payments.

Leaving enough scope for shareholders

The Federal Council's bill and the popular initiative correspond on several points. Where they differ, the draft bill is more moderate and less rigorous overall. It represents an appropriate response to the problem of excessive pay, but does not lay down restrictive provisions for the company's articles of association, neither does it determine any bans or penalties. This will ensure that, in the future as today, shareholders will have sufficient scope to structure the company according to their needs.

The Federal Council firmly believes that, were Switzerland to abandon its liberal company laws in favour of restrictive, heavy-handed regulation, it would lose its advantage over other countries as a business location. This would result in more firms being established outside Switzerland, companies moving their registered offices abroad, and fewer relocating to Switzerland. Jobs and tax revenues would then also be lost. In addition, were the popular initiative to pass into law, there would have be another major overhaul of company law, which would itself mean delays and legal uncertainty.

CORPORATE GOVERNANCE

The term "Corporate Governance" refers to all of the principles aimed at safeguarding shareholder interests. While maintaining decision-making capability and efficiency at the highest level of a company, these principles are intended to guarantee transparency and a healthy balance of management and control.

The Corporate Governance Directive requires issuers to disclose important information on their board and senior management (or to give substantial reasons why this information is not disclosed). The Directive itself establishes the basic principles. Details on what information needs to be published are indicated in the Annex to the Directive on Information Relating to Corporate Governance of the SIX Swiss Exchange.

The Corporate Governance Directive of the SIX Swiss Exchange entered into force on 1 July 2002. It first applied to annual reports for 2002 (for the financial year beginning on 1 January 2002 or later). The revised Corporate Governance Directive will enter into force on 1 January 2007. The Corporate Governance Directive that will remain in force until 31 December 2006 still applies for issuers whose financial year starts before 1 January 2007.

When the Corporate Governance Directive was first implemented, the SIX Swiss Exchange commissioned Prof. Dr Conrad Meyer (Institute of Accounting and Controlling of the University of Zurich) to carry out a study on how well it was complied with. The results are published in the study on its practical implementation (Studie zur praktischen Umsetzung der Corporate Governance-Richtlinie).

Description
Directive on Information Relating to Corporate Governance
(Corporate Governance Directive, DCG) of 17 April 2002 and 29 March 2006
(Entry into force on 1 January 2007, for financial years starting on or after
1 January 2007)
Commentary re Corporate Governance Directive, status as of 20 September 2007
Communiqué No. 09/2007 of 26.10.2007
Main focus for the review of annual reports for 2007 and 2007/2008 in terms of compliance with the Directive on Information relating to Corporate Governance
Checklist for the Corporate Governance Directive
Study on the practical implementation of the Corporate Governance Directive, as of 1 December 2003 (only in german)

OPENING A BANK ACCOINT IN SWITZERLAND: BASIC INFORMATION

BASIC ACCOUNTS

Choose the type of account that best fits your needs. By clicking on the account name you will see its full description.

Account name	Min. deposit	Internet banking	Set-up mode	Fee
				.
.				
Swiss Postal Account	none	Good	By mail	$459

The Swiss bank account for every pocket.This account is the most simple to open, is very cheap to use and offers the same total safety as our other accounts.

.				

Classic bank account	$3'500	Very good	By mail	$659.00
Opened with a major Swiss bank, this account will satisfy most needs you can have, be it in matters of investment, international trade or plain payment traffic.				
Internet banking account	$3,500	Excellent	By mail	$759.00
A favorite. Offered with a big Swiss bank, this it the ideal account for people who want to monitor their account entirely from the internet, using one of the best internet banking system in the world. Also possible for clients from Canada.				
Investment fund account	$5,000	Very good	By mail	$800.00
With this acccount you can automatically invest your deposits in a combination of investment funds without being penalized when you need to withdraw money.				
Swiss numbered account	$180,000	Possible	In person	$950.00
The mythic Swiss bank account, opened either with a true private bank or in the private banking section of a big bank according to your wished. Every imaginable service and access to the best people.				

POSTAL ACCOUNT

This is the simplest bank account you can open in Switzerland, but it already offers many possibilities and is very cheap. The Swiss postal service, an agency of the Swiss government now offers powerful bank accounts. Swiss francs accounts are the only to offer the full range of service, but you can set-up a foreign currency account.

Highlights	.	<ul><li>No minimum deposit</li><li>Account is free if you manage it through the internet</li><li>You can send cash in any currency to 130 countries</li><li>You can transfer money to more than 50 million bank and postal accounts all over the world</li></ul>
Type of bank	.	Swiss postal service (owned by the Swiss government). Over 40'000 employees in Switzerland, 3600 offices, Sfr.1'600 million in capital. Started operations in 1849.

Minimum deposits	.	None
Set up fee	.	$549.00
Set up mode	.	By mail or in person
Restricted countries	.	USA, Nigeria, Colombia
Internet banking	.	Available. You can monitor your account, make international bank transfers and order internatinal postal money orders. Internet banking is not available for people living in .
Banque restante	.	Not available
Credit cards	.	Mastercard / Eurocard if your account is in Swiss Francs
Investment options	.	Swiss treasury bills funds
Annual costs	.	• Standard account, no other accounts a year. • Same but with internet banking access • Savings account a year.

CLASSIC BANK ACCOUNT

This is our best selling account. It offers everything that investors and people trading internationally can desire. Its internet access lets you manage your account in its last details, trade online, transfer money, and very easily.

Highlights	.	• Our best selling account • Reasonable minimum deposit () • Award winning internet banking system • Extensive number of investment and international trade services
Type of bank	.	One of the biggest Swiss bank and among the ten biggest European banks. Over 60'000 employees, more than Sfr.900'000 millions of deposits and Sfr.28'000 millions of equity. Started operations in 1856.
Minimum deposits	-	$3,500
Set up fee	.	$659.00
Set up mode	.	By mail or in person
Restricted countries	.	. USA, Russia, Colombia, Nigeria, Albania, Armenia, Azerbaidjan, Bosnia, Bulgaria,

	.	Byelorussia, Croatia Estonia, Georgia, Kazhakstan, Kirghizia, Latvia, Lithuania, Macedonia, Moldavia, Uzbekistan, Rumania, Tadjikistan, Turkmenistan, Ukraine, Yougoslavia
Internet banking	.	Available - many powerful options Internet banking is not available for people living in Australia, Canada, Japan, Singapour, New-Zealand, USA.
Banque restante	.	Available for a year
Credit cards	.	Eurocard / Mastercard, Visa
Investment options	.	You can invest in any kind of security (stocks, bonds, options), in commodities, precious metals, investment funds, currencies. Anything traded on a public market.
Annual costs	.	for deposits below Sfr.15'000 for deposits below Sfr.25'000 Free---- for deposits above Sfr.25'000

INTERNET BANKING ACCOUNT

This is our best selling account. It offers everything that investors and people trading internationally can desire. Its internet access lets you manage your account in its last details, trade online, transfer money, and very easily. .		
Highlights	.	• Our best selling account • Reasonable minimum deposit ($3500) • Award winning internet banking system • Extensive number of investment and international trade services
Type of bank	.	One of the biggest Swiss bank and among the ten biggest European banks. Over 60'000 employees, more than Sfr.900'000 millions of deposits and Sfr.28'000 millions of equity. Started operations in 1856.
Minimum deposits	_	$3,500
Set up fee	.	$759.00
Set up mode	.	By mail or in person
Restricted countries	.	USA, Russia, Colombia, Nigeria, Albania, Armenia, Azerbaidjan, Bosnia, Bulgaria, Byelorussia, Croatia, Czechia, Estonia,

	.	Georgia, Hungary, Kazhakstan, Kirghizia, Latvia, Lithuania, Macedonia, Moldavia, Uzbekistan, Poland, Rumania, Slovakia, Slovenia, Tadjikistan, Turkmenistan, Ukraine, Yougoslavia.
Internet banking	.	Available - received several awards for its easy use and powerful options. International bank transfers only cost 4 SFR ordered through the internet - very cheap. Internet banking is not available for people living in and in the restricted countries (see above).
Banque restante	.	Available for $150 a year
Credit cards	.	Mastercard/Eurocard, Visa, American Express
Investment options	.	You can invest in any kind of security (stocks, bonds, options), in commodities, precious metals, investment funds, currencies. Anything traded on a public market.
Annual costs	.	SFR72 for deposits below Sfr.15'000 SFR 36 for deposits below Sfr.25'000 Free---- for deposits above Sfr.25'000

INVESTMENT FUND ACCOUNT

Opened in one of Switzerland's biggest bank, this account allows you to invest all the money you transfer to your account automatically, in a combination of investment funds suited to your investor profile. You get the advantage of a good yield while maintaining liquidity (no forenotice needed to withdraw money).

.

Highlights	.	• High yield with no liquidity constraints • Universal bank with all the banking services you can possibly need. • Internet access
Type of bank	.	One of the biggest banks in the world, with over 48'000 employees, Sfr.600'000 millions of deposits and more than Sfr.29'000 millions of equity. Started operations in 1912.
Minimum deposits	_	$5,000
Set up fee	.	$800.00
Set up mode	.	By mail or in person
Restricted countries	.	USA, Russia, Colombia, Nigeria, Albania, Armenia, Azerbaijan, Bosnia, Bulgaria, Byelorussia, Croatia Estonia, Georgia,

		Kazhakstan, Kirghizia, Latvia, Lithuania, Macedonia, Moldavia, Uzbekistan, Rumania, Tadjikistan, Turkmenistan, Ukraine, Yougoslavia
Internet banking	.	Available - many powerful options Internet banking is not available for people living in Australia, Canada, Japan, Singapour, New-Zealand, USA.. People from Canada, Australia, Singapour and New-Zealand who need internet access can open an Internet banking account which also offers excellent investment services.
Banque restante	.	Available for an annual SFR 200 charge.
Credit cards	.	Eurocard / Mastercard, Visa
Investment options	.	You define an investment strategy with your account officer and then all the money that is transferred on your account will automatically be invested in a combination of investment funds that reflects your profile. When you need to withdraw money, the necessary amount of fund's shares are sold automatically.
Annual costs	.	Free

NUMBERED ACCOUNT

This is the classic numbered Swiss bank account, the one that kings and tycoons have. Swiss private banks have 200 years of history in the business, and are the leader in the market..		
Highlights	.	• One account officer and his assistants will help you manage your money for the long term • Total discretion • The best people in the branch • Treated like a VIP in a palace when you come to the bank
Type of bank	.	We work with several leading private banks, each with its own specialty.
Minimum deposits	-	$180,000
Set up fee	.	$950.00
Set up mode	.	You must come in person to Switzerland
Restricted countries (opening of the account)	.	USA, Nigeria

Internet banking	.	Upon request
Banque restante	.	Available
Credit cards	.	All major credit cards
Investment options	.	The most complete range of securities (stocks, bonds, options), in commodities, precious metals, investment funds, currencies. Anything traded on a public market.
Annual costs	.	According to an agreement

For additional analytical, business and investment opportunities information,
please contact Global Investment & Business Center, USA
at (703) 370-8082. Fax: (703) 370-8083. E-mail: ibpusa3@gmail.com
Global Business and Investment Info Databank - www.ibpus.com

SWITZERLAND AS OFFSHORE JURISDICTION

Switzerland continues to be the jurisdiction of choice for rich individuals even in the wake of crackdowns against offshore financial centres, according to the Economist Intelligence Unit's publication, Tax Havens and Their Uses 2002.

About 35% of the US$3 trillion of individual wealth estimated to have been held in tax havens in 2000, was administered by Swiss-based wealth managers, according to Caroline Doggart, author of the report.

'Confronted with criticisms and ill-defined threats of economic sanctions from multilateral agencies representing the richest countries in the world, a slowdown in their main client economies, falling share prices, and a dearth of tourists, tax havens faced a lean future,' Doggart stated. 'Accused of money laundering and endangering world financial stability, the havens responded by tightening banking and financial supervision. After two years of hectic legislative changes, leading tax havens now have exemplary regulatory systems.'

Doggart now expects tax havens to see renewed growth in their share of the global investment industry, once the new procedures are in place.

The international campaign against tax havens also led to an increased interest in home-grown tax avoidance practices in countries where much of the tax haven business originates, she stated. High tax and red tape are mainly responsible for driving activities underground.

Switzerland is still the favourite destination for most individual-owned wealth in search of an offshore safe haven. The UK was the second most important centre for private offshore asset management, with 15% of the total. Caribbean havens jointly accounted for 10%.

Many tax havens also have seen an increase in interest from rich expatriates anxious to escape terrorist threats and urban crime, Doggart says. From Macau to Mustique, prices for seaside properties in low-tax and no-tax jurisdictions have been rising.

The most expensive locations are those with high levels of political stability, reliable business services, and sound property ownership regulations.

'Offshore centres would have good reason to worry about the future if company tax exemptions were all they had to offer to corporate business,' Doggart says. 'Finance ministers in most high-tax countries have been busily cutting company tax rates. Within the EU, the high-tax area par excellence, Ireland plans to unify its corporate income tax (CIT) rate at the bargain basement level of 12.5% from 2003. Denmark, Germany, Greece, and Portugal have rate reduction programmes under way. But CIT reductions in high-tax economies usually coincide with changes in tax bases, and reduced allowances and deductions, which help to preserve total CIT revenues despite lower tax rates. This sleight of hand does not fool corporate investors. Company tax havens like Luxembourg, the Channel Islands, the Isle of Man, Switzerland, and many others need not fear that their competitive advantages are eroded.'

She noted that some jurisdictions benefited from offering niche expertise, from Islamic banking in Labuan (Malaysia), captive insurance in Bermuda, and offshore funds in the Channel Islands.

'Rivalry is fierce as individual havens constantly improve their products and services, hoping to steal a march on their competitors,' she stated. 'No sooner has one jurisdiction come up with a promising idea for a niche product (protected cell companies and e-commerce legislation were all the rage in 2001), than copycat enabling laws pop up all over the globe. All tax havens and offshore finance centres are Internet connected (income tax-free Tokelau was the last one to link up). Their state-of-the-art websites have given even the smallest havens, like Anguilla, direct access to potential clients for offshore services, wherever they are.'

The book looks at the countries and businesses that play a part in this varied and important part of the world economy. It explores in depth those tax havens that combine the greatest number of attractive ingredients, particularly the Netherlands Antilles, the Bahamas, Bermuda, the Cayman Islands, the Channel Islands (Jersey and Guernsey), Cyprus, Hong Kong, Liechtenstein, Luxembourg, The Isle of Man, Mauritius, Switzerland, and the Virgin Islands.

'Whether market leaders can hang on to their shares and how the remainder is divided among other existing and aspiring tax havens in the future depends more on the evolution of fiscal policies in high-tax countries than on the economic and regulatory policies of individual tax havens,' Doggart says.

She noted that a rough and ready method for comparing national tax burdens relies on the use of tax ratios, shorthand for tax revenues calculated as a percentage of gross domestic product. In the OECD region as a whole, tax ratios rose throughout the 1990s, though not as fast as before. Fiscal reforms in the late 1980s concentrated on reducing top tax rates, yet tax ratios continued to rise, partly because rate reductions were offset by eliminating a wide range of tax reliefs, and partly because of soaring compulsory social security contributions.

The OECD average tax burden rose to 37% from 35% between 1990 and 2000, with 10 countries' governments taking charge of between 40% and 53% of their nations' incomes.

Doggart writes that International Monetary Fund research shows that for every one percentage point increase in industrialised countries' top corporate tax rates, capital inflows to offshore centres rose by 5% in general and by 19% for Caribbean centres.

The book is available from the Economist Intelligence Unit at +44(0)7830 1007 or at www.store.eiu.com. Price £95/US$150

Summary of taxes in the main tax havens

	Personal income tax	Estate duty	Corporation profits tax
Netherlands Antilles	Maximum marginal rate 60%	2-24%	34.5% incl surtax[a]
Bahamas	None	None	None
Bermuda	None	None[b]	None
Cayman Islands	None	None	None
Channel Islands	20%	None[b]	20%

For additional analytical, business and investment opportunities information, please contact Global Investment & Business Center, USA at (703) 370-8082. Fax: (703) 370-8083. E-mail: ibpusa3@gmail.com Global Business and Investment Info Databank - www.ibpus.com

Country			
Cyprus	20-40%[c]	Up to 30%	Up to 25%
Hong Kong	15%[d]	5-15%[d]	16%[d]
Liechtenstein	Up to 18.9%	1.5-27%	7.5-20%[a]
Luxembourg	Up to 43.05%	Up to 48%	26%
Isle of Man	12-18%	None	18%
Mauritius	15-25%	None	25%
Switzerland	Up to 11.5% plus cantonal taxes (35% max)	Differs according to cantonal laws	8.5% plus cantonal and communal taxes (effective rates of 14-30%)
British Virgin Islands	6-20%	None	15%

a Not applicable to offshore corporations. b Except in relation to local real estate. c Special rates for offshore entities and their employees. d Local-source income or assets only. Table produced by Economist Intelligence Unit.

IMPORTANT SWISS LAWS AND REGULATIONS

BUSINESS ENTITIES IN SWITZERLAND

INDIVIDUAL COMPANY

Under Neuunternehmerinnen and individual entrepreneurs, the company is still the most popular legal form you are legally if a natural person solely a commercial activity, so a business or a company operates. It is legally significant if a natural person solely a commercial activity, as a business or a company operates.

Owners of sole proprietorship enterprises shall bear the risk, for which she and her entire personal and business liability. Owners of sole proprietorship enterprises shall bear the risk, for which she and her entire personal and business liability. On the other hand they alone determine the business policy. On the other hand they alone determine the business policy. Has the company's success, it may be no big problems in a corporation to be converted. Has the company's success, it may be no big problems in a corporation to be converted. It fails, is the elimination easier than other legal forms. It fails, is the elimination easier than other legal forms.

For a sole proprietorship, there are no capital requirements, capital is only by the assets of the holder is limited. For a sole proprietorship, there are no capital requirements, capital is only by the assets of the holder is limited. A special constituent is not necessary. A special constituent is not necessary. The sole proprietorship then awakens to life when the owner or the owner with the business activity starts. The sole proprietorship then awakens to life when the owner or the owner with the business activity starts. A corporate and commercial contract it is not needed because the company only by the individual owners is kept. A corporate and commercial contract it is not needed because the company only by the individual owners is kept. The start-up procedures are correspondingly simple. The start-up procedures are correspondingly simple. The cost for advice and Handelsregistereintrag are hardly ever more than CHF 1'000 .-. The cost for advice and Commercial registration are hardly ever more than CHF 1'000 .-.

The name of the company must include the name of the founder or the founder - with or without forenames - exist. The name of the company must include the name of the founder or the founder - with or without forename - exist. Fantasy or Sachbezeichnungen are permitted only as a supplement. Fantasy Sachbezeichnungen or are permitted only as a supplement. The Werner Müller a carpenter could "Carpenter Smith" or "WM Werner Müller dipl. The Werner Müller a carpenter could "Carpenter Smith" or "WM Werner Müller dipl. Master Carpenter" hot. Master carpenter "hot.

If the annual turnover exceeds CHF 100,000 .-, the sole proprietorship must be registered in the commercial. If the annual turnover exceeds CHF 100,000 .-, the sole proprietorship must be registered in the commercial. With a lower sales, you can also voluntarily register. With a lower sales, so you can voluntarily register. The entry in the commercial has the consequence that the company's name is protected and that the Firmeninhabende of debt subject to bankruptcy. The entry in the commercial has the consequence that the company's name is protected and that the Firmeninhabende of debt subject to bankruptcy.

With the entry into the commercial register is the owner, the owner required to provide proper, ie, double bookkeeping to lead. With the entry into the commercial register is the owner, the owner required to provide proper, ie, double bookkeeping to lead. But even without commercial register entry is a record keeping requirement, so you need the tax authority for all receipts and expenditures and keep writing together with supporting documents to keep order. But even without commercial register entry is a record keeping requirement, so you need the tax authority for all receipts and expenditures and keep writing together with supporting documents to keep order.

EASY COMPANY

The company is simple - as the name suggests - the simplest form a partnership. The company is simple - as the name suggests - the simplest form a partnership. It is the conventional association of two or more persons to achieve a common purpose with common efforts or resources (OR Art. 530-551). It is the conventional association of two or more persons to achieve a common purpose with common efforts or resources (OR Art. 530-551).

Simple companies are often only for a certain period of time, eg a Baukonsortium, which after completion of the structure again dissolves. Simple companies are often only for a certain period of time, eg a Baukonsortium, which after completion of the structure dissolves again.

A simple partnership is only as to the outside community interests. A simple partnership is only as to the outside community interests. It has neither a separate legal entity, nor should it against the outside under a separate name. It has neither a separate legal entity, nor should it against the outside under a separate name. This results in practice often a simple partnership agreement without the parties are aware. This practice often results in a simple partnership agreement without the parties are aware. This ignorance may in liability cases to a nasty awakening lead. This ignorance may in liability cases to a nasty awakening lead.

Because liability in this form of society is not without pitfalls: The shareholders and partners are liable towards the outside of solidarity and for the unlimited liabilities of the entire society. Because liability in this form of society is not without pitfalls: The shareholders and partners are liable towards the outside of solidarity and for the unlimited liabilities of the entire society. A liability limit is only when a shareholder expressly in his own behalf. A liability limit is only when a shareholder expressly in his own behalf.

The creation of a simple society requires no special form. The creation of a simple society requires no special form, an entry in the commercial is not necessary nor possible. An entry in the commercial is not necessary nor possible. Highly recommended is the conclusion of a written contract, inter alia, the management, the division of labor and skills, the contributions and the profit and loss distribution regulates binding. Highly recommended is the conclusion of a written contract, inter alia, the management, the division of labor and skills, the contributions and the profit and loss distribution regulates binding.

PUBLIC LIMITED COMPANY

A joint stock company (Art. OR 620-763) can be replaced by one or more natural or legal persons are established. This brings or bring a certain capital, the subtotals (the shares) is decomposed. This brings or bring a certain capital, the subtotal (the shares) is Decomposed.

Together with the individual company (of which there are approximately 150,000) is the Aktiengesellschaft (AG) in Switzerland is the most common legal form (about 175,000) because they are classified liability, capital requirements, etc. for small business offers many advantages. Together with the individual company (of which there are approximately 150000) is the Aktiengesellschaft (AG) in Switzerland is the most common legal form (about 175000) because they are classified liability, capital requirements, etc. for small business offers many advantages.

For the liabilities of the corporation is liable only the company's assets in bankruptcy the shareholders will lose, and therefore exceed their shareholder equity capital. For the liabilities of the corporation is liable only the company's assets in bankruptcy the shareholders will lose, and therefore exceed their shareholder equity capital.

A shareholders' agreement provides clarity, if multiple parties in a company are involved. A shareholders' agreement provides clarity, if multiple parties in a company are involved. Establishing a joint stock company needs at least 1 shareholder, however, that natural or legal persons or other companies can be. Establishing a joint stock company needs at least 1 shareholder, however, that natural or legal persons or other companies can be. The formation process is more complex, the establishment costs are higher than for private companies. The formation process is more complex, the establishment costs are higher than for private companies.

Keyword: shareholders' agreement Keywords: Shareholders' agreement

The company name can be chosen freely, provided he is not already covered by another company is busy. The company name can be chosen freely, provided he is not already covered by another company is busy. The miller could carpentry of wood dream AG "or the" Müller AG "are. The miller could dream of wood Carpentry AG "or the" Müller AG "are.

Adverse Adverse double tax

The treasury of a public company distinguishes between private and business. The treasury of a public company distinguish between private and business. The AG is a legal person and how each person will be taxed separately. The AG is a legal person and how each person will be taxed separately. This gives us a disadvantage for shareholders: the power company profits, they pay out income taxes. This gives us a disadvantage for shareholders: the power company profits, they pay out income taxes. Paid in addition to the profit from a dividend to shareholders, they need the dividend again as personal income. Paid in addition to the profit from a dividend to shareholders, they need the dividende again as personal income. This is called double taxation. This is called double taxation.

Even when the share capital, the tax office twice: in the share capital is owed by the capital tax, while the shares as private assets of the shareholder are taxable. Even when the share capital, the tax office twice: in the share capital is owed by the capital tax, while the shares as private assets of the shareholder are taxable.

The disadvantages of the economic burden will double by the Parliament and adopted by the people at the ballot box in 2009 confirmed expected corporate tax reform taking effect will be mitigated II. The disadvantages of the economic burden will double by the Parliament and adopted by the people at the ballot box in 2009 confirmed expected corporate tax reform taking effect will be mitigated II The solution is as follows: The taxable portion of the future dividend of 60% in private assets and 50% in financial assets for shareholders with at least 10% participation is an approximation of the tax burden: companies that are financed through loans, will no longer be tax-advantageous treatment than those who are entrepreneurially active shareholders are looking for. The solution is as follows: The taxable portion of the future dividend of 60% in private assets and 50% for business assets for shareholders with at least 10% participation is an approximation of the tax burden: companies that are financed through loans, are no longer tax-favorable treatment than those entrepreneurially motivated the shareholders are looking for.

Federal Department of Finance: Corporate Tax Reform II (external link, new window) Federal Department of Finance: Corporate Tax Reform II (external link, new window)

Regulatory Scheme in the share capital into share capital

The share capital amounts to at least CHF 100'000 .-. The share capital amounts to at least CHF 100,000 .-. You must, however, only 20% of the planned share capital account (Liberia) - this is the minimum, regardless of CHF 50'000 .-. You must, however, only 20% of the planned share capital account (Liberia) - this is the minimum, regardless of CHF 50'000 .-. The rest later, but in any case still be paid - allerspätestens in liquidation or in bankruptcy cases. The rest later, but in any case still be paid - allerspätestens in liquidation or in bankruptcy cases.

The capital need not necessarily be paid in cash, but can also be in kind (eg real estate, machinery, etc.) are introduced. The capital need not necessarily be paid in cash, but can also be in kind (eg real estate, machinery, etc.) are introduced. The cash portion of share capital, you pay for the creation of a bank account lockout. The cash portion of share capital, you pay for the creation of a bank account lockout. There it remains until the publication of the foundation blocks in the Official Gazette. There it remains until the publication of the foundation blocks in the Official Gazette. Thereafter, it is by the bank to an account of the new company to be transferred. Thereafter, it is by the bank to an account of the new company to be transferred. From this time the management may dispose of the amount. From this time the management may dispose of the amount.

On share capital may be as many partners and associates participate. On share capital may be as many partners and associates participate. The shares may be in bearer form and / or run on the name of its nominal value must be at least 1 cents amount. The shares may be in bearer form and / or run on the name of its nominal value must be at least 1 cent amount.

In the case of bearer shares, the shareholders remain anonymous, and the respective owners of the shares is regarded as a shareholder. In the case of bearer shares, the shareholders remain anonymous, and the respective owners of the shares is regarded as a shareholder. Bearer shares, change the owner by mere delivery of the paper to another person. Bearer shares, change the owner by mere delivery of the paper to another person.

For registered shares, the share price to the actual name of the shareholder. For registered shares, the share price to the actual name of the shareholder. This person must also be in the share register of the company register. This person must also be in the share register of the company register. Shares the ownership change by signing the document by the transferor (the so-called "endorsement") and the entry in the share register of the company. Shares the ownership change by signing the document by the transferor (the so-called "endorsement") and the entry in the share register of the company.

Thus, the AG a certain control over the property: If shareholders know the name of society and its institutions as shareholders, for bearer shares is not necessarily. Thus, the AG a certain control over the property: If shareholders know the name of society and its institutions as shareholders, for bearer shares is not necessarily. For this reason, many opt for small business shares and place this example in their own family. That is why many opt for small business shares and place this example in their own family.

Your influence on the AG may be Founders of also about so-called right to vote shares they hold. Your influence on the AG may be of Founders thus about so-called right to vote shares they hold. These are stocks with low nominal and full voting rights, in the name of the Founders of loud.

These are stocks with low nominal and full voting rights in the name of the Founders of loud. This can be achieved, that a shareholder with 1,000 shares at CHF 10 - the company shareholders meeting compared to 100 with 100-franc shares may dominate, although both bearing the same amount of money (CHF 10'000 .-) have paid. This may be achieved, that a shareholder with 1,000 shares at C $ 10 - the company shareholders meeting compared to 100 with 100-franc shares may dominate, although both bearing the same amount of money (CHF 10'000 .-) have paid.

Board: oversight and design institution Board: oversight and body shaping

An AG must have a Board of Directors (BoD) for orders of 1 or more shareholders exists. An AG must have a Board of Directors (BoD) for orders of 1 or more shareholders exists. If the company legal persons are involved, these may be a representation on the Board represent. If the company legal persons are involved, these may be a representation on the board represent.

A representative of the corporation authorized person must be domiciled in Switzerland. A representative of the corporation authorized person must be domiciled in Switzerland. This person can be a member of the board or even a member of the Directorate. This person can be a member of the board or even a member of the Directorate.

The Board of Directors is the supreme supervisory body and design of the corporation. The Board of Directors is the supreme supervisory body and design of the corporation. Under the Code of Obligations (OR) leads the business of the Board himself, or he will transfer the management to a third party (which is the norm). Under the Code of Obligations (OR) leads the business of the Board himself, or he wants to transfer the management to a third party (which is the norm). Under the Act but the Board has seven non-transferable and irrevocable duties (Art. 716a CO). Under the Act, but the board has seven non-transferable and irrevocable duties (Art. 716a CO).

Duties of the Board Duties of the Board

I he names of the administrators will be published in the Commercial. The names of the administrators will be published in the Commercial. You personally liable for damages caused by intentional or negligent breach of duty have caused. You personally liable for damages caused by intentional or negligent breach of duty have caused.

A theme, which in recent years increasingly more important for SMEs has been (and will), is the corporate governance, ie the way a company will - or should be. A theme, which in recent years increasingly more important for SMEs has been (and will), is the corporate governance, ie the way a company wants - or should be.

Auditors and Auditors Annual Report and Annual Report

A joint stock company must have a review body that is at the foundation to be determined. A joint stock company must have a review body that is at the foundation to be determined. It has the General Assembly an annual written report on the accounts must. It has the General Assembly an annual written report on the accounts must. The Prüfprozedere provides for the proper revision for larger AGs (and limited) in which in 2 consecutive years, 2 of the 3 limit (total assets: CHF 10 million and turnover of CHF 20 million and 50 or more full-time equivalents) exceeded. The Prüfprozedere provides for the proper revision for larger AGs (and limited) in which in 2 consecutive years, 2 of the 3 limit (total assets: CHF 10 million and turnover of CHF 20 million and 50 or more full-time equivalents) exceeded. All other companies must go through a limited audit. All other companies must go through a limited audit.

For additional analytical, business and investment opportunities information, please contact Global Investment & Business Center, USA at (703) 370-8082. Fax: (703) 370-8083. E-mail: ibpusa3@gmail.com Global Business and Investment Info Databank - www.ibpus.com

New Rules for the New Rules for Audit Audit

Each stock has an annual report - consisting of annual accounts and annual report - to create. Each stock has an annual report - consisting of annual accounts and annual report - to create. The financial statements include the income statement, balance sheet and an annex with additional information, the minimum legal requirements are. The financial statements include the income statement, balance sheet and an annex with additional information, the minimum legal requirements are.

The highest authority: General Assembly The highest authority: General Assembly

The Annual General Meeting (AGM) of shareholders is the supreme organ of a public company. The Annual General Meeting (AGM) of shareholders is the supreme organ of a public company. The GM determines the statutes, elects the Board of Directors and the Auditors, approves or rejects the annual report and decide on the use of the company's profits. The GM determines the statutes, elect the Board of Directors and the Auditors, approves or rejects the annual report and decide on the use of the company's profits. In a subset of the PR balance must immediately convene a general meeting and rehabilitation measures. In a subset of the PR balance must immediately Convene a general meeting and rehabilitation measures. With an over-the Board of Directors has - or the review body - the judge must be notified. With an over-the Board of Directors has - or the review body - the judge must be notified.

COLLECTIVE SOCIETY

If two or more individuals (as opposed to legal persons, ie people of flesh and blood) together to create a joint according to commercial rules run company to operate, one speaks of a collective society (OR type 552-593).

Like the sole proprietorship, the name of one or more partners or shareholders in the company's name included. Like the sole proprietorship, the name of one or more partners or shareholders in the company's name included. The carpenter could Müller as a collective society that is "Müller Carpenter & Co." or "carpentry Müller & Suter" hot. The carpenter could Müller as a collective society that is "Miller Carpenter & Co." or "Carpentry & Müller Suter" hot.

Legally, the collective society has no legal personality, is not a legal person. Legally, the collective society has no legal personality, is not a legal person. You can, however, in commercial transactions under their own name and acquire rights, liabilities or processes occur as a party, for initiating and self-operated. You can, however, in commercial transactions under their own name and acquire rights, liabilities or processes occur as a party, for initiating and self-operated.

As a company, the collective society is not taxable, however, the individual partners and shareholders because of their wages, the potential profit, interest and equity of their property taxes directly. As a company, the collective society is not taxable, however, the individual partners and shareholders because of their wages, the potential profit, interest and equity of their property taxes directly.

The liability provisions for bringing the partners and shareholders some risks involved: They adhere to their own assets and unrestricted solidarity and this is up to 5 years after the dissolution of the company. The liability provisions for bringing the partners and shareholders some risks involved: They adhere to their own assets and unrestricted solidarity and this is up to 5 years after the dissolution of the company. The individual partners and shareholders will only have to pay if the collective society without success has been operated. The individual partners and shareholders will only have to pay if the collective society without success has been operated.

The collective society is a social contract between the parties was launched. The collective society is a social contract between the parties was launched. If you choose this legal decision, you should use the social contract in any event by a professional check. If you choose this legal decision, you should use the social contract in any event by a professional check. For public companies, the entry in the Commercial compulsory. For public companies, the entry in the Commercial compulsory.

KOMMANDIT SOCIETY

The Kommandit company OR art. 554-619) plays in the Swiss corporate landscape only a minor role. Currently there are about 3,000 in this country still limited. Currently there are about 3000 in this country still limited.

In principle, they are the same as the collective society: 2 or more individuals join together to create a rules-run on a commercial firm to operate. In principle, they are the same as the collective society: 2 or more individuals join together to create a rules-run on a commercial firm to operate.

A limited partnership is supported by a social contract between the parties was launched. A limited partnership is supported by a social contract between the parties was launched. The entry into the commercial register is compulsory. The entry into the commercial register is compulsory.

At least one of the shareholders - the so-called complementary - but is liable to unlimited private property for the debts of the company. At least one of the shareholders - the so-called complementary - but is liable to unlimited private property for the debts of the company. The other shareholders - the Kommanditäre - are liable only up to a certain deposit, known as the Kommanditsumme, and are not subject to the bankruptcy debt. The other shareholders - the Kommanditäre - are liable only up to a certain deposit, known as the Kommanditsumme, and are not subject to the bankruptcy debt. As Kommanditäre legal persons are also eligible. As Kommanditäre legal persons are also eligible. You may not entrusted with the management to discharge, they also have only limited rights of control and often are subject to a different profit and loss participation as complementary. You may not entrusted with the management to discharge, they also have only limited rights of control and often are subject to a different profit and loss participation as complementary.

A limited partnership is often chosen when a sole proprietorship or general partnership requires additional resources, without the management to a new partner or shareholder must be expanded. A limited partnership is often chosen when a sole proprietorship or general partnership requires additional resources, without the management to a new partner or shareholder must be expanded.

LIMITED LIABILITY COMPANY (GMBH)

The limited liability company (GmbH) (OR art. 772-827) describes a hybrid of equity and collective society. With over 60,000 GmbHs is this legal in third place in the Swiss corporate landscape, with the trend thanks to the low minimum capital of only CHF 20'000 .- steeply upward. With over 60,000 GmbHs is this legal in third place in the Swiss corporate landscape, with the trend thanks to the low minimum capital of only CHF 20'000 .- steeply upward.

Ltd. The new law is the beginning of the year 2008, in force and has brought significant innovations: A GmbH arises if one or more natural persons or commercial companies with a specific capital as a company constituted. Ltd. The new law is the beginning of the year 2008, in force and has brought significant innovations: A GmbH arises if one or more natural persons or commercial companies with a specific capital as a company constituted.

Each shareholder and each shareholder has at least 1 original capital of the capital (the capital) involved. Each shareholder and each shareholder has at least 1 original capital of the capital (the capital) involved. Strain deposits are now also tradable. Strain deposits are now therefore tradable. This can be a written agreement between the parties concerned. This can be a written agreement between the parties concerned. A public deed is no longer necessary. A public deed is no longer necessary.

The minimum capital of CHF 20,000 .- must be fully paid (Fachsprache: paid) or in kind covered. The minimum capital of CHF 20,000 .- must be fully paid (Fachsprache: paid) or with in kind covered. With the full payment of registered capital, the present solidarity among the members. With the full payment of registered capital, the present solidarity among the members. A ceiling on the share capital is no more. A ceiling on the share capital is no more. The minimum investment per shareholder in cash or in kind is CHF 100 -, while the number of deposits per ordinary shareholders are no longer restricted. The minimum investment per shareholder in cash or in kind is CHF 100 -, while the number of deposits per ordinary shareholders are no longer restricted. The owner of the deposits must be named in the Commercial Register. The owner of the deposits must be named in the Commercial Register.

Liability rule regime Liability

The term "limited liability" is slightly misleading, because the company is liable for its debts unlimited. The individual partners and shareholders are liable up to twice the maximum nominal value of their original capital. The margin and low performance for each tribe can share will be determined individually. The term " limited liability "is slightly misleading, because the company is liable for its debts unlimited. The individual partners and shareholders are liable up to twice the maximum nominal value of their original capital. The margin and low performance for each tribe can share will be determined individually .

The company name can be chosen freely, with the words "LLC" or "Ltd." to be seen. The company name can be chosen freely, with the words "LLC" or "Ltd". to be seen. Similar to AG, the GmbH, a government-supervised fiduciary and auditors to use. Similar to AG, the GmbH, a government-supervised fiduciary and auditors to use. Major corporations, which in 2 consecutive years, 2 of 3 exceed specified limits must have a full audit carried out. Major corporations, which in 2 consecutive years, 2 of 3 exceed specified limits must have a full audit carried out. As the limits apply to a balance sheet total of more than CHF 10 million, a turnover of more than CHF 20 million and 50 or more full-time positions. As the limits apply to a balance sheet total of more than CHF 10 million, a turnover of more than CHF 20 million and 50 or more full-time positions. All other corporations must provide for a partial revision process. All other corporations must provide for a partial revision process. If all shareholders agree, you can GmbHs small (less than 10 full-time equivalents) to waive the audit. If all shareholders agree, you can GmbHs small (less than 10 full-time equivalents) to the audit waiver.

Also the company is aware of the double taxation. So the company is aware of the double taxation. The net profit is taxable, and the profits must be distributed to shareholders as taxable income. The net profit is taxable, and the profits must be distributed to shareholders as taxable income. For the share capital of the GmbH are the shareholders and also property taxes owed. For the share capital of the GmbH are the shareholders and therefore property taxes owed.

For additional analytical, business and investment opportunities information, please contact Global Investment & Business Center, USA at (703) 370-8082. Fax: (703) 370-8083. E-mail: ibpusa3@gmail.com Global Business and Investment Info Databank - www.ibpus.com

Prerequisites for the creation Prerequisites for the creation

Establishing a GmbH requires one or more natural and / or legal persons. Establishing a GmbH requires one or more natural and / or legal persons. Would the investors to remain anonymous, they may under certain conditions, third persons as representatives to use. Would the investors to remain anonymous, they may under certain conditions, third persons as representatives to use.

The establishment costs of a GmbH are somewhat lower than in a stock, but higher than for a partnership. The establishment costs of a GmbH are somewhat lower than in a stock, but higher than for a partnership.

The management of the GmbH is the management board of a public company. The management of the GmbH is the management board of a public company. In principle, all common shareholders for the management and representation, the right and obligation, but they must be represented by a person leave the residence in Switzerland. In principle, all common shareholders for the management and representation, the right and obligation, but they must be represented by a person leave the residence in Switzerland. As board members are also liable Executive personally for damages caused by intentional or negligent breach of duty have caused. As board members are also executive personally liable for damages caused by intentional or negligent breach of duty have caused.

The supreme organ: The shareholders' meeting The supreme organ: The shareholders' meeting

The shareholders' meeting is the supreme organ of the GmbH and determines the Bylaws, the directors and the Auditors. The shareholders' meeting is the supreme organ of the GmbH and determines the Bylaws, the directors and the auditor. They also approved the profit and loss account and balance sheet, decide on the use of earnings and reduces the burden on the manager or managers. They also approved the profit and loss account and balance sheet, decide on the use of earnings and reduces the burden on the manager or managers. Even corporations are basically the same accounting rules that also apply for AGs. Even corporations are basically the same accounting rules that then apply for AGs.

COOPERATIVE

When the cooperative is the idea of encouraging, or economic self-help in the foreground, are examples of housing or purchasing cooperatives.

A business activity may also be under the legal form of a co-operative (OR Art. 828-926) be included. A business activity may also be under the legal form of a co-operative (OR art. 828-926) be included.

For a cooperative are also "internal" corporate values such as direct democracy and clearly defined participation rights (head vote principle). Is also a positive transparency on each hierarchy level, which roughly similar wage excesses largely avoiding. For a cooperative are also "internal" corporate values such as direct democracy and clearly defined participation rights (head vote principle). Is also a positive transparency on each hierarchy level, which roughly similar wage largely avoiding excess.

Hindrance, because slow, may be broad-based involvement of a cooperative effect. Hindrances, because slow, may be broad-based involvement of a cooperative effect. Is clearly detrimental to the co-operative legal form of company and capital market transactions: The head of vote principle excludes the one undesirable influences from competition, but also impossible because of alliances with financial obligations. Is clearly detrimental to the co-operative legal form of company and capital market transactions: The head of vote principle excludes the one undesirable influences from competition, but also impossible because of alliances with financial obligations. Because of the lack of fixed capital stock and thus a sufficient credit cooperatives have also only limited access to capital and can not in this way to obtain capital. Because of the lack of fixed capital stock and thus a sufficient credit cooperatives have also only limited access to capital and can not in this way to obtain capital.

Prerequisites for the creation Prerequisites for the creation

Establishing it needs at least 7 Genossenschafterinnen and cooperative, the natural or legal persons can be. Establishing it needs at least 7 Genossenschafterinnen and cooperative, the natural or legal persons can be. After the foundation can also be less cooperative, but there is the theoretical danger of a dissolution action. After the foundation can also be less cooperative, but there is the theoretical danger of a dissolution action.

A start-up capital is not required. A start-up capital is not required. If there is one thing, each cooperative is at least 1 share with a fixed nominal assume. If there is one thing, each cooperative is at least 1 share with a fixed nominal assume. The cooperative is liable for the company's assets. The cooperative is liable for the company's assets.

Statutory bodies of the cooperative are: Statutory bodies of the cooperative are:

• General Assembly

• Administration (at least three members)

• Control

The entry in the commercial is a must, the name of the cooperative but may be chosen freely. The entry in the commercial is a must, the name of the cooperative but may be chosen freely. Only for personal names, the words "cooperative" binding. Only for personal names, the words "cooperative" binding.

ASSOCIATION

Also an association (Civil Code Article 60-79), a species managed under commercial industry operate. But it must be a "perfect end" track. But it must be a "perfect end" track.

Who's with a club wants to be doing business, this must necessarily entered in the Commercial Register. Who's with a club wants to be doing business, this must necessarily entered in the Commercial Register. The association may end according to Civil Code (CC) but not for profit, so members of the asset benefits. The association may end according to Civil Code (CC) but not for profit, so members of the asset benefits. Since the association necessarily with an ideal end is connected, it is only very limited for the operation of a business. Since the association necessarily with an ideal end is connected, it is only very limited for the operation of a business.

For the club founded, at least 2 natural and / or legal persons is necessary. For the club founded, at least 2 Natural and / or legal persons is necessary. Capital formation is not required. Capital formation is not required. The foundation is made by the founding meeting that the statutes and to authorize the Board and any appropriate inspection to determine. The foundation is made by the founding meeting that the statutes and to authorize the Board and any appropriate inspection to determine. The necessary institutions are the Assembly and the Association Board of Directors (at least 1 member). The necessary institutions are the Assembly and the Association Board of Directors (at least 1 Members).

The Association is a separate legal entity. The Association is a separate legal entity. Therefore, the term club members are not personally responsible for the association's debts. Therefore, the term club members are not personally responsible for the association's debts. An exception exists only if the statutes provide otherwise. An exception exists only if the statutes provide otherwise. (Article 75a ZGB) (Article 75a ZGB)

FOUNDATION

With foundations will be assets for a fixed purpose verselbstständigt.

Assets can be in the form of a foundation (ZGB Art 80-89bis) independent. Assets can be in the form of a foundation (ZGB type 80-89bis) independent. The Foundation is a legal entity which the responsible body (board of trustees) applies. The Foundation is a legal entity which the responsible body (board of trustees) applies. The Foundation is supported by notarial deed or a will established. The Foundation is supported by notarial deed or a will established. You must - except for the Family Foundation and the Church's foundation - are entered in the commercial. You must - except for the Family Foundation and the Church's foundation - are entered in the commercial.

For the business activity within a foundation, the foundation charter in the fixed will of the founder or major donor. For the business activity within a foundation, the foundation charter in the fixed will of the founder or major donor. Responsible for compliance with this purpose is, depending on the nature and purpose of the community foundation (Confederation, cantons, municipalities). Responsible for compliance with this purpose is, depending on the nature and purpose of the community foundation (Confederation, Cantons, municipalities). With the exception of the Family Foundation and the Foundation of the Church (Art. 87 CC) are the foundations of regulatory oversight that is assumed. With the exception of the Family Foundation and the Foundation of the Church (Art. 87 CC) are the foundations of regulatory oversight that is assumed.

In business life, the Foundation organized a staff welfare facilities a great importance, as a legal enterprise is the foundation but is less suitable. In business life, the Foundation organized a staff welfare facilities a great importance, as a legal enterprise is the foundation but is less suitable. Conversely, the fate of a company with a foundation linked by appropriate purpose for a period longer be predetermined. Conversely, the fate of a company with a foundation linked by appropriate purpose for a period longer be predetermined

For additional analytical, business and investment opportunities information, please contact Global Investment & Business Center, USA at (703) 370-8082. Fax: (703) 370-8083. E-mail: ibpusa3@gmail.com Global Business and Investment Info Databank - www.ibpus.com

SUPPLEMENTS

BUSINESS TRAVEL

BUSINESS CUSTOMS

As a prosperous, highly developed Western democracy, Switzerland's business customs and practices are similar to those of other northern European countries. While some American business representatives may find their Swiss counterparts somewhat conservative and formal, business customs in Switzerland correspond generally to those of the United States. Punctuality, particularly in German-speaking areas, is very important. Allowing ample lead-time in setting up business appointments is expected and one should not expect to "drop in" without an appointment.

TRAVEL ADVISORY

A valid passport is required to enter Switzerland. Swiss residency and work permits for longer stays or employment are extremely difficult to obtain, as the Swiss government, at Cantonal level, imposes severe limitations on immigration and the country's foreign work force. All foreigners, including Americans, must have a work permit before commencing employment. The complicated process of obtaining a work visa can take several months.

For more information, contact the Consular Section of the Swiss Embassy in Washington, or the Swiss Consular Office in Atlanta, Boston, Los Angeles, New York, or San Francisco.

Swiss Official Representation in the USA:

Embassy of Switzerland, Washington DC

Swiss Consulate General Atlanta

Swiss Consulate General Boston - Swissnex Boston

Swiss Consulate General Los Angeles

Swiss Consulate General New York -- Swiss Business Hub USA

Swiss Consulate General San Francisco

Permanent Mission of Switzerland to the United States

Switzerland continues to have a very low rate of violent crime. However, pick pocketing and purse snatchings occur, especially during peak tourist periods and during major

conferences, shows, and exhibits. A typical scam used against businesspeople is for a thief to grab a briefcase in a hotel or airport while an accomplice distracts the victim. Loss or theft of a U.S. passport should be reported to the local police immediately and to the American Embassy in Bern at +41 (0) 31 357 7011. Under most circumstances, a replacement can be issued in the course of a working day.

For additional analytical, business and investment opportunities information,
please contact Global Investment & Business Center, USA
at (703) 370-8082. Fax: (703) 370-8083. E-mail: ibpusa3@gmail.com
Global Business and Investment Info Databank - www.ibpus.com

Countrywide emergency telephone numbers are police 117; Fire 118; and Ambulance 144. There is usually an English-speaking contact available.

VISA REQUIREMENTS

U.S. companies requiring travel to the United States of business-people resident in Switzerland should allow sufficient time for visa issuance, if required. Visa applicants should go to the following link:

http://bern.usembassy.gov/visas.html

Information about U.S. visa policy and procedures: http://travel.state.gov/visa/visa_1750.html

Information sheet for U.S. citizens traveling to Switzerland: http://travel.state.gov/travel/cis_pa_tw/cis/cis_1034.html

U.S. Companies that require travel of foreign businesspersons to the United States should be advised that security evaluations are handled via an interagency process. Visa applicants should go to the following links.

State Department Visa Website: http://travel.state.gov/visa/

TELECOMMUNICATIONS

Telecommunications are modern and, with on-going liberalization, dropping dramatically in price. Visiting U.S.-based business travelers may operate GSM-based cell phones in Switzerland. Cell phones are easily rented from vendors in Swiss airports.

TRANSPORTATION

The Swiss business infrastructure is excellent. There are major international airports in Zurich, Geneva and Basel as well as smaller airports throughout the country. Road and rail networks, despite the country's mountainous terrain, are very well maintained and efficient. High-speed trains link Zurich and Bern in less than one hour and Zurich and Geneva within two and one-half hours. Urban public transport is unsurpassed.

LANGUAGE

Switzerland is a multilingual country. Swiss-German is spoken by the majority of Swiss in the central and northeast portions of the country. French is the principal language of

Geneva and the western cantons, and Italian is spoken in the south, especially in the canton Ticino (Lugano/Locarno). English is widely spoken in business and tourist centers throughout the country.

HEALTH

Switzerland has excellent health care facilities. (Note: U.S. medical insurance is not always valid outside the United States. Travelers should check their insurance policies for specific overseas coverage.)

TEMPORARY ENTRY OF MATERIALS AND PERSONAL BELONGINGS

Personal effects, including laptop computers, do not need to be declared and can enter Switzerland freely. However, computer systems brought into Switzerland must be declared and a deposit must be paid covering the VAT and applicable customs duty, which is refundable upon leaving the country. ATA Carnets are used widely throughout Switzerland and Europe for products shown at trade exhibitions. Trade exhibit materials can enter freely with a Carnet as long as they leave the country after the event. If the product is sold at the exhibition, applicable duties and VAT must be paid. All international trade fairs in Switzerland have customs offices that facilitate the payment of fees and clearing of items in an expeditious fashion.

SELECTED GOVERNMENT AND BUSINESS CONTACTS

U.S. EMBASSY TRADE RELATED CONTACTS

U.S. Embassy Bern
Ambassador: Vacant
Deputy Chief of Mission: Vacant
Commercial Counselor: Michael Keaveny
Commercial Specialist: Werner Wiedmer
Commercial Specialist: Ernst Hegg
Commercial Assistant: Marianne von Känel
Economic/Political Counselor: Dennis Ortblad
Pol/Econ Officer: Richard O'Brien
Pol/Econ Specialist: Christian Kreis
Pol/Econ Specialist: Remy Delalande

Street/International Mail: U.S. Pouch Address:
Jubilaeumsstrasse 93-97 American Embassy Bern
P.O. Box U.S. Department of State
CH-3001 Bern 5110 Bern Place
Switzerland Washington, DC 20521-5110
Tel: (41-31) 357-7011
Fax: (41-31) 357-7336

Zurich America Center
Commercial Specialist: Sandor Galambos
Commercial Assistant: Elisabeth Mbitha-Schmid
Commercial Assistant: Philippe Mettler

International Mail:
Dufourstrasse 101
CH-8008 Zurich, Switzerland
Tel: (41-1) 422-2372
Fax: (41-1) 382-2655

America Center Geneva
Commercial Assistant: Georges Laurent

International Mail: U.S. Pouch Address:
ACG America Center Geneva ACG
Rue Versonnex 7 c/o U.S. Mission Geneva
CH-1207 Geneva, Switzerland Department of State
Tel: (41-22) 840 51 53 Washington, D.C. 20521-5110
Fax: (41-22) 840 51 67

AMCHAM AND SWISS CHAMBERS OF COMMERCE

There is no central chamber of commerce for all of Switzerland, rather each canton has its own chamber. There are also chamber associations covering business between Switzerland and most major trading partners. Following is the address of the Swiss-American Chamber of Commerce, as well as a selection of cantonal chambers.

Swiss-American Chamber of Commerce Contact: W. Diggelmann
Talacker 41 Tel: (41-1) 211 24 54
CH-8001 Zurich, Switzerland Fax: (41-1) 211 95 72
http://www.amcham.ch Email: info@amcham.ch

Aargau
Aargauische Industrie- Director: Dr. H. Suter
und Handelskammer Tel: (41-62) 837 18 18
Entfelderstrasse 11 Fax: (41-62) 837 18 19
CH-5001 Aarau, Switzerland

Basel
Handelskammer beider Basel Director: Dr. A. Burkhardt
St. Alban-Graben, P.O. Box Tel: (41-61) 272 18 88
CH-4001 Basel, Switzerland Fax: (41-61) 272 62 28

Bern
Berner Handelskammer Director: Dr. R. Portmann
Gutenbergstrasse 1 Tel: (41-31) 388 87 87
CH-3001 Bern, Switzerland Fax: (41-31) 388 70 70

Fribourg
Chambre Fribourgeoise du Director: Mr. A. Uebersax
Commerce et de l'Industrie Tel: (41-26) 347 12 20
37, rte. du Jura, Fax: (41-26) 347 12 39
CH-1706 Fribourg, Switzerland
http://www.cci.ch/fribourg

Geneva
Chambre de Commerce et de Director: P. Coidan
l'Industrie de Geneve Tel: (41-22) 819 91 11
Bd du Theatre 4, C.P. 5039 Fax: (41-22) 819 91 00
CH-1211 Geneve 11, Switzerland

Glarus
Glarner Handelskammer Secretary: Dr. K. Landolt

Spielhof 14a Tel: (41-55) 640 11 73
CH-8750 Glarus, Switzerland Fax: (41-55) 640 36 39

Graubunden
Bundner Handels- und Industrieverein Secr: Dr. M. Ettisberger
Poststrasse 43 Tel: (41-81) 252 63 06
CH-7002 Chur, Switzerland Fax: (41-81) 252 04 49

Jura
Chambre de Commerce et Director: Mr. J.-F. Gerber
d'Industrie du Jura Tel: (41-32) 421 45 45
Rue de l'Avenir 23, C.P. 274 Fax: (41-32) 421 45 40
CH-2800 Delemont 1, Switzerland

Luzern
Zentralschweiz. Handelskammer Secr: Mr. D. Schlatter
Kapellplatz 2 Tel: (41-41) 410 68 65
CH-6002 Luzern, Switzerland Fax: (41-41) 410 52 88
E-mail: info@hkz.ch

Neuchatel
Chambre Neuchateloise du Director: Mr. C. Bernoulli
Commerce et de l'Industrie Tel: (41-32) 722 15 15
Rue de la Serre 4, C.P. Fax: (41-32) 722 15 20
CH-2001 Neuchatel, Switzerland
E-mail: cnci@cci.ch

Solothurn
Solothurner Handelskammer Director: Dr. H.-R. Meyer
Grabackerstrasse 6 Tel: (41-32) 626 24 24
CH-4502 Solothurn, Switzerland Fax: (41-32) 626 24 26
E-mail: info@sohk.ch

St. Gallen
Industrie- und Handelskammer Director: Dr. H. Schmid
St. Gallen - Appenzell Tel: (41-71) 223 15 15
Gallusstrasse 16, P.O. Box Fax: (41-71) 222 47 27
CH-9001 St. Gallen, Switzerland
www.ihk.ch

Thurgau
Thurgauer Industrie- und Director: Mr. M. Fehle
Handelskammer Tel: (41-71) 622 19 19
Schmidstrasse 9, P.O. Box 317 Fax: (41-71) 622 62 57
CH-8570 Weinfelden, Switzerland
E-mail: info@ihk-thurgau.ch

Ticino
Camera di Commercio del Director: Mr. C. Camponovo
Cantone Ticino Tel: (41-91) 911 51 11
Corso Elvezia 16 Fax: (41-91) 911 51 12
CH-6901 Lugano, Switzerland

**For additional analytical, business and investment opportunities information,
please contact Global Investment & Business Center, USA
at (703) 370-8082. Fax: (703) 370-8083. E-mail: ibpusa3@gmail.com
Global Business and Investment Info Databank - www.ibpus.com**

Valais/Wallis
Chambre Valaisanne de Commerce Director: Mr. T. Gsponer
et de l'Industrie Tel: (41-27) 327 35 35
Rue Pre-Fleuri 6, C.P. 288 Fax: (41-27) 327 35 36
CH-1951 Sion, Switzerland
E-mail: cvsci@cci.ch

Vaud
Chambre Vaudoise du Commerce Director: J.-L. Strohm
et de l'Industrie Tel: (41-21) 613 35 35
Avenue d'Ouchy 47, P.O. Box 205 Fax: (41-21) 613 35 05
CH-1000 Lausanne 13, Switzerland
http://www.cvci.ch

Winterthur
Handelskammer & Arbeitgebervereinigung Secretary: Mr. C. Modl
Winterthur (HAW) Tel: (41-52) 213 07 63
Neumarkt 15, P.O. Box 905 Fax: (41-52) 213 07 29
CH-8401 Winterthur, Switzerland

Zurich
Zurcher Handelskammer Director: Mr. C. Boesch
Bleicherweg 5, P.O. Box 4031 Tel: (41-1) 221 07 42
CH-8022 Zurich, Switzerland Fax: (41-1) 211 76 15
http://www.zurichcci.ch

SWISS TRADE OR INDUSTRY ASSOCIATIONS

The following lists trade associations most relevant to U.S. companies pursuing business in Switzerland. For a complete listing of associations, please consult the Publicus 2001 "Schweizer Jahrbuch des oeffentlichen Lebens", published by Schwabe & Co. AG Verlag, Farnsburgerstr. 8, CH-4132 Muttenz, Switzerland; Tel: (41-61) 467-8575; Fax: (41-61) 467-8576.

SHIV Schweizerischer Handels- und Pres: Dr. A. F. Leuenberger
Industrieverein (Vorort) Dir: Dr. R. Ramsauer
(Swiss Union of Commerce and Industry Assn) Tel: (41-1) 389 93 00
Hegibachstrasse 47, P.O. Box 1072 Fax: (41-1) 389 93 89
CH-8032 Zurich, Switzerland
Email: vorort@vorort.ch

Schweizerische Zentrale U.S. Desk: Ms. Kuenzli
fuer Handelsfoerderung (OSEC) Tel: (41-1) 365 51 51
(Swiss Office for Trade Promotion) Fax: (41-1) 365 52 21
Stampfenbachstrasse 85, P.O. Box 492
CH-8035 Zurich, Switzerland

Vereinigung des Schweizerischen Director: Dr. Zeller
Import- und Grosshandels (VSIG) Tel: (41-61) 228 90 30
(Swiss Fed.of Importers & Wholesalers) Fax: (41-61) 228 90 39
Güterstrasse 78, P.O. Box 656
CH-4010 Basel, Switzerland
http://www.vsig.ch

For additional analytical, business and investment opportunities information,
please contact Global Investment & Business Center, USA
at (703) 370-8082. Fax: (703) 370-8083. E-mail: ibpusa3@gmail.com
Global Business and Investment Info Databank - www.ibpus.com

Schweizerischer Verband der Secretary: Dr. M. Pfeifer
Internationalen Handelsfirmen Tel: (41-61) 279 33 91
(Swiss Assn. of Intl. Trading Houses) Fax: (41-61) 279 33 10
Aeschenvorstadt 4
CH-4010 Basel, Switzerland

H+ Hospitals of Switzerland Dir: Dr. C. Haudenschild
Rain 32 Tel: (41-62) 824 12 22
CH-5001 Aarau, Switzerland Fax: (41-62) 822 33 35

Verband des Schweiz. Versandhandels (VSV) President: H.M. Meier
(Mail Order Association) Tel: (41-1) 830 16 02
Brandenbergstrasse 30 Fax: (41-1) 830 16 08
CH-8304 Wallisellen, Switzerland
http://www.vsv-versandhandel.ch

Swissmem Director: Mr. T. Daum
Verein Schweizerischer Tel: (41-1) 384 44 11
Maschinenindustrieller (VSM) Fax: (41-1) 384 42 42
(Machinery Manufacturers Association)
Kirchenweg 4, P.O. Box
CH-8032 Zurich, Switzerland
http://swissmem.ch

Vereinigung fuer Schweiz. Luft- Pres: Mr. H. Kobelt
fahrtindustrie Tel: (41-1) 384 41 11
(Swiss Aeronautical Industries Group) Fax: (41-1) 384 42 42
Kirchenweg 4
CH-8032 Zurich, Switzerland

Verband des Schweiz. Maschinen- Pres: Mr. U. Luther
und Werkzeughandels Tel: (41-1) 940 93 36
(Machine & Tool Trade Association) Fax: (41-1) 940 93 44
Buchhaldenstrasse 10
CH-8610 Uster, Switzerland

Verein Schweiz. Metallwarenfabrikanten Secretary: P. Schnadt
(Metal Product Mfr's Association) Tel: (41-41) 711 61 34
Gartenstrasse 3, P.O. Box 4754 Fax: (41-41) 711 88 43
CH-6304 Zug, Switzerland

Schweiz. Elektrotechnischer Verein Director: Dr. E. Jurczek
Luppmenstrasse 1 Tel: (41-1) 956 11 11
CH-8320 Fehraltorf, Switzerland Fax: (41-1) 956 11 22

Schweizerische Normen-Vereinigung (SNV) Director: Dr. H.P. Homberger
(Standards Association) Tel: (41-1) 254 54 54
Muehlebachstrasse 54 Fax: (41-1) 254 54 74
CH-8008 Zurich, Switzerland

Schweiz. Technischer Verband (STV) Secretary: S. Schwitter
(Technical Association) Tel: (41-1) 268 37 11

For additional analytical, business and investment opportunities information,
please contact Global Investment & Business Center, USA
at (703) 370-8082. Fax: (703) 370-8083. E-mail: ibpusa3@gmail.com
Global Business and Investment Info Databank - www.ibpus.com

Weinbergstrasse 41, POB Fax: (41-1) 268 37 00
CH-8006 Zurich, Switzerland
http://www.swissengineering.ch

Schweizer Automatik Pool (SAP) Contact: Mr. R. Schmid
(Electronics, Automation Equipment & Tel: (41-1) 286 31 11
Computer Manuf. & Distr. Association) Fax: (41-1) 202 92 83
c/o ATAG Ernst & Young AG
P.O. Box 5272
CH-8022 Zurich, Switzerland
http://www.sap-verband.ch

ProTelecom Director: Mr. J. Wilhelm
(Telecommunication Association) Tel: (41-31) 390 40 40
Laupenstrasse 18a, P.O. Box Fax: (41-31) 390 40 41
CH-3001 Bern, Switzerland
E-mail: office@protelecom.ch

ASUT Contact: Dr. C. Bolla-Vincenz
(Swiss Telecommunications Users Assoc.) Tel: (41-31) 328 27 27
Kramgasse 5, P.O. Box 515 Fax: (41-31) 328 27 37
CH-3000 Bern 8, Switzerland
www.asut.ch

SWICO Director: Mr. B. Baumann
(Information, Communication, Software Tel: (41-1) 445 38 00
& Business Organization Association) Fax: (41-1) 445 38 01
Technopark 1
CH-8005 Zurich, Switzerland

Verband Schweiz. Firmen fuer Secretary: Mr. J. H. Schnetzer
Arzt- und Spitalbedarf (FAS) Tel: (41-31) 380 85 87
(Medical & Hospital Supply Assoc.) Fax: (41-31) 380 85 96
Monbijoustrasse 22, P.O. Box
CH-3001 Bern, Switzerland
E-mail: fasmed@medical-devices.ch

Schweiz. Ingenieur & Architekten Verein (SIA) GenSecr: Mr. E. Mosimann
(Society of Engineers and Architects) Tel: (41-1) 283 15 15
Selnaustrasse 16, P.O.Box Fax:(41-1) 201 63 35
CH-8039 Zurich, Switzerland
http://www.sia.ch

Swiss Textiles Federation Director: Mr. T. Isler
P.O. Box 4838, Beethovenstr. 20 Tel: (41-1) 289 79 79
CH-8022 Zurich, Switzerland Fax: (41-1) 289 79 80
E-mail: contact@tvs.ch

Schweiz. Gesellschaft fuer Chemische Director: Dr. B. Moser
Industrie (SGCI) (Chemical Ind. Assoc.) Tel: (41-1) 368 17 11
P.O. Box, Nordstrasse 15 Fax: (41-1) 368 17 70

For additional analytical, business and investment opportunities information,
please contact Global Investment & Business Center, USA
at (703) 370-8082. Fax: (703) 370-8083. E-mail: ibpusa3@gmail.com
Global Business and Investment Info Databank - www.ibpus.com

CH-8035 Zurich, Switzerland
http://www.sgci.ch

Schweizerische Bankiervereinigung Contact: Prof. N. Blattner
(Swiss Banking Association) Tel: (41-61) 295 93 93
P.O. Box 4182, Aeschenplatz 7 Fax: (41-61) 272 53 82
CH-4002 Basel, Switzerland
E-mail: office@sba.ch

Schweizer Hotelierverein Contact: Dr. C. Juen
Swiss Hotel Association Tel: (41-31) 370 41 11
Monbijoustrasse 130, P.O. Box Fax: (41-31) 370 44 44
CH-3001 Bern, Switzerland
http://www.swisshotels.ch

Verband Elektronischer Zahlungsverkehr President: P.-A. Steim
(Electronic Payment Systems Assoc.) Tel: (41-1) 363 14 00
Frohburgstrasse 98 Fax: (41-1) 363 15 25
CH-8006 Zurich, Switzerland
E-mail: vez@ku-law.ch

Schweizer Börse SWX President: Dr. J. Fischer
(Swiss Exchange SWX) Tel: (41-1) 229 21 11
Selnaustrasse 30 Fax: (41-1) 229 22 33
8021 Zurich
E-mail: swx@swx.com

SWISS GOVERNMENT AGENCIES

The following list of Swiss government agencies may be of relevance to U.S. companies doing business in and with Switzerland. The "Eidgenoessischer Staatskalender", published by Eidg. Drucksachen- und Materialzentrale (Federal Printing Office), CH-3000 Bern, Switzerland, provides a comprehensive listing of Swiss government departments and officials.

Eidgenoessische Departement des Innern:
(Federal Department of Home Affairs)
Bundesamt fuer Statistik Director: C. Malaguerra
(Federal Office for Statistics) Tel: (41-32) 713 60 11
Espace de l'Europe 10 Fax: (41-32) 713 60 02
CH-2010 Neuchatel, Switzerland

Bundesamt fuer Gesundheitswesen (BAG) Director: Prof. T. Zeltner
(Federal Office for Public Health) Tel: (41-31) 322 21 11
Schwarzenburgstrasse 165 Fax: (41-31) 322 95 07
CH-3097 Liebefeld, Switzerland

Eidgenoessische Justiz- und Polizeidepartement:
(Federal Department of Justice and Police)
Eidg. Amt fuer Messwesen Director: Dr. W. Schwitz
(Fed. Office for Weights and Measures) Tel: (41-31) 323 31 11

For additional analytical, business and investment opportunities information,
please contact Global Investment & Business Center, USA
at (703) 370-8082. Fax: (703) 370-8083. E-mail: ibpusa3@gmail.com
Global Business and Investment Info Databank - www.ibpus.com

Lindenweg 50 Fax: (41-31) 323 32 10
CH-3003 Bern-Wabern, Switzerland

Eidg. Institut fur Geistiges Eigentum Dir: Dr. R. Grossenbacher
(Fed. Inst. for Intellectual Property) Tel: (41-31) 325 25 25
Einsteinstrasse 2 Fax: (41-31) 325 25 26
CH-3003 Bern, Switzerland
http://www.ige.ch

Eidg.Departement für Verteidigung, Bevölkerungsschutz und Sport:
(Fed. Dept. of Defence, Protection of the Population and Sport)
Gruppe fuer Ruestungsdienste (Armaments Group) Director: Mr. T. Wicki
Kasernenstrasse 19 Tel: (41-31) 324 57 01
CH-3003 Bern, Switzerland Fax: (41-31) 324 57 63

Eidegenoessische Finanzdepartement:
(Federal Department of Finance)
Eidg. Zollverwaltung Director: Dr. R. Dietrich
(Federal Customs Office) Tel: (41-31) 322 65 11
Monbijoustrasse 40 Fax: (41-31) 322 78 72
CH-3003 Bern, Switzerland

Eidgenoessische Volkswirtschaftsdepartement:
(Federal Department of Economic Affairs)
Staatssekretariat für Wirtschaft (SECO) Secretary: Dr. D. Syz
(State Secretariat for Economic Aff.) Tel: (41-31) 322 56 56
Bundeshaus Ost Fax: (41-31) 322 56 00
CH-3003 Bern, Switzerland

Bundesamt fuer Wirtschaft und Arbeit Director: J.-L. Nordmann
(Fed. Office for Econ. Dev. & Labor) Tel: (41-31) 322 29 09
Bundesgasse 8 Fax: (41-31) 322 27 49
CH-3003 Bern, Switzerland

Bundesamt fuer Berufsbildung & Technology Director: Prof. H. Sieber
(Fed.Off. for Prof. Training & Technology) Tel: (41-31) 322 21 29
Effingerstrasse 27 Fax: (41-31) 324 96 15
CH-3003 Bern, Switzerland

Eidg. Dept. fuer Umwelt, Verkehr, Energie und Kommunikation:
(Fed. Dept. of Environment, Transport, Energy and Communications)
Bundesamt fuer Zivilluftfahrt Director: Andre Auer
(Federal Office for Civil Aviation) Tel: (41-31) 325 80 39
Maulbeerstrasse 9 Fax: (41-31) 325 80 32
CH-3003 Bern, Switzerland

Bundesamt fuer Umwelt, Wald & Landschaft Director: Dr. P. Roch
(Fed. Office for the Environment, Tel: (41-31) 322 93 11
Forestry and the Landscape) Fax: (41-31) 322 79 58
Papiermuehlestrasse 172
CH-3063 Ittigen, Switzerland

For additional analytical, business and investment opportunities information,
please contact Global Investment & Business Center, USA
at (703) 370-8082. Fax: (703) 370-8083. E-mail: ibpusa3@gmail.com
Global Business and Investment Info Databank - www.ibpus.com

Bundesamt fuer Kommunikation Director: Mr. M. Furrer
Federal Office for Communications Tel: (41-32) 327 55 11
Zukunftstrasse 44 Fax: (41-32) 327 55 55
CH-2501 Biel, Switzerland

Quasi Public Organization:
Swiss Post Director: Mr. U. Gygi
Viktoriastrasse 21 Tel: (41-31) 338 28 16
CH-3030 Bern, Switzerland Fax: (41-31) 338 56 00

Mixed Private/Public Sector:
Swisscom AG Director: Mr. Jens Alder
Alte Tiefenaustrasse 6 Tel: (41-31) 342 11 11
CH-3050 Bern, Switzerland Fax: (41-31) 342 25 49
http://www.swisscom.com

SWISS MARKET RESEARCH FIRMS

Following are some of the major Swiss companies performing market research. Terms and fees must be solicited by the U.S. company. The U.S. Embassy cannot recommend one firm over another.

Consultex SA Director: A. Sundberg
157 Rte du Gd-Lancy Tel: (41-22) 792 16 59
CH-1213 Onex-Geneva, Switzerland Fax: (41-22) 793 39 15
http://www.consultex.ch

A.C. Nielsen S.A. Director: Mr. Ittensohn
Nielsenstrasse 8, Postfach Tel: (41-41) 445 64 64
CH-6033 Buchrain, Switzerland Fax: (41-41) 440 17 07
http://www.acnielsen.ch

Battelle-Europe Director: Raffael Nicolini
Geneva Research Centers Tel: (41-22) 827 27 27
7 route de Drize Fax: (41-22) 827 20 22
CH-1227 Carouge-Geneva, Switzerland

IHA - GFM Contact: Herbert Gnos
Institut fuer Marktanalysen AG Tel: (41-41) 632 91 11
Obermattweg 9 Fax: (41-41) 632 91 23
CH-6052 Hergiswil, Switzerland
http://www.ihagfm.ch

Real Marketing AG Director: A. Bassi
Dufourstrasse 107, P.O. Box 1226 Tel: (41-1) 383 08 83
CH-8034 Zurich, Switzerland Fax: (41-1) 383 08 84

Admerca AG Director: P. Betschart
Telecom Consultants Tel: (41-1) 422 41 77
Arosastrasse 25 Fax: (41-1) 422 97 77
CH-8008 Zurich, Switzerland

For additional analytical, business and investment opportunities information,
please contact Global Investment & Business Center, USA
at (703) 370-8082. Fax: (703) 370-8083. E-mail: ibpusa3@gmail.com
Global Business and Investment Info Databank - www.ibpus.com

Trimedia Communications AG Dir: Mr. T. C. Maurer
Zollikerstrasse 141, P.O. Box Tel: (41-1) 388 91 11
CH-8034 Zurich, Switzerland Fax: (41-1) 388 91 12

SWISS COMMERCIAL BANKS

Following are the head offices of the two largest commercial banks in Switzerland. Each has numerous branches throughout the country. For additional information on these and other banks, please consult the Swiss Financial Yearbook, published by Elvetica Edizioni SA, P.O. Box 134, Via Vela 6a CH-6834 Morbio-Inferiore, Switzerland; Tel: (41-91) 683 50 56; Fax: (41-91) 683 76 05.

UBS AG Pres: Mr. M. Ospel
Bahnhofstrasse 45, P.O. Box Tel: (41-1) 234 11 11
CH-8021 Zurich, Switzerland Fax: (41-1) 236 51 11
http://www.usb.com

Credit Suisse CEO: Mr. L. Mühlemann
Paradeplatz 8 Tel: (41-1) 333 11 11
P.O. Box 100 Fax: (41-1) 332 55 55
CH-8070 Zurich, Switzerland
http://www.csg.ch

U.S.-BASED MULTIPLIERS RELEVANT FOR SWITZERLAND

The Swiss-American Chamber of Commerce, in addition to its head office in Zurich (see Chamber heading above), maintains offices in four U.S. locations:

New York Chapter Chairman: R. C. O'Brien
Credit Suisse First Boston Corp. Tel: (212) 325-9100
Eleven Madison Ave. Fax: (212) 325-8326
New York, NY 10010-3629

Southeast U.S.A. Chapter Chairwoman: Janis H. Cannon
C/o Swissotel Tel: (404) 760-1692
3391 Peachtree Road N.E. Fax: (404) 760-1802
Atlanta, GA 30326

Southeast U.S.A. Chapter Chairman: Heinz Roth
Carolina Division Tel: (704) 292-1237
2208 Houston Branch Road Fax: (704) 292-1137
Charlotte, NC 28270

Southeast U.S.A. Chapter Chairman: L. S. Burkhardt
Florida Division Tel: (407) 645-3500
1201 South Orlando Ave., P.O. Box 8181 Fax: (407) 645-3529
Winter Park, FL 32790-8181

California - San Francisco Chapter Chairman: P. Kaempfen
P.O. Box 26007 Tel: (415) 433-6679
San Francisco, CA 94126-6007 Fax: (415) 433-6601

California - Los Angeles Chapter Chairman: R. Wacker
c/o Julius Baer Rep. Office Tel: (626) 974-5429
1900 Avenue of the Stars, Ste. 2701 Fax: (626) 974-5439
Los Angeles, CA 90067

The Swiss government maintains official representation in the U.S. through its Embassy in Washington and Consulates General in six locations:

Embassy of Switzerland Amb: Vacant
2900 Cathedral Avenue, N.W. Tel: (202) 745-7900
Washington, D.C. 20008-3499 Fax: (202) 387-2564
http://www.swissemb.org

Swiss Consulate General Consul: Alexander Kubli
1275 Peachtree Street, N.E., Ste. 425 Tel: (404) 870-2000
Atlanta, GA 30309-3555 Fax: (404) 870-2011
E-mail: vertretung@atl.rep.admin.ch

Swiss Consulate General Consul: Eduard Jaun
737 N. Michigan Ave, Ste. 2301 Tel: (312) 915-0061
Chicago, IL 60611-0561 Fax: (312) 915-0388
E-mail: vertretung@chi.rep.admin.ch

Swiss Consulate General Consul: W. Simmen
Wells Fargo Bank Plaza Tel: (713) 650-0000
1000 Louisiana, Suite 5670 Fax: (713) 650-1321
Houston, TX 77002-5006
E-mail: vertretung@hou.rep.admin.ch

Swiss Consulate General Consul: H.-P. Egger
11766 Wilshire Boulevard, Suite 1400 Tel: (310) 575-1145
Los Angeles, CA 90025 Fax: (310) 575-1982
E-mail: vertretung@los.rep.admin.ch

Swiss Consulate General Amb: Jacques Reverdin
633 Third Ave., 30th Floor Tel: (212) 599-5700
New York, NY 10017-6706 Fax: (212) 599-4266
E-mail: vertretung@nyc.rep.admin.ch

Swiss Consulate General Consul: R. Quillet
456 Montgomery Street, Suite 1500 Tel: (415) 788-2272
San Francisco, CA 94104-1233 Fax: (415) 788-1402
E-mail: vertretung@sfr.rep.admin.ch

OTHER MULTIPLIERS RELEVANT FOR SWITZERLAND

Some 30 U.S. states maintain their own offices in Europe for economic development and trade promotion. Most are members of the Council of American States in Europe (CASE). While these offices often focus on attracting European, including Swiss, investment to their respective states, they also provide trade assistance. Many sponsor group participation at major trade events or organize trade and investment missions, led by prominent state officials. A list of CASE offices is available from the Chairman: Paul Zito, Director, State of Ohio, European Office, Rue de la Pépinière 1, 4th Floor, 1000 Brussels, Belgium Tel. (32-2) 512 86 87, Fax. (32-2) 512 66 14.

TPCC Trade Information Center in Washington: 1-800-USA-TRADE

U.S. Department of State
Bureau of Economic and Business Affairs
Tel: (202) 647-7971
Fax: (202) 647-5713

U.S. Department of Commerce
Country Desk Officer
(for market access and regulatory problems only)
Tel: (202) 482-2434
Fax: (202) 482-2897

U.S. Department of Agriculture (USDA)
Foreign Agricultural Service (FAS)
South Agricultural Bldg., Room 5071
Washington, D.C. 20250
Tel: (202) 720-3935
Fax: (202) 790-2159
http://www.fas.usda.gov

Overseas Private Investment Corporation
1100 New York Ave. N.W., 12th floor
Washington, DC 20527
Tel: (202) 336-8799
Fax: (202) 408-9859
http://www.opic.gov

USEFUL BUSINESS AND GOVERNMENT CONTACTS

In the U.S.:

Embassy of Switzerland
2900 Cathedral Avenue N.W.
Washington, DC 20008-3499
Telephone: (202) 745-7900
Telefax: (202) 387-2564
Telex: (023) 44 00 55 AMWN UI
Swiss consulates are located in most major U.S. cities: Atlanta, Miami, Chicago, Cincinnati, Cleveland, Columbus, Detroit, Kansas City, Minneapolis, St. Louis, Houston, Dallas, Denver, New Orleans, Los Angeles, Phoenix, New York, Boston, Buffalo, Philadelphia, Pittsburgh, San Juan, San Francisco, Honolulu, Salt Lake City and Seattle.

In Switzerland:

For additional analytical, business and investment opportunities information, please contact Global Investment & Business Center, USA at (703) 370-8082. Fax: (703) 370-8083. E-mail: ibpusa3@gmail.com
Global Business and Investment Info Databank - www.ibpus.com

Swiss Federal Government
Bundeshaus
CH-3000 Bern
Telephone: (011 41) 31/ 61 24 11

U.S. Embassy
Jubil„umsstrasse 93
CH - 3005 Bern
Telephone: (011 41) 31/ 43 70 11
Telefax: (011 41) 31/ 43 73 44

The U.S. Embassy in Switzerland has two specialized trade officers. Currently, Mr. Reichenbach is the Commercial Consul and Mr. Scarlis is the Economic Consul.

U.S. Consulate in Zurich

Zollikerstrasse 141
CH-8001 Zurich
Telephone: (011 41) 1/ 55 25 66

SWISS-AMERICAN CHAMBER OF COMMERCE

Mr. Walter Diggelmann
Talacker 41
CH-8001 Zurich
Telephone: (011 41) 1/ 211 24 54
Telefax: (011 41) 1/ 211 95 72
The Port Authority of New York and New Jersey, European Office

John P. Cannizzo, General Manager
Leutschenbachstrasse 45
CH-8050 Zurich
Telephone: (011 41) 1/ 302 13 10
Telex: (011 41) 1/ 823 678

Official information on investments in Switzerland is available from:

Bundesamt f r Industrie, Gewerbe und Arbeit (Federal Office for Industry, Trade and Labor)
Bundesgasse 8
CH-3003 Bern
Telephone: (011 41) 31/ 61 29 44
Telefax: (011 41) 31/ 61 27 49
Telex: (011 41) 31/ 913 280

Unofficial information is available from:

Schweizerische Zentrale f r Handelsf"rderung
Stampfenbachstr. 85
CH-8035 Zurich

For additional analytical, business and investment opportunities information,
please contact Global Investment & Business Center, USA
at (703) 370-8082. Fax: (703) 370-8083. E-mail: ibpusa3@gmail.com
Global Business and Investment Info Databank - www.ibpus.com

Telephone: (011 41) 1/ 365 51 51
Telefax: (011 41) 1/ 365 52 21

ZURICH CHAMBER OF COMMERCE

P.O. Box, CH-8022 Zurich
Telephone: (011 41) 1/ 221 07 42
Telefax: (011 41) 1/ 221 76 15
Geneva Chamber of Commerce

Boulevard du Th,ftre 4
CH-1204 GenŠve
Telephone: (011 41) 22/ 21 53 33
Telefax: (011 41) 22/ 20 03 63

SELECTED BANKING CONTACTS IN SWITZERLAND

Working group members	Contacts
Swiss Bankers Association	Working Group on Banks and the Environment Postfach 4182 CH-4002 Basel Switzerland Tel: ++41 61 / 295 93 93 Fax: ++41 61 / 272 53 82 E-Mail: silvia.matile@sba.ch
CREDIT SUISSE	Environmental Management (CCUE) Postfach 100 CH-8070 Zurich Switzerland Tel: ++41 1 / 333 73 33 Fax: ++41 1 / 333 76 33 E-Mail: eco@credit-suisse.ch Internet: http://www.csg.ch/eco_performance_97
UBS	UBS AG, Environmental Risk Management Services Bahnhofstrasse 45 8098 Zürich Switzerland Tel: ++41 1 / 234 39 28 Fax: ++41 1 / 234 34 15 E-Mail: fachreferat-umwelt@ubs.com
Verwaltungs- und Privat-Bank AG	Specialist Committee on the Environment Im Zentrum FL-9490 Vaduz Fürstentum Lichtenstein Tel: ++41 75 / 235 64 34 Fax: ++41 75 / 235 77 64
Zürcher Kantonalbank	Specialist Environmental Unit Postfach CH-8010 Zurich

	Switzerland Tel: ++41 1 / 802 53 38 Fax: ++41 1 / 802 58 13 E-Mail: umwelt@zkb.ch Internet: http://www.zkb.ch
Bank Sarasin & Cie	Andreas Knörzer u. Hans Weber Postfach 4002 Basel Tel: ++41 61 / 277 74 77 or ++41 61 / 277 72 61 Fax: ++41 61 / 277 76 88 or ++41 61 / 277 76 62 E-Mail: research_bs@sarasin.ch

Working group members	Contacts
Investment business: • Environmental equity analysis	Zürcher Kantonalbank Sabine Döbeli Environmental Research Postfach CH-8010 Zurich Switzerland Tel: ++41 1 / 220 24 13 Fax: ++41 1 / 220 32 12 E-Mail: sabine.doebeli@zkb.ch
Investment business: • Environmental equity analysis and sustainable investment strategies	Bank Sarasin & Cie Andreas Knörzer and Frank Figge Postfach CH-4002 Basel Switzerland Tel: ++41 61 / 277 74 71 or ++41 61 / 277 77 68 Fax: ++41 61 / 277 76 88 E-Mail: research_bs@sarasin.ch
Investment business: • Environmental equity analysis	CREDIT SUISSE Dr. Bernd Schanzenbächer Environmental Management (CCUE 4) Postfach 100 CH-8070 Zurich Switzerland Tel: ++41 1 / 333 80 33 Fax: ++41 1 / 333 76 33 E-Mail: bernd.schanzenbaecher@credit-suisse.ch
Investment business: • Environmental equity analysis • Eco Performance • Portfolio	UBS AG Gianreto Gamboni Environmental Performance Analysis Gartenstrasse 9 CH-4002 Basel Switzerland Tel: ++41 61 / 288 33 09 Fax: ++41 61 / 288 55 24 E-Mail: gianreto.gamboni@ubs.com

For additional analytical, business and investment opportunities information,
please contact Global Investment & Business Center, USA
at (703) 370-8082. Fax: (703) 370-8083. E-mail: ibpusa3@gmail.com
Global Business and Investment Info Databank - www.ibpus.com

Structural biology	Interest Group of Private Professional Builder-Owners (IPB) Postfach 523 CH-8045 Zurich Switzerland Tel: ++41 1 / 468 24 61 Fax: ++41 1 / 451 34 56
Corporate ecology	CREDIT SUISSE Patrik Burri Environmental management (CCUE 1) Postfach 100 CH-8070 Zurich Switzerland Tel: ++41 1/ 332 70 03 Fax: ++41 1/ 333 76 33 E-Mail: patrik.burri@credit-suisse.ch
Corporate ecology	Bank Sarasin & Cie Hans Weber Postfach CH-4002 Basel Switzerland Tel: ++41 61 / 277 72 61 Fax: ++41 61 / 277 76 62
Corporate ecology	UBS AG Corporate ecology Martin Schürmann Aeschenplatz 6 CH-4002 Basel Switzerland Tel: ++41 61 / 288 22 94 Fax: ++41 61 / 288 53 56 E-Mail: martin-za.schuermann@ubs.com
Energy management	UBS AG Energy management Martin Bänninger Bahnhofstrasse 45 CH-8098 Zurich Switzerland Tel: ++41 1 / 236 33 40 Fax: ++41 1 / 236 67 13 E-Mail: baenninger@ubs.com
Lending operations: • Environmental risks in loan assessment	CREDIT SUISSE Elizabeth Casal Specialist Ecological Risk Unit (CKKA 3) Postfach 100 CH-8070 Zurich Switzerland Tel: ++41 1 / 333 48 54 Fax: ++41 1 / 333 75 84 E-Mail: elizabeth.casal@credit-suisse.ch

For additional analytical, business and investment opportunities information,
please contact Global Investment & Business Center, USA
at (703) 370-8082. Fax: (703) 370-8083. E-mail: ibpusa3@gmail.com
Global Business and Investment Info Databank - www.ibpus.com

Lending operations: • Environmental risks in loan assessment	Zürcher Kantonalbank Andreas Brühlmann Specialist Ecological Loan Assessment Unit Postfach CH-8010 Zurich Switzerland Tel: ++41 1 / 220 31 54 Fax: ++41 1 / 220 39 10
Lending operations: • Environmentally-friendly loans	Basellandschaftliche Kantonalbank Kaspar Schweizer Rheinstrasse 7 Postfach CH-4410 Liestal Switzerland Tel: ++41 61 / 906 36 36 Fax: ++41 61 / 901 36 06
Lending operations: • Environmentally-friendly loans	Luzerner Kantonalbank Heidi Scherrer / ISM Postfach CH-6002 Lucerne Switzerland Tel: ++4141 / 206 21 04 Fax: ++41 41 / 206 30 18
Lending operations: • Environmentally-friendly loans	Thurgauer Kantonalbank Herbert Blatter Postfach CH-8570 Weinfelden Switzerland Tel: ++41 71 / 626 63 88 Fax: ++41 71 / 626 64 07
Lending operations: • Environmentally-friendly loans	Zürcher Kantonalbank René Beeler Fachstelle Umwelt Postfach 8010 Zürich Tel: ++41 1 / 802 53 38 Fax: ++41 1 / 802 58 13 E-Mail: umwelt@zkb.ch Internet: http://www.zkb.ch
Swiss Association for Environmentally Aware Corporate Management (öbu)	Öbu Gabi Hildesheimer Obstgartenstrasse 28 CH-8006 Zurich Switzerland Tel: ++41 1 / 364 37 38 Fax: ++41 1 / 364 37 11 E-Mail: oebuinfo@oebu.ch
Environmental management in banks (Germany)	Association for Environmental Management in Banks, Savings Banks and Insurance Companies (VfU)

For additional analytical, business and investment opportunities information,
please contact Global Investment & Business Center, USA
at (703) 370-8082. Fax: (703) 370-8083. E-mail: ibpusa3@gmail.com
Global Business and Investment Info Databank - www.ibpus.com

	Wilhelmstrasse 28 D-53111 Bonn Germany Tel: ++49 228 7668494 Fax: ++49 228 7668496 E-Mail: 101330.3112@compuserve.com
United Nations Environment Programme (UNEP)	United Nations Environment Programme (UNEP) Economics, Trade and Environment Unit (ETEU) Palais des Nations CH-1211 Geneva 10 Switzerland Tel: ++41 22 / 917 81 78 Fax: ++41 22 / 796 92 40 E-Mail: eteu@unep.ch
Editorial control of guide to environmental management	E2 Management Consulting AG Oliver Schmid-Schönbein Höhenweg 18 CH-9000 St. Gallen Switzerland Tel: ++41 71 / 220 91 44 Fax: ++41 71 / 220 91 45 E-Mail: oliss@e2mc.com Internet: http://www.e2mc.com

SWITZERLAND LARGEST LAW FIRMS

- **Bar & Karrer**, Seefeldstrasse 19, Zürich, CH-8024, Switzerland, Tel: (41) 1-2615150, Fax: (41) 1-2513025, Contact: Christian Steinmann
- **Borel & Barbey**, 2 rue de Jargonnant, PO Box 6045, Geneva 6, CH-1211, Switzerland, Tel: (41) 22-7361136, Fax: (41) 22-7364588, Contact: Nicolas Pierard
- **Brunschwig Wittmer**, 13 Quai de L'ile, PO Box 5245, Geneva 11, CH-1211, Switzerland, Tel: (41) 22-7813322, Fax: (41) 22-7813100, Contact: Francois Brunschwig
- **Crosier & Gillioz**, 61, rue du Rhone, PO Box 3127, Geneva, CH - 1204, Switzerland, Tel: (41) 223101233, Fax: (41) 223108192, Contact: Jean-Paul Croisier
- **Froriep Renggli**, Bellerivestrasse 201, Zürich, CH-8034, Switzerland, Tel: (41) 1-3866000, Fax: (41) 1-3836050, Contact: Walter J. Weber
- **Hartmann Müller Partner**, Zürichbergstrasse 66, Zürich, CH-8044, Switzerland, Tel: (41) 1-251-77-12, Fax: (41) 1-251-78-11, Contact: Niklaus B. Müller
    - Hartmann Müller Partner offers a full range of legal services with an emphasis on corporate law. With attorneys fluent in English, German French and Italian, the firm represents a range of international clients. The firm has offices in Zürich and Zug and is a Switzerland member of Multilaw, a global association of 49 independent law firms.
- **Haymann & Baldi**, Hottingerstrasse 17, PO Box 7033, Zürich, CH-8023, Switzerland, Tel: (41) 1-2621010, Fax: (41) 1-2621822, Contact: Michael Haymann
- **Henrici, Wicki & Guggisberg**, Hottingerstrasse 21, Zürich, CH-8032, Switzerland, Tel: (41) 1-2516655, Fax: (41) 1-2525984, Contact: Dr. A. Wicki
- **Homburger Rechtsanwalte**, Weinbergstrasse 56/58, P.O.Box 326, Zürich, CH-8035, Switzerland, Tel: (41) 1-2653535, Fax: (41) 1-2653511, Contact: Prof. Dr. Eric Homburger

For additional analytical, business and investment opportunities information,
please contact Global Investment & Business Center, USA
at (703) 370-8082. Fax: (703) 370-8083. E-mail: ibpusa3@gmail.com
Global Business and Investment Info Databank - www.ibpus.com

- **Lalive & Partners**, 6, Rue de l'Athenee, Geneva 12, 1211, Switzerland, Tel: (41) 22-3198700, Fax:, Contact: Dr. Jean-Flavien Lalive
- **Lenz & Staehelin**, Nleicherweg 58, Zürich, 8027, Switzerland, Tel: (41) 1-2041212, Fax: (41) 1-2041200, Contact: Willy Staehelin
- **Magnin, Dunand & Partners**, 2 Rue Charles-Bonnet, Geneva, 1206, Switzerland, Tel: (41) 22-3476262, Fax: (41) 22-3476796, Contact: Dr. Jean-Jacques Magnin
- **Meyer Lustenberger & Partner**, Forchstrasse 452, PO Box, Zürich, CH-8029, Switzerland, Tel: (41) 1-3914161, Fax: (41) 1-3912781, Contact: Dr. Ferdinand Meyer
- **Niederer Kraft & Frey**, Bahnhofstrasse 13, Zürich, 8001, Switzerland, Tel: (41) 1-2171000, Fax: (41) 1-2171400, Contact: Dr. Hugo A. Frey
- **Pestalozzi Gmuer & Patry**, Loewenstrasse 1, CH-8001 Zürich, Switzerland, Tel: (41) 228094500, Fax: (41) 41228094501, Contact: Dr. Robert Furter
  - Pestalozzi Gmuer & Patry is one of the largest firms in Switzerland and was established in 1911. The firm has offices in Zürich and Geneva, Switzerland, and Brussels, Belgium. It is the Martindale-Hubbell reviser. Pestalozzi Gmuer & Patry is the member for Switzerland of Lex Mundi, a global association of 152 independent law firms.
- **Pirenne Python Schifferli Peter & Partners**, 3 rue Bellot, Geneva, CH-1206, Switzerland, Tel: (41) 22-3474645, Fax: (41) 22-3468576, Contact: Yves Pirenne
- **Poncet Turrettini Amaudruz & Neyroud**, 8 - 10 rue de Hesse, PO box 5715, Geneva 11, CH-1211, Switzerland, Tel: (41) 22-3191111, Fax: (41) 22-3121431, Contact: Robert Turrettini
- **Prager Dreifuss & Partner**, Zollikerstrasse 183, Zürich, 8008, Switzerland, Tel: (41) 1-4227711, Fax: (41) 1-4227714, Contact: Eric L. Dreifuss
- **Schellenberg & Haissly**, Lowenstrrasse 19, PO Box 6333, Zürich, 8023, Switzerland, Tel: (41) 1-2116040, Fax: (41) 1-2211165, Contact: Dr. Georg von Segesser
- **Secretan Troyanov & Partners**, 2 rue Charles-Bonnet, Geneva 12, CH-1211, Switzerland, Tel: (41) 22-7897000, Fax: (41) 22-7897070, Contact: Tikhon Troyanov
- **Stoffel & Partner**, Dufourstrasse 40, Zürich, CH-8008, Switzerland, Tel: (41) 1-2521616, Fax: (41) 1-2522700, Contact: Dr. Marco Stoffel
- **Tavernier, Gillioz, de Preux, Dorsaz**, 11 rue Toepffer, Geneva, CH-1206, Switzerland, Tel: (41) 22-3477707, Fax: (41) 22-3479789, Contact: Edmond Tavernier
- **Umbricht Baderscher & Roesle**, Bahnhofstrasse 22, PO Box 4174, Zürich, CH-8022, Switzerland, Tel: (41) 1-2112550, Fax: (41) 1-2212552, Contact: Dr. Robert P. Umbricht
- **von Erlach Klainguti Stettler Wille & Partners**, Dreikonigstrasse 7, PO Box 4088, Zürich, CH-8022, Switzerland, Tel: (41) 1-2832111, Fax: (41) 1-2020707, Contact: Fursprecher Dietrich Stettler
- **Walder Wyss & Partners**, Munstergasse 2, P. O. Box 4081, Zurich, CH-8022, Switzerland, Tel: (41) 1 265-75-11, Fax: (41) 1-265-260-20-10, Contact: Dr. Didier Sangiorgio
- **Wenger Mathys Plattner**, Aeschenvorstadt 55, Basel, CH-4010, Switzerland, Tel: (41) 61-2716262, Fax: (41) 12610788, Contact: Dr. Werner Wenger

MAJOR SWISS NEWSPAPERS AND PERIODICALS

Der Bund
Type: Daily Newspaper
P.O. Box
Language: German
CH-3001 Bern, Switzerland
Circulation: 64,685
Editor-in-Chief: Dr. Konrad Stamm

Tel: (41-31) 385 11 11
Fax: (41-31) 385 11 12

Berner Zeitung
Type: Daily Newspaper
P.O. Box CH-3001
Bern, Switzerland
Language: German

For additional analytical, business and investment opportunities information, please contact Global Investment & Business Center, USA at (703) 370-8082. Fax: (703) 370-8083. E-mail: ibpusa3@gmail.com
Global Business and Investment Info Databank - www.ibpus.com

Circulation: 132,555
Editor-in-Chief: Andreas Z'Graggen
Tel: (41-31) 330 31 11
Fax: (41-31) 332 77 24

Basler Zeitung
Type: Daily Newspaper
P.O. Box CH-4002 Basel, Switzerland
Language: German
Circulation: 117,417
Editor-in-Chief: Hans-Peter Platz
Tel: (41-61) 639 11 11
Fax: (41-61) 631 15 82

Neue Zuercher Zeitung
Type: Daily Newspaper
P.O. Box CH-8021 Zurich, Switzerland
Language: German
Circulation: 160,335
Editor-in-Chief: Dr. Hugo Buetler
Tel: (41-1) 258 11 11
Fax: (41-1) 252 13 29

Tages-Anzeiger
Type: Daily Newspaper
P.O. Box CH-8021 Zurich, Switzerland
Language: German
Circulation: 282,222
Editor-in-Chief: Dr. Esther Girsberger
Tel: (41-1) 248 44 11
Fax: (41-1) 248 44 71

Blick
Type: Daily Newspaper
P.O. Box CH-8021 Zurich, Switzerland
Language: German
Circulation: 373,354
Editor-in-Chief: Wolfram Meister
Tel: (41-1) 259 62 62
Fax: (41-1) 262 29 76

24Heures
Type: Daily Newspaper
P.O. Box 585 CH-1001 Lausanne, Switzerland
Language: French
Circulation: 92,605
Editor-in-Chief: Gian Pozzy
Tel: (41-21) 349 44 44
Fax: (41-21) 349 41 10

Le Matin
Type: Daily Newspaper

P.O. Box 1095
CH-1001 Lausanne, Switzerland
Language: French
Circulation: 54,476
Editor-in-Chief: A. Exchaquet
Tel: (41-21) 349 49 49
Fax: (41-21) 349 41 10

LE TEMPS
Type: Daily Newspaper
29, rte de l'Aeroport
CH-1215 Geneva, Switzerland
Language: French
Circulation: 50,000
Editor-in-Chief: Eric Hoesli
Tel: (41-22) 819 88 88
Fax: (41-22) 819 89 89

Tribune de Geneve
Type: Daily Newspaper
P.O. Box 434
CH-1211 Geneva 11, Switzerland
Language: French
Circulation: 60,480
Editor-in-Chief: Marco Cattaneo
Tel: (41-22) 322 40 00
Fax: (41-22) 781 01 07

La Liberte
Type: Daily Newspaper
P.O. Box 1056
CH-1701 Fribourg, Switzerland
Language: French
Circulation: 35,753
Editor-in-Chief: Roger de Diessbach
Tel: (41-37) 86 44 11
Fax: (41-37) 86 44 00

Corriere del Ticino
Type: Daily Newspaper
Ai Mulini
CH-6933 Muzzano, Switzerland
Language: Italian
Circulation: 36,521
Editor-in-Chief: Giancarlo Dillena
Tel: (41-91) 58 31 31
Fax: (41-91) 58 29 77

Giornale del Popolo
Type: Daily Newspaper
Via San Gottardo 50
CH-6903 Lugano, Switzerland
Language: Italian

For additional analytical, business and investment opportunities information, please contact Global Investment & Business Center, USA at (703) 370-8082. Fax: (703) 370-8083. E-mail: ibpusa3@gmail.com
Global Business and Investment Info Databank - www.ibpus.com

Circulation: 23,725
Editor-in-Chief: Filippo Lombardi
Tel: (41-91) 23 22 72-75
Fax: (41-91) 23 28 05

Die Weltwoche
Type: Weekly Magazine
Postfach
CH-8021 Zurich, Switzerland
Language: German
Circulation: 106,511
Editor-in-Chief: Fredy Gsteiger
Tel: (41-1) 207 73 11
Fax: (41-1) 202 61 27

Sonntags-Zeitung
Type: Newsmagazine
Postfach
CH-8021 Zurich, Switzerland
Language: German
Circulation: 122,881
Editor-in-Chief: Andreas Durisch
Tel: (41-1) 248 40 40
Fax: (41-1) 242 47 83

Sonntags-Blick
Type: Newsmagazine
Dufourstrasse 23
CH-8008 Zurich, Switzerland
Language: German
Circulation: 360,477
Editor-in-Chief: Bernhard Weissberg
Tel: (41-1) 259 62 62
Fax: (41-1) 251 80 06

Schweizer Illustrierte
Type: Weekly Magazine
Dufourstrasse 23
CH-8008 Zurich, Switzerland
Language: German
Circulation: 196,265
Editor-in-Chief: Peter Rothenbuehler
Tel: (41-1) 259 63 63
Fax: (41-1) 262 04 42

Cash
Type: Weekly News
Hohlstrasse 192

CH-8021 Zurich, Switzerland
Language: German
Circulation: 50,000
Editor-in-Chief: Markus Gisler
Tel: (41-1) 242 80 77
Fax: (41-1) 242 90 41

L'Hebdo
Type: Monthly Mag.
P.O. Box 3153
CH-1005 Lausanne, Switzerland
Language: French
Circulation: 55,000
Editor-in-Chief: Ariane Dayer
Tel: (41-21) 320 36 11
Fax: (41-21) 320 36 17

Bilanz
Type: Monthly Mag.
Edenstrasse 20
CH-8021 Zurich, Switzerland
Language: German
Circulation: 70,000
Editor-in-Chief: Medard Meier
Tel: (41-1) 207 72 21
Fax: (41-1) 201 59 16

Schweizer Handels-Zeitung
Type: Weekly News
Seestrasse 37
CH-8027 Zurich, Switzerland
Language: German
Circulation: 37,025
Editor-in-Chief: Dr. K. Speck
Tel: (41-1) 201 35 55
Fax: (41-1) 202 01 26

Bilan
Type: Monthly Mag.
Av. de la Gare 33
P.O. Box 585
CH-1001 Lausanne, Switzerland
Language: French
Circulation: 21,528
Editor-in-Chief: Max Mabillard
Tel: (41-21) 349 48 22
Fax: (41-21) 349 40 80

For additional analytical, business and investment opportunities information,
please contact Global Investment & Business Center, USA
at (703) 370-8082. Fax: (703) 370-8083. E-mail: ibpusa3@gmail.com
Global Business and Investment Info Databank - www.ibpus.com

BANKS WITH CORRESPONDENT U.S. BANKING ARRANGEMENTS

The Swiss banks listed in Appendix E have correspondent relationships with U.S. banks, as do most other large Swiss banks. More importantly, the following U.S. banks have offices or representatives in Switzerland and are quite interested in trade and project financing.

American Express Bank (Switzerland) SA T. Graeme Haig
16, rue de Contamines   General Manager
P.O. Box 351
Tel:(41-22) 702 08 08
CH-1211 Geneva 12, Switzerland   Fax:(41-22) 789 22 23

Bank of America NT & SA   Nancy Ferroggiaro
40, rue du March   Vice President
P.O. Box 3042   Tel:(41-22) 318 89 11
CH-1211 Geneva 3, Switzerland   Fax:(41-22) 318 69 00

Bank Morgan Stanley AG   Adolf Bruendler
Bahnhofstrasse 92   General Manager
P.O. Box 6740   Tel:(41-1) 220 91 11
CH-8023 Zurich, Switzerland   Fax:(41-1) 211 98 07

Bankers Trust AG   Roberto Martinez
Stauffacherquai 42   General Manager
P.O. Box   Tel:(41-1) 639 25 00
CH-8002 Zurich, Switzerland   Fax:(41-1) 639 29 00

The Chase Manhattan   Georges Vergnion
Private Bank (Switzerland)   General Manager
63, rue du Rhone   Tel:(41-22) 787 91 11
P.O. Box 257   Fax:(41-22) 736 24 30
CH-1204 Geneva, Switzerland

Citibank (Switzerland)   Philippe Holderbeke
Bahnhofstrasse 63   Country Corporate Officer
P.O. Box 3760   Tel. (41-1) 205 71 71
CH-8021 Zurich, Switzerland   Fax. (41-1) 205 86 06

J.P. Morgan (Suisse) SA   William L. Oullin
3, place des Bergues   Managing Director
P.O. Box 1864   Tel. (41-22) 739 11 11
CH-1211 Geneva 1, Switzerland   Fax. (41-22) 732 26 55
Republic National Bank of New York   Sem Almaleh
(Suisse) SA   General Manager
2, place du Lac   Tel. (41-22) 705 55 55
P.O. Box 3580   Fax. (41-22) 311 99 60
CH-1211 Geneva 3, Switzerland

SWITZERLAND: STRATEGIC STATISTICS

Economic indicators	Date	Unit	Value
National consumer price index (change over previous year)	Feb 00	in %	1.6
Index of producer and import prices (change over previous year)	Feb 00	in %	2.7
Industry: production (change over previous year)	3.1999	in %	4.1
Industry: sales (change over previous year)	3.1999	in %	4.5
Retail trade: Development of sales (change over previous year, nominal value)	Jan 00	in %	2.9
Employed persons (change over previous year)	3rd quart. 99	in %	0.3
Unemployment rate	Dec 99	in %	2.5
Gross Domestic Product (change over previous year, real increase, provisional)	1998	in %	2.1

Date	Unit	Value		Date	Unit	Value
Municipalities			01.01.98	Number	2,915
Representatives in Lower House of Parliament			1995	Number	200
Surface area			1995	in sq. km	41,284
-	Agricultural land		1979/85	in %	38.3

Date	Unit	Value		Date	Unit	Value
Main resident population			31.12.98	in 1000s	7,123.5
Percentage of foreigners			1998	in %	19.4
Population density			1998	per sq. km	173
Live births			1998	in 1000	78.4
Deaths			1998	in 1000	62.6
Excess of births over deaths			1998	in 1000	15.8
Immigration/emigration			1998	in 1000	11.3

Date	Unit	Value		Date	Unit	Value
Housing stocks			31.12.97	Number	3,472,355
Housing construction permits issued			1997	Number	33,284
Newly built dwellings			1997	Number	35,961

Empty dwellings	01.06.98	in %	1.85
Housing under construction	31.12.97	Number	39,426

Date	Unit		Value			
Enterprises			1998	Number	312,449
Establishments			1998	Number	379,358
Number of jobs (Fully and partly employed persons)			1998	Number	3,471,428
Number of jobs (in %) by NOGA (Fully and partly employed persons)			1998	in %	100.0
-	Industry, manufacturing, energy supply		1998	in %	21.0
-	Construction		1998	in %	8.5
-	Sail, repair, hotels and restaurants		1998	in %	23.7
-	Transport and communication		1998	in %	6.8
-	Financial intermediation, insurance, business services		1998	in %	5.4
-	Public administration		1998	in %	4.0
-	Education		1998	in %	6.0
-	Health and social work		1998	in %	10.6
-	Other community and personal services		1998	in %	4.1

Date	Unit		Value			
Unemployed (annual average)			1998	Number	139,660
-	Men		1998	in %	55.2
-	Women		1998	in %	44.8
-	Totally unemployed		1998	in %	84.3
-	Partially unemployed		1998	in %	15.7
-	Foreigners		1998	in %	47.2
Unemployment rate (annual average)			1998	in %	3.9
-	Men		1998	in %	3.5
-	Women		1998	in %	4.4

Date	Unit		Value			
Nights spent in hotels			1998	Number	31,817,059
-	%age of foreigners		1998	in %	58.8
-	Cars [1]		30.09.98	Number	3,383,273

For additional analytical, business and investment opportunities information, please contact Global Investment & Business Center, USA at (703) 370-8082. Fax: (703) 370-8083. E-mail: ibpusa3@gmail.com
Global Business and Investment Info Databank - www.ibpus.com

-	Doctors per 100 000 inh.	1996	Number	178.9
-	Dentists per 100 000 inh.	1996	Number	48.7
-	Chemists per 100 000 inh.	1996	Number	22.2
[1]	vehicles of the Federal Administration included			

Date	Unit	Value		
National income (provisional figure)		1997	in mill. CHF	316,542
National income per capita (provisional figure)		1997	in CHF	44,500
Cantonal expenditure		1997	in mill. CHF	56,790.0
Cantonal revenue		1997	in mill. CHF	53,722.4
Balance of revenue/expenditure		1997	in mill. CHF	-3,067.6

Date	Unit	Value		
Taxation [2]				
-	Income of CHF 30 000	1997	in %	3.32
-	Income of CHF 50 000	1997	in %	7.22
-	Income of CHF 100 000	1997	in %	13.67
-	Income of CHF 200 000	1997	in %	22.72
Financial strength (CH=100)		1998/99	Figure	100
[2]	Federal, cantonal and municipal tax on gross income of a married man with no children living in cantonal capital			

For additional analytical, business and investment opportunities information, please contact Global Investment & Business Center, USA at (703) 370-8082. Fax: (703) 370-8083. E-mail: ibpusa3@gmail.com Global Business and Investment Info Databank - www.ibpus.com

BASIC TITLES FOR SWITZERLAND
IMPORTANT!
All publications are updated annually!
Please contact IBP, Inc. at ibpusa3@gmail.com for the latest ISBNs and additional information

Title
Switzerland A "Spy" Guide - Strategic Information and Developments
Switzerland A Spy" Guide"
Switzerland Air Force Handbook
Switzerland Air Force Handbook
Switzerland Army Weapon Systems Handbook
Switzerland Army Weapon Systems Handbook
Switzerland Army Weapon Systems Handbook
Switzerland Army, National Security and Defense Policy Handbook
Switzerland Army, National Security and Defense Policy Handbook
Switzerland Banking & Financial Market Handbook
Switzerland Banking & Financial Market Handbook
Switzerland Business and Investment Opportunities Yearbook
Switzerland Business and Investment Opportunities Yearbook
Switzerland Business and Investment Opportunities Yearbook Volume 1 Strategic Information and Opportunities
Switzerland Business Intelligence Report - Practical Information, Opportunities, Contacts
Switzerland Business Intelligence Report - Practical Information, Opportunities, Contacts
Switzerland Business Law Handbook - Strategic Information and Basic Laws
Switzerland Business Law Handbook - Strategic Information and Basic Laws
Switzerland Business Law Handbook - Strategic Information and Basic Laws
Switzerland Business Law Handbook - Strategic Information and Basic Laws
Switzerland Clothing & Textile Industry Handbook
Switzerland Company Laws and Regulations Handbook
Switzerland Constitution and Citizenship Laws Handbook - Strategic Information and Basic Laws
Switzerland Country Study Guide - Strategic Information and Developments
Switzerland Country Study Guide - Strategic Information and Developments
Switzerland Country Study Guide - Strategic Information and Developments Volume 1 Strategic Information and Developments
Switzerland Customs, Trade Regulations and Procedures Handbook
Switzerland Customs, Trade Regulations and Procedures Handbook
Switzerland Diplomatic Handbook - Strategic Information and Developments
Switzerland Diplomatic Handbook - Strategic Information and Developments
Switzerland Directory of Diplomatic and Consular Corps
Switzerland Ecology & Nature Protection Handbook
Switzerland Ecology & Nature Protection Handbook
Switzerland Ecology & Nature Protection Laws and Regulation Handbook
Switzerland Economic & Development Strategy Handbook
Switzerland Economic & Development Strategy Handbook
Switzerland Emission Trading Laws, Regulations and Programs Handbook

Title
Switzerland Energy Policy, Laws and Regulation Handbook
Switzerland Export-Import and Business Directory
Switzerland Export-Import and Business Directory
Switzerland Export-Import Trade and Business Directory
Switzerland Export-Import Trade and Business Directory
Switzerland Foreign Policy and Government Guide
Switzerland Foreign Policy and Government Guide
Switzerland Government and Business Contacts Handbook
Switzerland Government and Business Contacts Handbook
Switzerland Healthcare Sector Organization, Management and Payment Systems Handbook - Strategic Information, Programs and Regulations
Switzerland Immigration Laws and Regulations Handbook - Strategic Information and Basic Laws
Switzerland Industrial and Business Directory
Switzerland Industrial and Business Directory
Switzerland Insolvency (Bankruptcy) Laws and Regulations Handbook - Strategic Information and Basic Laws
Switzerland Intelligence & Security Activities & Operations Handbook
Switzerland Intelligence & Security Activities & Operations Handbook
Switzerland Intelligence, Security Activities & Operations Handbook
Switzerland Intelligence, Security Activities & Operations Handbook
Switzerland Internet and E-Commerce Investment and Business Guide - Strategic and Practical Information: Regulations and Opportunities
Switzerland Internet and E-Commerce Investment and Business Guide - Strategic and Practical Information: Regulations and Opportunities
Switzerland Investment and Business Guide - Strategic and Practical Information
Switzerland Investment and Business Guide - Strategic and Practical Information
Switzerland Investment and Business Guide - Strategic and Practical Information
Switzerland Investment and Business Guide - Strategic and Practical Information
Switzerland Investment and Trade Laws and Regulations Handbook
Switzerland Labor Laws and Regulations Handbook - Strategic Information and Basic Laws
Switzerland Land Ownership and Agriculture Laws Handbook
Switzerland Nuclear Energy Sector Laws, Regulations and Policies Handbook
Switzerland Offshore Investment and Business Guide - Strategic and Practical Information
Switzerland Offshore Investment and Business Guide - Strategic and Practical Information
Switzerland Offshore Investment Guide
Switzerland Offshore Investment Guide
Switzerland Offshore Tax Guide
Switzerland Offshore Tax Guide
Switzerland Parliament Guide
Switzerland Parliament Guide
Switzerland Recent Economic and Political Developments Yearbook
Switzerland Recent Economic and Political Developments Yearbook
Switzerland Recent Economic and Political Developments Yearbook
Switzerland Space Programs and Exploration Handbook
Switzerland Space Programs and Exploration Handbook

Title
Switzerland Starting Business (Incorporating) in Switzerland Guide
Switzerland Starting Business (Incorporating) in....Guide
Switzerland Tax Guide
Switzerland Tax Guide
Switzerland Taxation Laws and Regulations Handbook
Switzerland Telecom Laws and Regulations Handbook
Switzerland Telecommunication Industry Business Opportunities Handbook
Switzerland Telecommunication Industry Business Opportunities Handbook
Switzerland Transportation Policy and Regulations Handbook
Switzerland: How to Invest, Start and Run Profitable Business in Switzerland Guide - Practical Information, Opportunities, Contacts

BASIC LAWS AND REGULATIONS AFFECTING BUSINESS[3]

COUTRY	LAW TITLE
Switzerland	Act of 18 December 1970 the Federal fight against diseases transmissible Rights (Act epidemics)
Switzerland	Act of 18 December 1998 on the Federal assisted ProCreation (LPMA)
Switzerland	Act of 18 March 1994 on federal funds (Act funds, LFP)
Switzerland	Act of 18 March 1994 on the Federal Sickness Insurance (KVG)
Switzerland	Act of 20 December 1946 on federal insurance and Survivors (LAVs)
Switzerland	Act of 24 March 1995 on federal grants and trade of securities (Stock Exchange Act, SESTA)
Switzerland	Act of 9 October 1992 on federal and common objects Commodities Feed Additives (Act Commodities Feed Additives, LDAI)
Switzerland	Act of June 25, 1930 on the issuance of letters of guarantee (LLG)
Switzerland	Act of March 24, 2006 Federal Family Allowances (LAFam) RO
Switzerland	Act on Data Protection (DSchG) (canton of Fribourg)
Switzerland	Act on the Swiss National Federal Bank (National Bank Act)
Switzerland	Act on the University (Canton Fribourg)
Switzerland	Antitrust law, KG
Switzerland	Asylum Act 1998
Switzerland	Chemicals Fees Regulation (ChemGebV)
Switzerland	Chemicals Ordinance (chemo)
Switzerland	Civil Rights Act
Switzerland	Clean Air Act (LRV)
Switzerland	CO_2 law
Switzerland	Collective Investment Schemes Act, CISA
Switzerland	Collective Investment Schemes Ordinance, CISO
Switzerland	Construction Products Act, BauPG
Switzerland	Consumer Information Act, KIG
Switzerland	Copyright Act, the Copyright Law

---

[3] For ordering tests of specific laws in English or French, Please contact Global Investment Center USA at ibpusa3@gmail.com

For additional analytical, business and investment opportunities information,
please contact Global Investment & Business Center, USA
at (703) 370-8082. Fax: (703) 370-8083. E-mail: ibpusa3@gmail.com
Global Business and Investment Info Databank - www.ibpus.com

Switzerland	Copyright Act, the Copyright Law
Switzerland	Criminal Code 1937
Switzerland	Criminal Law, SGG
Switzerland	Cultural Promotion Act, KFG
Switzerland	Customs Regulation (ZV) on 1 November 2006
Switzerland	Customs Tariff Act of 9 October 1986 (CTA)
Switzerland	Decree of 14 November 1973 Aviation (Aviation Ordinance, LFV)
Switzerland	Decree of 4 April 2007 on safety rules for piping systems
Switzerland	Design Act, DESG
Switzerland	EDI Ordinance of 23 November 2005 on alcoholic beverages
Switzerland	EDI Ordinance of 23 November 2005 on drinking, spring and mineral water
Switzerland	Electricity Supply Ordinance of 14 March 2008 (Electricity Supply) and revised Energy Regulation
Switzerland	Energy Act (EnG) of 26 June 1998
Switzerland	Energy Act dated 26 June 1998
Switzerland	Energy Ordinance (Ordinance) of 7 December 1998
Switzerland	Energy Ordinance dated 7 December 1998 (ENO)
Switzerland	Environmental Protection Act (EPA)
Switzerland	Environmental Protection Act (EPA)
Switzerland	Federal Act of 10 October 1997 on Combating Money Laundering and Terrorist Financing in the Financial Sector (Anti-Money Laundering Act, AMLA)
Switzerland	Federal Act of 10 October 1997 on Combating Money Laundering and Terrorist Financing in the Financial Sector (Anti-Money Laundering Act, AMLA)
Switzerland	Federal Act of 10 October 1997 on the fight against money laundering in the financial sector (Money Laundering Act, AMLA)
Switzerland	Federal Act of 13 June 2008 on the Police Information Systems Association (BPI)
Switzerland	Federal Act of 13 March 1964 on work in industry, commerce and trade (Labor)
Switzerland	Federal Act of 14 December 2001 on Film Production and Film Culture (film Act, FIA)
Switzerland	Federal Act of 14 March 2006 on family allowances (Family Allowances Act, FamZG) AS
Switzerland	Federal Act of 15 June 1934 on federal criminal justice
Switzerland	Federal Act of 16 December 1994 on public procurement (BoeB)
Switzerland	Federal Act of 16 December 1994 on public procurement (BoeB)
Switzerland	Federal Act of 18 March 1994 on Health Insurance (KVG)
Switzerland	Federal Act of 18 March 1994 on investment funds (investment funds law, AFG)
Switzerland	Federal Act of 19 December 2003 on Research Involving Embryonic Stem Cells (Stem Cell Research Act, STRA)
Switzerland	Federal Act of 19 June 1959 on invalidity insurance (LAI)
Switzerland	Federal Act of 19 June 1992 on Data Protection (FADP)
Switzerland	Federal Act of 19 March 1976 on the safety of technical installations and equipment
Switzerland	Federal Act of 20 June 1930 on the expropriation
Switzerland	Federal Act of 20 June 1986 on the hunting and the protection of wild mammals and birds (hunting law, JSG)
Switzerland	Federal Act of 20 June 2003 on the Annulment of the Convictions of Persons who assisted Refugees at the time of the Nazi regime
Switzerland	Federal Act of 20 June 2003 on the use of DNA profiling in criminal proceedings and for the identification of unknown or missing persons (DNA-profile-law)

For additional analytical, business and investment opportunities information,
please contact Global Investment & Business Center, USA
at (703) 370-8082. Fax: (703) 370-8083. E-mail: ibpusa3@gmail.com
Global Business and Investment Info Databank - www.ibpus.com

Switzerland	Federal Act of 20 March 1975 on the Protection of Plant Varieties (Plant Variety Protection Act)
Switzerland	Federal Act of 20 March 1981 on International Mutual Assistance in Criminal Matters (Mutual Assistance Act, IRSG)
Switzerland	Federal Act of 20 March 2008 on the application of police coercion and policing measures within the jurisdiction of the federal government (coercion law, ZAG)
Switzerland	Federal Act of 21 June 1991 on Fisheries (BGF)
Switzerland	Federal Act of 21 June 1991 on Fisheries (BGF)
Switzerland	Federal Act of 22 June 1877 the police Hydraulic
Switzerland	Federal Act of 22 June 1979 on spatial planning (spatial planning law, RPG)
Switzerland	Federal Act of 22 June 2001 on cooperation with the International Criminal Court (ZISG)
Switzerland	Federal Act of 22 June 2007 on the Federal Census (Census Act)
Switzerland	Federal Act of 22 June 2007 on the Swiss Federal Nuclear Safety Inspectorate (ENSIG)
Switzerland	Federal Act of 22 June 2007 on the Swiss Financial Market Supervisory Authority (Financial Market Supervision Act, FINMASA)
Switzerland	Federal Act of 23 June 2006 on Medical
Switzerland	Federal Act of 23 March 2007 on the power supply (Electricity Supply Act, Electricity Supply)
Switzerland	Federal Act of 24 June 1902 concerning the electric light and heavy current installations (Electricity Act, Electricity Act)
Switzerland	Federal Act of 24 March 1995 on Gender Equality (Gender Equality Act, GEA)
Switzerland	Federal Act of 24 March 1995 on Stock Exchanges and Securities Trading (Stock Exchange Act, Stock Exchange Act)
Switzerland	Federal Act of 24 March 2006 on Radio and Television (RTVA)
Switzerland	Federal Act of 25 June 1982 on Occupational Retirement, Survivors' and Disability Pension Plans (BVG)
Switzerland	Federal Act of 26 June 1998 on Archiving (Archiving Act, Archa)
Switzerland	Federal Act of 28 September 1923 on the ship register
Switzerland	Federal Act of 3 October 1951 on the narcotic and psychotropic substances (narcotics law)
Switzerland	Federal Act of 3 October 1975 on the inland waterway (BSG)
Switzerland	Federal Act of 3 October 1975 Treaty with the United States of America on Mutual Legal Assistance in Criminal Matters
Switzerland	Federal Act of 4 October 1963 laying pipelines for transport of liquid or gaseous fuels or fuels (pipeline law, RLG)
Switzerland	Federal Act of 4 October 1985 on footpaths and hiking trails (FWG)
Switzerland	Federal Act of 4 October 1991 on the Forest (Forest Act, WaG)
Switzerland	Federal Act of 4 October 2002 on the Civil Protection and Civil Protection (Population and Civil Protection Act, BZG)
Switzerland	Federal Act of 5 October 1984 on the Federal government for the penalties and measures
Switzerland	Federal Act of 7 October 1983 on Environmental Protection (Environmental Protection Act, USG)
Switzerland	Federal Act of 7 October 1983 on the Protection of the Environment (Environmental Protection Act, EPA)
Switzerland	Federal Act of 7 October 1994 on central criminal police bodies of the Federation

For additional analytical, business and investment opportunities information,
please contact Global Investment & Business Center, USA
at (703) 370-8082. Fax: (703) 370-8083. E-mail: ibpusa3@gmail.com
Global Business and Investment Info Databank - www.ibpus.com

Switzerland	Federal Act of 8 October 1999 relating to construction products (Construction Products Act, BauPG)
Switzerland	Federal Act of 8 October 2004 on Human Genetic Testing (GUMG)
Switzerland	Federal Act of 8 October 2004 on transplantation of organs, tissues and cells (Transplantation Act)
Switzerland	Federal Act of October 3, 1951 on narcotics and psychotropic substances (Narcotics Act, Narcotics Act)
Switzerland	Federal Act on Aircraft Record
Switzerland	Federal Act on Cartels and Other Restraints of Competition
Switzerland	Federal Act on Collective Investment Schemes (CISA)
Switzerland	Federal Act on Currency and Payment Instruments
Switzerland	Federal Act on Fisheries (BGF)
Switzerland	Federal Act on Political Rights
Switzerland	Federal Act on Railways Noise Abatement
Switzerland	Federal Act on Stock Exchanges and Securities Trading
Switzerland	Federal Act on the Federal Criminal Justice
Switzerland	Federal Act on the Protection of Waters (WPL)
Switzerland	Federal Act on the Swiss National Bank (National Bank Act)
Switzerland	Federal Code on Private International Law (CPIL)
Switzerland	Federal Constitution of the Swiss Confederation
Switzerland	Federal Court Act, BGG
Switzerland	Federal Law of 06.27.1973 on Stamp Duty (StG)
Switzerland	Federal Law of 1 July 1966 on the Nature and Cultural Heritage (NCHA)
Switzerland	Federal Law of 10 October 1997 on the fight against money laundering in the financial sector (LBA Act money laundering)
Switzerland	Federal Law of 10.13.1965 on Withholding Tax (WHT)
Switzerland	Federal Law of 14.12.1990 on Direct Federal Tax (DBG)
Switzerland	Federal Law of 15 December 2000 on medicinal products and medical devices (Therapeutic Products Act, HMG)
Switzerland	Federal Law of 15 December 2000 on protection against dangerous substances and preparations
Switzerland	Federal Law of 18 December 1970 on the control of communicable human diseases (Epidemics Act)
Switzerland	Federal Law of 18 December 1998 on medically assisted reproduction (reproductive medicine)
Switzerland	Federal Law of 18 February 1878 concerning handling of Railway Police
Switzerland	Federal Law of 19 December 1958 on the road (SVG)
Switzerland	Federal Law of 19 December 2003 on research on embryonic stem cells (Law on research on stem cells, LRCS)
Switzerland	Federal Law of 19 December 2003 on research on embryonic stem cells (Stem Cell Research Act)
Switzerland	Federal Law of 21 December 1948 concerning aviation (LFG)
Switzerland	Federal Law of 22 December 1916 on the utilization of the water forces (Water Act, WRG)
Switzerland	Federal Law of 23 June 2006 on Collective Investment Schemes (Collective Investment Schemes Act, CISA)
Switzerland	Federal Law of 23 June 2006 on the University Act (the medical profession, MedBG)

For additional analytical, business and investment opportunities information,
please contact Global Investment & Business Center, USA
at (703) 370-8082. Fax: (703) 370-8083. E-mail: ibpusa3@gmail.com
Global Business and Investment Info Databank - www.ibpus.com

	medical professions
Switzerland	Federal Law of 24 January 1991 concerning the protection of waters (WPL)
Switzerland	Federal Law of 8 November 1934 on Banks and savings banks
Switzerland	Federal Law of 8 November 1934 on Banks and Savings Banks (Banking Act, BA)
Switzerland	Federal Law of 8 October 2004 on human genetic analyze (Lagh)
Switzerland	Federal Law of 8 October 2004 on transplantation of organs, tissues and cells (Act transplantation)
Switzerland	Federal Law of 9 October 1992 on foodstuffs and consumer goods (food law, LMG)
Switzerland	Federal law on acquisition and loss of Swiss nationality (nationality law)
Switzerland	Federal Law on Aviation
Switzerland	Federal Law on Banks and Savings Banks (BankL)
Switzerland	Federal Law on Cartels and Other Constraints on Competition (Law on Cartels, LC)
Switzerland	Federal Law on Consumer Credit
Switzerland	Federal Law on Copyright and Neighbouring Rights of October 9, 1992
Switzerland	Federal Law on Criminal Procedure
Switzerland	Federal Law on Currency and Payment Instruments (CI)
Switzerland	Federal Law on Industrial Designs and Models of March 30, 1900, as last Amended on March 24, 1995
Switzerland	Federal Law on Medicinal Products and Medical Devices
Switzerland	Federal Law on Medicinal Products and Medical Devices
Switzerland	Federal Law on Old-Age and Survivors Insurance (AHVG)
Switzerland	Federal Law on Old-Age and Survivors Insurance (AHVG)
Switzerland	Federal Law on Patents for Inventions of June 25, 1954
Switzerland	Federal Law on Political Rights
Switzerland	Federal Law on Rural Land Rights (BGBB)
Switzerland	Federal Law on Stock Exchanges and Securities
Switzerland	Federal Law on the Protection of Nature and Cultural
Switzerland	Federal Law on the Protection of New Plant Varieties of March 20, 1975
Switzerland	Federal Law on the Protection of Topographies of Semiconductor Products of October 9, 1992
Switzerland	Federal Law on the reduction of CO2 emissions
Switzerland	Federal Law Relating to Non-human Gene Technology
Switzerland	Federal Law Relating to the Protection of the Environment
Switzerland	Federal Statistics Act of 9 October 1992 (FStatA)
Switzerland	Fight against terrorism in Switzerland - Provisions of national and international law (2004).
Switzerland	FMG Telecommunications Act of 30.04.1997
Switzerland	Food and Commodities Regulation of 23 November 2005 (LGV)
Switzerland	Forest Act, WaG
Switzerland	Forest Regulation (WaV)
Switzerland	Genetic Engineering Act (GTG)
Switzerland	Hunting Act (JSG)
Switzerland	Hunting Regulation (JSV)
Switzerland	Hydraulic Engineering Act
Switzerland	Insurance contract law, SG
Switzerland	Insurance Supervision Act

For additional analytical, business and investment opportunities information,
please contact Global Investment & Business Center, USA
at (703) 370-8082. Fax: (703) 370-8083. E-mail: ibpusa3@gmail.com
Global Business and Investment Info Databank - www.ibpus.com

Switzerland	January 17, 1961 Regulations you Disability Insurance (DI)
Switzerland	Law of 15 December 2000 on Federal Drug and Medical Devices (Law on Therapeutic Products LPTH)
Switzerland	Law of 15 December 2000 on federal protection against dangerous substances and preparations (Law on Chemicals, Chemicals Act)
Switzerland	Law of 19 June 1959 Federal Disability Insurance (AIA)
Switzerland	Law on Court Organization (Canton Solothurn)
Switzerland	Law on direct cantonal taxes (DSTG) (canton of Fribourg)
Switzerland	Legge sulle Federal borse di Commercio e il valori Mobiliari
Switzerland	Legge tributaria (Canton Ticino)
Switzerland	Loi sur les contributions directes (canton of Neuchâtel)
Switzerland	LRTV Loi sur la radio du 21.06.1991 et la télévision (RS 784.40)
Switzerland	LTC Loi sur les télécommunications du 30.04.1997 (RS 784.10)
Switzerland	Maritime law
Switzerland	Merger Act of 3 October 2003
Switzerland	Military Criminal Law dated 23 March 1979
Switzerland	Military Criminal Law of 13 June 1927
Switzerland	Money Laundering Act, AMLA
Switzerland	Money Laundering Act, AMLA; SR 955.0
Switzerland	Mortgage Regulation of 23 January 1931 (PFV)
Switzerland	National Park Act
Switzerland	Nature and Cultural Heritage Protection Act (NHG)
Switzerland	New Customs Law of 18 March 2005 -
Switzerland	Noise Abatement Ordinance
Switzerland	Noise Abatement Ordinance (NAO)
Switzerland	November 7, 2007 by order of federal subsidies for the reduction of health insurance premiums (ORPM)
Switzerland	Nuclear Energy Act
Switzerland	Nuclear Energy Act of 21 March 2003 (KEG)
Switzerland	Nuclear Energy Liability Act of 18 March 1983 (KHG)
Switzerland	Nuclear Energy Liability Regulation of 5 December 1983 (KHV)
Switzerland	Nuclear Energy Ordinance of 10 December 2004 (KEV)
Switzerland	Order of 16 March 2007 on the transplantation of organs, tissues and manmade Order (transplantation) cells
Switzerland	Order of 17 October 2001 on the drugs (OMED)
Switzerland	Order of 18 May 2005 on protection against dangerous substances and preparations (Ordinance on chemicals, Chemicals Ordinance)
Switzerland	Order of 2 February 2005 on research on embryonic stem cells (Order on stem cell research, ORCS)
Switzerland	Order of 23 November 2005 on DFI of Alcoholics drinks
Switzerland	Order of 23 November 2005 on Foodstuffs and Utility Articles Feed Additives (LGV)
Switzerland	Order of 27 June 1995 on the Sickness Insurance (KVV)
Switzerland	Order of 27 October 2004 on tobacco products and of products containing tobacco substitutes intended to be Fumes (Ordinance on tobacco OTAB)
Switzerland	Order of 29 May 1996 on narcotics and psychotropic substances (Ordinance on drugs, Ostup)

For additional analytical, business and investment opportunities information, please contact Global Investment & Business Center, USA at (703) 370-8082. Fax: (703) 370-8083. E-mail: ibpusa3@gmail.com Global Business and Investment Info Databank - www.ibpus.com

Switzerland	Order of 31 October 2007 on family benefits (OAFam) RO
Switzerland	Order of 4 December 2000 on medically assisted ProCreation (OPMA)
Switzerland	Order of 8 March 1999 on the medical prescription of heroin
Switzerland	Ordinance Concerning the Federal Act on Fisheries (VBGF)
Switzerland	Ordinance of 14 June 1993 to the Federal Act on Data Protection (OFADP)
Switzerland	Ordinance of 14 June 2002 on Telecommunications Installations (TIO)
Switzerland	Ordinance of 2 February 2000 on the utilization of the water forces (water ordinance, WRV)
Switzerland	Ordinance of 2 February 2005 on research on embryonic stem cells (stem cell research regulation)
Switzerland	Ordinance of 7 November 2007 on Parks of National Importance (Parks Ordinance, Parko)
Switzerland	Ordinance of 7 November 2007 on the federal contribution to health insurance premium (VPVK)
Switzerland	Ordinance of 9 March 2007 on Radio and Television (RTVO)
Switzerland	Ordinance of 9 March 2007 on Telecommunications Services (OTS)
Switzerland	Ordinance of the FDF of 30 January 2002 on Electronic Data and Information (OEIDI)
Switzerland	Ordinance of the FDHA of 10 December 2007 on Combined Warnings on Tobacco Products
Switzerland	Ordinance of the Swiss Federal Banking Commission Concerning the Prevention of Money Laundering (MLO SFBC)
Switzerland	Ordinance of the Takeover Board on Public Takeover Offers (Takeover Ordinance, TOO)
Switzerland	Ordinance on Air Pollution,
Switzerland	Ordinance on Banks and Savings Banks (Banking Ordinance, Banko)
Switzerland	Ordinance on Banks and Savings Banks of 17 May 1972 (Bank Regulation, BO)
Switzerland	Ordinance on Beverage Containers (VGV)
Switzerland	Ordinance on Beverage Containers (VGV)
Switzerland	Ordinance on Collective Investment Schemes (CISO)
Switzerland	Ordinance on Environmental Impact Assessment
Switzerland	Ordinance on Hydraulic Engineering (WBV)
Switzerland	Ordinance on Insurance Old Age, Survivors and Disability (OFA)
Switzerland	Ordinance on Noise Abatement Railways
Switzerland	Ordinance on Plant Protection Products (psmv)
Switzerland	Ordinance on Sanctions for Unlawful Restraints of Competition (KG Sanctions Regulation, SVKG) of 12 March 2004
Switzerland	Ordinance on Sanctions for Unlawful Restraints of Competition (KG Sanctions Regulation, SVKG) of 12 March 2004
Switzerland	Ordinance on Stock Exchanges and Securities Trading (Stock Exchange Ordinance)
Switzerland	Ordinance on the Control of Mergers of Enterprises of 17 June 1996 (position as at 23 March 2004)
Switzerland	Ordinance on the control of Mergers of Enterprises of June 17, 1996 (position as at 23 March 2004)
Switzerland	Ordinance Regarding the Sanctions for Unlawful Restrictions of Competition 2004
Switzerland	Ordinance Relating to Impacts on the Soil (OIS)
Switzerland	Ordinance Relating to Protection from Non-Ionizing Radiation (decree)
Switzerland	Ordinance to the Federal Law on Fisheries (VBGF)

For additional analytical, business and investment opportunities information,
please contact Global Investment & Business Center, USA
at (703) 370-8082. Fax: (703) 370-8083. E-mail: ibpusa3@gmail.com
Global Business and Investment Info Databank - www.ibpus.com

Switzerland	Patent Law, Patent Law
Switzerland	Penal code
Switzerland	Pesticide regulation
Switzerland	Pipeline Ordinance of 2 February 2000 (RLV)
Switzerland	Planning Regulation of 28 June 2000 (RPV)
Switzerland	Plant Protection Ordinance (PSV)
Switzerland	Privacy Policy (DSG)
Switzerland	Radiation Protection Act of 22 March 1991 (RPA)
Switzerland	Railway Act of 20 December 1957 (EBG)
Switzerland	Regulation of 11 December 1995 on public procurement (VoeB)
Switzerland	Regulation of 12 February 1918 on the calculation of the water rate (water rate regulation, TM)
Switzerland	Regulation of 12 June 1995 on the safety of technical installations and equipment (STEV)
Switzerland	Regulation of 14 February 2007 on Human Genetic Testing (GUMV)
Switzerland	Regulation of 14 February 2007 on the creation of DNA profiles in civil and administrative area (VDZV)
Switzerland	Regulation of 16 March 2007 on the allocation of organs for transplantation (organ allocation Regulation)
Switzerland	Regulation of 16 March 2007 on the transplantation of human organs, tissues and cells (transplantation Regulation)
Switzerland	Regulation of 17 January 1961 concernant the Invalidity insurance (IVV)
Switzerland	Regulation of 17 May 1972 on Banks and Savings Banks (Banking Ordinance, BO)
Switzerland	Regulation of 17 October 2001 on the drug (drug prescription, VAM)
Switzerland	Regulation of 17 October 2007 on the Emergency Organisation Radioactivity (VEOR)
Switzerland	Regulation of 18 May 2005 on Protection against Dangerous Substances and Preparations (Chemicals Ordinance)
Switzerland	Regulation of 2 December 1996 on Stock Exchanges and Securities Trading (Stock Exchange BEHV)
Switzerland	Regulation of 21 November 2007 on the Federal government for the penalties and measures (LSMV)
Switzerland	Regulation of 22 November 2006 on the organization of public procurement of Federal (Org-VoeB)
Switzerland	Regulation of 22 October 2003 on the cost of the federal criminal justice
Switzerland	Regulation of 24 February 1982 on International Mutual Assistance in Criminal Matters (Mutual Assistance Regulation, O-IMAC)
Switzerland	Regulation of 24 October 1979 on the Military Criminal
Switzerland	Regulation of 25 October 1995 on the compensation of losses in hydropower use (VAEW)
Switzerland	Regulation of 26 November 1986 on footpaths and hiking trails (FWV)
Switzerland	Regulation of 27 June 1995 on health insurance (KVV)
Switzerland	Regulation of 27 November 2000 relating to construction products (Construction Products Regulation, BauPV)
Switzerland	Regulation of 27 October 2004 on tobacco products and tobacco products with tobacco substitutes (Tobacco Regulation, OTab)
Switzerland	Regulation of 29 May 1996 concerning narcotic and psychotropic substances (narcotics regulation, BetmV)

Switzerland	Regulation of 29 September 2006 on Capital Adequacy and Risk Diversification for Banks and Securities Dealers (Capital Adequacy Ordinance, ERV)
Switzerland	Regulation of 30 March 1994 on electrical power installations (power regulation)
Switzerland	Regulation of 30 March 1994 on low-voltage electrical systems (low current regulation)
Switzerland	Regulation of 31 October 1947 on the Old Age and Survivors Insurance (Rav)
Switzerland	Regulation of 8 March 1999 on the medical prescription of heroin
Switzerland	Regulation of the EDI of 14 February 2007 on Human Genetic Testing (GUMV-EDI)
Switzerland	Regulation on CO2 tax (CO2 Regulation)
Switzerland	Regulation on Nature and Cultural Heritage (NHV)
Switzerland	Regulation on protection against non-ionizing radiation (decree)
Switzerland	Regulation on Soil Pollution (OIS)
Switzerland	Regulation on the age and survivors' insurance (AHVV)
Switzerland	Regulation on the age and survivors' insurance (AHVV)
Switzerland	Regulation on the collection of fees in antitrust law (KG Fee Ordinance) of 25 February 1998
Switzerland	Regulation on the control of concentrations between undertakings (VKU) of 17 June 1996
Switzerland	Regulation on Voluntary Retirement, Survivors and Disability Insurance (VFV)
Switzerland	Regulations of the Takeover Board (Regulations-TB, TB-R)
Switzerland	Reproductive Medicine Regulation of 4 December 2000 (FMedV)
Switzerland	Road Traffic Regulations of 13 November 1962 (VRV)
Switzerland	RTA Federal Law of 21.06.1991 on Radio and Television
Switzerland	SFBC Money Laundering Decree of 18.12.2002 (MLO SFBC)
Switzerland	Swiss Civil Code
Switzerland	Swiss Federal Nuclear Energy Act dated 21 March 2003
Switzerland	Takeover Ordinance-TB
Switzerland	Tax Act 1976 (Canton of Valais)
Switzerland	Tax Act 1992 (Canton Thurgau)
Switzerland	Tax Act 1994 (Canton Obwalden)
Switzerland	Tax Act 2000 (Canton train)
Switzerland	Tax Act Nidwalden
Switzerland	Tax and Finance Law (Canton Basel Land)
Switzerland	Tax Law
Switzerland	Technical Ordinance on Waste (TVA)
Switzerland	Telecommunications Act of 30 April 1997 (TCA)
Switzerland	Trademark Law, Trademark Law
Switzerland	Transport Act, TG
Switzerland	Transport Insurance Ordinance of 20 November 1959 (VVV)
Switzerland	Vocational Training Act, BBG
Switzerland	Water Protection Act (WPL)
Switzerland	Water Protection Ordinance (WPO)
Switzerland	Water Protection Ordinance (WPO)
Switzerland	Water Use Act (WNG) (Canton Aargau)
Switzerland	Waterways Act (WBG)
Switzerland	Waterways Regulation (WBV)

Switzerland	Youth criminal law, JStG

For additional analytical, business and investment opportunities information,
please contact Global Investment & Business Center, USA
at (703) 370-8082. Fax: (703) 370-8083. E-mail: ibpusa3@gmail.com
Global Business and Investment Info Databank - www.ibpus.com

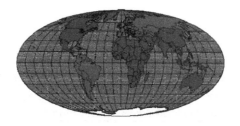

DOING BUSINESS AND INVESTING LIBRARY

World Business Information Catalog, USA: http://www.ibpus.com
Email: ibpusa@comcast.net.

Price: $99.95 Each

TITLE
Abkhazia (Republic of Abkhazia): Doing Business and Investing In...Guide - Practical Informtion, Regulations, Opportunities
Afghanistan: Doing Business and Investing In...Guide - Practical Informtion, Regulations, Opportunities
Aland: Doing Business and Investing In...Guide - Practical Informtion, Regulations, Opportunities
Albania: Doing Business and Investing In...Guide - Practical Informtion, Regulations, Opportunities
Algeria: Doing Business and Investing In...Guide - Practical Informtion, Regulations, Opportunities
Andorra: Doing Business and Investing In...Guide - Practical Informtion, Regulations, Opportunities
Angola: Doing Business and Investing In...Guide - Practical Informtion, Regulations, Opportunities
Anguilla: Doing Business and Investing In...Guide - Practical Informtion, Regulations, Opportunities
Antigua and Barbuda: Doing Business and Investing In...Guide - Practical Informtion, Regulations, Opportunities
Antilles (Netherlands): Doing Business and Investing In...Guide - Practical Informtion, Regulations, Opportunities
Argentina: Doing Business and Investing In...Guide - Practical Informtion, Regulations, Opportunities
Armenia: Doing Business and Investing In...Guide - Practical Informtion, Regulations, Opportunities
Aruba: Doing Business and Investing In...Guide - Practical Informtion, Regulations, Opportunities
Australia: Doing Business and Investing In...Guide - Practical Informtion, Regulations, Opportunities
Austria: Doing Business and Investing In...Guide - Practical Informtion, Regulations, Opportunities
Azerbaijan: Doing Business and Investing In...Guide - Practical Informtion, Regulations, Opportunities
Bahamas: Doing Business and Investing In...Guide - Practical Informtion, Regulations, Opportunities
Bahrain: Doing Business and Investing In...Guide - Practical Informtion, Regulations, Opportunities
Bangladesh: Doing Business and Investing In...Guide - Practical Informtion, Regulations, Opportunities
Barbados: Doing Business and Investing In...Guide - Practical Informtion, Regulations, Opportunities
Belarus: Doing Business and Investing In...Guide - Practical Informtion, Regulations, Opportunities
Belgium: Doing Business and Investing In...Guide - Practical Informtion, Regulations, Opportunities
Belize: Doing Business and Investing In...Guide - Practical Informtion, Regulations, Opportunities
Benin: Doing Business and Investing In...Guide - Practical Informtion, Regulations, Opportunities
Bermuda: Doing Business and Investing In...Guide - Practical Informtion, Regulations, Opportunities
Bhutan: Doing Business and Investing In...Guide - Practical Informtion, Regulations, Opportunities
Bolivia: Doing Business and Investing In...Guide - Practical Informtion, Regulations, Opportunities
Bosnia and Herzegovina: Doing Business and Investing In...Guide - Practical Informtion, Regulations, Opportunities
Botswana: Doing Business and Investing In...Guide - Practical Informtion, Regulations, Opportunities
Brazil: Doing Business and Investing In...Guide - Practical Informtion, Regulations, Opportunities
Brunei: Doing Business and Investing In...Guide - Practical Informtion, Regulations, Opportunities
Bulgaria: Doing Business and Investing In...Guide - Practical Informtion, Regulations, Opportunities
Burkina Faso: Doing Business and Investing In...Guide - Practical Informtion, Regulations, Opportunities
Burundi: Doing Business and Investing In...Guide - Practical Informtion, Regulations, Opportunities
Cambodia: Doing Business and Investing In...Guide - Practical Informtion, Regulations, Opportunities

For additional analytical, business and investment opportunities information,
Please contact Global Investment & Business Center, USA
at (202) 546-2103. Fax: (202) 546-3275. E-mail: rusric@erols.com

TITLE
Cameroon: Doing Business and Investing In...Guide - Practical Informtion, Regulations, Opportunities
Canada: Doing Business and Investing In...Guide - Practical Informtion, Regulations, Opportunities
Cape Verde: Doing Business and Investing In...Guide - Practical Informtion, Regulations, Opportunities
Cayman Islands: Doing Business and Investing In...Guide - Practical Informtion, Regulations, Opportunities
Central African Republic: Doing Business and Investing In...Guide - Practical Informtion, Regulations, Opportunities
Chad: Doing Business and Investing In...Guide - Practical Informtion, Regulations, Opportunities
Chile: Doing Business and Investing In...Guide - Practical Informtion, Regulations, Opportunities
China: Doing Business and Investing In...Guide - Practical Informtion, Regulations, Opportunities
Colombia: Doing Business and Investing In...Guide - Practical Informtion, Regulations, Opportunities
Comoros: Doing Business and Investing In...Guide - Practical Informtion, Regulations, Opportunities
Congo: Doing Business and Investing In...Guide - Practical Informtion, Regulations, Opportunities
Congo, Democratic Republic: Doing Business and Investing In...Guide - Practical Informtion, Regulations, Opportunities
Cook Islands: Doing Business and Investing In...Guide - Practical Informtion, Regulations, Opportunities
Costa Rica: Doing Business and Investing In...Guide - Practical Informtion, Regulations, Opportunities
Cote d'Ivoire: Doing Business and Investing In...Guide - Practical Informtion, Regulations, Opportunities
Croatia: Doing Business and Investing In...Guide - Practical Informtion, Regulations, Opportunities
Cuba: Doing Business and Investing In...Guide - Practical Informtion, Regulations, Opportunities
Cyprus: Doing Business and Investing In...Guide - Practical Informtion, Regulations, Opportunities
Czech Republic: Doing Business and Investing In...Guide - Practical Informtion, Regulations, Opportunities
Denmark: Doing Business and Investing In...Guide - Practical Informtion, Regulations, Opportunities
Djibouti: Doing Business and Investing In...Guide - Practical Informtion, Regulations, Opportunities
Dominica: Doing Business and Investing In...Guide - Practical Informtion, Regulations, Opportunities
Dominican Republic: Doing Business and Investing In...Guide - Practical Informtion, Regulations, Opportunities
Ecuador: Doing Business and Investing In...Guide - Practical Informtion, Regulations, Opportunities
Egypt: Doing Business and Investing In...Guide - Practical Informtion, Regulations, Opportunities
El Salvador: Doing Business and Investing In...Guide - Practical Informtion, Regulations, Opportunities
Equatorial Guinea: Doing Business and Investing In...Guide - Practical Informtion, Regulations, Opportunities
Eritrea: Doing Business and Investing In...Guide - Practical Informtion, Regulations, Opportunities
Estonia: Doing Business and Investing In...Guide - Practical Informtion, Regulations, Opportunities
Ethiopia: Doing Business and Investing In...Guide - Practical Informtion, Regulations, Opportunities
Falkland Islands: Doing Business and Investing In...Guide - Practical Informtion, Regulations, Opportunities
Faroes Islands: Doing Business and Investing In...Guide - Practical Informtion, Regulations, Opportunities
Fiji: Doing Business and Investing In...Guide - Practical Informtion, Regulations, Opportunities
Finland: Doing Business and Investing In...Guide - Practical Informtion, Regulations, Opportunities
France: Doing Business and Investing In...Guide - Practical Informtion, Regulations, Opportunities
Gabon: Doing Business and Investing In...Guide - Practical Informtion, Regulations, Opportunities
Gambia: Doing Business and Investing In...Guide - Practical Informtion, Regulations, Opportunities
Georgia: Doing Business and Investing In...Guide - Practical Informtion, Regulations, Opportunities
Germany: Doing Business and Investing In...Guide - Practical Informtion, Regulations, Opportunities
Ghana: Doing Business and Investing In...Guide - Practical Informtion, Regulations, Opportunities
Gibraltar: Doing Business and Investing In...Guide - Practical Informtion, Regulations, Opportunities
Greece: Doing Business and Investing In...Guide - Practical Informtion, Regulations, Opportunities
Greenland: Doing Business and Investing In...Guide - Practical Informtion, Regulations, Opportunities
Grenada: Doing Business and Investing In...Guide - Practical Informtion, Regulations, Opportunities
Guam: Doing Business and Investing In...Guide - Practical Informtion, Regulations, Opportunities

For additional analytical, business and investment opportunities information,
Please contact Global Investment & Business Center, USA
at (202) 546-2103. Fax: (202) 546-3275. E-mail: rusric@erols.com

TITLE
Guatemala: Doing Business and Investing In...Guide - Practical Informtion, Regulations, Opportunities
Guernsey: Doing Business and Investing In...Guide - Practical Informtion, Regulations, Opportunities
Guinea: Doing Business and Investing In...Guide - Practical Informtion, Regulations, Opportunities
Guinea-Bissau: Doing Business and Investing In...Guide - Practical Informtion, Regulations, Opportunities
Guyana: Doing Business and Investing In...Guide - Practical Informtion, Regulations, Opportunities
Haiti: Doing Business and Investing In...Guide - Practical Informtion, Regulations, Opportunities
Honduras: Doing Business and Investing In...Guide - Practical Informtion, Regulations, Opportunities
Hungary: Doing Business and Investing In...Guide - Practical Informtion, Regulations, Opportunities
Iceland: Doing Business and Investing In...Guide - Practical Informtion, Regulations, Opportunities
India: Doing Business and Investing In...Guide - Practical Informtion, Regulations, Opportunities
Indonesia: Doing Business and Investing In...Guide - Practical Informtion, Regulations, Opportunities
Iran: Doing Business and Investing In...Guide - Practical Informtion, Regulations, Opportunities
Iraq: Doing Business and Investing In...Guide - Practical Informtion, Regulations, Opportunities
Ireland: Doing Business and Investing In...Guide - Practical Informtion, Regulations, Opportunities
Israel: Doing Business and Investing In...Guide - Practical Informtion, Regulations, Opportunities
Italy: Doing Business and Investing In...Guide - Practical Informtion, Regulations, Opportunities
Jamaica: Doing Business and Investing In...Guide - Practical Informtion, Regulations, Opportunities
Japan: Doing Business and Investing In...Guide - Practical Informtion, Regulations, Opportunities
Jersey: Doing Business and Investing In...Guide - Practical Informtion, Regulations, Opportunities
Jordan: Doing Business and Investing In...Guide - Practical Informtion, Regulations, Opportunities
Kazakhstan: Doing Business and Investing In...Guide - Practical Informtion, Regulations, Opportunities
Kenya: Doing Business and Investing In...Guide - Practical Informtion, Regulations, Opportunities
Kiribati: Doing Business and Investing In...Guide - Practical Informtion, Regulations, Opportunities
Korea, North: Doing Business and Investing In...Guide - Practical Informtion, Regulations, Opportunities
Korea, South: Doing Business and Investing In...Guide - Practical Informtion, Regulations, Opportunities
Kosovo: Doing Business and Investing In...Guide - Practical Informtion, Regulations, Opportunities
Kurdistan: Doing Business and Investing In...Guide - Practical Informtion, Regulations, Opportunities
Kuwait: Doing Business and Investing In...Guide - Practical Informtion, Regulations, Opportunities
Kyrgyzstan: Doing Business and Investing In...Guide - Practical Informtion, Regulations, Opportunities
Laos: Doing Business and Investing In...Guide - Practical Informtion, Regulations, Opportunities
Latvia: Doing Business and Investing In...Guide - Practical Informtion, Regulations, Opportunities
Lebanon: Doing Business and Investing In...Guide - Practical Informtion, Regulations, Opportunities
Lesotho: Doing Business and Investing In...Guide - Practical Informtion, Regulations, Opportunities
Liberia: Doing Business and Investing In...Guide - Practical Informtion, Regulations, Opportunities
Libya: Doing Business and Investing In...Guide - Practical Informtion, Regulations, Opportunities
Liechtenstein: Doing Business and Investing In...Guide - Practical Informtion, Regulations, Opportunities
Lithuania: Doing Business and Investing In...Guide - Practical Informtion, Regulations, Opportunities
Luxembourg: Doing Business and Investing In...Guide - Practical Informtion, Regulations, Opportunities
Macao: Doing Business and Investing In...Guide - Practical Informtion, Regulations, Opportunities
Macedonia: Doing Business and Investing In...Guide - Practical Informtion, Regulations, Opportunities
Madagascar: Doing Business and Investing In...Guide - Practical Informtion, Regulations, Opportunities
Madeira: Doing Business and Investing In...Guide - Practical Informtion, Regulations, Opportunities
Malawi: Doing Business and Investing In...Guide - Practical Informtion, Regulations, Opportunities
Malaysia: Doing Business and Investing In...Guide - Practical Informtion, Regulations, Opportunities
Maldives: Doing Business and Investing In...Guide - Practical Informtion, Regulations, Opportunities
Mali: Doing Business and Investing In...Guide - Practical Informtion, Regulations, Opportunities

For additional analytical, business and investment opportunities information,
Please contact Global Investment & Business Center, USA
at (202) 546-2103. Fax: (202) 546-3275. E-mail: rusric@erols.com

TITLE
Malta: Doing Business and Investing In...Guide - Practical Informtion, Regulations, Opportunities
Man: Doing Business and Investing In...Guide - Practical Informtion, Regulations, Opportunities
Marshall Islands: Doing Business and Investing In...Guide - Practical Informtion, Regulations, Opportunities
Mauritania: Doing Business and Investing In...Guide - Practical Informtion, Regulations, Opportunities
Mauritius: Doing Business and Investing In...Guide - Practical Informtion, Regulations, Opportunities
Mayotte: Doing Business and Investing In...Guide - Practical Informtion, Regulations, Opportunities
Mexico: Doing Business and Investing In...Guide - Practical Informtion, Regulations, Opportunities
Micronesia: Doing Business and Investing In...Guide - Practical Informtion, Regulations, Opportunities
Moldova: Doing Business and Investing In...Guide - Practical Informtion, Regulations, Opportunities
Monaco: Doing Business and Investing In...Guide - Practical Informtion, Regulations, Opportunities
Mongolia: Doing Business and Investing In...Guide - Practical Informtion, Regulations, Opportunities
Montserrat: Doing Business and Investing In...Guide - Practical Informtion, Regulations, Opportunities
Montenegro: Doing Business and Investing In...Guide - Practical Informtion, Regulations, Opportunities
Morocco: Doing Business and Investing In...Guide - Practical Informtion, Regulations, Opportunities
Mozambique: Doing Business and Investing In...Guide - Practical Informtion, Regulations, Opportunities
Myanmar: Doing Business and Investing In...Guide - Practical Informtion, Regulations, Opportunities
Nagorno-Karabakh Republic: Doing Business and Investing In...Guide - Practical Informtion, Regulations, Opportunities
Namibia: Doing Business and Investing In...Guide - Practical Informtion, Regulations, Opportunities
Nauru: Doing Business and Investing In...Guide - Practical Informtion, Regulations, Opportunities
Nepal: Doing Business and Investing In...Guide - Practical Informtion, Regulations, Opportunities
Netherlands: Doing Business and Investing In...Guide - Practical Informtion, Regulations, Opportunities
New Caledonia: Doing Business and Investing In...Guide - Practical Informtion, Regulations, Opportunities
New Zealand: Doing Business and Investing In...Guide - Practical Informtion, Regulations, Opportunities
Nicaragua: Doing Business and Investing In...Guide - Practical Informtion, Regulations, Opportunities
Niger: Doing Business and Investing In...Guide - Practical Informtion, Regulations, Opportunities
Nigeria: Doing Business and Investing In...Guide - Practical Informtion, Regulations, Opportunities
Niue: Doing Business and Investing In...Guide - Practical Informtion, Regulations, Opportunities
Northern Cyprus (Turkish Republic of Northern Cyprus) Doing Business and Investing In...Guide - Practical Informtion, Regulations, Opportunities
Northern Mariana Islands: Doing Business and Investing In...Guide - Practical Informtion, Regulations, Opportunities
Norway: Doing Business and Investing In...Guide - Practical Informtion, Regulations, Opportunities
Oman: Doing Business and Investing In...Guide - Practical Informtion, Regulations, Opportunities
Pakistan: Doing Business and Investing In...Guide - Practical Informtion, Regulations, Opportunities
Palau: Doing Business and Investing In...Guide - Practical Informtion, Regulations, Opportunities
Palestine (West Bank & Gaza): Doing Business and Investing In...Guide - Practical Informtion, Regulations, Opportunities
Panama: Doing Business and Investing In...Guide - Practical Informtion, Regulations, Opportunities
Papua New Guinea: Doing Business and Investing In...Guide - Practical Informtion, Regulations, Opportunities
Paraguay: Doing Business and Investing In...Guide - Practical Informtion, Regulations, Opportunities
Peru: Doing Business and Investing In...Guide - Practical Informtion, Regulations, Opportunities
Philippines: Doing Business and Investing In...Guide - Practical Informtion, Regulations, Opportunities
Pitcairn Islands: Doing Business and Investing In...Guide - Practical Informtion, Regulations, Opportunities
Poland: Doing Business and Investing In...Guide - Practical Informtion, Regulations, Opportunities
Polynesia French: Doing Business and Investing In...Guide - Practical Informtion, Regulations, Opportunities
Portugal: Doing Business and Investing In...Guide - Practical Informtion, Regulations, Opportunities

For additional analytical, business and investment opportunities information,
Please contact Global Investment & Business Center, USA
at (202) 546-2103. Fax: (202) 546-3275. E-mail: rusric@erols.com

TITLE
Qatar: Doing Business and Investing In...Guide - Practical Informtion, Regulations, Opportunities
Romania: Doing Business and Investing In...Guide - Practical Informtion, Regulations, Opportunities
Russia: Doing Business and Investing In...Guide - Practical Informtion, Regulations, Opportunities
Rwanda: Doing Business and Investing In...Guide - Practical Informtion, Regulations, Opportunities
Sahrawi Arab Democratic Republic : Doing Business and Investing In...Guide - Practical Informtion, Regulations, Opportunities
Saint Kitts and Nevis: Doing Business and Investing In...Guide - Practical Informtion, Regulations, Opportunities
Saint Lucia: Doing Business and Investing In...Guide - Practical Informtion, Regulations, Opportunities
Saint Vincent and The Grenadines: Doing Business and Investing In...Guide - Practical Informtion, Regulations, Opportunities
Samoa (American): Doing Business and Investing In...Guide - Practical Informtion, Regulations, Opportunities
Samoa (Western): Doing Business and Investing In...Guide - Practical Informtion, Regulations, Opportunities
San Marino: Doing Business and Investing In...Guide - Practical Informtion, Regulations, Opportunities
Sao Tome and Principe: Doing Business and Investing In...Guide - Practical Informtion, Regulations, Opportunities
Saudi Arabia: Doing Business and Investing In...Guide - Practical Informtion, Regulations, Opportunities
Scotland: Doing Business and Investing In...Guide - Practical Informtion, Regulations, Opportunities
Senegal: Doing Business and Investing In...Guide - Practical Informtion, Regulations, Opportunities
Serbia: Doing Business and Investing In...Guide - Practical Informtion, Regulations, Opportunities
Seychelles: Doing Business and Investing In...Guide - Practical Informtion, Regulations, Opportunities
Sierra Leone: Doing Business and Investing In...Guide - Practical Informtion, Regulations, Opportunities
Singapore: Doing Business and Investing In...Guide - Practical Informtion, Regulations, Opportunities
Slovakia: Doing Business and Investing In...Guide - Practical Informtion, Regulations, Opportunities
Slovenia: Doing Business and Investing In...Guide - Practical Informtion, Regulations, Opportunities
Solomon Islands: Doing Business and Investing In...Guide - Practical Informtion, Regulations, Opportunities
Somalia: Doing Business and Investing In...Guide - Practical Informtion, Regulations, Opportunities
South Africa: Doing Business and Investing In...Guide - Practical Informtion, Regulations, Opportunities
Spain: Doing Business and Investing In...Guide - Practical Informtion, Regulations, Opportunities
Sri Lanka: Doing Business and Investing In...Guide - Practical Informtion, Regulations, Opportunities
St. Helena: Doing Business and Investing In...Guide - Practical Informtion, Regulations, Opportunities
St. Pierre & Miquelon: Doing Business and Investing In...Guide - Practical Informtion, Regulations, Opportunities
Sudan (Republic of the Sudan): Doing Business and Investing In...Guide - Practical Informtion, Regulations, Opportunities
Sudan South: Doing Business and Investing In...Guide - Practical Informtion, Regulations, Opportunities
Suriname: Doing Business and Investing In...Guide - Practical Informtion, Regulations, Opportunities
Swaziland: Doing Business and Investing In...Guide - Practical Informtion, Regulations, Opportunities
Sweden: Doing Business and Investing In...Guide - Practical Informtion, Regulations, Opportunities
Switzerland: Doing Business and Investing In...Guide - Practical Informtion, Regulations, Opportunities
Syria: Doing Business and Investing In...Guide - Practical Informtion, Regulations, Opportunities
Taiwan: Doing Business and Investing In...Guide - Practical Informtion, Regulations, Opportunities
Tajikistan: Doing Business and Investing In...Guide - Practical Informtion, Regulations, Opportunities
Tanzania: Doing Business and Investing In...Guide - Practical Informtion, Regulations, Opportunities
Thailand: Doing Business and Investing In...Guide - Practical Informtion, Regulations, Opportunities
Timor Leste (Democratic Republic of Timor-Leste): Doing Business and Investing In...Guide - Practical Informtion, Regulations, Opportunities
Togo: Doing Business and Investing In...Guide - Practical Informtion, Regulations, Opportunities
Tonga: Doing Business and Investing In...Guide - Practical Informtion, Regulations, Opportunities
Trinidad and Tobago: Doing Business and Investing In...Guide - Practical Informtion, Regulations, Opportunities

For additional analytical, business and investment opportunities information,
Please contact Global Investment & Business Center, USA
at (202) 546-2103. Fax: (202) 546-3275. E-mail: rusric@erols.com

TITLE
Tunisia: Doing Business and Investing In...Guide - Practical Informtion, Regulations, Opportunities
Turkey: Doing Business and Investing In...Guide - Practical Informtion, Regulations, Opportunities
Turkmenistan: Doing Business and Investing In...Guide - Practical Informtion, Regulations, Opportunities
Turks & Caicos: Doing Business and Investing In...Guide - Practical Informtion, Regulations, Opportunities
Tuvalu: Doing Business and Investing In...Guide - Practical Informtion, Regulations, Opportunities
Uganda: Doing Business and Investing In...Guide - Practical Informtion, Regulations, Opportunities
Ukraine: Doing Business and Investing In...Guide - Practical Informtion, Regulations, Opportunities
United Arab Emirates: Doing Business and Investing In...Guide - Practical Informtion, Regulations, Opportunities
United Kingdom: Doing Business and Investing In...Guide - Practical Informtion, Regulations, Opportunities
United States: Doing Business and Investing In...Guide - Practical Informtion, Regulations, Opportunities
Uruguay: Doing Business and Investing In...Guide - Practical Informtion, Regulations, Opportunities
Uzbekistan: Doing Business and Investing In...Guide - Practical Informtion, Regulations, Opportunities
Vanuatu: Doing Business and Investing In...Guide - Practical Informtion, Regulations, Opportunities
Vatican City (Holy See): Doing Business and Investing In...Guide - Practical Informtion, Regulations, Opportunities
Venezuela: Doing Business and Investing In...Guide - Practical Informtion, Regulations, Opportunities
Vietnam: Doing Business and Investing In...Guide - Practical Informtion, Regulations, Opportunities
Virgin Islands, British: Doing Business and Investing In...Guide - Practical Informtion, Regulations, Opportunities
Wake Atoll: Doing Business and Investing In...Guide - Practical Informtion, Regulations, Opportunities
Wallis & Futuna: Doing Business and Investing In...Guide - Practical Informtion, Regulations, Opportunities
Western Sahara: Doing Business and Investing In...Guide - Practical Informtion, Regulations, Opportunities
Yemen: Doing Business and Investing In...Guide - Practical Informtion, Regulations, Opportunities
Zambia: Doing Business and Investing In...Guide - Practical Informtion, Regulations, Opportunities
Zimbabwe: Doing Business and Investing In...Guide - Practical Informtion, Regulations, Opportunities

For additional analytical, business and investment opportunities information,
Please contact Global Investment & Business Center, USA
at (202) 546-2103. Fax: (202) 546-3275. E-mail: rusric@erols.com